Economics and Diplomacy

MEMOIRS AND OCCASIONAL PAPERS SERIES
ASSOCIATION FOR DIPLOMATIC STUDIES
AND TRAINING

Series Editor: MARGERY BOICHEL THOMPSON

In 2003, the Association for Diplomatic Studies and Training (ADST) created the Memoirs and Occasional Papers Series to preserve firsthand accounts and other informed observations on foreign affairs for scholars, journalists, and the general public. Sponsoring publication of book series is one of numerous ways in which ADST, a nonprofit organization founded in 1986, seeks to promote understanding of American diplomacy and those who conduct it. Together with the Foreign Affairs Oral History program and ADST's support for the training of foreign affairs personnel at the State Department's Foreign Service Institute, these efforts constitute the Association's fundamental purposes. Deane Hinton's memoir, the twenty-eighth volume in the series, follows the career of a talented negotiator who was one of a handful of diplomatic experts on international economic issues.

Claudia Anyaso, ed., *Fifty Years of US Africa Policy*
Diego and Nancy Asencio, *The Joys and Perils of Serving Abroad: Memoirs of a US Foreign Service Family*
Janet C. Ballantyne and Maureen Dugar, eds., *Fifty Years in USAID: Stories from the Front Lines*
Thompson Buchanan, *Mossy Memoir of a Rolling Stone*
J. Chapman Chester, *From Foggy Bottom to Capitol Hill: Exploits of a GI, Diplomat, and Congressional Aide*
John Gunther Dean, *Danger Zones: A Diplomat's Fight for America's Interests*
Robert E. Gribbin, *In the Aftermath of Genocide: The US Role in Rwanda*
Allen C. Hansen, *Nine Lives: A Foreign Service Odyssey*
John G. Kormann, *Echoes of a Distant Clarion: Recollections of a Diplomat and Soldier*
Nicole Prévost Logan, *Forever on the Road: A Franco-American Family's Thirty Years in the Foreign Service*
Armin Meyer, *Quiet Diplomacy: From Cairo to Tokyo in the Twilight of Imperialism*
William Morgan and Charles Stuart Kennedy, eds., *American Diplomats: The Foreign Service at Work*
John David Tinny, *From the Inside Out*
Theresa Tull, *A Long Way from Runnemede: One Woman's Foreign Service Journey*
Daniel Whitman, *A Haiti Chronicle: The Undoing of a Latent Democracy, 1999–2001*
Virginia Carson Young, *Peregrina: Unexpected Adventures of an American Consul*

For a complete list of series titles, visit http://adst.org/publications/memoirs-and-occasional-papers/.

Economics and Diplomacy

A Life in the Foreign Service of the United States

Deane Roesch Hinton

MEMOIRS AND OCCASIONAL PAPERS SERIES
ASSOCIATION FOR DIPLOMATIC STUDIES AND TRAINING

Washington, DC

Library of Congress Control Number: 2015935365
ISBN 978-0-9864353-2-4 paperback (alk. paper)

 An imprint of New Academia Publishing

 New Academia Publishing
P.O. Box 24720, Washington, DC 20038-7420
info@newacademia.com - www.newacademia.com

Dedicated to the Men and Women of the American Foreign Service

This memoir, as a memoir should be, is basically written from memory. I did, however, use clips from media to trigger my memory. The only significant exception, where I wrote from notes, is the discussion of my failed effort with Foreign Secretary Abdul Sattar to convince him that Pakistan would be better off without nuclear weapons.

From family and friends I have received much help. My wife Patricia was an inspiration. My son Deane Patrick typed parts of the manuscript and contributed to the index. ADST Publishing Director Margery Thompson not only encouraged me to continue when I was discouraged; she also gave me much editorial advice and kept track of drafts I misplaced. ADST interns Eli Rau, Batul K. Sadliwala, Caroline Wallace, Mary Larson, and Reanna Suela helped in converting and copyediting the manuscript and index. David Beall read and commented on the entire text. Needless to say, I alone am responsible for any errors.

Contents

Part One: Beginnings   1

  1. Early Days   3

  2. Soldiering (1943–1945)   37

Part Two: Foreign Service Officer Years   49

  3. Critical Decisions (1945–1946)   51

  4. Damascus (1946–1949)   59

  5. First Intermission (1949)   91

  6. Mombasa (1949–1951)   97

  7. Fletcher and Harvard (1951–1952)   121

  8. Paris (1952–1955)   129

  9. INR – Washington (1955–1958)   147

10. USEC – Brussels (1958–1961)   157

11. National War College (1961–1962)   175

12. Commodity Policy (1962–1963)   183

13. Atlantic Political Economic Affairs (1963–1967)   199

14. Guatemala (1967–1969)   211

15. Chile (1969–1971)   231

16. Council on International Economic Policy (1971–   247
1974)

PART THREE: Ambassadorial Years   265

17. Zaire (1974–1975)   267

18. Washington (E) (1975–1976)   289

19. USEC (1976–1979)   297

20. Washington (EB) (1979–1981)   313

21. El Salvador (1981–1983)   329

22. Intermission (1983)   365

23. Pakastan (1983–1987)   369

24. Costa Rica (1987–1989)   401

25. Panama (1990–1994)   415

Index   439

Part One

Beginnings

1

Early Days

Fort Missoula

A sign at Fort Missoula, Montana, where I was born on March 12, 1923, read, "Prohibited to Kill Buffalo on the Parade Ground." Or so my mother told me much later.

Established in 1877, Fort Missoula and the 7th Infantry, based there for years, played a role in the wars against the Nez Perce Indians, led by Chief Joseph and Chief Looking Glass. Thus I was tied to the West from the beginning.

My earliest memory is of taking advantage of a technicality at age three or four. Mother had told me to come home from play "when the flag comes down." On the day in question, the Fort Missoula retreat gun fired, but the flag somehow stuck. I played on with my friends until an annoyed Mom came to pull me home.

This bad habit of looking for loopholes in laws and regulations stuck with me for better or worse. It was one way of reconciling respect for authority, taught to every Army brat, with my independent streak.

That independent streak runs deep in families that moved steadily west from Europe, through the eastern and central United States, to Arizona and Colorado. My father, Joe Arthur Hinton, was born November 29, 1895, in Phoenix, Arizona. My mother, Doris Eileen Roesch Hinton, was born January 20, 1897, at in Denver, Colorado. Mother, who attached importance to such things as becoming a Daughter of the American Revolution, traced one side of the family back to a Nathaniel Phelps, who in 1775, although already in his seventies, served as a private revolutionary soldier during the "Lexington Alarm."

Mother was a gentle soul who had great difficulty birthing me. I was a one-month premature "blue baby." My start in life was precarious and not eased by location. It was deathly cold in Montana when I joined the army family—so cold that the wooden floors in the kitchen froze.

Dad had certainly not planned to be a soldier, but fate intervened. Having grown up in Arizona, he perversely wanted to go to sea. He was given an appointment to the Naval Academy and traveled east in 1914 only to be rejected at Annapolis because of color blindness. When his congressional sponsor asked if he were interested in West Point, he replied "No." Rather than study for the Army, he entered the University of Arizona, where he studied mining engineering. But war intervened. Immediately after the United States entered World War I, Dad enlisted. He attended and graduated from Officer Candidate School (OCS) as a Second Lieutenant. Assigned to the 27th Infantry, he found himself a member of the American Siberian Expeditionary Force. He did not return home until 1922 after serving in Siberia, Manchuria, the Philippines, and Hawaii. Deeming it too late to return to school, he signed up for the regular army. He also married my mother. He had known her, but not well, before the war in high school in Douglas, Arizona.

Grandpa Joe, as my children affectionately knew him, was a soldier's soldier, an athlete, and a sportsman. The hunting and fishing in Montana in the 1920s was like nowhere else in America. Dad missed Montana, as it was unique, but he hunted and fished wherever he could for years and years. He taught me what I know of fishing in Arizona in the early 1930s, off Quaymas and Acapulco in the mid-1930s, and in Michigan, Wisconsin, and Maine in the late 1930s. I was not as avid a fisherman as he. A memory of an early fishing trip and an often- repeated story is how I, a boy of eight, saved him from a rattlesnake. We were fishing for bass and perch in the Theodore Roosevelt Lake in Arizona. Dad beached our rowboat and wandered up the bank, casting. When he started back there was a much-annoyed coiled rattler right smack in his path. Dad yelled that I should push off and row the boat around to him. It was easily enough done, but magnified into the tale of how brave little Deane saved his dad from the threatening rattler.

When I was five, Dad gave me my first gun, a single shot .22. Soon I was a fair shot. One summer near Flagstaff, Arizona, I regularly brought home squirrels for dinner. I also got lost in the forest that year, having wandered away from Dad and his party, who were surveying land controlled by the National Guard. It is hard to say if I was more frightened than my mother, but all ended well, as eventually I found a track that led me home.

Still later, I received a .410 lever-action shotgun, my pride and joy, good for quail and dove hunting. When I was eleven, I was turned over to a veteran sergeant in Dad's company of the 25th Infantry at Fort Huachuca, Arizona, to be taught how to shoot a standard-issue army rifle. As a reward for diligent effort and somewhat improved marksmanship, Dad and friends took me along on a deer hunt in Northern Sonora. I did not get even one shot, but in the cold I froze and returned home so exhausted from the uphill-downhill chase that I lost the considerable enthusiasm with which I had started out that morning at 2 a.m. Never again did I go on a deer hunt. I could claim I was protecting endangered wildlife, but that wasn't it at all. One deer hunt was enough.

Dad and l last fished together in southern Chile in 1979. It had been a terrible year for me, as Miren, my wonderful Chilean wife, slowly died of cancer. Fishing with my "old man," a very spry 84, after the funeral provided the only good memories of that heart-rending year.

Chicago

When I was four, Dad was transferred from the 4th Infantry at Missoula to the Infantry School at Fort Benning, Georgia. We drove there in the family Hupmobile, stopping en route to visit my mother's parents in Chicago. With awful roads and occasional breakdowns, the trip took weeks, but oh what fun.

My Grandma Roesch had helped my mother get me through the tough early days. I knew and loved her. Grandpa Roesch, however, was an unknown quantity to me.

His was quite a story. In 1868 his parents emigrated from Germany to the United States. They settled in Trenton, Missouri, where Grandpa grew up.

Grandpa always maintained that he was born in Alsace, which was part of France when he was born on April 14, 1864. We were led to believe it was somewhere near Riquewihr. Recently, however, I have seen convincing evidence that he was actually born in Kaiserslautern, Germany. My guess is that he cooked up the Alsace story during World War I. Nor did it hurt during World War II to claim Alsace rather than Germany as one's birthplace.

Truthfully, there is a fascinating real connection to France. My great-great-grandfather was François Pierre Roquette. As a youth of sixteen he fought for France at Waterloo. After Napoleon's defeat, he accompanied Marshal Soult to what is now Germany. There he changed his name to Roesch and became a professional soldier, eventually receiving command of a fortress on the Rhine. He kept his connection to France by marrying a French girl, Elise Garnier.

Grandpa Roesch graduated from Trenton High School, distinguishing himself as class valedictorian. However, long before graduating he went to work as a machinist apprentice on the Chicago, Rock Island & Peoria Railroad. From that point on his life was railroading. He was a machinist, locomotive fireman, and locomotive engineer for the Denver & Rio Grande as well as for the Atchison, Topeka and Santa Fe (at that time called the Atlantic and Pacific), foreman for the Florida Central and Peninsular Railroad, and roundhouse foreman for the Denver and New Orleans. He then went into management positions in Chicago, Alton, Birmingham, Spencer, North Carolina, and Douglas, Arizona.

Early on, or so family legend has it, Grandpa tired of shoveling coal into steam boilers. As he told the story, one day watching Grandma grind hamburger, he decided the screw principle would work just as well to move coal from the coal car to the locomotive furnace. Thus, the stoker was invented. Grandpa took out the first of his patents.

In 1920, he joined the Standard Stoker Company, headquartered in Chicago. He lived there until his death in 1951 at age 87. The record shows he was a Mason and an inveterate joiner of countless associations of railroad people. He left Grandma, my uncle Rudolf, and my mother a modest inheritance.

My earliest memory of Grandpa dates to our passage through Chicago en route to Fort Benning in 1927. I was thrilled to walk alone down Lake Park Avenue to the 47th Street Illinois Central stop to meet Grandpa descending from the platform every evening at precisely 5:35. He would greet me and walk me to the candy store for a treat. Then we went to the corner cigar store, run even then by Cubans, where he would replenish his supply of smokes. Perhaps my love of good cigars was born then and there.

My last memories of Grandpa date to 1945–46, after my return to Chicago from the war. He was still writing columns on "Locomotive Running and Repairs" for *The Engine Man's Magazine*. Unlike earlier years, he was now having trouble with the math. He sought my help. While I also had trouble with the math, far more troubling was Grandpa's persistence in writing "proofs" that steam locomotives would never be lastingly replaced by either diesel or electric locomotives. Sadly, his identification with steam was too deep for his intelligence, early inventiveness, and imagination to overcome.

Although I was oblivious to it at the time, Grandpa's relation with Grandma Roesch was cold and distant. He slept in a front bedroom of the apartment at 1413 50th Street into which they had moved in the early 1930s. She slept in a small room off the kitchen, probably meant to be servants' quarters. He gave her money. She ran the house and cooked wonderful meals. Her Sunday chicken and dumplings were unsurpassed. Once a week, Grandpa took us all to the movies. Apart from meals and movies they did nothing together, not even talking. Grandma cared for him in his last illness, even while writing that she hated him. What went wrong with that marriage?

Interestingly, my mother only learned after Grandma's death that she had married and divorced a Fred W. Tuttle in Colorado before her marriage to Grandpa Roesch. Divorce in the 1880s was scandalous. That family skeleton was well concealed. Nor did my mother tell me. As she had before me, I learned of all this after my mother's death from papers she had put away. I also came upon the observation that Grandma would not talk of her youth and indeed became quite agitated when Mother tried to draw it out of her.

Born in Elkader, Iowa, on December 18, 1871, Minnie Louise Rolf moved early on to Chaffee County, Colorado. Records indicate that her father, Milton Rolf, one day just up and left his family. Some thought he went to Mexico, but in any case he simply disappeared. Did Grandma's first husband also abandon her? Or what led to the divorce? Apparently Grandpa Roesch provided Minnie a safe haven from a stormy, unhappy upbringing and a bad first marriage, but sadly she seems not to have been happy with him either.

With me, however, Grandma and Grandpa were loving. To them I was "Sonny." Grandma introduced her "Sonny" to baseball. She was a rabid Cubs fan, as I am to this day thanks to her. When Grandma Roesch wasn't at the ballpark, she listened, without fail, to radio broadcasts of Cubs games. She took me to Wrigley Field many, many times, and also to the first All-Star Game at Comiskey Park. I wrote my dad about that game, telling him how the American League won, about Babe Ruth's homer, and the fine catch Babe made to end the game. For a Cubs fan it was disappointing, but what great baseball. And I saw Babe Ruth's homer!

Grandma also traipsed me through the educational sights of Chicago. She taught me a lot and she taught me well. I liked the woolly mammoth, the dinosaurs, and the mummies in the Field Museum even more than the paintings at the Art Institute. When I return to Chicago, I still like to wander through both institutions. But my sons, Sebastian and Deane Akbar, while they tolerate the Art Institute and the Field Museum, far prefer the Museum of Science and Industry.

Fort Benning

After our short stay in Chicago we drove on to Fort Benning, Georgia. My memories of Benning are few. However, I will never forget the red mud. Nor will I forget my mother yelling at me to take off my muddy shoes before coming into the house. Then too, there was a preschool play in which I had to wear a ridiculous green string bean costume, to my great discomfort.

Dad recounted later that he almost failed the Infantry School because of his poor horsemanship! That passing a course in equitation was a prerequisite for graduating from the Infantry School in 1927 says something about the army's slow reaction to change and its love of tradition.

But graduate he did. Then Dad was assigned as Instructor of the Arizona National Guard in Phoenix. So we traveled west in the faithful Hupmobile. Later I discovered Dad used what influence he had to get the Arizona job because doctors said a dry climate was what I needed to put my bronchitis behind me. This was a career-sacrificing move, since it involved five years away from regular troops. In Phoenix, I was treated like a frailer kid than I think I was. Mother forced me to take long naps every afternoon and almost always sent me to bed early. Now I welcome naps and early bedtimes, but I hated it as an eight- or nine-year-old.

Arizona

After countless flat tires Dad expertly changed, the Hinton Hupmobile reached Douglas, Arizona, where we stayed with Dad's mother and father. Grandpa Hinton was then mayor of Douglas. The wonderful result for me was that he arranged for me to tour the city on a big, bright red fire engine. What an exciting ride!

Grandpa Arthur Hinton came west in 1883, first working for an uncle engaged in ranching and freighting out of Globe, Arizona. Once riding the range, he and another cowboy had a run-in with some Indians and killed an Apache. Grandpa suffered a wound. Until his death he carried the physical scar and also a scar on his conscience about the death of the Indian. Most Westerners would not have given a hoot about one less Apache, but Grandpa was different.

Moving to Phoenix, he went into merchandising with farming and cattle raising as additional pursuits. In 1895, the year of my dad's birth, Grandpa was elected to the Territorial Legislature. Later he worked as a self-taught mining engineer in the Bisbee copper mines and Douglas smelter. He also worked in mining camps in Mexico until revolutionaries chased his family and him back to Douglas. From that period my father, then a teenager, recalled and recited to the end of his ninety-six years the revolutionary *dicho* (saying or slogan):

Mucho trabajo, poco dinero,
déme frijoles, viva Madero.

After four terms as mayor of Douglas, in 1928 Grandpa was elected to the State Legislature. With FDR's overwhelming victory in 1932, Grandpa and many other Republicans were retired from politics.

In the meantime, however, tragedy struck. Driving from Douglas to Phoenix to spend Christmas with us, Grandpa lost control of his car in a blizzard in the mountains above Bisbee. It teetered on the edge of a canyon for a minute or two then rolled over and down. Grandma Hinton died of her injuries a few days later. Grandpa was hardly bruised. I was told of his bravery and the importance of marital togetherness, both illustrated by Grandpa staying in the car, although he had had plenty of time to step out. Loyal to his wife, he chose to remain with her as the car rolled over and down. Fortunately, his life was spared.

Grandpa Hinton was probably born in Kansas, possibly in Concordia. Why he came to Arizona is not entirely clear. One story, probably apocryphal, but much bandied about in the family, has it that he was run out of Kansas as a horse thief. It seems more likely he came to Arizona in search of opportunities that simply did not exist in Kansas. This conclusion is fortified by the fact that Arthur Elmer Hinton married a Harbert. The Harberts, one of Arizona's leading families, probably would not have permitted their daughter Emma to marry a reputed horse thief. In any case, Arthur and Emma, who had been born in Colorado, were married in October of 1888. They had two sons, Clarence, the elder, known as Hogan, and Joe Arthur, my father, born November 29, 1895.

Arthur Hinton's great-grandfather reportedly came to America from France. He settled briefly in what is now Louisville, Kentucky. His luck ran out when Indians killed him as he was crossing a river in a canoe. Family survivors retreated to Vincennes, Maryland. Indeed, Jeremiah Hinton and Nancy Moore, his wife, raised most of their family in Maryland before moving west to Kansas. The couple had twelve children, most of whom died young. When Jeremiah reached Kansas, he had only two girls and four boys with him.

The Harbert family went west right after the Civil War. They briefly settled in Virginia City, Montana, a rough frontier town if ever there was one. After five persons were hanged from the rafters of City Hall, the Harberts moved on to Oregon. There they became well off as owners of considerable rich agricultural land. The family split, however, with some Harberts staying in Oregon and others moving south to California, Colorado, and Arizona.

The Harberts were real entrepreneurs. For example, they imported ostriches. In fact, the Harbert ostrich farm in Arizona was one of the largest, if not the largest, in the nation. Money poured in until one day ladies stopped putting feathers in their bonnets. Fickle fashion! The ostrich business collapsed, but Harbert land holdings, including a good part of Phoenix, more than saw the family through the rough period.

As far as I know, except for a small "quit claim" settlement relating to part of what was then the Phoenix fairgrounds, Dad got nothing from the Harbert family. His father moved to California after the Roosevelt landslide of 1932 and worked a small gold mine. When my folks and I were in San Francisco in 1936, waiting to sail to Hawaii, Grandpa Hinton came down from the hills to have dinner with us. He showed me a leather bag of gold dust and a couple of nuggets from the mine. I was mightily impressed. There was gold in "them thar hills." Unfortunately, we never saw Grandpa again. He died December 1, 1937, while visiting Clarence. He was virtually impoverished. He made enough to eat on at his mine, but without a big strike, gold mining had proven to be a terribly tough business. His body was returned to and buried in Douglas. A public day of mourning was declared, and the whole town turned out to honor him at his funeral. He had been an extremely popular mayor and citizen.

Phoenix

In Phoenix, Mom and Dad rented a small house at 715 West Culver. At the time I did not think it was small. Indeed, when Dad and I returned to Phoenix in 1987, I was surprised the house was not bigger.

School caught up with me in Phoenix. Kenilworth Elementary was about a block and a half from our house, across a busy street. Although there was a crossing guard, "Be Careful" was drilled into me.

Thanks to wonderful teachers, I loved school. Through the fifth grade I did well. After Dad was transferred to Fort Huachuca in 1933, school was never the same. On my last day at Kenilworth, my favorite teacher, Miss Meredith Bishop, gave me a rabbit's foot for good luck as a farewell gift. I carried it for years, but finally—I think during World War II—it disappeared, lost in time.

The years in Phoenix were good ones. My folks gave me loving, but overly sheltering, care, so it seems to me now. Mother read to me every night at bedtime, and soon I was reading widely myself. A lavishly illustrated *Pinocchio* was my favorite book, followed closely by *Treasure Island*. Mother and I read them together until I could virtually recite the stories.

When I was seven, my folks took me to hear Admiral Richard Byrd lecture. I was enthralled. The famous Antarctic explorer inscribed a copy of his *Little America* for me on January 27, 1931. To this day it's a prize possession.

My desire to explore the world dates from that period. It was nourished later by the Halliburton travel adventure books, starting with *The Royal Road to Romance*. Another travel book that somewhat later had an impact on me was *East of the Sun and West of the Moon*, an account of a Roosevelt big game hunt in the Karakorams. Years later, while ambassador to Pakistan, I saw for myself the Karakorams, one of the world's greatest mountain ranges, but no big game hunting for me. I have yet to visit Antarctica.

Summers were scorching hot in Phoenix. My mother managed to get away with me for part of the hot season. We went twice back to Chicago, once to Flagstaff, where Dad was surveying a National Guard facility (that's the year I got lost in the forest!), and twice to

Prescott. There were also shorter breaks from Phoenix heat with camping in the White Mountains and stays at Frank and Ruby's ranch near Mayer.

The round trip to Chicago on the Southern Pacific Limited was a real adventure: days and nights in Pullman sleepers; the swaying jolting walk to the diner; lots of rummy with Mom; much time to read; and, when no one beat me to it, a seat on the rear platform, where I could try to protect my eyes from flying cinders as I watched America roll by.

Frank's cattle ranch was even more of an adventure. There I "learned" to ride. The ranch was also the locale for two family legends. One had it that Frank could flip pancakes off the stove and up the chimney, then catch them with one step outside. The other: in a brotherly roughhouse Dad threw Hogan right through the wall. Ruby had to have a window installed to fill the breach.

I regret that I did not have Dad explain our relation with Frank, Ruby, and the numerous Hintons I later encountered in Los Angeles. There was also a Jim Hinton, who showed up in Chicago to entertain me in grand style while I was at the university. He said he lived in St. Louis and had made a killing in the shoe business.

My guess is that Frank was Dad's uncle, a brother of Grandpa Hinton, but I really don't know. How foolish of me not to ask more questions and take notes when there was still a chance to have Dad explain these relations. We saw my uncle Hogan, my aunt Clara, and my cousin Patty just a few times before they moved to Oregon in the early 1930s.. There they barely made ends meet raising chickens, but still it was better than being unemployed in Douglas. Our two families corresponded, but less and less frequently as time passed. Then the correspondents, mainly my mother and Aunt Clara, passed on.

In 1980 Dad and I meant to stop in Oregon to see Aunt Clara, who had outlived Hogan, before proceeding to Seattle, where we were to begin our Alaskan cruise. The Cadillac broke down in Yellowstone, and we lost a day getting it fixed. After studying maps and taking into account the latest we could get to Seattle, we decided we had to skip seeing Aunt Clara. It was just as well. The day we would have stopped by was the day she died!

After a number of years, I re-established enough contact with Patty, long since married into the Raetz family, for us to exchange Christmas cards and for her to inform me in no uncertain terms that she was no longer to be called Patty. She had legally changed her name to Annette Raetz. No explanation for the switch from Patty to Annette has yet been provided.

Sadly, it is difficult to maintain coherent extended families in modern America. How different it was when I married into a Chilean family and discovered how close and rewarding the ties of an extended Latin family could be.

Summers in Prescott stand out in my memory. I had my first "job" there. We kids would hang out around the telegraph office. When a cable came in the first boy in line "volunteered" to deliver it. Maybe I'm stretching things to call this a job; certainly the telegraph company considered us to be helpers not employees. Moreover, some miserly recipients gave the delivery boy nothing. Generally, however, one was rewarded with a dime, very occasionally a quarter. A quarter was big money in those days.

These were the years of the Great Depression. Fortunately, Dad, as an officer of the regular Army, had job security. Unfortunately, as a mere first lieutenant, he earned very little. We weren't starving, but money was short. Dad supplemented his pay by officiating at high school and college football games for $5.00 or $10.00 a game. Also, he earned psychic income and supplemented our diet by bringing home sea bass from fishing trips to the Gulf of California and venison from hunting trips in the White Mountains. Still, had it not been for Grandpa Roesch's financial help, Mother and I would not have traveled to Chicago nor summered in Prescott.

I was uneasy about the seemingly unending number of unshaven men in tattered clothes who rang our doorbell. They looked like bums to me, but mother saw individuals down on their luck. She turned no one away without a sandwich and a cup of coffee, not even those she, too, thought were bums. Word of her generosity naturally got out. Our house became a favorite stop for those with enough gumption to walk fairly far from the railroad tracks. Mother said as long as we had what we did, we could not turn away these men, most of whom would have much preferred a job to a handout. But there were virtually no jobs, at least until the PWA (Public Works Administration) created the CCC (Civilian Conservation Corps) and other public works programs.

Mother was a serious woman with a real puritan streak in her. It seems to me, as I think back, that she largely lacked a sense of humor. But I do remember one joke she played on Dad, with my collusion. To help meet expenses he tried, without much success, to install a vegetable garden in our backyard. His major ambition was to grow asparagus. He tilled and tilled the soil, carefully adding sand, fertilizer, and seed. One day, just before he was due to return from an extended National Guard inspection trip, mother bought some asparagus, which we pushed into the soil. Dad returned, went to inspect his vegetable garden, and with a shout of joy and amazement called to us to come see how his asparagus had grown!

One of Dad's friends was Colonel Goodale, a retired Army officer, who was a renowned stamp collector, specializing in French colonial issues. The colonel took an interest in me, acquainting me in particular with the joys of collecting those tiny pieces of paper from which one could learn so much history and geography. Those stamps influenced my interest in the world beyond my horizon. The knowledge I gained from them doubtless helped me pass the Foreign Service examination years later.

While Colonel Goodale's gifts of stamps got my collection started, they were soon supplemented by Mother buying me "Mission Mixtures," which we culled together. What a thrill it was to find a stamp that would completely fill an album page. Later Mother allowed me to send off for books of penny approvals. Thus began a hobby that gives me much pleasure to this day.

It is, however; a hobby that has become much less manageable as postal authorities the world over, including prominently the United States Postal Service, pour out new stamps. Collectors are now often overwhelmed. In addition to trying to improve my holding of U.S. stamps, I took refuge for some years in a fairly specialized collection of stamps relating to the unification of Europe, building on my professional interest in European integration. Even so, I found that I simply could not keep up. As the twentieth century comes to an end, I plan to stop acquiring new U.S. issues. There are simply too many.

In the future, however, I'll concentrate on filling gaps in my U.S. collection. Unfortunately this becomes more and more expensive as the gaps grow fewer. Lots of stamps I am missing will forever be beyond my means, but careful bidding in auctions should slowly fill many album pages to my great delight. One of these days I'll have to go for broke and acquire the Zeppelins, the $5.00 Columbian, and the $2.00 Trans-Mississippian.

With or without these gems, I have dozens, if not hundreds, of cigar boxes and a couple of locker trunks filled mostly with ordinary stamps waiting to be soaked and sorted. The good ones should someday go into albums and the duplicates in a system to facilitate trading. The task is virtually endless, and it's certain I will not complete it.

This is what Colonel Goodale started me on. It has given me hundreds, nay thousands, of hours of pleasure through the years. Sadly, none of my children or stepchildren have taken stamps up seriously, a bit of dabbling, nothing more. Thus, I worry some about what will happen to my collection when I'm gone—should I try to dispose of it while I have time or leave it for someone else to dispose of, someone without appreciation of its sentimental value, to say nothing of knowledge of its now considerable monetary value? Oh, how I wish Akbar, my youngest, would take an interest in stamps, but I know better than to try to force him in that or any other direction.

In June of 1933, Dad proceeded to his new assignment at Fort Huachuca, Arizona, while Mother and I once again boarded the train for Chicago. I was excited. In addition to my new rabbit's foot, I had been given my first camera, a Brownie Box. Dad told me he wanted me to photograph the Chicago World's Fair, "A Century of Progress."

Thinking back now, over sixty year later, it is hard to recall the thrill of the 1933 World's Fair, but it was undoubtedly the most exciting and stimulating event of my young life. Since Grandma and Grandpa Roesch lived near the Illinois Central tracks, we had an easy train ride directly to the fair. I wanted to go every day. For weeks, we went almost every day. I wore out my mother and my grandmother exploring the fair. I visited many exhibits again and again. I missed nothing other than a few sideshows into which ten-year-old boys were not admitted. The spectacular night show spotlighting a hundred years of progress in transportation was my favorite. It was a memorable last hurrah for the great steam locomotives and a moving tribute to the railroads that opened up the American West. Grandpa Roesch also loved the display of locomotives. Sadly, I thought, he did not much care for or want to see most of the other exhibits.

I took lots of appallingly bad pictures. Strangely, at the time, I thought they were great. After all, I had taken them with my very own camera. Then, too, I made a great discovery that summer— hamburgers—which we ate for lunch every day, since I would eat nothing else at the fair.

Another memorable treat in Chicago was to visit Marshall Fields and ride the escalator. I loved that. Moreover, we inevitably arrived at the floor with a square city block of toys. I still ride the Marshall Fields escalator to the ninth floor and back down to the basement when I visit Chicago. It helps to keep good childhood memories alive. Sadly, however, the toy department is no more.

The summer of 1933 was capped off for me when Grandpa Roesch bought me a Pointer puppy. I named him "Spot," after the first dog in my life, also named "Spot," at Fort Missoula. His memory had been kept alive both by Dad's stories of hunting with Spot and by family pictures. In fact, one of the earliest pictures of me, taken by my folks, showed me with Spot.

Fort Huachuca, Arizona

At Fort Huachuca I came face to face with the hard fact that life can be difficult. A small, isolated army post was an entirely different experience from Phoenix, where I had grown into boyhood and had many friends. To make matters worse, officers and their families were sharply separated from the vast majority of individuals at Huachuca. The usual caste division between army officers and enlisted men was magnified by racial discrimination. The 25th United States Infantry was a segregated black regiment.

Soon my new playmates were regaling me with horror stories of how a deranged soldier had systematically gone around the loop of officer quarters, killing whomever he found. My folks eventually calmed my fearful nights, but a ten-year-old's imagination needs little stimulus to run wild.

The post school for whites was a three-room affair with three badly overtaxed teachers. I struggled through sixth and seventh grades in what approached the fabled one-room school of frontier days. It was more of a struggle, since I had no good friends and had problems with some of the boys and girls. I lost my first few fights to bigger boys who liked to bully me. I was frankly baffled by the carrying on of some of the girls.

Perhaps one of the incentives to pick on me, as I saw it, was that my folks were known to disapprove of drinking. Prohibition was over, and there was some serious drinking at the Fort Huachuca Officer's' Club.. Mother was opposed, and Dad respected her view, although he had drunk in Siberia and drank moderately after Mother's death many years later. Thus, Lt. and Mrs. Hinton stood out as the only officer couple not indulging at the Club. I credit mother for the courage of her convictions. She probably did not realize how painful it was for me to be marked as different.

But I have happy memories of other aspects of Huachuca. I learned to handle a Springfield, coached by a kindly but firm sergeant serving in the rifle company led by my dad. The Springfield's recoil bruised my shoulder but burnished my pride.

The pond, "my pond," was a hundred yards or so below our house. Some of us built a raft and stayed on the alert for rattlesnakes after one scary encounter. The raft and pond provided hours and hours of fun. What a rude shock, almost fifty years later, when Dad and I returned for a visit to find "my pond" incorporated into a new Officers' Club landscaping.

I learned to play tennis on the post court with my first racquet (steel springs, believe it or not) and took evening car trips with Mother and Dad. Sometimes we went to a whistle stop to watch a Southern Pacific train go by and sometimes to the desert to hunt quail, I with my 410.

I faked illness so I could stay home from school to listen to radio accounts of Dizzy Dean pitching in the World Series. I had my first regular paying job delivering *The Saturday Evening Post* and *Ladies Home Companion*. I didn't make much, just a few cents a copy, but oh, was I proud to be earning something.

By now we had two dogs, my Spot and Dad's Bolshevik, an older bird dog Dad had inherited from a departing officer. While I was at school and at night, our dogs were wired to the clothesline. One of my chores was to "police" after them. Fortunately, I loved the dogs dearly, so I did my job. Each day, however, I was amazed at how much dog doo I collected.

My folks recognized that the post school was not much of an educational institution. Perhaps they were also cognizant of my relational problems with the other kids, perhaps not. In any case, in 1935 they sent me off to the California Preparatory School, a private school near Covina, California, a town of comic strip fame. I surmise that Grandpa Roesch financed my stay at Cal Prep, where I completed eighth grade and my elementary education.

It was not a happy time for me. Separated from my parents, I joined a class where almost everyone had known each other for several years. My first night, my roommate, Thomas Ames, established his place in the pecking order by beating me up. After that, however, we got along fine. Tom went so far as to tell other boys not to pick on me.

Educationally, Cal Prep was definitely a step up. I did well with class work. Athletics, especially football, were something else.

I was small for my age, a real lightweight. So the stupid coach designated me as the team center! I was not bad on offense, but defense was something else again. In those days, you played both ways until you dropped, which was considered very bad form. Cal Prep was a school of privileged white kids. Our opponents were mostly public schools whose teams were stuffed with big, tough Mexicans. We fought hard and won not a single game, but were immensely proud of a 0-0 tie: our best game of the season.

I'll never forget those big offensive linemen blowing me out of the center of our defense and those tremendous fullbacks gaining big yards over my position as they trampled me into the mud. I never played tackle football again, nor did I want to. I had earned my letter; that was enough. Still, I love to watch the game. Wistfully, I think I might not have done too badly as a linebacker, or better, as a corner, where I could have used my brains and speed. But center playing a seven- man defensive line, no way!

The record shows that I also won a letter in basketball, but I have no recollection of this. Moreover, until Michael Jordan came along, I thought basketball was too boring to watch. The only other sport I recall from my Cal Prep days was archery, at which I was pretty good.

The Thanksgiving after my arrival at Cal Prep, "Aunt Jenny," one of Dad's relatives, who lived in Los Angeles, invited me to a monster family dinner. It was a memorable feast. Unfortunately, however, I do not recall ever again seeing any of these great-uncles, great-aunts, and even more distant family members.

After the school year was completed, I set out with my parents for Hawaii. Dad had been transferred to the 21st Infantry at Schofield Barracks.

Hawaii

I was excited by the promise of Hawaii. Reputedly an island paradise, it meant even more to me. I was escaping from the travails of Fort Huachuca and Cal Prep. Hawaii meant a chance to start again.

Many are the advantages and disadvantages of an itinerant life, but one great advantage is the chance to start over: being able to put what you have learned from experience into play in a new locale with new people, who may be prejudiced against newcomers but who at least have nothing in particular against you.

We sailed from San Francisco on the U.S. Army Transport *Republic*. It was not a modern cruise ship, but not bad either. Parental supervision relaxed, and we kids had a great time. My folks even let me wager a daily dime on the ship's sea mileage pool. I bet on a number at which I thought the daily mileage, calculated at noon, would end. It probably gave me a distorted view of gambling. Since all pool proceeds were distributed to the winners, the odds were fair.

Our reception in Honolulu was memorable. I had never seen anything like it. Bands played, and flower leis were placed around the necks of all newcomers, including thirteen-year-old boys. There were blue skies with puffy white clouds and an ideal temperature. Then we moved into temporary quarters, a sort of motel at Fort De Russy, right on famed Waikiki Beach. De Russy's coastal defense guns were impressive, but nothing could match the overall setting.

Mother and I lived on the beach for about six weeks while waiting for our family quarters at Schofield. Dad joined his new regiment, the 21st Infantry, but came to Honolulu to spend weekends with us on the beach.

Eventually, quarters became available, and we moved into our assigned house at Schofield Barracks. It was fairly small but comfortable. Notably, we had our own banana tree, with lots of fruit, in our patio.

When school opened, I was tormented by Latin but not, as often before, by my classmates. Best of all, Russ Graf and I became close friends—biking together, studying together, playing sports together, playing chess together, and enjoying life together. Russ and I corresponded for years, as I did for some time also with his sister, Barbara. The last time I saw Dr. Graf, as he had become, was in Paris in 1954. Christmas card exchanges petered out. After retiring, I tried, at first unsuccessfully, to find him. The anger of losing touch with good friends is probably the principal disadvantage of the itinerant life. I should have taken more care to stay in touch, but at the time I did not realize how important it was to maintain contact.

Several years after my retirement, one of my stepdaughters, who had access to a computer data bank, pulled up for me the addresses and telephone numbers of every listed Russell Graf in the United States. Since my last address for Russ was in Indiana, I sent letters to every one of that name there and in surrounding states. "Bingo," Russ replied from Bowling Green, Kentucky. We have agreed on a reunion, but Russ cannot yet leave his wife, Lois, who is suffering from Alzheimer's.

In addition to commanding a company, Dad was regimental athletic director. As a result, he spent far more time training soldier athletes than he did teaching military skills. He coached and managed the 21st Infantry baseball, football, basketball, and boxing teams. Competition among regimental teams was fierce. Scouts were somehow inserted in troop transports leaving the States to try to identify good athletes among transferees and recruits. Based on scout's reports and other information, there was a fierce struggle in the assignment process to get talent to the "right unit." Dad's regiment was not the best at recruiting, but his teams were competitive. He was a hell of a coach. Better than just cheering for the baseball team, I was named (nepotism at play) regimental batboy. As such I got in considerable fielding practice. It was not enough, to become a really good player, but enough to nourish a lifelong passion for the game.

We took in all of the beauties of Oahu, since my folks loved to drive, picnic, and walk the beaches. In addition, one holiday we flew over to visit the "Big Island." It was fabulous: fewer people, wider vistas, many more waterfalls, and, best of all, volcanoes. We walked in the Kilauea Crater. Elsewhere we watched lava flows from so close up the heat staggered us. In the rain forests, the giant ferns were unforgettable. Mother Nature's power and majesty were on display; volcanoes, earth tremors, and incredible rainstorms could not have made a stronger impression on me.

On Oahu, I communed with nature from time to time, lying in the grass on a hill not too far from our house, watching the clouds roll by. After all, one couldn't be with one's friends, play tennis, carry bats, ride bicycles, and study all of the time. Sex was coming noticeably in my life, but I was not prepared. I had heard Mother ask Dad if he should have a talk with me about life. Dad had replied that Deane knew all he needed to know from other boys. But I didn't. Moreover, I was afraid to ask. By myself, I mooned for hours over a photographic murder mystery in which a beautiful young girl's nude body had been found on a beach. The curves of her breasts entranced me, but I knew not why.

Girls were hardly in my life; I scarcely recognized their existence. Barbara Graf, Russ' sister, was a friend. Otherwise, except for organized teenage dances at the Officers' Club, where I was expected to dance with a different girl each dance, I had nothing to do with the fair sex. Nor did I consciously recognize a connection between my fascination with exposed breasts and these immature young ladies. A chaste goodnight kiss might be exchanged with my dance date, as dates were virtually mandatory, but that was it. Somehow, I was shielded from or blind to the petting and sexual exploration in which many teenagers engage.

Fort McKinley, Maine

Inevitably, transfer orders arrived for Dad, putting the family in motion again. Our new destination was Fort McKinley, Maine, home of the 5th Infantry. To get there, we traveled by an army troop transport from Hawaii to New York via San Francisco and the Panama Canal. For me, the trip was memorable. For one thing, I more or less learned to play bridge, a game I enjoy to this day. It's a great way to while away time on a long sea voyage or in retirement. For another, I threw such a scene in Panama, shameful in retrospect, that my folks gave in and parted with $100,an enormous sum for them in those days, to buy me a quality 35mm camera. I had outgrown my box cameras and my Argus and was into developing, printing, enlarging, and coloring my own photos. To move up, I had my heart set on a Leica or a Contax. These, however, were financially out of reach. The Contaflex I ended up with met my needs, brought happiness to my heart, and gave peace to my parents.

When we reached New York, or rather Brooklyn, where army transports docked, we lost no time in getting aboard a train for Chicago. It was so good to see Grandma and Grandpa Roesch again after almost three years.

The next adventure was going with Dad to Detroit to take delivery at the factory of our new Packard, then back to Chicago via the Northern Peninsula and Wisconsin, with Dad fishing all the way. Then, with Mother aboard, we headed east to Maine. En route we stopped to visit Uncle Rudolph, as everyone called mother's brother George, and Aunt Erdine in Syracuse, New York.

The best part of our visit with Rudolph and Erdine was at a cabin deep in the woods on a private lake Uncle Rudolph co-owned with a number of friends. Unfortunately, financial difficulties forced him to sell his share of what I remember as a paradise. Among other points in its favor was the strange fact that the fish in that lake seemed to like my lures, whereas I had had virtually no success as a fisherman in northern Michigan.

Once in Maine, Mother and I moved into a hotel in Portland, while once again Dad occupied bachelor quarters on post with his regiment, waiting for family quarters to become available for us. In the hotel, I stayed glued to the radio.

It was 1938. As we had driven across the country, alarming reports of developments in Europe had filled the airwaves. Hitler was threatening Czechoslovakia, alleging mistreatment of a German minority. War seemed imminent. The crisis erupted as I listened on the hotel radio. British Prime Minister Neville Chamberlain and French Premier Pierre Daladier flew to Munich to meet with Hitler and Mussolini. Chamberlain emerged to announce "peace in our time." He and Daladier had sold out their ally, the Czechs, ceding to Hitler what was not theirs to cede, the Sudetenland section of Czechoslovakia.

A longtime cover-to-cover reader of *Time*, I had followed closely the Japanese invasion of China, the Italian invasion of Ethiopia, the German reoccupation of the Rhineland, and German and Italian backing for Franco in Spain's Civil War. For a boy of fifteen, I looked at this latest crisis with a considerable historical background. Although I hoped peace would be preserved, I did not expect Munich to be the last crisis in Europe. Hitler looked insatiable to me.

Soon we moved into our new quarters at Fort McKinley on Great Diamond Island in Casco Bay. Built as a coastal defense facility, the fort's big guns, in deep concrete emplacements, were strategically placed but totally inoperative.

Living on an island, I found getting to and from school a real trial. While I didn't have to walk ten miles through snowdrifts, as I occasionally told my children I had, the trip was nevertheless demanding. Army trucks, open to the elements, picked us kids up in front of our houses and took us to the military dock on the island. There we boarded an army packet that took us to the dock of another fort in South Portland. From that dock, another open truck took us to South Portland High School. We were late every morning as well as frozen most winter mornings.

After school, out at three p.m., we took another truck to the fishing docks of Portland itself, where we boarded an island-to-island commercial ferry. There we waited in relative comfort for it to sail at about five p.m. Eventually, this ferry docked at the civilian end of Great Diamond Island, where yet another army truck was waiting to take us home. Four truck rides, two boat rides, and school occupied almost twelve hours door-to-door. Fortunately, the wait for the ferry in Portland gave us time to do our homework, although I never seemed to have enough time to master Latin and Julius Caesar's Gallic Wars. We also had some time for cards and jacks. I learned how to play jacks waiting for that damned ferry to sail, but not well enough to beat most of the girls, who had been playing all of their lives.

The hurricane of 1938 was memorable. Apparently convinced hurricanes were not allowed in Maine, our ferryboat skipper sailed as usual, despite warnings. Portland Bay was not at all as usual. We had seasick passengers, lots of them, as the ferry gyrated every which way. Somehow we made it to the dock on Great Diamond Island, but it took forever to tie up, as fierce winds and high waves buffeted the ferry. After dropping us off, the ferry hove to in a fairly sheltered spot between two islands and rode out the storm. Many other boats were not so lucky, to say nothing of trees and rooftops.

Another memorable event of that year's transport was a tragedy. One winter day our favorite truck driver, coming to pick us up at the civilian dock, skidded on ice, lost control, and plunged into the water. Trapped in the cab of his truck, he drowned in the frigid water. We students were shocked and saddened, but the incident brought home to us that the unexpected can always intervene.

Even worse was the sudden death of a friend's mother from pneumonia. I was learning at age fifteen that life could be filled with unpleasant surprises. Fortunately, my folks and I stayed in good shape.

While I got along with the other kids, I had no friend as close as Russ Graf. However, one beautiful girl, Peggy Wilson, attracted me. Sadly for me, she had a steady boyfriend. I could only tease her a bit while I admired her from a distance.

Apart from my studies, which except for Latin, did not greatly complicate my life, I devoted my free time to reading, walking the island with my dog, Bolshevik II,, and competing on the South Portland High School debate team. I enjoyed the give and take of argumentation and ended the year by winning the State of Maine Individual Debating Championship. With it came a $100 scholarship to Bates. The topic for debate in 1939 was "An Anglo-American Alliance." I defended the affirmative. In my talking points appeared the following rather prescient question: "What policy would the United States pursue if we saw the Japanese empire-builders move toward Singapore, the Malay Peninsula, the Dutch Indies, and eastward halfway across the Pacific?" I argued that an Anglo-American alliance would preclude such a tragic development, just as it would deter Hitler.

My folks were proud of my success as a debater. Better, I had accomplished something of significance on my own, even if it was far from as glamorous as being a hero on the football team. I looked forward to my senior year at South Portland and to the challenge of defending my championship.

But it was not to be. War clouds once again were growing over Europe, as Hitler annexed all of Czechoslovakia and threatened Poland over Danzig. On September 1, 1939, Hitler invaded Poland. Soon thereafter, Britain and France, finally awake to the threat, declared war on Germany. With that, the United States implemented its contingency plan, deploying the 5th Infantry from Maine to the Canal Zone to strengthen the defenses of the Panama Canal.

As a result of Hitler's aggression, I was separated from my father, my mother, my school, my debate team, and my dog.

Elgin Academy

Although it was already September and school had started, my folks somehow managed to enroll me in the Elgin Academy. It, as well as the state reformatory, was located in Elgin, Illinois. This coincidence inspired many poor jokes and much kidding.

Elgin Academy had an advantage other than just having an opening for an additional boarder. I was near Chicago and Grandma Roesch. That helped, but did not offset the separation from my parents, my dog, and my debate team colleagues.

Elgin Academy was not as bad as Cal Prep, which is not to say that it was much better. Once again, I was a new boy thrust into a group where almost everyone had known each other for years. My roommate was a rich kid from Chicago's North Shore. He had started high school at the snotty but educationally excellent New Trier High. For disciplinary reasons, his parents had enrolled him at Elgin. He had an incredible collection of jazz records, which he played full blast until lights-out. Gene Krupa was his favorite, and his drums reverberated throughout the residence hall. We got along by ignoring each other, but it was impossible for me to study in our room with that music blaring. So off I went to study hall. It was some, but not much, better.

Latin was finally behind me. I had passed Latin III unconditionally and knew when to quit. Now French was causing me similar problems. This worried me. Latin had been a pain, but French was a concern. I had made up my mind to be a Foreign Service Officer and knew from perusal of the three day written examination, at that time probably the most difficult exam given in the U.S., that I had to have at least one foreign language under control and preferably two. I figured I could learn enough history, economics, and international law to pass, but I was worried by my seemingly poor capacity for languages.

Except for French, I did well academically at Elgin. Socially, life lacked a good deal. While I was not an unwelcome newcomer, my classmates certainly did not go out of their way to try to get me to fit in. In fact, I did not fit in well. My only real friend was my history professor, who was as concerned about what was happening in Europe as I was. In the spring of 1940, we hung by his radio as the Wehrmacht rolled over Western Europe. The fall of France was a staggering, unbelievably depressing blow.

Apart from school, following world events, and fairly regular weekends in Chicago, where I made up for the poor food of the Academy, my passion became tennis. I played every minute I could. I might have developed into a good player, had there been a decent coach. To get more time on the courts, I attended Catholic mass at 6 a.m. each Sunday. Attending a church service was an Academy requirement, but the requirement did not specify which church one was to attend. It was convenient for me to get the requirement out of the way early in the day. For this, the Catholic Church was the most attractive. By attending 6 a.m. mass, I was on the court by 7 a.m. for a full day of tennis.

Graduation finally came, but not before one more traumatic event. I had been chosen to deliver Lincoln's Gettysburg Address to a Memorial Day assembly of the student body, relatives, and friends. I knew it well and anticipated no problems. Inexplicably, however, my mind went blank halfway through. While I closed with a strong "government of the PEOPLE, by the PEOPLE, and for the PEOPLE shall not perish from the earth," I was mortified. I feared everyone was laughing at me, which of course they were not.

Along with other seniors, I had been thinking about college. I decided to apply to M.I.T., Stanford, and the University of Chicago. M.I.T. said "okay," but for admission in the fall of 1941. Stanford and Chicago accepted me. My folks pushed for Stanford. In a show of independence and confidence in Grandma, I chose the University of Chicago.

University Years

Before entering the University of Chicago, I had a great summer. Dad had arranged for me to sail to Panama from Brooklyn on an Army transport. But first, I was able to visit the New York World's Fair. I ate it up, as I had the Century of Progress in Chicago. After watching a demonstration of TV, I decided it had a future. The Futurama and various sideshows were also enjoyable, with few restrictions on my attendance this time. The city itself, too, was not Chicago, but not bad, pulsating with life.

The voyage up Panama was notable for an evening out in San Juan, Puerto Rico. My somewhat older shipmates introduced me to Cuba Libres—lots of Cuba Libres, far too many Cuba Libres. I was drunk for the first time. My buddies, enjoying it more than I, got me safely back to ship, but the hangover ruined some otherwise pleasant days at sea. It was years before I tried another rum and coke.

In Panama, Dad's unit was stationed up the Canal from the Pacific at Paraíso. Mother had rooms at the Tivoli Hotel, where I joined her. With a defense construction boom underway, anyone, even seventeen-year-old boys, could get work. Thus I began my years as a government employee with the Constructing Quartermaster Corps. I was timekeeper for a small project within walking distance of the hotel. Putting in ten hours a day in the sun and rain left me drained. At night, when I had the strength, I would explore Central Avenue, just across the fence separating the Canal Zone from the rest of Panama. There, Chinese and Indian stores were filled with items I had never seen before. There were ivory carvings, bronze gongs, incense, camphor wood chests, intricate puzzle boxes, silks and many more wonders. When I decided to spend some of my hard earned cash, I bought a red Buddha on a black stand and a Dunhill pipe.

Mother had forbidden cigarettes, but said nothing about pipes. When she saw me puffing away, she told me to stop until she could discuss pipe smoking with Dad. Their joint verdict was favorable. I smoked pipes for the next thirty-nine years. The Buddha was a treasure I gave to Peggy Zimmer to keep for me during the war. I came home safely just as Peggy was getting married to Webb Fiser, so I parted with it for good, making it their wedding present. I wonder what happened to it.

Other teenagers in Panama that summer chose not to work. Thus they were free to enjoy the lively social life, complete with bars, many parties, and lots of girls. My social development was delayed, but I really did not know what I was missing. I was proud of my job; I was saving money for extras at school and feeling good about it. In fact, I even proposed to my folks that I delay school and go on helping the defense effort. Fortunately, they talked the silly boy out of that.

I think my mother enjoyed Panama more than any other assignment. Why?

For one thing, she was in better health than she had been for a long time. From my birth on, Mother was frequently in and out of hospitals. Her fragile health was, I think, the reason I never had a brother or sister. Regrettably, my parents were too reticent about such things to explain why my pleas for a sibling were in vain.

For another, in Panama she found a cause outside the home to which to devote herself. She threw herself into Red Cross work, first heading the unit devoted to helping the British, then serving as chairman for all voluntary services in the Canal Zone. Fund raising, collecting clothing, and bandage rolling were key tasks. Mother was a good organizer and thrived on the challenge. It didn't hurt that she was comfortably ensconced in the Hotel Tivoli, dedicated to gracious colonialist living, or that she was now less preoccupied about my health, which was robust.

When the time came to leave Panama, I had another wonderful trip, this time to San Francisco, again on an Army transport. Since the ship was scheduled to stay docked for a few days, I was allowed to sleep onboard. I explored San Francisco and the San Francisco World Fair. Two World Fairs in one year was really something.

Overall, I liked the city more than I had New York. Although the setting for the San Francisco Fair was spectacular, I thought the New York Fair was more educational and fun.

From California, I took a train to Chicago, where l moved in with Grandma Roesch for a few days of waiting for the dorms to open.

The magic day of entering the university arrived. What excitement: new faces, new places, new challenges. I had a room to myself in Judson Court, a men's residence hall across the Midway from the main campus. Orientation activities dominated the first week, complete with lectures, mixers, dances, fraternity house visits, and receptions, at one of which I shook President Robert Maynard Hutchins' hand. We were left in no doubt that the University of Chicago was a serious educational institution, best symbolized, I guess, by President Hutchins' decision to abolish intercollegiate football. He is also known for his not-very-clever declaration that when he felt like exercising, he lay down until the feeling went away. If the abolition of football was a symbol, the educational reality was an incredibly strong faculty and a comprehensive curriculum.

After careful contemplation, I decided not to pledge to a fraternity. It was a good decision from the academic and financial points-of-view, but less good from the social adaptability point-of-view.

My faculty advisor urged me to pursue intermediate French even though I had done badly with first-year French at Elgin Academy. Since I was still dreaming of a Foreign Service career, he easily convinced me. I struggled with French all year, but at least I did not fail. Nevertheless, my "D" in French was the worst grade I would get at the university. English also proved to be difficult. I barely scraped out a "C." As a freshman, I took two of the famous College core courses, Biological Sciences and Social Sciences. The lectures, readings, and discussions were designed primarily to teach us to think. Physiologist Anton Carlton, among others, never tired of asking us to ask "What is the evidence?" The approach was entirely different from what I had known in high school. I was fascinated, but the volume of reading, often hundreds of pages a week, overwhelmed me. I didn't do too well on quizzes and quarterly exams. However, in the Chicago system your grade for the year depends entirely on how you do in the final course comprehensive examination. By dint of many extra hours of hard study and careful review of key concepts, I earned As in BiSci and SocSci, thereby salvaging the year and my pride.

Living on the same floor of Judson were, among others: Herb Madison, who became a lifelong friend and best man at my marriage; Bertrand Dreyfus, a refugee from German-occupied France, who when not studying physics spent countless hours in the stacks of Harper Library reading whatever he could find about the famous Dreyfus case and Emile Zola's courageous denunciation of the French government in his article "J'Accuse"; and Stu Schulberg, the younger brother of Budd Schulberg, whose book, *What Makes Sammy Run*, was a bestseller we all read. I met most of my friends, however, not in the dorm or in class, but at Student Forum. The Forum was a university-sponsored group devoted to debates and talks about any subject under the sun. Because the university seemingly built obstacles to my ambition to make the freshman tennis team, I eventually concentrated my extra-curricular efforts on Student Forum. There I made a number of lifelong friends.

One friend, Bill Durka, a brilliant pre-law student, won election as the Forum President in 1942. I probably would have succeeded him in 1943 had I not entered the Army. Bill, unable to serve because of a physical handicap, finished law school, practiced communications law for a while, and then joined the General Counsel's office of GE. Thereafter he became President of a GE subsidiary making movies and still later represented GE on trade issues being negotiated in the Tokyo round of multilateral trade talk. Now retired, he alleges he is writing a "great book." He's been at this for years, which makes me wonder if he will ever finish. I hope so, since I would like to read it.

Another lifetime friend was Don Dewey. His passion was and is the movies. Don served as a military policeman during the war. After postgraduate study at home and in England, where he met and married his wife Ruth, as well as academic stints here and there, he retired as a professor of economics at Columbia University. His work undermining the case for government regulation and applying economic analysis to anti-trust issues drew much praise.

Gordon Tullock, an abrasive genius type, was my frequent debate partner. After obtaining a postwar law degree, Gordon scored the highest grade ever on the Foreign Service written examination. Temperamentally unsuited for a bureaucratic career, Gordon left the Service, but not before studying Chinese at Yale and serving in China. From his China years, he drew unusual material for his books on bureaucracy and economics. His most memorable achievement, however, was applying elements of economic theory to develop the theory of public choice with James Buchanan. Buchanan was awarded the Nobel Prize for Economics; sadly, his collaborator went without even a nod. Gordon, bitter, nevertheless carried on as Professor of Economics and Political Science at the University of Arizona.

Now retired after a distinguished career as a sociologist, Joe "Jerry" Kahl took me into his home in Chicago. Jerry's mother set a much more elegant table in their Chicago Gold Coast apartment than I was accustomed to from Army family life, at Grandma's, or at school. I was embarrassed, for example, by not knowing how to handle a fish knife or eat poached eggs, but the gracious senior Kahls both reassured me and advanced my education in "proper" social behavior. Jerry is unique among my friends in that he went to the university with socialist leanings, emerged with his beliefs unscathed, and today brags about being a lifelong Democrat, except for once when he strayed to vote for Henry Wallace.

It seems to me that there is something intrinsically wrong with most sociologists. Jerry is no exception. He wrote me in many of my posts, partly to congratulate me on position, but principally, it seemed to me, to criticize U.S. policy. He was, like so many sociologists in Latin America, attracted to Marxism and blinded by Fidel Castro. Sociologists seem to focus on the ills of society, rather than on resource constraints or limitations of the political system. As a result they are prone to softheaded thinking. For all of this, there are few people I would rather spend time with than Jerry Kahl. He is wrong about many things, but he is stimulating.

Warren Nutter was a totally different case. He entered Chicago with strong leftist leanings, did a hundred and eighty degree about face, and became a militant rightist. Warren and I each admired, almost to the point of worship, Henry C. Simons. Simons was a major intellectual influence on us both. It seemed to me, however, that Warren became a rabid extremist. I doubt Simons would have approved. In any case, Warren had a strong academic career and also served as an Assistant Secretary of Defense in the Nixon administration, where we were colleagues. Sadly, he passed on prematurely.

Other good university friends, with most of whom, to my deep regret, I am no longer in touch, included Dick Hill, Dick Emmet, Peggy and Webb Fiser, they of the Red Buddha, and George Probst, the faculty supervisor of Student Forum.

We Student Forum members had fun. Talking to a labor union group about the Nazi and fascist menace, I was astonished to hear from the floor an impassioned defense of the Italian invasion of Greece on the grounds that Greek cooking had to be eliminated. To my chagrin, more of the audience agreed with this gastronomic view than with my political points.

In the spring of 1941, our debate team went to Madison, Wisconsin for the Big Ten debate championships. Gordon Tullock and I won both of our debates, beating Wisconsin and Northwestern, but the rest of the team did badly. Still, for the first time in years, the

University of Chicago did not finish in the cellar. The more notable part of the trip, however, was "motoring" back to Chicago.

Eight of us in two cars had driven the 150 miles to Madison, Wisconsin, with no serious problems. However, what should have been a four-hour return trip turned into a twelve-hour endurance test. The car I was traveling in had used two gallons of oil to get to Madison, so we were ready with extra oil for the return trip. But we were not ready for a car with a dead battery that had to be towed to a filling station. Nor were we ready for a flat tire in the middle of the night in a blizzard. Then, on the outskirts of Chicago, I shouted that it sounded to me like a wheel was coming off. Our driver, without slowing, announced that wheels never came off when it sounded like they might. Only it did. So we abandoned the car. All eight of us, crammed into the second car, returned safely, if belatedly, to the university.

Politics was a growing interest. I liked FDR, but I didn't like his third-term ambitions. Moreover, Wendell Willkie made sense to me. He was the first of a long line of losers I have supported. But I did agree with Roosevelt's efforts to aid the Allies. By early 1941, I was advocating American entry into the war. As the debate between America First and Aid the Allies raged, I passed out handbills at train stations urging aid for the Allies. I also enrolled in two extracurricular military courses: one simple drilling and tactics, the other military history and strategy. Our drills, and particularly the one maneuver we attempted, were hilarious farces. However, reading great military thinkers from Sun Tzu to Clausewitz was fascinating, as were the lectures given without notes by William H. McNeill, a young historian later to become famous.

To my surprise, Dad extended his tour of duty in Panama. He could not resist the offer to form and train one of the first, if not the first, air-borne units in the U.S. Army, the 550th Air Borne Battalion. Its mission was to move into any country near the Canal should known German sympathizers threaten to gain control. As C.O. of this reaction force, Dad visited nearby countries, up to Guatemala in the North and down to Peru in the South. While this was a great job for Dad, it posed problems for me, especially when the War Department informed me that transportation for dependents to Panama would not be available in 1941. Herb Madison, who was planning a camping trip in the Rockies, invited me to join him. For a while it looked like I would spend my summer in a tent, despite my hopes of returning to Panama for the summer. At the last moment, however, my mother decided she had to see me. So I received a PanAm ticket from Brownsville, Texas to Albrook Field in the Canal Zone. How my folks financed this I do not know. Money was tight. Indeed, I had to submit monthly accounts of all of my expenditures at the university. Maybe Grandpa Roesch helped once again. Who knows?

After a slow, hot train ride from Chicago to Brownsville, clearly a non-place with an airport, I took off in a Pan-American DC-3. In 1941 there were no night flight facilities, no radio beacons, and no runway lights. Consequently, we overnighted in Guatemala City well before dark after puddle jumping south through Mexico. PanAm lodged us in a modest hotel, where we had an excellent dinner of chicken, beans, rice, and tortillas. Only later did we learn the chicken was iguana. Psychological conditioning might have kept us from eating a large lizard had we known. However, we didn't know until later. Best of all, the iguana was delicious. In the future, when others looked askance at iguana, I enjoyed my meal. This acquired taste increased my popularity with *guatemaltecos* when years later I returned as an American diplomat. My colleagues might gag, but I enjoyed myself at iguana feasts.

After dinner, some heavy equipment operators, also en route to the Canal Zone, invited me to see the town with them. We started at the Plaza Central where a colorful fiesta in celebration of who-knows-what was underway. It was like the 4th of July, complete with fireworks, only in this case skyrockets were mounted on paper mache bullheads. When the individuals inside the make-believe bulls saw fit, they fired the rockets into the crowd. It was lots of fun if you didn't get hit. My friends and I took refuge behind a large tree on the corner of the square. I've been back many times to admire that tree. Years later, when I lived in Guatemala, I saw much violence but never again *toros* armed with skyrockets.

When the excitement in the Plaza died down, the tough construction workers, no doubt influenced by hormonal surges, decided it was time for some action. We toured the brothels of Guatemala City in two taxis. I was disgusted by the whores and amazed at the stamina of the men. They thought I was a wimp not to participate, but I wanted nothing of such a sad spectacle. Brawny as they were, they were kind enough not to insist that I lose my virginity then and there. We took off for Panama bright and early the next morning, with stops en route in San Salvador, El Salvador, Managua, Nicaragua, and San Jose, Costa Rica.

Back in the Canal Zone, I passed the summer of 1941 much as I had that of 1940. This time I was a materials expediter on a large construction project. I rode a truck all day from site to site taking notes on what was needed. Then I saw to it that the materials arrived where needed on time. The driver of my truck was an Italian. Of course, he told me his life story. His ambition was to reach the States, but he went to Chile when he escaped Fascist Italy. It was clear to me from his stories of the wondrous women and wonderful wines that he was sorry he had not stayed there. However, he had chosen to work his way north. He didn't think much of Peru, Ecuador, or Panama. They couldn't compare with Chile. Now he was counting on earning enough money on defense construction sites to see him safely to the States. I lost touch with him, so I do not know if he made it, but I bet he did.

I have often thought it was indeed a strange coincidence that when the Foreign Service sent me to Latin America years later my first post was in the Guatemala of my memorable early adventures in eating and carousing. From there I was transferred to the Chile of the Arabian Nights stories told by my Italian friend. Believe it or not, the summer of 1941 foreshadowed my future by more than twenty-five years, to say nothing of the beautiful Chilean lady I was to marry thirty years later.

The Army Transport *Siboney* on which it was somehow arranged I should return to New York was nowhere near as comfortable as the *Republic* had been. Worse, it was September and hurricane season in the Caribbean. We caught the fringes of a major one. How the Siboney rolled. Waves broke clear over her. For the first, but not the last, time in my life I was seasick, real seasick.

New York City was more fascinating than ever and I was better able to enjoy it. I met Bertrand Dreyfus and some of his French friends for a night of good eating and camaraderie. Then I went on to see Uncle Rudolf and Aunt Erdine in Syracuse. I also saw another university friend, Walt Grody, in Syracuse. I then went back to Chicago to the by-now familiar dorm life and academic grind.

Only 1941 was different. Pearl Harbor changed almost everything. I was assiduously studying, with the radio playing classical music softly, when the program was interrupted by the startling news of the Japanese attack. Soon the Army would take over Judson Court. Herb Madison and I would briefly room together at International House, only to be bounced by the Navy. But first, Herb took me downtown for a steak dinner. I had won my bet that we would be at war by the end of the year.

Now I and millions of other young men agonized over what to do. Enlist? Wait for the draft? Which service? Robert Hutchins encouraged us to wait, saying Government should call and place each one where best he could serve.

My decision was to increase my already heavy course load and attend school year-round. I wanted to be as far along toward my degree as possible before putting on my uniform. Then the Army announced its Enlisted Reserve Program, designed to give students enough time to finish their degree work while also making them available for immediate service if needed. This program made sense to me. A number of my friends and I signed up.

At registration time, I substituted Social Science II for the Spanish course I had planned to take as more preparation for the Foreign Service career of which I still dreamed. I kept alive some hope of mastering a foreign language by monitoring the French course that had given me so much pain my freshman year. This helped, but clearly I was not cut out to be a linguist.

About this time, I decided I might become an economist. One source of inspiration was Henry C. Simons. Likable, caustically critical of such as Alvin Hansen of Harvard, and enormously talented as an expositor, Simons brought economics alive. On the other hand, Frank Knight, far more famous an economist, induced sleep, at least in me. With Knight we spent months on a chapter or two of Ricardo's *Principles*. With Simons we slew Keynesian dragons with time left over for *A Positive Program for Laissez-Faire*. My appreciation for Simons grew during the war, when he corresponded with me and sent me reprints of his articles. No other of my professors paid attention to me once I was a GI.

Economics was part of the Social Science program. It had to be supplemented with other SocSci courses by university rule. A European History course was a snap for me, but a graduate course in Eastern European History required a major research paper. I did mine on Czechoslovakian foreign policy pre-Munich, paying much attention to the role of Foreign Minister Edvard Beneš. This paper, which still reads well, was my first serious study of a foreign policy issue.

Despite the war, Student Forum carried on. Only now, a University Steering Group largely set our agenda. Our lectures and roundtables, presented to church groups, social clubs, labor unions, and what have you, were now focused on war-related subjects, such as civil defense and how individuals could help the war effort, for example, by conservation. What time I had left over after studies and the Student Forum war effort was devoted to bridge and theater-going. Gertrude Lawrence in "Lady in the Dark" was a high point of 1942. Sadly, the debate team foundered and tennis was a memory.

When bounced from International House to make room for the Navy, I finally found a room in, of all places, the Chicago Theological Seminary. No theology for me, but there was a bad bed in a convenient location between classes and eating establishments. The monk-like silence of the Theological Seminary did facilitate studying. Perhaps it also stimulated me to write a serious birthday letter to mother.

Like most young people, I was both idealistic and naive. Still, my letter contained some significant insights. "'There is today," I wrote, "such a close interrelationship existing between the activities, social, political, and economic, of the peoples of the world that the situation anywhere will ultimately affect America and vice versa." The doctrine of interdependence came naturally to me.

For the solution of the horrendous postwar problems I foresaw, I proposed applying social controls to the process of change while respecting individual rights. As I think of this now, I recognize I was much too much enthralled by government social engineering. Although faithful to Simon's doctrine of positive laissez-faire, I had much too positive a view of government controls. In my letter, I concluded I intended to devote my life to helping make the required changes, either as a U.S. or international civil servant or by influencing public opinion by working in radio, publishing, or politics. Blindly, despite my exposure at the New York World Fair, I did not mention television as a molder of public opinion.

Mother replied I should understand the fundamental ills of the world came from human selfishness. Human nature, she asserted, was immutable. I disagreed. I thought human nature could be changed with education and improved living conditions. Thus we pursued an argument about the nature of men that has been raging at least since the great Greek philosophers and perhaps well before them.

On March 26, 1943, at just twenty years old and some two and a half years after starting a four-year degree program, I received my Bachelor of Arts degree from the University of Chicago at a solemn Commencement in Rockefeller Chapel. Less than a week later, I reported for active duty as a soldier.

2

Soldiering (1943–1945)

My goals when I reported for active duty were two. Young and foolish, I wanted to fight and I wanted to be an officer. My father had enlisted in the infantry and gone to Officer Candidate School (OCS). Clearly, I should do as my old man. Like most twenty-year-olds, if I thought about it at all, I assumed I was immortal, the one who would survive intact, come what may.

Thus I was disappointed when after a short period at Scott Field I was sent to Miami Beach for Army Air Corps basic training. I had asked for the infantry, but my letter home on April 17 notes, "The interviewer didn't even write it down. He told me the classifying officer would put me where I fitted."

Disappointed or not, bunking on the seventh floor of the St. Moritz Hotel with an ocean view wasn't hard to take, especially after freezing all winter at the Chicago Theological Center. Moreover, the physical activity connected with training, even KP, screen washing details, and bakery oven cleaning were a welcome change from the endless grind of books and paper writing. Just joking about oven cleaning—one of the nastiest, dirtiest, hottest jobs I've ever had.

Air Force basic training, processing included, was supposed to last a bit less than a month. However, that allowed no time for disorganization. Having arrived in Miami April 17, 1943, I should have gone on long before June, but in fact it was the end of July before I was transferred to the Citadel to join the Army Specialist Training Program (ASTP). In the meantime, I had been moved out of the St. Moritz and indeed out of almost a dozen other makeshift barracks, one week being moved three times. In early May I wrote home, "By a queer piece of paper work, yesterday we were in the 9th day of 18 days of training, today we finished the 16th day of 56 days of training." I completed basic training, completed it again, and was shuffled from the 412th Training Group Flight N-2 to Flight L of the 412th to the 416th Training Group, starting in Flight K before being moved to Flight L. It was confusion magnified to the point of chaos. We learned to sing "Off we go into the wild blue yonder" at the top of our voices. Units were judged on noise volume, not artistry.

Through it all I kept pushing for OCS. Writing Dad, I noted only ten days service was required before applying and "I'm a veteran of almost three weeks." In May, I went before the OCS Board and passed for the Field Artillery with "flying colors." The next day my colors were shot away when I failed the eye examination. My reapplication for the Engineers, Chemical Warfare, or Ordnance did not look promising, and soon I withdrew it to concentrate on ASTP.

However, ASTP was not to pan out either. Sent to the Citadel for exams, all of which I did well on, the placement officers ruled I was overqualified for Basic Engineering and under qualified for Advanced Engineering, despite my test scores, since I lacked a college-level course in physics. It was a real catch-22 situation. At the end of my letter home about this disappointment, I noted that while the Army fidgets deciding what to do with me, "I'll have a fine time goofing off here." And I did, Charleston being one of the better U.S. cities for "goofing off."

Herb Madison, stationed at Camp Jackson, also had some free time, so we arranged to meet for a weekend in Columbia, South Carolina. However, unbeknownst to us, there was a curfew in Columbia. So we had an adventurous night dodging military policemen (MPs), eventually sleeping a bit in a union hall down by the railroads, where a kindhearted night w a t c h m a n took pity on us. Great fun, no harm done, and we both got back where the Army thought we belonged without more problems.

After two weeks of "goofing off" and eating Citadel grits at every meal, I was transferred to the 1189th Training Group in Greensboro, North Carolina. For a while it looked like I would once again do basic training, but somehow I talked myself into a cushy desk job typing up furloughs. Best of all, there was time for reading at a good post library, where I soon finished Lee's *Lieutenants*, all three volumes. Finally, over six months after I had gone on active duty, the Army decided I was to be a cryptographer. Accordingly, in mid-September I started school at Chanute Field, Illinois.

School was tough, but being with Pep Paulson, a friend from college with lots of free time to play bridge, made up for it. Of course, the Army, or more accurately an officer thereof, screwed up after promising to assign Pep and me to the same unit. There went our bridge partnership. Worse, Pep didn't make it home from the war.

One good thing about Chanute Field was it was not far from Chicago. It was a joy to get back to see Grandma, the university, which sure looked good after seven months in the Army, and lots of old friends, most also with weekend passes.

At the end of October, I received a furlough and headed to Fort Meade, South Dakota, where Dad commanded the 88th Glider Infantry. Of course, the regiment had no gliders, but they were supposed to come later. What Fort Meade did have was bitterly cold weather. It also had a young officer who, to brownnose his C.O., my dad, invited me to go horseback riding with him. Not wanting to disgrace Dad, I accepted even though I had had it with horses years before in Arizona. It was awful; the horses, Calvary mounts, had not been ridden in months. The ground was frozen and the temperature was somewhere near zero. So with skittish horses on icy ground, the problem was not to enjoy a ride, but to stay on. Eventually we got safely back to the stables, but I resolved then and there to avoid horses in the future. My other memory of that leave was the parlous health of Mother. Shortly thereafter she went into the Mayo Clinic for a successful operation.

From Chanute, I was transferred to the Salt Lake City Base Air Corps replacement depot. I was getting closer to being assigned to a unit, but bureaucratic snafus delayed me in Salt Lake for an extra two weeks. It turned out there was another Hinton at the base. I received his pay (great, since he was a sergeant), but he received my transfer orders, not so great for either of us. With all of this straightened out, in early December I took a train to Denver and then to Harvard, Nebraska, where a newly constructed air base was home to the 484th Heavy Bombardment Group, scheduled to fly B-24s. Only two of these were at the base when I arrived.

After getting off the train at Harvard one cold morning, a buddy also assigned to the 484th and I could see nothing but blowing snow. In a few minutes a truck arrived and hauled us out to the base. One reason we couldn't see anything in town besides the snow was because there was nothing to see. Reportedly Harvard had a population of 787, but they were not to be seen. The base was not much either: low lying barracks, a flight control tower, and a couple of small operations buildings, in one of which I would work as a cryptographer. Flatter country I had never seen and would never see again. Flat, desolate, and cold, oh so cold.

Somehow, however, we got through our training program, which stepped up in intensity week by week as aircraft arrived and flying time mounted. More flying, more time on duty for cryptographers. Still I got away occasionally to Hastings and once to Lincoln. A buddy and I hitchhiking to Lincoln were picked up by a couple of young fellows who kindly passed around their fifth of whiskey. We drank more than our share in hopes of keeping our driver sober enough to get us to Lincoln. Years later in Guatemala, I had a similar experience, but with a pilot in a small plane. Both were memorable days that I was lucky to survive.

In early March 1944 after weeks of speculation about where in the Pacific we were headed, the Group's ground personnel were trucked to the Harvard station (still nothing in Harvard), where a troop train headed east awaited us.

The long ride to a staging area near Norfolk left me with another memory. One early morning we pulled into Hinton, West Virginia, a coal-mining center. Someone woke me to see my namesake of a town. In the early morning mountain mist, it was squalid, dirty, rundown, and generally a disgrace to the family name. Whether my side of the Hinton clan could trace roots back to Hinton, West Virginia, I know not; but if so, I know why they moved on west.

My twenty-first birthday was passed somewhere near Norfolk. Few of my fellow soldiers could understand how it was possible I was twenty-one and still a virgin. Clearly they thought I had been missing out on something important. I was less inclined to argue with each passing day.

With that milestone behind me, the Army, as a birthday present, gave me a trip to Italy. We traveled in a Liberty ship in a slow convoy that zigged and zagged across the Atlantic. We were jammed in the hold with hardly room to move. The bunks were stacked five high with about two feet of headroom in each. The brief time we were allowed on deck each day was eagerly looked forward to, whatever the weather. Some were even allowed to sleep on deck, as I did on a number of nights. But the most memorable of nights found me below, sleeping soundly, when all hell broke loose. Off Algeria at dawn, the Germans attacked our convoy with submarines and torpedo aircraft. The hell that reverberated through our tub of a Liberty ship was the antiaircraft fire from the fleet, including some from our ship. The squadron adjutant used the public address system to tell us to keep calm, but his voice broke. Most of us laughed at the poor fellow. We kept calm since there was nothing else to do. Had we taken a torpedo that would have been the end. No real way out of a Liberty ship. Post

action accounts from those on deck told of a torpedo just yards off our stern. Was this so or was it a storyteller's invention? In any case, we didn't get hit, but we did learn in a hurry the war was for real.

Our convoy paused a day or so at Valletta, Malta, breaking up into smaller convoys. Then our tub sailed around the boot of Italy and landed us one sunny day at Brindisi. A small engine pulling a number of dilapidated boxcars awaited us. Once loaded, we chugged slowly northward, stopping quite a while in Bari where air raid sirens howled, but without an air raid. Eventually we disembarked from trucks near Cerignola and trucked west of town to what euphemistically was called Torretta Air Base. It was part of the large Foggia complex of 15th Air Force bases. Once out of our trucks, we were ordered to dig foxholes first, then erect tents. As it got darker, we concluded on our own tents were a better idea than foxholes.

Few foxholes were ever finished. Fortunately, Jerry never paid us a visit. Had he bombed or strafed our field and tents, the survivors would have quickly become as adept at foxhole digging as were those of our colleagues who had liberated Tunisia, where the German Air Force harassed the Allies day in and day out for months.

Fifty-one years later, I returned to Brindisi, Bari, Cerignola, and Foggia. Apart from the cathedral in Cerignola, nothing looked as I remembered it. To my annoyance, I could not even find remnants of Torretta airfield, much less the large stone farmhouse that had been group headquarters and had housed the code room I had manned.

We were located in a poor farming area. When we arrived at Easter, the fields were as lush and green as they ever got. Soon, however, the nearly perpetual wind kicked up tons of dust. It seeped into everything, everywhere. In the fall and winter, with rain and snow, we bogged down in mud. My letters home to Mother, five or six a month, are dull reading: complaints about the wind, the dust, the mud, the cold, and requests for chocolates, books, pipe tobacco, cookies, cheese, and film. When I tried to tell her something interesting, the censor intervened. I pushed so hard that at one point I was made to read the regulations governing censorship. They were overdone, but I came to recognize I could not win. Mother once asked me to explain the (P) in my address: 825th Bomb Squadron, 484th Bomb Group (P). Of course, the Germans knew as well as I the P stood for Pathfinder, but my explanation of this was cut out of the letter. Our group, which was to win two presidential citations and seven battle stars, had the honor, perhaps dubious given the extra risks involved, of leading the 49th Wing on raids. Our navigators were the best.

Incredibly, although I had a safe job way behind the lines, I was also awarded seven battle stars. It did not matter that I had not been within a thousand miles of the battle in Normandy. It counted, since the 484th Group had dropped bombs on Normandy. The real benefit was each battle star turned out to be worth five points toward early discharge when the war in Europe ended.

We had not been in Italy long when I and two other cryptographers were sent to Algiers for advanced training. Specifically, we were taught how to use British Second Cipher, a machine system nowhere near as easy to use as the U.S. machine system. It was just as well that we mastered the system, since during the landings in southern France and the push up the Rhone our group flew support for a British headquarters using Second Cipher. The three of us who knew it worked around the clock for days. I felt we were making a contribution during that period. Among other drawbacks, the British system produced endless garbles unless you typed exactly fifty characters a minute to match the fifty-cycle current. Be that as it may, Algiers was a most welcome break. We were housed in a decent school in Maison Carrée, had good food, and got frequent passes into town. Eventually upon my return to Italy, the censors even passed my description of the kasbah as a sixteenth-century village set in the middle of a twentieth-century city. I couldn't get that out of North Africa, even though the war had moved on a year before, but my group censor in Italy was more relaxed, at least as far as the kasbah of Algiers was concerned.

On the flight back from Algiers to Tunis to Caserta, I had a long talk with a Foreign Service Officer. Whoever he was, he encouraged me to keep my ambition to join the Service alive. He also encouraged me to study Italian. I tried, even taking classes in Cerignola, half an hour away from our base by bouncy truck if you could get a ride, but I just didn't have the willpower to stay with it. One of my many mistakes.

Back at our base, I found myself "volunteered" to help run our small squadron store, our Post Exchange (PX). Once hooked, I worked hard at it. Unfortunately it took a lot of extra time, time therefore unavailable for language study, but my efforts may have helped me win the designation as the senior cryptographer in the squadron, which carried with it a "rocker" under my sergeant's stripes, making me a staff sergeant, no less. Moral: Do more than just your job and you may be noticed favorably by higher-ups.

The PX job also got my buddy Dave Miller and me out of tent life, although I'm not sure that bunking in our small PX was a real improvement. The PX was a former pigpen, "modernized" with a door and a roof. Its advantage was that it was far more weather proof than our tent; its disadvantage was that the PX goodies attracted rats, large rats, very large rats that often jumped on you in your bunk at night. One night when I was working the code room, Dave shot at one with his 45mm pistol, missing, but deafening himself in the constrained quarters. Not a good idea!

However, the rats encouraged us to improve our living conditions by building our own house. Winter was coming so five of us pooled our resources, bought "Tufa blocks," stole beams to support the inadequately waterproofed old tenting we used for a roof, and salvaged from crashed aircraft flow valves, aluminum tubing, and plastic for windows. The tubing ran from a fifty gallon drum of aviation fuel to our stove, the fire box of which was the base end of a shell casing sitting in half an empty fifty gallon drum, from which a chimney pipe protruded through the roof. Burning 100-octane aviation fuel, mixed with fuel oil when we could get it, and dripping it drop by drop into the shell casing kept us warm the winter of 1944.

Such stoves were illegal. With more reason than was usual, the powers that be thought aviation fuel should be reserved for airplanes bombing Germany. However, our officers and flight crews liked to keep warm on the ground, just as we did, so they perforce looked the other way. Worse than illegal, these stoves were dangerous. Many tents and houses burned during the winter, with some casualties. I singed my eyebrows relighting an upscale model installed in the group code room. My burns would have been serious had I not been shielded from the explosion by a doorway.

When we decided to build our house, I wrote Mother it might take a week or so. Of course, it took almost two months. Officers with easy access to vehicles could more easily find and "requisition" materials for their houses. It was much harder for us. Acquiring the roof rafters was critical but required real stealth and a bit of bribery. Even hiring workers, so-called masons, was not easy, given that almost everyone had decided to build at the same time. Still the effort was worthwhile. We were warmer, drier, and had much more light through our windows than ever we had had in our tent or the PX hut. And the toasted Velveeta cheese sandwiches from the top of our stove were out of this world. Mothers could not send us enough cheese.

Although I had gotten to Naples, it was November before I snagged a coveted pass for a visit to Rome. What a city. The visit was worth two twelve-hour truck rides through the snow-covered Apennines. One memory: a pit stop that led to an invitation from members of the 10th Indian Division to join them "for a spot of tea." I still had that memory when I inspected its successor division in 1985, the 10th Pakistani in Lahore.

The Red Cross was well established in Rome. Their tours for GIs were great. They even got me into a papal audience for U.S. troops. I figured the Pope's blessing wouldn't hurt, but was far more impressed with St. Peter's and especially Michelangelo's Sistine Chapel. I thought the chapel just about the greatest thing I had ever seen. Hardly an original thought, but a sincere one. Also in Rome I had a most satisfying and instructive night with an attractive lady who convinced me sex could be more than physical relief from hormonal pressures. My letters home, however, were silent on this, so I write only from memory.

I reflected about the papal ceremony, "The pomp and pageantry is one more reminder of the ritual which the Catholic Church insists upon. It is beautiful, but a poor substitute for bread. Or maybe the people wouldn't have bread anyway, so ritual is better than nothing."

While in Rome I stopped by the Headquarters for American Military Government, hoping my qualifications might land me a job. I got no further than the sentry at the gate of what later I came to know as the American Embassy on Via Veneto. "Soldier, just head back to your unit," he said. My hopes ended right there.

As the year ended, we had a Christmas tree in our house, lots of packages with most welcome edibles, and concern over the German offensive in the Ardennes. Still looking for a way out of the boring life of a code clerk, I was busy studying administrative regulations and procedures in preparation for an examination for appointment as a Warrant Officer. I also contemplated applying for an Infantry Officer Candidate School in response to a circular. Shavetails, as second lieutenants were called, didn't last too long in the infantry, so it's just as well that idea came to naught.

On New Year's Eve I drank too much, far too much, Italian gin. Staggering home at about 2 a.m., I fell into a slit trench filled with water. I might have drowned except the water was so cold it revived me and I crawled to safety. For years after that I couldn't drink gin, even good gin.

A cryptographer's life at an air base was not all that exciting. Most of our work came in the early evening when the orders for the next day's missions were received. We cryptographers were the first at the base to know if targets were hard ones or if, for a change, the group was to have a milk run. When I walked the orders into the flight crew's briefing room, many were those, it seemed to me, who looked at me to see if I would give a sign of what was coming.

Apart from work, I gradually fell into a study routine of some Italian, some French, some international law from a correspondence course (unfinished), and some mathematics for economists. But I probably spent more time playing poker, bridge, and chess. When the group bridge and chess championships came along, it was announced the champions would get leave and a trip to the Air Force Rest Camp in Nice, France. Joe Egan and I won the enlisted bridge tournament, only to be badly beaten by the winning officer pair. I won the enlisted chess championship, but once again was beaten by an officer, a B-24 navigator. Sadly, the next day the Group Chess Champion was killed on a mission. Nowhere near as sad, but nevertheless sad for me, I was not sent to Nice in his place.

Then came the Warrant Officer (W.O.) exams, oral and written. Somehow I passed. On April 24, I was awarded an honorable discharge and took the oath as a W.O. Regretfully but proudly, I said goodbye to my buddies in the 484th Bomb Group, including especially my dog George, and headed for Rome. Why Rome? Because I was to be an Information and Education Officer and for that I needed to attend an army education staff school. Thus I was on the banks of the Tiber when on May 8, 1945, the war in Europe ended. My fellow classmates and I were among the few in uniform in Italy who were not given the day off to celebrate. The school was judged by some idiot to be on too tight a schedule. Still we lifted a few in the evening.

Just as WWI was won because the Germans were surrounded by my dad in Siberia and his brother in France, so WWII was won because the Germans recognized the futility of continuing when surrounded by Dad in the Supreme Headquarters Allied Expeditionary Force (SHAEF) in France and I in Italy. Or so we tell ourselves in the Hinton family.

To my delight, and in accordance with the best Army traditions, having qualified as an I&E officer I was assigned not to I&E work, but as Assistant Adjutant of the Army Air Corps Rest Camps, with headquarters in Naples. There I was billeted in an apartment building on the waterfront and put to work writing citations so deserving and undeserving officers could receive decorations for their magnificent contributions to winning the war. Citation writing apart, I now had one of the cushiest jobs in Europe. I was at work about eight hours a day. I was living well and eating better than ever before in the Army. Moreover, in May I "had" to spend some time at a rest camp on Capri. Tough duty. Then I was sent to Venice to oversee payroll day. More tough duty. Venice was in its way as impressive as Rome. At the same time, it is, of course, utterly different. Venice is a city I never tire of revisiting. Our hotel on the beach was great, even if the swimming was restricted since few of the German mine fields had been cleared. For the first time in two years, there was all the ice cream one could eat. And it was good.

So, why on July 25, did I leave all of this to become a 2nd Lt. in the Signal Corps, assigned as Message Center Officer (Cryptographic) of the 875th Signal Depot Company, scheduled to ship out directly to the Pacific within a couple of weeks? Why, indeed? My friends thought I was crazy, but the call had come for someone to fill a job for which I was as well qualified as anyone. Moreover, as I wrote at the time, "the war is the dominant movement of our lives....To live fully one must participate in the main act." And so I became an officer after all and also one of the few soldiers during the war to have held three different serial numbers: 160881219 as an enlisted man, W2131656 as a warrant officer, and 02 039 653 as a commissioned officer.

I wrote home that I was back in the Army, living in a tent in a hot, dusty staging area near Naples, washing in my helmet, and eating out of a mess kit. What a letdown from Air Force Rest Camp life. But it wasn't really a letdown. I was delighted with my men (God knows what they thought of me) despite their poor morale. Some of them had started in the Pacific, worked their way to Europe via India and the Red Sea, and were now, lacking a few points for redeployment to the States, on their way back to the Pacific. My fellow officers cordially welcomed me. They promptly set about showing me why war for officers is a better deal than for enlisted men or even warrant officers. They took me various places reserved for officers, the most memorable of which were the downtown transient mess in the Terminus Hotel and the Orange Club overlooking the Bay of Naples. I wrote it had the best dance music, the best view, and the prettiest girls in town. In 1995, I tried and failed to locate it again, but I did find a superb restaurant, more or less in the area where the Orange Club must have been.

On August 6, 1945, en route to the docks in an Army truck convoy, I read in *Stars and Stripes* about the dropping of an atomic bomb on Hiroshima.

The transport we boarded was the Norwegian M.S. *Torrens*. With 1,800 troops aboard, it was far more commodious and comfortable than the Liberty ship that had brought me to Europe. Moreover, we were not slowed by a convoy and cruised at night with lights on. Once settled in, we played cards and speculated incessantly about whether or not the war was almost over.

If the war ended, we asked ourselves, what would happen to us? Would we still go to the Pacific or would we be sent home? With each new radio bulletin, our spirits waxed or waned. Then, at 5:17 a.m. on August 16, about one sailing day from the Panama Canal, the ship's loudspeaker blared out, "Now hear this. Now hear this. By order of the Commander in Chief, we are changing course and proceeding to New York."

No one minded being awakened for that news. What pandemonium. The shouting in the hold must have shaken the bridge. We were elated. It was the most exciting single moment of my life. Going home! What's more I was going home before all of those wise guys in Europe who had told me what a fool I was for signing up for the Pacific. Such a lucky roll of the dice for me.

We disembarked somewhere up the Hudson, where we were the first unit to arrive with full field equipment, including weapons. Units like my dad's regiment, redeploying from Europe, left their field equipment behind, took leave, and were reequipped on the West Coast before proceeding to the Pacific theater of operations. The port authorities were accustomed to putting returning GIs onto the right troop train to get them to an Army facility near their homes, but they wanted nothing to do with our weapons. That is until our C.O. told them off and threatened to just leave our field equipment unattended. At least, we admiringly believed the story of his threat.

So I went on leave to Chicago, where I first lived at Grandma Roesch's with my mother and her parents. On October 28, 1995, at Camp Grant, Illinois, I was paid off and transferred into the reserves. I was a civilian again.

Mine had been an easy war. I was under fire only once, off Algiers in our Liberty ship. I drew blood only once, with my trench knife trying to open a C ration. No Purple Heart for self-inflicted wounds, accidental or otherwise. The only place I began to appreciate the full horror of war was at Casino. I visited after the fighting was over. The crowded temporary military cemeteries, German as well as Allied, made clear the cost of war in lives. The destruction of the town, to say nothing of the Abbey we had futilely bombed to bits, mistakenly thinking it was the key to the German defense, was unlike anything I had seen before. I marveled that the French Moroccans and the Polish Brigade, after numerous failures by others, including U.S. divisions, had finally taken the dominating position held so long by the Germans, which to me looked impregnable. That battlefield visit, reinforced by shocking photos of other battles and consecrated by the atomic destruction at Hiroshima and Nagasaki, left no doubt in my mind about the need to build a lasting peace.

My interest in foreign policy was very much alive. While still in Europe, Mother had been sending me releases of the Commission to Study the Organization of the Peace and the American Association for the United Nations at my request. Nevertheless, whatever my interest in foreign policy, my immediate plan was to return to the University of Chicago to study for a PhD in economics with the help of the GI bill.

PART TWO

Foreign Service Officer Years

3

Critical Decisions (1945–1946)

There were two major developments in my life while I was on terminal leave from the Army. These days such developments are called "defining events." First, my mother introduced me to Angela Peyraud. Second, the State Department announced a special examination for servicemen and women to qualify for entry into the Foreign Service of the United States. Both Angela and State's announcement intrigued me. Soon Angela and I were dating frequently. I was also studying French vocabulary like mad. I made up thousands of cards, French on one side, English on the other, and went over and over them. It was basically impossible to study for the general parts of the Foreign Service examination; you either knew it or you didn't. However, I thought a serious effort on French was needed. I knew my French was poor and I was painfully aware that a grade below 70 on my foreign language test would disqualify me from the Service, however well I might do on the rest of the examination.

Angela worked as a research assistant with Dr. Halstead, an authority on the brain at the University of Chicago. She was good company, intelligent, and modestly ambitious. She and I shared a liking for good food, the theater, and music. By and large, I found her circle of friends to be fine people: the Druids, including her best friend Leslie Sissman, James Foote Adams, and Johnny Lister, a gay pianist. As my college buddies, including Herb Madison, drifted back to the university from the War, they too became Druids.

Al and Bettie Peyraud, Angela's parents, were wonderful hosts to the group. Al mixed a fine rum shrub, much appreciated by all. This type of social life was new to me. I had not had time for it at the university and it simply was not available in the Army. I was enjoying myself, despite my problems with French, and planned to return next academic quarter to the university.

Angela's father, Al Peyraud, edited a dental trade magazine for Coe Laboratories to earn a living, but was in reality a frustrated classical scholar. His father, an excellent landscape painter, had come to the States from Switzerland and settled in the Midwest. Al had married Bettie Grey in Harrisburg, Pennsylvania, just before going to France in World War I. The Greys were a well-known Iowa family.

On November 19 and November 20, 1945, I took the Foreign Service Examination. It was reduced from the prewar three-day test to two days of six hours each, if you were examined in two modem languages. Since I was only trying in French, my second day of exams was only four and a half hours. The results of these stressful ten and half hours were not to be made known for three months.

On November 26, 1945, Angela's 23rd birthday, after a good dinner downtown, I asked her to marry me. The site was hardly romantic. We were sitting on a step in the stairwell leading up to her parents' apartment. Even though she knew I would not know about a job in the Foreign Service for months, she accepted. We were in love, or thought we were, and that was all that mattered.

It is hard more than fifty years later to remember how things were between us at that time. We seemed to enjoy each other's company greatly. We talked fairly freely and necked more freely.

Since life at Grandma Roesch's was confining, Mother had rented an apartment in Cottage Grove. It was a horrible place filled with awful statuary, lamps, cherubs, and an awful assortment of bric-a-brac. Angela and I made good use of the sofa, petting up a storm. But she put strict limits on how far we could go. "That, Deane pie, is for when we are married."

I was back at the university, crowded now with ex-GIs taking advantage of the GI Bill. I registered for a public finance course being given by my favorite professor, Henry C. Simons. He had been good enough to write me and send me some of his articles about taxation while I was overseas. The course was jammed. After the first session, Simons asked Warren Nutter, another student Simons had befriended, and me to see him in his office. There he noted the class was too large for good discussion, asked us to drop out, and promised he would schedule a seminar next quarter for just a few students including Warren and Deane. We agreed, but he welshed, committing suicide (allegedly from worry over Sterling balances, but that makes no sense to me) before we had the promised seminar. It was a sad and strange ending to a brilliant career. Simons's little pamphlet, *A Positive Program for Laissez-Faire*, Friedrich Hayek's *The Road to Serfdom*, and John Stewart Mill's essay *On Liberty* were by far the most important academic influences on my thinking.

In early February I learned I had passed the Foreign Service written examination. I squeaked through with a 70 in French, the minimum acceptable, but did so well on the general sections that I ended up with an 84 average overall. Not bad, but the oral exam still lay before me. Angela was pleased. She said she liked the idea of an overseas life better than being married to a dull, old economist. In any case, my problems with calculus were beginning to dim my enthusiasm for economics. And when Frank Knight, recognized as a deep thinker and great economist, spent an entire quarter of a course entitled "The History of Economic Thought" without getting beyond a chapter or two of Ricardo, my ardor for economics dimmed further.

As the date chosen for our wedding, May 10, 1946, approached, I was having qualms about the whole business. Exactly why, I do not know; I was conscious of the fact that Angela was the first girl I had met upon my return from Europe. Indeed she was the first American girl with whom I had ever had a "hot date." My relations with my lady friends from my university years, including Mary Colley, with whom I corresponded until she informed me she had married another soldier, had been basically platonic. Now the hormones had taken over. I wondered, should I have gotten to know other girls before taking the plunge? Perhaps Angela too had doubts, but we never discussed it. I told Bill Durka a couple of days before the wedding I was troubled, but I couldn't explain why. We concluded that before major changes in life, concern about an uncertain future was natural.

In April I passed the oral examination for the Foreign Service and began the wait for an appointment, not as long in those days as now. The lengthy oral before four examiners was rough, but I knew I had at least one vote when a general asked me, "Who wrote *Lee's Lieutenants*?" "Douglas Southall Freeman, sir," I replied. The general grinned. I later learned he had tried that question many times and few were those who knew the answer. How did I learn this? I learned when years later he told my father about the question. I think the answer, not the general's acquaintanceship with Dad, carried the day. But maybe the connection between the two soldiers, about which I knew nothing, also helped. Who knows?

Angela and I were married in the lovely Episcopal Church of

the Redeemer only a few blocks from the Peyrauds' apartment. It was not close enough, however, that lots of us, including bride and groom, did not get wet from a steady rain. Sadly my dad was still in the Philippines. The reception at the Peyrauds', at which Peyraud friends must have outnumbered Hinton friends by at least four to one, seemed interminable to me. Eventually, the cake cut, the toasts toasted, hands shaken, mothers and mothers-in-law kissed, we slipped away in the old Packard Mother had kindly lent me. We drove only a few blocks to the Windermere East for our first night as a married couple.

It did not go as well as I had thought it would and I dare say Angela felt the same, but sadly we weren't able to talk about it. Puritan upbringing, I suppose. In fact, both of us cooed and talked of love while wondering privately why sex was not up to its reputation. I was not a practiced lover and clearly was impatient after so many months of petting and frustration. Except for a few wonderful occasions, Angela was passionate neither then nor later. Sex for her seemed something she would put up with for me. Even before our honeymoon was over at a state park in southern Indiana she was asking to skip sex some nights.

Whatever that means and whatever our initial problems, our married life fell into a pleasant groove. We had been lucky enough to find an apartment on S. Harper. It was dark and dingy, but to locate an apartment within walking distance of the university in 1946 was a small miracle. We just got by on Angela's earnings and my GI Bill stipend, but we got by, helped no doubt by frequent meals with the Peyrauds, who lived more or less around the corner at 5411 S. Blackstone. Invitations from my mother and grandparents at 1413 East 50th Street also helped. I studied, perhaps not as hard as I might have had I not known I was going into the Foreign Service, but still hard. I particularly enjoyed Ted Schultz's far ranging course about the economics of agriculture. From it grew what became a lifelong interest in the economics of development.

The one course other than Calculus where I only received a C was Hans Morgenthau's exploration of modem European totalitarianism, Marxism, Nazism, and fascism. I knew the material and thought I did well on the exam. Why the C? My explanation was I had argued with the professor in class and he didn't like it. Despite my annoyance with Morgenthau, I have to admit his *Politics Among Nations*, which came out two years later, was superb.

Finally word came that I was to report to Room 936 in the State

Department in Washington. Mother once again lent me the old Packard and we drove east to a new life.

On September 26, 1946, I took three separate oaths: one as a Foreign Service officer, another as a Secretary in the Diplomatic Service of the United States, and a third as Vice Consul of Career of the United States of America. I also paid $5 to a bonding company for a $5,000 bond to be held by the Treasury Department. I had become a Foreign Service officer, Unclassified C, Salary $3,271.80 a year. I was at the bottom of the Service, but I was in it. A dream of mine had been realized.

Angela and I moved into a conveniently located boarding house on F Street, Northwest. I could easily walk to the department, now the Old Executive Office Building, and a streetcar took me to Lothrop House where most courses for junior officers were held.

I found the Foreign Service School, as it was known before evolving into the Foreign Service Institute, dull and boring. It would take a Charlie Chaplin to hold one's attention to discussions of the organization of the government, of the State Department, and of an embassy. Then, too, our course coordinator, Larry Taylor, thrilled and motivated us by explaining that almost all officers could expect to serve about twenty years before reaching a responsible position. It had taken him that long to become Consul General in Brazzaville. There was a heavy dose of the consular regulations: citizenship, visas, shipping; some administration, including FS accounting, some cryptography (easy for me), a bit of attention to commercial promotion, a few lectures on reporting (Marshall Greene, talking about Embassy Tokyo in the pre–Pearl Harbor period, was one of the few lecturers to make us think life in the Foreign Service could be interesting), and some extraordinary discussions of protocol.

Never will I forget, nor ever would I ever use, what we were taught about the sofa shift. Reportedly, the hostess would take her place on the sofa with a guest on either side. As a new guest arrived, he or she would displace the guest on the hostess's left, which guest would move to her right, and so on until no more guests arrived!

Another unforgettable memory of those days involved Dean Acheson. Our cryptography class met in the basement of the southwest corner of the State Department. One day the teacher was late, the classroom locked, and we had no place to sit and wait other than on the corridor floor. There we were when Dean Acheson, then the Under Secretary of State, strode by. Since he was easily recognizable, we students jumped to our feet, then settled back down when he was gone. This happened six times, as he came down the corridor three times, went out the door leading to the White House, and then returned. Eventually we got into class. Soon, however, to our great surprise a senior officer arrived and announced that we were a disgrace to the Service! Why? Dean Acheson had reported that a strange group was shooting craps in the State Department corridor! Crap shooting in the State Department was not allowed, at least not with dice. All of the class loudly and vociferously denied the charge. The official left, but soon returned to present Mr. Acheson's apologies. The official explained Acheson was rather tense, as we would understand if we looked toward the White House, where Soviet Foreign Minister Molotov was being met by Acheson, who would take him to see President Truman.

Apart from such a bonding experience, there was little that held our class together. We seldom met outside of class. A welcoming cocktail by Selden Chapin, soon to be Director General, and a graduation reception by Lawrence Taylor, our course chairman, is all I can remember. Angela and I did see a good deal of another married couple, Bob and Louise Stookey, but the bachelors went in every direction. One late arrival in our class, Dave Mark, became a close friend. Overall, however, no attempt was made to develop an esprit de corps.

The Foreign Service was and is more a grouping of talented individuals than a cohesive institution. This is one of the many things wrong, but given the nature of our Service it is hard to correct. Still, more of an effort to develop an esprit de corps should be made.

Early in our training we were asked to list our top three choices by country for our first overseas post. Assignments were to be given out on the last day of the roughly one month course. A sense of tense anticipation smothered our class that day. After talking at length with Angela, I had put Turkey at the top of my list. I forget what else I listed, but I know the list did not include the post to which I was assigned: the United States Legation, Damascus, Syria. Nor was I ever assigned to Turkey. I came close after Islamabad in 1987, but that is another story.

Damascus sounded exotic, as it proved to be. Also, Syria was next door to Turkey, so I guess our wishes were not totally ignored.

In those days our smaller diplomatic posts were legations. Today we have no more legations. It gradually dawned on our leaders that smaller countries had lots of pride. They did not appreciate legations, a symbol of second-class status. They wanted an American

embassy. Ambassadors headed embassies, ministers headed legations. While the State Department planned to make Damascus an
independent legation soon, in 1946, Minister George Wadsworth,
resident in Beirut, was accredited to both Lebanon and Syria. Except when the minister was in Syria, Legation, Damascus was run
by a charge d'affaires.

Once graduated, I was assigned to the Lebanon-Syria desk,
where Adrian Colquitt took my Foreign Service education in hand.
Read this, read that; talk to so and so; visit the Defense Mapping
Agency, visit Commerce, visit Agriculture, visit the Tariff Commission, saturate yourself in Syria and U.S. relations with Syria. One
jarring note was an indignant phone call one afternoon from whoever was in charge of seamen's affairs demanding to know why
I had not called for an appointment for consultation. I suggested
the caller look at a map and tell me if there were likely to be many
problems in the Syrian desert involving American seamen.

One of my first tasks was to write the traditional letter to the
charge d'affaires expressing pleasure at my assignment to Damascus and offering to be of any assistance to him or his. Gordon Mattison, then charge, replied graciously that he looked forward to the
arrival of the Hintons and appreciated my offer to be of service,
but had no requests. One slightly different note was his comment
that he had trouble understanding how at 23 I had done what I had
already done, i.e. a B.A. degree, thirty months of military service,
marriage, and an academic year of graduate studies in economics.

Angela and I were faced with the challenge of buying household items for living quarters we would have to find for ourselves
once in Damascus. Kerosene heaters and a Servel kerosene refrigerator were high on our list, but nowhere near as high as food and
drink. We knew little to our taste would be available in postwar
Syria and were advised by all concerned to buy and ship. Going
over our weight allowance and into debt was better than having no
canned spaghetti. So we ordered a two year supply of toilet paper,
booze, and just about everything else we thought we might need or
miss, including lots of long-playing records.

After a month of school and a month of consultations, we went
back to Chicago on leave. From my standpoint, the best part of the
leave was again seeing Dad, finally home from the Philippines, and
introducing Angela to him. A worrisome aspect of the leave was
wondering how we were to get to Damascus. That question was
finally answered when a telegram from the department arrived

informing me that passage for us to Beyrouth, as Beirut was then sometimes spelt, had been secured. Having left Angela in Chicago to enjoy a long visit with her folks, I returned to duty in Washington and met Angela in New York just before we sailed on December 20, 1946, on the *Marine Carp* for the Levant.

4

Damascus (1946–1949)

The *Marine Carp*, on which we sailed for Beirut, was still configured as a wartime Army Transport. Angela and I were separated, each of us in a cabin for eight men or women with a shower and toilet shared by sixteen of us, or more exactly fifteen and a baby. Still it was much better than bunking in the hold where hundreds of Greeks, Jews, and Arabs were crowded in just as troops had been the year before. Bill Porter, the senior Foreign Service officer on board, en route to Jerusalem, and his bride were in the only private cabin. Moreover, they were not given to mixing with the rest of us.

Our voyage started badly. The American Export Line told us only when we arrived at the dock that we were limited to one suitcase per person in our cabin. We frantically repacked on the pier, opening Christmas packages and stowing gifts in what now had to be hold baggage. To make matters worse it was snowing and blustery cold on the pier. By the time we sailed the weather had deteriorated further. The first few days out it was so rough the captain even acknowledged in his log that it was rough. Nevertheless I tried to eat and paid the price. Angela stuck to her bunk and could claim later not to have been sick. She did confess, however, not having before been to sea and therefore not knowing how ships behave in storms, that she had been terrified we would capsize, my reassurances as a veteran of a hurricane at sea notwithstanding.

Christmas was cheery by dint of our will to be cheerful. We sixteen cabin mates opened our few accessible presents in common and, led by missionaries among us, sang carols. Singing helped.

By New Year's Eve we were well into the Mediterranean and able to celebrate on smooth seas. The feared outbreak of violence between the Arabs and Jews in the hold did not occur despite clear signs of tension. Somehow peace prevailed, even with alcohol easily available to celebrate the coming of the New Year. Beirut, usually the last of four ports of call for American Export Line ships, was first this time. Angela and I lamented not seeing Haifa, Alexandria, and Piraeus. We were cheered, however, when upon arrival in Beirut we observed with admiration how effective Foreign Service personnel are in helping colleagues clear immigration and customs. We were cleared, driven to our hotel, and had our baggage (most of it at least) delivered to our rooms, while other passengers, including our non-official cabin mates, struggled with Lebanese bureaucratic chaos.

While it is a Foreign Service tradition to help one's colleagues, we had it even better.

Dania Brewster, a friend of Angela's from their days together at the University of Chicago, was married to Dan, a Foreign Service Officer stationed at Beirut. The Brewsters took particularly fine care of us. We became good friends, exchanging visits, a weekend in Damascus for a weekend in Beirut, sharing service gossip, keeping in close touch after Dan and Dania were transferred to Athens, and serving together again in Paris and Washington. Dania was short, vivacious, and an extrovert. Dan was tall, handsome, and taciturn. He spoke fluent Greek. As a result, much of his career was oriented toward Greek-Turkish affairs. Sadly after some fifteen years of marriage, Dania left Dan for a lively CIA type. Dan plodded on but failed to fulfill his Foreign Service ambitions.

Gordon Mattison, my chief-to-be in Damascus, was visiting Beirut that weekend. He kindly offered Angela and me a ride to Damascus. Mattison's driver, like most Lebanese and Syrian drivers, was a speed demon for whom the rules of the road existed only to be broken. Nevertheless, with Mattison repeatedly cautioning him to take it easy, we arrived safely after a harrowing drive in ice and snow over the Lebanon and Anti-Lebanon mountains. Chargé Mattison stopped the car on the outskirts of Damascus and had the driver display the Stars and Stripes. People along the road applauded wildly as we rode into town. It was a moving experience, especially for a Foreign Service couple arriving at their first post.

Before the year was out, however, Syrians would tear our flag off the Legation flagpole and burn it. These contrasting experiences were unforgettable.

Other memorable experiences were walking down "The Street Called Straight" and visits to the great Omayyad Mosque and nearby tomb of Saladin, who had driven the Crusaders out of the Holy Lands in the 12th Century. Eventually we also visited Roman ruins at Baalbek and Palmyra, Phoenician ruins at Arwad, and Crusader castles. Add in the first Palestine war complete with air raids, my first political job, our first diplomatic reception, our first diplomatic dinner, the crash of an American civil airliner, a wedding in Quneitra that I attended as a Consular observer, our first encounters with a chief of state, our first car (our own, not borrowed from my mother), first brushes with the CIA, our first anti-American riots, our first refugee tragedy, our first coup d'état, and my first promotion. Lots of firsts. Many would have been memorable in any case, but firsts at a first post are special firsts!

Our first visit to the souks was special, but there we could and did return and return. Shopping on foot in the souks, no cars allowed, but look out for donkeys, carts, and bicycles; it was so different from shopping Marshall Field's! Teeming with activity, the souks were pungent with varied odors, not all agreeable. There were streets dedicated to leather workers, metal workers, spice merchants, fruit and vegetable shops, rug dealers, used clothing hawkers, everything imaginable. Fabulous fun to visit.

Damascus asserts a claim to being the oldest continually inhabited city in the world, tracing its history back to some 2,000 years before Christ. And what a history. Strategically, Damascus is the gateway to the desert beyond which lies Baghdad and Mecca. It also sits astride north-south land routes between two cradles of civilization, Egypt and Mesopotamia. It was conquered in turn by the Assyrians, Alexander the Great, the Seleucides, the Romans, the Arabs, the Mongols under Tamerlane, who burned the city and deported its skilled artisans to Samarkand, and then the Ottomans. After World War I and the breakup of the Ottoman Empire, Damascus was ruled by the French under a League of Nations mandate until Syria achieved independence in 1946.

We are told in the Bible Paul, on the road to Damascus, was converted by a vision of Jesus into the greatest of Christian missionaries. Mohammed, approaching Damascus from the desert, overwhelmed by its great beauty, turned back, reputedly remarking, "One cannot enter paradise twice."

Driven that first day to our hotel, the Orient Palace, about which it was said, "Lots of Orient, Damn Little Palace.", we had no illusions we had entered paradise. Although the hotel was one of four or five buildings in Damascus designed for steam heating, the heating was rarely on. While I worked at the Legation, Angela, if not exploring the souks with new friends, tried to keep warm by living in her fur coat. Nor initially was the food much to our liking. In time, however, we came to appreciate Arab cuisine, if never the Orient Palace versions thereof, and learned to go easy on the greasier dishes. In all of Damascus there was only one restaurant, aptly named "The Oasis," that tried to serve Western food. That winter we ate a lot of scrambled eggs and ravioli at "The Oasis."

Obviously, in these circumstances our first priority was to find our own place to live. This was the Foreign Service before housing normally comes with the job. So we set out every chance we had to find a suitable house or apartment, walking through neighborhoods where construction was underway. Early on we saw a beautiful large apartment with a fountain on a magnificent terrace. Way above budget, it nevertheless persuaded Angela that we, too, had to have a fountain on a terrace. She wrote home:

> We felt a definite obligation to look at every empty apt in town to be sure we found one that exactly suited our needs. During the process of looking those needs began to increase in number at an alarming rate. I became convinced of the absolute necessity of a terrace - preferably a large terrace equipped with a fountain....Having made up my mind, I was immediately faced with the problem of winning my husband over to my way of thinking. Unfortunately, my husband is one of the tough-minded sort on whom other people's terraces have little effect. The best I could do was to get him to agree to putting up with one if it just happened to be attached to an otherwise acceptable apartment.

This is not the way I remember it. It's slander since I like terraces and fountains, but Angela's account is contemporaneous and in writing so I defer to it. I guess her repeated references to her "husband" rather than to "Deane" signify something else. In any case, we eventually found and, after interminable construction delays, moved into a small third floor apartment with a lovely terrace and fountain on a hillside overlooking all of Damascus. Ideal, except for one drawback about which we learned later.

Our landlord, who lived in one room on the roof, was a devout Moslem. As such, in accordance with religious practice he was supposed to sacrifice a ram on the Eid al-Adha, the yearly Feast of the Sacrifice. Our landlord bought a goat, supposedly a ram, a month before the holy day. That bleating goat, penned on the roof directly above us, drove us nuts. As sorry as we were for his sacrifice, it was a welcome day indeed when he served his purpose.

At the Legation, I was asked to assist the assistant commercial attaché. Based in Beirut, the commercial attaché, Clayton Lane, came infrequently to Damascus, but when he did he made an impression. Clayton was an old style Foreign Service Officer. He never went out without his homburg; ridiculous for a business call in Damascus, but that was Clayton. My first immediate boss was Alex Davit, also a first tour officer, with whom it was a delight to work. There was, however, hardly enough work for one commercial officer to say nothing of two. Accordingly, I was set to straightening out the files. Not too challenging, but soon Charge Mattison tapped Alex to be the administrative officer, leaving me as the commercial officer. Economic issues, at least the important ones, like negotiations for new oil pipelines across Syria, were handled by the minister or chargé. At least they were until the oil companies, which kept their own counsel and most American diplomats in the dark, ran into a serious roadblock. Then and only then would they ask for the assistance of the U.S. Government.

My duties were more routine than pipeline negotiations. I broke in writing World Trade Directory reports, usually requested by Washington, on Syrian firms that seemed to be nothing more than a shop in the Souks, a shop for which credit references were nonexistent. Another task was to seek, usually in vain, to settle trade complaints from U.S. exporters of used clothing who had not been paid. Statistical reports were more fun. When Washington wanted to know how many sheep and goats there were in Syria, I would visit the Ministries of Economy and of Agriculture. Received graciously after coffee, it would be suggested that I come back next week or the week thereafter. When I duly returned, sure enough I was given data on the sheep and goat population of Syria. I then fulfilled my reporting requirement. Of course, the statistics were invented to please the foolish foreigner, but Washington seemed not to know the difference or care.

The Palestine question was before the General Assembly of the United Nations. When hasn't it been? The U.S., as always, had a position. We liked the draft agenda. The Legation was instructed to seek Syrian support. Charge Mattison called on Prime Minister Jamil Mardam Bey, who was also foreign minister, and returned triumphant to the Legation to send a telegram reporting that Syria was with us. His reporting cable had an element of crowing about it. Of course, Syria and Jamil Bey led the charge later in the week that produced the Arab League's decision to oppose the agenda we favored. This was the first political demarche of which I had knowledge. I learned two lessons:

First, don't believe everything you are told. It ain't necessarily so.

Second, report what was said, keeping to the facts, but don't crow.

I, and presumably Mattison as well, had been brought up in a Puritan-American context, taught to emulate George Washington's "I cannot tell a lie." Slowly it would dawn on me that while America has its share of liars, in many other cultures lying is a way of life.

George Wadsworth, Envoy Extraordinary and Minister Plenipotentiary, resident in Beirut, was, as I noted above, accredited to both Lebanon and Syria. He was a legend in the Service both for his pursuit of golf (he fostered the construction of golf courses wherever he served), and for his lengthy and flowery reports, which he repeated all around the Middle East to the annoyance of some of his colleagues and all communication clerks. To his great credit, Wadsworth had played a significant role in bringing about French withdrawal from the Levant. Now he was leaving for a new assignment as ambassador to Baghdad.

As is customarily the practice, Minister Wadsworth came to Damascus for a final round of calls and a final reception in his honor offered by Gordon Mattison. Gordon explained to us that Wadsworth expected upon his return to "his residence," in which, in the Minister's absence the Mattisons were "allowed" to live, to find everything exactly as he had left it. Gordon confided in us he had never gotten it right, lived in dread that something would be wrong this time also, but he and his wife, using a diagram prepared after Wadsworth's last departure, thought for once they had "his residence" in the order the Minister would want.

Wadsworth's farewell reception was the Hintons' first diplomatic reception. Gordon Mattison gave explicit instructions to his staff. Basically, we were to play a zone defense. Angela, for example, was to entertain all who ventured into an area around the piano. I, however, was to play the Minister man-to-man, one-on-one. I was to do what he wished done. More specifically, I was to see that he did not want for martinis. All seemed to be going well, the Minister's martini glass did not wont, when about an hour into the affair the Minister, pointing across the room, said, "Hinton, see that lamp. It belongs in the corner over there." I moved the lamp, but seldom have I felt more ridiculous than carrying that floor lamp from one corner of the living room to another through a hundred or so guests jammed one against the other in the residence living room.

Our fist diplomatic dinner, also in honor of Wadsworth, was hosted by British Minister and Mrs. Broadmead, a rather stuffy couple it seemed to Angela and me. As was British custom, after dinner the men left the ladies and adjourned to the study for brandy and cigars. While I had smoked an occasional White Owl during the war, I had not before encountered a Havana. I was almost sick on the Minister's carpet. Valiantly, however, I made it home without disaster. Moreover, I resolved then and there to enjoy the strong cigars proper diplomats apparently smoked. To this day, some fifty-five years later, despite repeated warnings from doctors, I enjoy few things more than a good cigar, especially a Havana.

When Wadsworth left, Legation, Damascus became independent of Beirut. I was now the de facto commercial attaché, since Clayton Lane, the Homburg Man, was no longer accredited to Damascus and the newly designated attaché, Fritz Alfsen, who turned out to be another nut at least by my standards, had not yet arrived. When he did arrive, he made the appropriate calls on Syrian cabinet ministers. What was nutty was he delivered to them long flowery speeches about friendship, common values, and peaceful cooperation between our two countries. Nuttier still, he drafted long telegrams reporting his eloquent remarks. His drafts, however, went no further, since the new chargé, James S. Moose, would not have his name signed to such foolishness.

Most junior officers, apprentices in their profession, then as now, are rotated from section to section in a legation or embassy. The quite sensible idea is to give the juniors as wide an experience as possible in the various functions of a diplomatic office. Much of this seasoning I missed. Instead I had the good fortune to have my bosses rotated. In two plus years at Damascus I served under two ministers (Wadsworth and Keeley) and three chargés. Each of my chiefs was quite different and each a valued teacher.

My favorite and the most influential on my own thinking about the Service and its functions was Jimmy Moose. Mattison had been helpfully friendly but was relaxed about work. Concerning Moose, I wrote home, "He knows exactly how things are supposed to be done and insists that they be done that way."

Moose, unlike the others rotated above me, spoke Arabic. Immersed in the history of the Near East, his favorite recreation was to visit archeological sites in the desert. He kindly included me when he drove to Latakia in early May of 1946 to welcome an American destroyer making a courtesy port call. En route he taught me more about most of the ruins we passed than I wanted to know. About Arwad, however, now an island and once a Phoenician seaport, I could not hear enough. As we visited the seawalls, constructed some fifteen hundred years before the birth of Christ, to our astonishment Syrian police stopped us from taking photos and took us into custody. They alleged we were spying on Syria's defenses. We were returned to the mainland where Moose, on his best diplomatic behavior, using his Arabic talked a more senior policeman into freeing us and returning our films and cameras. I asked Moose if he would lodge a diplomatic complaint. No, he replied, there was nothing malicious involved, just ignorant overzealous police inherently suspicious of foreigners. Had there been reason to believe there was a planned Government intent to harass, a protest would have been much in order. I admired the cool way Moose handled the whole business and learned an important lesson: one should avoid turning minor incidents into significant issues.

The visit of the U.S. *Gainard* was a great success with the Syrians. It was especially impressive for me. The three of us from the Legation, Moose, Political Officer Ralph Barrow, and I, were piped aboard and rendered honors, and the Charge was saluted with eleven guns upon our departure. Ahmad al-Sharabati, the Syrian Defense minister, received a nineteen-gun salute upon completion of his call

Commander Gustin, Captain of the *Gainard*, flew to Damascus with Ralph and myself in a small plane. No sooner were we airborne than Ralph sickened. I gave him an 8-by-10 envelope to serve as a sickness bag. As we were approaching the Damascus airport, the envelope was full and I saw Ralph trying to open the side window to dump it. I yelled "No" and grabbed at the bag. Too late. The wind blew the contents of the envelope back into our faces. As I was about to puke in turn, the plane hit the runway, blew a tire, and cartwheeled to a stop. I was so glad to be intact that I forgot all about being sick. But Ralph and I were terribly messy and smelly.

Gustin, already contemplating a career change, was so impressed by the Legation and what we did that he soon left the Navy. Not long thereafter he became a Foreign Service Officer.

Ralph Barrow was a bachelor. In Syria, a conservative religious country where Moslem wives seldom ventured into public, this was a professional advantage it would not have been in Western Europe.

It meant he could circulate in political circles without concern he was abandoning a wife at home. The hard truth is Damascus was a difficult post for Angela and other Western women. Generally their social life was restricted to the small foreign community. But naturally they wanted to get out and see what men were seeing. Ralph had taken up with Alice Bracken, who with her mother had been in Angela's cabin on the Marine Carp. When the Government invited diplomats to celebrate "National Evacuation Day," commemorating the first anniversary of the French withdrawal, Ralph told me he could and would sneak Alice and her mother undetected into the stands to watch the scheduled tribal dances. He invited Angela to join them. With misgivings, I agreed.

Trying to make an inconspicuous approach to a sheltered viewing spot, Ralph and the three ladies encountered the Minister of Defense. Ahmad al-Sharabati promptly led them to the diplomatic section where President Shukri al-Quwatli took over. He gave them robes to keep them warm. Later he invited the ladies to eat with him off of his platter. Somehow he even produced forks so they did not have to handle the greasy rice and lamb with their right hands, as did the rest of us. The President's graciousness made quite an impression, but I was still worried about possible repercussions. They came. The Foreign Office Chief of Protocol told us it had just never occurred to them to invite ladies. In the future, he said, they would; and they did. Moose, instead of reprimanding us, congratulated Ralph and the ladies for having pulled off a coup. Indeed they had, striking a real and successful, if accidental, blow for women's liberation.

Moose critiqued his officers' work with handwritten notes. Sometimes I argued back; sometimes I just hung my head in shame. Once he stung my pride. At long last I had had to make a real demarche about a trade issue. I carried out my instructions, noted the Syrian oral response, and ended the reporting cable with my opinion of the General Agreement on Tariffs and Trade (GATT) principles involved. Moose dropped the opinion paragraph. I protested that I knew a great deal about trade and the GATT and thought my opinion should be sent. Moose said he thought I was right, but I might be wrong. The deciding factor, however, was simply that my opinion about the GATT would not matter one way or another in Washington. He told me neither I nor the Legation should run the risk of being discredited by advancing an immaterial point. He was, of course, right. A reporting officer may well opine about other country's policies and attitudes, even discreetly about U.S. policy, but should avoid asserting views on matters that are basically none of one's business.

Moose impressed upon us that to know a country one had to travel widely outside of the capital. Since I was his commercial-economic officer, he sent me to Aleppo, Syria's second city and a commercial center. The most memorable event of Angela's and my visit, apart from the Citadel and the magnificent souks, was a moderately strong earthquake that shook the fabled Baron's Hotel early one morning. Our first earthquake!

Moose also sent me back to Latakia with instructions to learn about and report on Latakian tobacco, a rich smoke cured leaf generally used in pipe tobacco mixtures. My report, complete with photos of primitive smoke houses, was published by the Department of Agriculture under my by-line. It was my first and as far as I can recall last by-line article.

I agree completely with Moose's views concerning travel. An officer who just sits on his or her butt in an office will miss much that someone who circulates throughout the country talking to a wide swath of people, not just Government officials, will come to understand and appreciate.

Travel became much easier with the arrival of our new Chevrolet sedan. Angela and I visited the Krak des Chevaliers, the largest Crusader castle in the Levant, where we spent a cold night camping on the battlements. With our friends the Fergusons we visited the fabled Roman temples at Baalbek. For a change of pace, we went to Malula, a small village of whitewashed houses north of Damascus in a lovely, isolated mountain valley, where Aramaic, believed to be the language of Christ, is still spoken. Fergie, a linguist, was fascinated by the sounds. Joanna, his delightful, if odd, Austrian wife, was enthusiastic about the village.

Fergie, who had helped me with French in Washington, was now living in Beirut, teaching Arabic to Foreign Service Officers. On one leave, Angela and I drove to Alexandretta (Iskunderun) in Turkey over roads hardly worthy of the name and only after convincing a dubious Turkish frontier guard that our diplomatic passports with Turkish visas actually authorized our entry into Turkey. Our accommodations were primitive, but we did not mind in those days. As souvenirs we brought back some distinctive ceramics.

Our most exciting trip, this time with the Fergusons and many others, was to the incredibly impressive ruins of Palmyra. To get there we navigated across the desert for five hours, guided (when we could see them) by sparsely placed fifty-gallon gasoline drums along an almost invisible track. Queen Zenobia of Palmyra had successfully broken from Rome in 270 A.D. For a time she and the Palmyran armies ruled a vast Levantine empire that even stretched beyond the Levant to include Egypt. Her empire, however, did not last long. Roman Emperor Aurelian organized a counter-effort. Zenobia was defeated and taken in chains to be exhibited in Rome. Palmyra thereupon lost its political significance, but remained an important city on major trade routes for many more centuries. Eventually, however, the desert prevailed, leaving the great Columnar and the Great Temple standing, seemingly in the middle of nowhere. The night of our arrival Fergie and Angela, cowed by the hordes of mosquitoes, stayed at what was called a hotel. Joanna and I walked totally enthralled, enchanted, and innocent in the moonlight among the ruins. We paid a price of raised eyebrows and enormous welts from countless bites, but it was worth it.

Thrice I rode on the Air Attaché's DC-3. Angela, others, and I flew with Colonel Brown to Baghdad, Iraq and then to Tehran, Iran. In Tehran we stayed with Ed Waggoner, our suave FSO friend from the Marine Carp, who was a wonderful guide. While there, we bought two beautiful carpets and a striking silver cigarette case. We had a fright en route to Dhahran, Saudi Arabia. Somehow our pilots lost track of our exact location—not good in a mountainous area, with one peak about 15,000 feet and, further south, one over 17,000.

We climbed and climbed as high as the plane would go, not quite 17,000 feet, and headed southwest to the Gulf. We passengers froze, developed king size headaches, and nearly passed out from lack of oxygen. The few oxygen bottles on board were wisely reserved for our pilots. Believe me, unrestrained was our joy when the lights of Abadan finally hove into view below.

A flight to Nicosia, where we overnighted, convinced us Cyprus was well worth a return visit. Sadly, I have yet to make it.

My third trip with Colonel Brown was most memorable. A few days before the British Mandate for Palestine was to end, Washington directed Brown to fly to Haifa, pick up Consul General Designate Tommy Wasson, and fly him to a Royal Air Force fighter strip near Jerusalem. Given the breakdown of public order, road travel from Haifa to Jerusalem was deemed inadvisable. Haifa presented no problem, but the fighter strip at Jerusalem was a tight fit for a

DC-3. Wasson was waiting for us at the Haifa airport. He had a number of suitcases and a few cases of liquor. Brown said he was sorry, but only half of Wasson's possessions could come with us. Without hesitation, Wasson had the booze loaded. We landed safely, left the Consul General in good British hands, and took off, only to receive a burst of machinegun fire, presumably Arab generated, through our right wing. No great harm done. Sadly, however, in the aftermath of the first Palestine War Wasson was killed by a sniper, presumably Israeli.

Days before the Jerusalem flight I wrote Mother, "There are some conditions that just might take me away from Damascus for some time." In fact, I had been instructed to be ready "until further notice" to join within twenty-four hours an envisaged observer group in Palestine. I was on a flight where every pound counted to learn a bit about the lay of the land. Incidentally, to this day my orders have not been rescinded. I'm still ready to go.

The Legation was moving into a new building on Avenue Bustan Sabbagh. Now, happily, it would be a short walk from our apartment. As the staff prepared to move out of our rented former Legation building, we learned the Soviets would be the next tenants. What an opportunity thought Peter Male, a British third secretary, and I. There were so many things we wanted to know and did not know about what the Soviets were up to in the Middle East. We might learn something from planted listening devices. Messages went off to London and Washington. They generated some interest, but when Miles Copeland, the first CIA station chief in Syria, arrived, he explained, as had British intelligence, that a risk-gain calculation ruled out establishment of a listening post. Miles did agree, however, there was no harm in letting the Russians think differently. At a Soviet reception later that year celebrating the "XXX Anniversary of the Great Socialist Revolution of October," by prearrangement Peter whispered to me, just loud enough to be overheard by one of our hosts, "Do you think they found them?" Indignantly I hushed up Peter. Later we fantasized about the Soviets taking the building apart looking for bugs. But who knows what, if anything, happened.

The following year, 1948, Ted Burgess and I struck a low blow in the Cold War at a similar Soviet reception. Stationing ourselves on either side of the door from which goodies emerged, we significantly reduced the caviar supply reaching other guests. Childish, but such good eating, and perhaps the Soviet Minister was embarrassed his supply ran out before many of his guests had lost their appetite for caviar.

Angela had a much harder time in Damascus than I. Other Western ladies were few and compatible ones even fewer. Her best friend, Peggy Davit, was a new mother busy with her baby boy, Sandy. Margie Garrett, an old time Middle East hand, whose father, a Bliss, was President of the American University of Beirut, could not have been nicer. Margie, however, traveled a lot. She could often ride for free, since her husband, PanAm Station Chief Johnson Garrett, had airline privileges. Before long as the novelty of prowling the Souks wore off, Angela began to teach English to Syrians and Calvert system materials to some American children. She liked it and was good at it.

Angela also began to spend more weekends in Beirut. I often went with her, but not often enough. One Saturday night late I got a call from Beirut saying she was returning to Damascus that night. Early the next morning she came in close to tears with black and blue marks on her arms and other bruises elsewhere. An American official in Beirut had been telling her she looked great in a bathing suit. True. Apparently he decided she would be even better in bed without it. Angela resisted; hence the bruises.

The beaches and bright lights of Beirut still attracted us, but if we stayed in Damascus on weekends we used what free time we had for local sightseeing and shopping. Just strolling the covered markets was great fun. Shopping was even more fun, but budgetary stringency limited our buying. One day with the Fergusons we discovered a wonderful woodcarver deep behind the souks. For a few Syrian pounds he made us magnificent cigarette boxes: great gifts. Arab coffee pots, some in matched sets, from the copper souk, also appealed. Mostly we could only admire the carpets and brocades at Asfar & Sarkis, an upscale shop where we were always welcome, even those of us who rarely bought items. George, their number one salesman, knew full well that in return for coffee and carpet viewing we would steer our visitors to Asfar & Sarkis. Moreover, as Christmas approached we actually bought their brocade ties, intricately woven with strands of gold and silver using a centuries old technology, for friends and family back home.

Our favorite shopping was for Druze chests. These are substantial pieces of furniture, the fronts of which are hand-carved into fantastic patterns. Buying such a chest was a real challenge. Those in shops were very expensive, so one wanted to cut out the middleman and find a Druze wanting to sell one of his chests. He would have loaded his chest on his burrow well before dawn, then walked seventy miles or so to the Damascus market. When you spotted such a seller, much patience was required. Bargaining, of course, was essential, but your Druze artisan would not even suggest an outlandish price for hours, and certainly would not sell until dusk. For him, the day was as much to socialize in town as it was to sell his chest. Moreover, the bargaining dance was as important, if not more important, than the result. The three cup coffee rule was often in effect, with both would-be seller and would-be buyer taking turns buying coffee from passing vendors. Angela and I successfully bought four of these wonderful artifacts: one for each set of parents and two for us. To this day mine serves me well.

To my surprised delight, my name was on the 1948 promotion list. To Alex Davit's chagrin and my horror, since Alex clearly deserved promotion more than I, his name was not. A gentleman, he grimly congratulated me. Reportedly Peggy was not only understandably bitter, but also nasty in her comments about the Hintons. Fortunately the following day a corrected list arrived in another cable. Alex Davit was also promoted to Class 5. Both families had something about which to cheer. Better yet, our friendship, if it had been in danger, was safe.

It is perhaps inevitable in a highly competitive service, but the tension surrounding issuance of the annual promotion list has to be lived to be believed. Particularly when officers approach time in class limits, lifetime careers are at risk. In these circumstances most nerves are extra taunt. But it is worth it. The promotion system recognizes outstanding performance, not always, but most of the time. In due course, almost all capable officers receive their promotions. In some cases, poorly performing officers "are selected out." At Damascus, our superiors must have identified one junior officer misfit since he was selected out several years later. Apparently he failed a second chance at another post. The Foreign Service promotion system has many defects and needs reform in some respects. Nevertheless, the basic concept has served the Republic well.

In the summer of 1947, the Mooses were replaced by the Memmingers, who brought with them their son, Tito, a holy terror. Bob Memminger, a frustrated Shakespearian actor, was more hyper than either of his predecessors. This had its good and bad points. He wanted reporting from Damascus stepped up. While I am eternally grateful to him for his decision in September of that year to make me responsible "for all reports of a political nature" upon Ralph Barrow's departure, a real career boost, his insistence that I and Fuad Ghamayan, the Syrian political assistant, report on an

Arab League meeting at Sofar in the Lebanese mountains had less happy results. Obviously we could not get into the meetings. I knew hardly anyone outside of the session to talk to, could communicate well only in English, and was viewed with suspicion, as was Fuad, by the Arab leaders and their staffs. If that were not enough, our new Minister in Beirut, Lowell Pinkerton, while he had acquiesced to my presence at the meeting, clearly thought we were out of line. He was right we had no business trying to operate on another mission's turf.

Fortunately Minister Pinkerton did not hold this incident against me. Just as Pinkerton though Memminger was too active, Memminger thought the trouble with Pinkerton was he seldom reported. Quite a change from Wadsworth. I discovered during a courtesy call on the Minister that to talk with Pinkerton was to tap a gold mine of valuable information and insightful interpretations of Near East developments. He knew a great deal precisely because his widespread sources trusted him. Thereafter I made it a point to call on the American Minister to Lebanon as often as possible. I used what he told me to enhance my reporting, being careful, of course, not to compromise Pinkerton or his sources. Actually, he seldom revealed his sources, so I could concentrate on getting the story right.

Trying to get back to Damascus from Beirut one March afternoon with the Davits as passengers, I had an accident in a blinding snowstorm. A car coming down the mountain smacked me on my side of the road. Fortunately neither or us was going very fast, but Peggy suffered a painful bruise. When I challenged the other driver, the damn fool replied, "We always drive on the inside in a blizzard."

I maintain I have not had a moving automobile accident since that winter day in 1948. However, my sons, Chris and Joe, maintain I bumped a policeman on a motorcycle after a Redskins game at Kennedy Stadium in the 1960s. Memory is a selective phenomenon. Surely their story is an invention. Or is it?

Another night we were luckier in returning to Damascus from Beirut. To put it mildly, Angela and I had had too much to drink at a farewell party for the Fergusons. I had to be at work, so foolishly we headed home at 2 a.m. While Angela taught me the words to the Marseilles, my guardian angel steered me onto the Beirut-Tripoli road, which was nowhere near as dangerous as the mountain route to Damascus. When we began to sober up, we recognized we were on the wrong road. Thank God. By the time we turned around I was able to drive safely to Damascus.

Memminger named me his political officer, not because I was qualified. Clearly I was not, not speaking Arabic and having virtually no experience, but *faute de mieux*, as the French would say. The Foreign Service lacked officers who could speak Arabic. My friend Fergie Ferguson was busy trying to remedy this, but in 1947 the shortage persisted. I worked hard to develop secondary sources to overcome my language deficiencies as best I could. The press, even the abysmal Syrian press, given to hyperbole and often paid either to publish or not to publish journalistic inventions, was of course useful. Careful reading between the lines was, of course, essential. Visiting American journalists could often tell me more than I could tell them. They were well worth talking to, if just to get a more balanced view of the world than was prevalent in Damascus. Some of our British colleagues were helpful, especially "Flux" Dundas, their legation's "Oriental Secretary." Flux had all of the qualification I lacked for a political job, as well as a keen sense of humor, a love of pink gins, and a cynical view of the world. He was not stuffy like so many of his British colleagues. I attribute his openness to the fact that he was not of the Foreign Office career service, but rather was seconded to the legation from the British Council, a cultural information service. The legendary Colonel Sterling, who had entered Damascus with Lawrence in 1918 and was presumed to head British intelligence, was an incomparable source on the Bedouin tribes, their leaders, and their loyalties. And his stories of the Levant, what stories! This elder Arabist fascinated me, but in one area I had to discount his views. He made no effort to conceal his admiration for the Hashemite King Abdullah of Transjordan, nor his belief that "Greater Syria" was just a matter of time. The French Minister, Jean Serres, considered Sterling dedicated to promoting British primacy in Syria and the "Greater Syria" scheme little more than a plot to further diminish French influence. Across a chessboard, I also got to know the Turkish Consul General. He was perhaps the best-informed foreigner in Syria. We had many games. While I generally lost at chess, I certainly gained in information and understanding. My friend was a wise and helpful man.

There were two important foreign policy issues confronting Syria when I assumed the political job. Above all else there was the "Palestine Question." Likewise, of great concern to the Syrian leadership was the so-called question of "Greater Syria." Questions of lesser importance included Kurdish separatism, tensions in the Syrian-Lebanese economic relation, especially relating to exchange rates and the tie to the French franc, the so-called Alexandretta question, water rights issues, and countless issues arising in or out of the United Nations system.

The United States, as a world power, takes an interest in just about everything. Instructions flow endlessly from Washington. As the Political Officer, unless a high level demarche was specifically requested I carried out our instructions at the Foreign Ministry, usually at the level of the United States desk; sometimes with Ibrahim Ishwani, the able and personable Secretary General. Most of these instructions dealt with matters of little interest to Syria. After a while it was easy for me to carry out an instruction, say about Korea, quite casually, since there seemed to be no way to engage Syrian interest. Thinking about it at my next post in 1950 after North Korea attacked South Korea, I recognized how wrong I had been. Clearly I should have tried harder to stimulate Syrian interest in that distant peninsula.

In mid-1947 King Abdullah of Transjordan proclaimed that the Hashemite Kingdom of "Greater Syria" would shortly be established, uniting Iraq, Jordan, and Syria under his rule. Abdullah was a son of Sharif Hussein, who had allied the Arabs with the British in World War I. He was a younger brother of King Feisal of Iraq, who for a few months in 1920, before Britain and France combined to overthrow him, had been king of Syria. Many Arabs recognized Abdullah as a legitimate defender of the Moslem Holy Places, even though his family had been displaced from that role by Ibn Saud, now King of Saudi Arabia. Abdullah's ambitious proclamation frightened most Syrians. They valued their hard won independence. The proclamation also elicited strong anti-Abdullah reactions from King Ibn Saud and the Egyptians, to say nothing of the Grand Mufti Husseini of Jerusalem and the French. The latter, of course, saw a British plot to supplant what influence they had left in Syria. Thereafter periodic reports that Abdullah was trying to subvert the Druze as well as various Bedouin tribal leaders kept the pot boiling. For me, the "Greater Syria" issue illuminated the deep splits in the Arab world while suggesting the fissures among Western powers.

However divided the Arabs might be on other issues, they were united—Moslem Arabs, Christian Arabs, even Jewish Arabs—in opposition to a Zionist state in Palestine. The conflict between Arab nationalism and Zionism was implacable and, as time has shown, close to irresolvable. While some Arabs would acknowledge the horrors of the Nazi Holocaust and of Russian pogroms, none thought a Jewish homeland in Palestine was acceptable, much less desirable. Why should Palestinians pay for European crimes? Why should Arabs, who had lived in Palestine for hundreds of years, be forced to turn over their lands to the returning Jewish Diaspora?

The Arabs felt betrayed by the West, especially by "perfidious Britain." During World War I the British had promised Sharif Hussain independence if the Arabs would join the British and fight with them to defeat the Ottoman Turks. The same British promised Zionists "their best endeavors" to facilitate "the establishment in Palestine of a national home for the Jewish people" in the Balfour Declaration. Then, too, the British and French defined their future spheres of influence in the Ottoman Empire in the Sykes-Picot Agreement. When the Arabs learned of this secret agreement, they viewed it as further proof of British betrayal.

By the time I assumed the political job in Damascus, the British, exhausted by their efforts in World War II, had decided to leave Palestine. Their often futile efforts to keep the peace between Jews and Arabs and control, also often in vain, the influx of Zionists and arms into Palestine had convinced them it was time to lay down their League of Nations Mandate. The issue of what would replace the Mandate was before the United Nations. A Special U.N. Commission of Inquiry had recommended partition. The Arabs were adamantly opposed. Nevertheless, on October 31, 1947, the General Assembly of the United Nations voted in favor of partition between Arabs and Zionists. The United States, the Soviet Union, Britain, and France voted with the majority.

Early the next morning, a Sunday, I was informed by telephone that a large crowd egged on by inflammatory speeches was on the march from the center of Damascus toward foreign missions. As I watched the thousands of chanting marchers from my terrace, the police cordon in front of the United States Legation melted away. One remaining police officer, brave or foolish or both, stood blocking the entrance. Perhaps because of his stand, perhaps at his suggestion, some hotheads, including turbaned members of the Moslem Brotherhood, surged to the rear of the Legation, forcibly entered, vandalized an office, then made their way to the roof where they tore down our flag. As I watched in a cold fury, our flag was burned as were three Legation vehicles parked in front. A Syrian national manning our switchboard and one of our Arab drivers were cursed, but not harmed.

The demonstration continued to the French Legation. There, after vandalizing offices, some of the mob broke into the Minister's wine cellar. That was too much for Madame Serres. Wielding a broom, she drove the rabble away from her champagne! Demonstrations against the Soviets, the British, and the Belgians, who had also voted for partition, were little more than verbal. An attack, however, on the office of the Communist newspaper was resisted, a mistake. At least three persons were killed in the resulting melee.

The Syrian Government, although clearly involved in organizing the crowd, hypocritically blamed "foreign agents." Nevertheless, the President and Prime Minister appeared to recognize matters had gone much too far. They personally apologized to Chargé Memminger and agreed the Syrian Government would pay compensation for damage. A company of Gendarmes presented arms as the Stars and Stripes was formally raised at the Legation.

My first orchestrated riot left me with a number of reactions. Watching the surging, chanting mob of thousands climb toward our legation had been frightening. I was impressed, however, with how many Syrians had not joined the demonstrators, who were largely organized students and disciplined Moslem Brotherhood members. Maybe the common people did not care so much about Palestine after all. How representative was the firebrand, Fawzi al-Qawuqji, who had assured the crowd "We shall fight to keep Palestine for the Arabs." He bragged of having organized a private Arab intervention force. We believed he was advised in this effort by Nazi Germans who had found refuge in Syria. We were certain the Syrian Government was encouraging his efforts with covert finance. But, I wondered, could this unofficial army fight as well as Qawuqji could orate?

Monday, Colonel McGrath, the Army Attaché, arrived at work with his service 45mm automatic on his hip. He drew up and somehow sold the chargé a "Defense Plan" for the Legation. I was assigned to the first floor team. According to the plan, to repel a mob trying to enter the building our "principal weapon will be staves." If unable to hold the mob off with staves and with a few tear gas grenades controlled by the colonel, we were to fall back to the second floor, and then to the third floor, the last line of defense for our Alamo. It was absurd. Worse it was dangerous to an idiotic degree. After all, lives are far more important than property. McGrath's plan, in my judgment, was fatally flawed. It lacked even one word about the desirability of trying to evacuate the Legation prior to an attack. Silver eagles do not necessarily evidence common sense.

The sight of the disciplined march of turbaned members of the Moslem Brotherhood toward our Legation spurred me to complete a study of the Brotherhood I had begun shortly after assuming the political job. The resulting lengthy analytical despatch (State Department nomenclature for such a document) drew much praise from readers in Washington as well as in other Near Eastern posts and London. I had scored. The report looked hard at the best-organized, toughest, anti-foreign, anti-secular organization in Syria. The Brotherhood aimed at nothing less than reform of the entire Arab world by a return to the fundamental beliefs of Islam, including religious toleration. The Brotherhood made a sharp distinction between Jews, to be respected, and Zionists, to be driven into the sea. I noted that while the group's "Doctrine" made much of individual personal rights, it appeared not to consider women to be persons. My report also reviewed prewar antecedents in Syria, noting, however, that postwar organizational and financial help from Egypt's Moslem Brotherhood was far more important.

Early on in my political job I wrote Grandpa Roesch, "Life here is utterly confusing. Names are different, ideas are different, and the attitude of the people to politics is different in Syria than in the U.S. Moslems believe Allah will take care of everything....'Burka', tomorrow, is when things will be done. That little, in fact, is done seems to be of no concern." But by early 1948 I wrote home, "The steady grind of telling Washington what goes on in Syria is becoming an obnoxious routine. I can write the editorials of any paper in town, predict exactly what any politician will say, before he says it. Syrian attitudes toward the United States have turned cold. The mess is discouraging....Too much of this business consists of listening to damn fools inventing reasons for not doing the obvious."

As spot reporting became an "obnoxious routine," I spent more time on biographical reporting and thinking about an analytical approach to political reporting. I was collecting data on (1) key groups, religious sects, political parties, leadership cliques, (2) institutions, (3) attitudes, e.g. degrees of xenophobia, and (4) problems, e.g. "Greater Syria," currency stability, industrial development. Then I thought I should ask, "What group has what attitude to what problem within what institutional setting?" or for a new problem, "What institutions, groups, and attitudes are relevant?"

This was a big order. Bigger than I could handle on my own. Unfortunately money for a research assistant was not available until my successor, Roger Davies, arrived. Consequently even with encouragement from Bob Sethian, head of Near Eastern Research in the Department of State, I only made a beginning on it before moving on to a new post.

Notwithstanding my frustrations with the required routine reporting, with Arabic, with a male-dominated society, and with corruption (every Syrian appeared to have his price, be he for sale or rent), I really loved my work. I began to think of becoming an Arabist. Before asking for language training, I talked it over with Fergie, my linguist friend. He reminded me of my problems with French and my pronunciation of Arabic. He recalled my inability to master the sound described in class in Washington as the last gasp of a drowning man. Fergie told me I could be taught to read Arabic, but he honestly thought the effort required would be disproportionate to the results. Moreover, he doubted I would ever speak Arabic reasonably well. After thinking over this forthright advice, I applied for advanced economic training. My post selection was Istamboul, Strasbourg, and Kabul. While I knew, or thought I knew, no attention was paid to our request list, submitted interestingly enough on April Fool's Day, my seniors told me anyone foolish enough to list Kabul would promptly have his wish fulfilled. Apparently not, since I have yet to see Kabul.

Fergie's advice was good advice. It spared me years of inevitable frustration in dealing with Arabs and Israelis. As an economic specialist I would serve almost worldwide rather than focusing on the Middle East. I often thought of my good fortune as I watched my Arabist friends struggle fruitlessly with the Palestine problem. Thirty years would pass before Anwar Sadat broke the mold. His initiative in going to Jerusalem breathed life into the peace process. Who will sustain it to produce peace?

About this time I was involved in an incident that left a lasting mark on me. It dramatically reinforced by parents' teaching about truthfulness.

Each month a warrant officer in the Army Attaché's office asked two of us to count his cash on hand, verify his accounts, and certify we had done so. The amounts involved were relatively small, but the count took quite a while to complete. Eventually we just took the officer's word for it and signed. Mistake, big mistake. A visiting inspector turned up a shortage of several hundred dollars. The

Army Inspector launched a formal inquiry. I was to testify under oath. In an informal chat beforehand I said I planned to admit I had certified the accounts to be correct without having done the requisite counting. The Inspector then advised my errant colleague and me that if we wanted to avoid more trouble, we should decline to answer under oath his central questions. He pointed out that a truthful answer would incriminate us in another crime: false certification. Taking his advice, "we took the Fifth." From this extremely painful situation, I learned again what I should have known: don't stray from the truth.

The British Mandate for Palestine was to end at midnight on May 14, 1948. As this moment approached, the United Nations Assembly was still debating. A United Nations Trusteeship seemed to be a viable option. In Washington, Secretary of State Marshall opposed early recognition of the new state of Israel certain to be proclaimed by the Zionists. President Truman was listening to various options but had not declared himself. When he did, the United States was the first country in the world to recognize Israel.

In Damascus we knew Fawzi al-Qawuqji's irregulars had disappeared from their training area at the Syrian army base in Katana. We soon learned the small Syrian army was also moving toward the frontier with Palestine. Inside Palestine the security situation was out of anyone's control. When the British unexpectedly abandoned Haifa, the Zionists moved in. President Shukri al-Quwatli of Syria called in the American chargé. But Memminger was out of town. In the absence of a more senior officer, I went to the Presidency. Not only did the President receive me, but also key members of the Cabinet. I learned quickly my French was not up to catching the full tenor of an agitated president's remarks. Clearly, however, Syria was withdrawing its consul from Haifa. Eventually, feeling most inadequate in my first ever substantive conversation with a chief of state, I confirmed in my poor French that Syria was asking the United States to assume protection of its interests in Haifa. My cable to Washington containing this request drew an immediate "Thanks but no thanks" answer. To my relief, Bob Memminger returned in time to deliver the reply.

On the morning of May 13, an urgent cable from the Department of State asked the Legation to comment on a report from our Army Attaché that the Syrian army had entered Palestine and war had broken out. This report from Colonel McGrath, about which the Legation learned from Washington, was wrong. McGrath had sought a "scoop," neglecting in the process even to mention to the chargé his premature report that Syria was at war. Two days later he would have been right. By then Memminger had laid down the law: the regulations concerning coordination of reporting would be observed by all, including Army attachés.

Personally, I am all in favor of independent reporting by the various elements of a mission, provided and only provided the chief of mission is informed of the report and given an opportunity to comment on it before it is sent.

Syria's war effort fizzled. One Israeli kibbutz in Galilee held off the entire Syrian army and al-Qawuqji irregulars, repulsing attack after attack. Syria's political leadership was shaken and discredited.

A first Israeli air raid on Damascus was a token affair. A lone single-engine plane overflew in the middle of the night, dropping several small bombs. Syrian jitters escalated, but there were no casualties. The only reported damage was to the Irish Protestant Mission to the Jews! Our friend Mina Christe, the delightful Irish lady heading the Mission, thought it rather ironic she had been bombed by the Jewish state. I thought it rather odd that there was an Irish Protestant Mission to the Jews in Damascus.

Our two mutt dogs reacted quite differently to the attack. Pasha went out on the terrace and barked. Hareem dove under our bed.

The next and last Israeli air raid was a different matter. At noon on July 18, an Arab-Israeli armistice was to enter into effect. The night before, intense pain from an abscessed tooth kept me from sleeping. At dawn in anticipation of driving to Beirut for an emergency dental appointment, Angela joined me on our terrace. Just then an Israeli B-17 came in low out of the sun. It was headed our way, spewing bombs across the city. As the explosions climbed toward us, we headed downstairs to an irrigation ditch. In mid-town, hundreds of civilians were wounded or killed. One bomb fell directly across from Charge Memminger's residence, killing the English Director of the Bank of Iran and blowing in all of the residence windows. Fortunately he and his family were in the back of the house. Apart from a few scratches, they were not harmed. Another American house took a direct hit, but luckily the family was in Beirut. Needless to say, my departure for Beirut was delayed as we rushed to help the Memmingers and to console, as best we could, the British widow.

Finally in Beirut, I had my first root canal operation. Then while Angela and the Arthur D. Allens went to the beach I polished off a large pitcher of whiskey sours and napped. Man, did I nap!

I could see no excuse for the Israeli attack on a defenseless city. The war was to end in a few hours. Why did Israel strike Damascus? Perhaps to terrorize Syria's inhabitants. Whatever the rationale, I feared the raid induced hatred.

Tel Aviv radio carried an Israeli communiqué boasting of a successful air strike against the Mezze airport. Lying propaganda. Mezze was ten miles from where the B-17's bombs hit. However, in Damascus there were no Western journalists to report the truth. Syria's censors had long since persuaded foreign newsmen to go elsewhere.

In early August of 1948, Minister James Hugh Keeley, Jr. presented his credentials to President al-Quwatli as Envoy Extraordinary and Minister Plenipotentiary of the United States of America to Syria. The Minister and his staff were dolled up in tails and white ties for the ceremony. It was a scorcher of a day. Tails did not help. I felt I was in a Turkish bath. The Syrians appeared delighted to have a resident American minister. The contractors building the Minister's residence even made an extra effort to finish the job. An extra effort, yes, but too late to finish the project on schedule. Still an unfinished home was better than the Orient Palace Hotel, so the Keeleys moved in anyway.

Jim Keeley, my fourth boss in less than three years, had many of the best traits of the Irish and at least one of the worst. Sometimes his emotions got the better of his reason. Jim was personable, immensely likable, with a wonderful sense of humor. He told great stories. He flawlessly and hilariously mimicked French, Greek, Russian, and British diplomats. A fabulous party giver, Jim had a knack for making his guests feel at home, even guests with whom he shared no language. One of his more entertaining ways of breaking down barriers was to have his guests try to trace a path through of maze drawn on a paper they could only see in a mirror.

Jim was quite different from Bob Memminger and Jimmy Moose, to say nothing of the relaxed Gordon Mattison. Moose had wanted quality reporting. He was a stickler for getting the facts right. Memminger wanted quality, but quantity was perhaps more important to him. Jim Keeley was a fighter, a man of convictions, not a seeker of objective truth. He wanted reporting from his legation to fit the way he saw the world.

Keeley's first direct order shocked us. We were told, after it became apparent that not everyone was equipped with what Keeley considered proper outfits for the credentials ceremony, to get complete sets of formal clothes: tux, white and black jackets, striped pants, morning coats, grey ties, top hat, the works. Diplomats, he said, had to have diplomatic uniforms. To be sure we complied, the minister personally took our measurements and submitted a joint order to Swartz Brothers of Baltimore. He told us prices would be reasonable. He was right about the prices, but reasonable prices for unneeded accouterments still left a sour taste. There were parts of my new diplomatic uniforms that in the next forty years I wore only to costume parties. I next needed white tie and tails six years later in Paris. However, another twenty-five years would pass before they were needed again. When that time came, I discovered that moths had holed my uniform. I had to rent the proper attire to attend President Reagan's 1981 white tie reception for the diplomatic corps. Ronald Reagan, incidentally, was the first president in many years to host white tie events.

The Palestine War had generated an enormous tide of Arab refugees. Before the British Mandate ended, some Israelis, including the Stern Gang led by Menachem Begin, had carried out a campaign of terror, including the Deir Yassin massacre. The Stern Gang apparently wanted to induce Arabs to flee, leaving their homes for Israelis to occupy. A number of Arab leaders, miscalculating badly, encouraged an Arab flight. The result was hundreds of thousands of displaced persons seeking refuge in Jordan, Syria, and those parts of Palestine still controlled by Arab Governments.

I visited a number of camps established in Syria. Conditions were appalling. The Syrians, with extraordinary budget appropriations supplemented by private relief efforts, were doing what they could for their Arab brethren. Still they could barely keep alive the estimated 90,000 refugees in Syria. We knew U.N. assistance was being organized but had no idea when it would arrive. My reports, endorsed enthusiastically by Minister Keeley, encouraged American generosity. The U.S. had supported Israel as refuge for Jews worldwide, but in so doing had contributed to new Diaspora, this time of Arabs. It seemed to us we had a moral and humanitarian obligation to help. Help we did. Indeed, fifty years and three or four generations of Palestinian refugees later, we are still helping finance a U.N. relief effort.

Following up on U.N. Under Secretary Ralph Bunche's successful efforts to arrange an armistice between the Arab states and Israel, Count Folke Bernadotte of Sweden was appointed U.N. Mediator. His task was to achieve a lasting peace. To put it mildly, the odds were heavily against success. He worked with dedication, however, and put forward a proposal to the parties. Keeley asked me to analyze it with particular attention to acceptability to Syria.

I wrote, "Because the Bernadotte Plan calls for implicit recognition of Israel, it is certainly unacceptable to the Arab Higher Committee, Syria, and Iraq." I had no doubt Syria was what later came to be called a "rejectionist state." But, I asked, what could be done to bring Syria to accept the Bernadotte Plan? As unlikely as I knew it to be, I suggested answers to Syria's principal concerns might be persuasive. Syria, frightened by the talk of Israeli extremists that Israel's natural frontier was on the Euphrates, to say nothing of King Abdullah's pretensions to rule "Greater Syria," would surely see a United States guarantee of its frontiers as highly attractive. Help in stabilizing the Syrian currency would also be attractive to Damascus. Of course, Washington understandably was not ready to think in terms of either aid or security guarantees. More than fifty years later, the peace process is incomplete and Syria is still a "rejectionist state."

Suddenly I was sick, desperately sick. Typhoid fever was the diagnosis. I was paying the price for my refugee visits. Had I not had my shots, I doubt I would be writing this.

While in bed at home slowly recovering, Minister Keeley paid me a surprise visit. He wanted my reaction to a cable he had drafted. To this day I regret not advising him to change the draft radically. I would like to think I would have done so had it not been for my high fever and weakened condition.

Jim's cable was a strident call for a U.S. policy review, not necessarily an unacceptable idea, but one of his reasons was unacceptable. He asked for a review, to the best of my recollection, taking into account Jewish history, "from the crucifixion of Christ the Messiah to the assassination of Bernadotte the Mediator." That ringing phrase drew attention, including White House attention. Jim never again served as a chief of mission.

Ralph Barrow, from the Syria desk in the State Department, wrote warning me that Damascus, under Keeley, was getting a bad reputation for clientitis. He urged me to cool it, to employ a modern phrase, not his I'm sure. On December 8, 1948, I wrote back, "We feel someone has to try to dramatize the issues. In conversations locally we are fighting the good fight for a reasoned compromise solution, but elsewhere the extremist view may help correct a bias which seems to us to be on the wrong side." The use of "we" and "us" reflected the fact that Minister Keeley, to whom I felt obligated to share both Ralph's and my letters, had reworked my draft reply. I now recognize that "we" was a mistake. The extremist view, if it had any effect, probably served to discount the view from Damascus. We would have had more effect, for example, had we simply drawn attention to the Syrian reactions to the Israeli foreign minister's statement that the frontiers recommended by the United Nations Security Council Observer Mission were "unacceptable" and to Zionist assertions that all of Galilee and Judea, in accordance with Abraham's Biblical injunction, were to be incorporated into Israel. To associate the Legation with Syrian outrage over such statements was simply wrong.

Syria's position on Palestine remained rock hard in opposition to Israel and most U.N. efforts at peacemaking. Moreover, Count Bernadotte's talks with King Abdullah of Transjordan fanned the flames of Syrian suspicions. Splits among the Arabs grew. Syria backed Mufti Haj Amin al-Husseini in calls for the establishment of a Palestine Government in Gaza. The Egyptians were furious. More ominously, the Soviets were moving away from Israel to a pro-Arab position. A Syrian-Soviet rapprochement seemed unlikely, but before it had not even been mentioned outside of Communist circles.

A visit of Habib Bourguiba to Syria provided a welcome break from the incessant focus on Palestinian and Arab internal squabbles was . To my delight, Bourguiba talked with me at some length about his struggle to end French colonial rule in Tunisia. Of course, to advance his cause he exploited my interest in his views. While I recognized Bourguiba was using me, I could not help but be impressed. Personally, he struck me as far more sophisticated and cultured than the Syrian leadership.

Evan Wilson, political counselor in Tehran, also visited Damascus about this time. He took me aside to say he hoped I would be interested in opening a consulate in Meshed as principal officer. After talking it over with Angela, who was in an adventurous frame of mind, I told Evan we were intrigued by the idea but needed to know more about what was involved. After exploration, I wrote Evan, "As much as I recognize the worthwhile work done by the C.I.A., I have no desire to be a front man." That was that.

Yet another visitor to Damascus was Ambassador George McGhee. His role in the Greek-Turkish Aid Program under the Truman Doctrine had made his reputation. He came to Damascus to explore solutions to the Palestinian refugee problem. At a long working dinner at Jim Keeley's, I was more outspoken about what I viewed as our obligation to help substantially than is expected of a junior officer. McGhee took it, but advised me that while he personally appreciated frank talk, were I not to curb my ways I would not be long in the Foreign Service. Good advice. Maybe I should have taken it.

By late 1948 the Legation's number one Communist watcher, C.I.A. Station Chief Miles Copeland, was well established. He and his wife Lorraine had rented a house only a bit smaller than the minister's residence. Miles did not hide his role as the head of U.S. intelligence in Syria. While this raised eyebrows, he and Lorraine were great people well liked by us all. Their parties, often complete with Iranian caviar and Russian vodka flown in from Tehran, were outstanding.

Miles was learning Arabic. To my mind, he was making amazing progress. Early in our relation he had been unable, he said, to bug the building we were moving out of and the Soviets were moving into. Otherwise, as far as I could judge, he was doing a good professional job. He had established contact with some Kurdish leaders. He put several of these in touch with me. I appreciated that. Then he and Steve Meade, the assistant army attaché, began to go off the deep end, it seemed to me.

Miles announced Lorraine and his kids would go to Beirut for a weekend, ostensibly accompanied by Miles. In fact, Miles and Steve planned to sneak back into Mile's house after dark. Miles told me he expected Syrian counterintelligence to raid his house. He put bars on the windows—not to keep robbers out, but to keep in these Syrians. He also installed internal floodlights he and Steve could turn on from their hiding place. It sounded nutty to me. I asked, "Why?" Miles condescendingly explained to me, a neophyte in intelligence matters, that catching the Syrian counterintelligence agents in his house would persuade Syrian intelligence that Miles and the C.I.A. were all-knowing! The plan still seemed nutty to me, but if the Minister was willing to have some of his people play cops and robbers, who was I to object?

The first weekend came and went without a Syrian break-in. The following weekend three toughs entered Miles' darkened house. Miles turned on the floodlights and called for the surrender of the intruders. They started shooting. Miles and Steve fired back. Then the intruders, strengthened by fear, broke the recently installed bars on a window and fled. Although the walls were pockmarked by bullets, miraculously no one was hurt in "The Battle of Copeland Manor." Miles telephoned the police to report an attempted robbery.

The next day senior government officials, some of whom knew the truth, sanctimoniously expressed their deep regret at this criminal break-in of a diplomat's residence. The police promised to track down the robbers. While surveying the crime scene, a police officer opened a desk drawer in Miles' study. It was booby-trapped! Tear gas flooded the study. A weeping police officer ran out, no doubt cursing the crazy Americans.

I concluded that "The Battle of Copeland Manor" failed to convince Syrian intelligence that American agents were all that clever, to say nothing of "all-knowing."

Early in 1949, Miles consulted me about his plan to work with a Major Husni Zaim to overthrow Shukri al-Quwatli, the elected president of Syria. In telling me of the plot, Miles also showed me a cable from Archie Roosevelt in Beirut. Archie, the agency's regional coordinator, did not want Hinton, "a bull in a china shop," to be advised of what was under consideration. While I appreciated Miles's forthrightness, I reacted strongly against the plan. I could see no reason whatsoever to interfere in the internal power structure of Syria. I did not believe Major Zaim would run Syria better than Quwatli. Nor did I think his Syria would act more in our interest than Quwatli's. Vociferously I made my case to Minister Keeley. It seemed to me he was not enthusiastic about the Zaim option, but neither was he disposed to call off Copeland and Meade. Miles argued the U.S. would have great influence after the coup. Major Zaim, he pointed out, was a good friend of our Major Steve Meade. Steve, I thought, had sold the idea to Miles, but I was not certain. I wondered: Had Zaim recruited Steve to advance his ambition or had Steve recruited Zaim?

In 1969 when Miles published his book *The Game of Nations*, he claimed he had organized the Zaim coup, alleging it was part and parcel of a broad C.I.A. plan to experiment with "political action." I am still not sure where the truth lies.

On March 30, 1949, Zaim and the Syrian army overthrew the Quwatli Government. I went to the Legation early to start work on reporting cables. At the entrance I was met by a little soldier with a big Tommy gun, which he aimed at my belly button. I got the idea I was not to enter. I therefore proceeded to the Minister's residence and told Jim Keeley all about the soldier and his gun. Jim said, "I'll show you how to do it." He had his Dragoman put on full uniform, climbed into his limousine, flew our flag, and rapidly pulled up in front of the Legation. The splendid Dragoman opened the car door with a flourish. His Excellency, the Minister of the United States, stepped out. The soldier stuck his gun in Jim's gut! Back in the car, Jim asked the driver to take him to the Defense Ministry. There we were quickly ushered into the presence of Zaim. Keeley smoothly said, "Major, there seems to be a misunderstanding. Your soldiers won't let me into my legation." Zaim agreed there was a misunderstanding, telling us the soldier was there for our protection. He ordered a lieutenant to go with us to the Legation, where he called off our "protector."

Once inside, we still could not report because we could not find our code clerk-communicator. He was not at home nor anywhere else we looked for him. After some speculation that the Syrians had kidnapped him to delay our reporting, he appeared. He was a ham radio operator. After hamming all night he had fallen asleep in the locked communications area. He had been in the Legation during the coup and during our search for him! We felt a little silly, but were back in business.

After an initial burst of popular enthusiasm for the Army takeover, an unusual calm descended on Damascus. Soon, however, Zaim's lack of capacity to govern was evident. Rumors of new coup plotting began to circulate.

I longed to see what new disasters would next befall Syria, but time was running out for the Hintons in Damascus. My replacement, Roger Davies, arrived, but I still had no orders. Roger told me I had made a few enemies in the department with my forthright reporting and links to Keeley's policy recommendations. There was, he added, a plot afoot to send me to Luanda. I had to ask him where that was and recoiled when I found out, not at the thought of Africa, but at the thought of having to try to learn Portuguese. A few days later a cable arrived assigning me as Consul and Principal Officer at Mombasa. Where was Mombasa? When I learned it was in East Africa, the combination of Swahili and English sounded much better to me than Lwena, Kongo, and Portuguese. And I was to have my own post. That the consulate was small and distant from the main foreign policy arena was immaterial. The idea of our own post was enormously appealing to Angela and to me.

Lots of hurried farewells were highlighted by Minister Keeley presenting us a treasured souvenir of a wonderful first Foreign Service post: a sword and scabbard, inscribed in silver:

To Deane and Angela
With the Affection of Their Colleagues
American Legation, Damascus
April 9, 1949

5

First Intermission (1949)

We sailed from Beirut to New York on the S. S. *Excambion* with calls at Alexandria, Piraeus, Naples, and Marseille. This time we were comfortably installed in our own cabin, the weather was excellent, the food not too bad, and the sightseeing at ports-of-call fascinating. We even had time for a few days in Rome, where Bob Brand of the embassy and Alfred Scherck, an extremely knowledgeable Austrian survivor of the Holocaust, were our wonderful guides. In 1949 the dollar was riding high. We stayed, therefore, at the Hassler in Rome. Located just above the Spanish Steps, it is a premier European hotel. Never again, when in Rome, could I afford it.

That trip provided much psychic income. The sea voyage also gave me a chance to decompress. Travel in later years was rush-rush by air. A more hectic pace is hardly an improvement. But in some other areas, life in the Foreign Service has greatly improved.

In the 1940s there really was no State Department medical service. We got our shots and physicals at Navy or Public Health Service clinics. When I contracted typhoid fever, instead of being medically evacuated to a first class hospital, as I would have been by the 1970s, Angela and a Syrian doctor took care of me. I was lucky to be reimbursed the $41.19 in charges for the doctor and medicine. Even that took a formal finding by the department that my illness "was not the result of vicious habits, intemperance or misconduct on (my) part."

Angela came down with hepatitis in Damascus. No reimbursement for her medical expenses. Fortunately it was a mild case, but I had to listen to her complain for the more than six weeks she was forbidden alcoholic beverages.

Suffering from an energy letdown, I pressed in Washington for more than the routine physical tests. Reluctantly the department agreed. I had amoebic dysentery. Belatedly convinced by blood tests, the department redeemed itself by sending me to George Washington Hospital for treatment. In those days, since the treatment was drastic and capable of inducing heart disorders, sufferers were hospitalized.

Typhoid, hepatitis, and amoebic dysentery at our first post were part of the price we paid for a Foreign Service career. And congressional critics talked and still talk of tea drinking diplomats in cushy posts!

By and large, the Foreign Service now provides housing or support for overseas personnel. Assigned to Mombasa as Principal Officer, I thought the department's Office of Foreign Building Operations (FBO) would help us establish ourselves. Specifically we hoped we would have a government-supplied refrigerator in a private house we would rent for ourselves while the search, never successful, for a Principal Officer's Residence to be bought or leased by FBO continued. FBO ruled they would only supply a refrigerator where there was a Government owned or leased house.

So I went into debt for a refrigerator and other things needed to outfit ourselves for tropical Africa. I owed about a third of a year's salary when we sailed for Mombasa.

Apart from hospitalization, frustration with FBO, and naive surprise that no one in Washington wanted to know my views about Syria or the Palestine question, our return home was great.

Angela went straight from New York to Al and Bettie Peyraud's Chicago apartment. She was home and happy, although she professed to miss me. I certainly missed her while I struggled with Washington.

The struggle was made easier staying with the Fergusons. Joanna, the Joanna of the moonlight stroll in Palmyra, was enchanting. Beautiful; a superb cook; master of single line drawings; mistress of Gerald, an imaginary cuddly Panda; given to strumming a lute while she sang folk music, American and Russian; she was a wonderful hostess. That it also seemed to me she was trying to seduce me almost right in front of Fergie added zest to the situation. It was generally believed she had had a torrid affair with one of Fergie's Arabic students in Beirut and rumors about other adventures were circulating. Tempted I was, but resist I did. It just was not right, but, to be honest, my memories are tinged with regret.

The first weekend my folks came for me and drove me back to Channelside, their new home in Cardinal, Virginia.

When Dad had returned from the Philippines, where his regiment had rounded up Japanese stragglers and skirmished with the Hukbalahap, he was assigned to Richmond, Virginia, to advise on the training of a reserve Airborne Division. It was a non-job. So with over thirty years' service, he decided to retire. But where? He and Mother began to scout for property. They saw Channelside in Tidewater, Virginia, early on and liked it and its wonderful location on a spit of land surrounded on three sides by water, but could not afford it. Months later the agent called to say the price had been greatly reduced. Keeping a small reserve to put the rundown house in shape, my parents became landowners.

Dad soon learned being a gentleman farmer was one hell of a hard job. He worked about twenty acres; reinvigorated an orchard; planted flower and vegetable gardens; seeded berry patches, blue berries and strawberries; kept pigs, geese, ducks, and chickens; culled his own oyster bed in the bay; and, if this were not enough, established bee hives. He thrived on it. Mother, still in precarious health, ran the house, fussed with a dog and various cats, and puttered in the garden. She liked to pick string beans, little stooping required, and flowers, worth stooping for. All in all, Channelside, if isolated, was a wonderful place. I loved it, especially since I was not pushed to work too hard.

After that weekend I returned to Washington and my hospital cure for amoebic, then headed west to Chicago. Angela and I enjoyed our visit. Bettie and Al treated me exceedingly well. They were, however, so solicitous that after a while in their not-too-large apartment I began to feel smothered.

Then after a visit to the doctor Angela announced she was pregnant. That was great news in itself, but all the more so because we had begun to wonder after three years of marriage if something was wrong.

While in Chicago I spent time with Grandpa and Grandma. Grandpa, but not Ma Roesch, had failed noticeably. He was gone by the time I returned from Mombasa. In his last days, he gave both Grandma and my mother, who had come to Chicago to help with the place, an extremely hard time. We had a great week of rest before heading for New York. There we saw a hit musical, *Kiss Me Kate*, and, as in 1946, dined with Bill Durka the night before sailing on the S.S. *Robin Kettering*, a freighter with passenger accommodations for twelve.

Our passage was marred by lousy food, no other bridge players, and a small, nauseating selection of long-playing records (LPs), except for one Mozart concerto, *Kiss Me Kate*, and *South Pacific*. After listening to *Kiss Me Kate* forty or fifty times, even it wears on one. We breathed a sigh of relief when the phonograph broke down. While our days were normally uneventful, we had an exciting August 9 passing the equator. With ceremony in the name of Neptunus Rex, his Commodore Glen D. Webster, who just happened also to be master of the *Robin Kettering*, awarded parchment diplomas, admitting us to the "Solemn mysteries of the Ancient Order of the Deep."

It was eighteen days from New York to Cape Town. Unfortunately Captain Webster estimated at least another month to reach Mombasa due to port congestion. He could not take his ship directly into a dock to unload; first, there was a wait offshore or in the harbor for a berth. It bothered me that this port congestion would greatly delay my arrival at my new post. So during my call on the Consul General in Cape Town, I asked him if he thought I should disembark and fly to Mombasa. He replied with a categorical "No." Mombasa would be fine without me, I should stay with Angela, and I would get to know various ports during the slow voyage up the east coast of Africa. This answer did nothing to strengthen my self-esteem or persuade me of my own essentiality for the Foreign Service, but it was a good answer. I took advantage of the situation and explored Cape Town, Port Elizabeth, Durban (including a trip into Zululand), and Lourenco Marques with Angela. Alex and Peggy Davit were stationed in Port Elizabeth. It was great fun to see them again and recount the good old days in Damascus.

The forty-nine days between New York and Mombasa had one great advantage. There was plenty of time to read. I read everything I could get my hands on about Africa. Particularly useful were Elspeth Huxley's *Race and Politics in Kenya* and Margery Perham's *Africans and British Rule*. The *South and East African Year Book and Guide*, published by the Union Castle Line, was a first class source of basic data, as were the official annual Colonial Reports. I thought them more useful in a practical sense than Lord Hailey's monumental *An African Survey*.

As time dragged on, I began to fear I would run out of reading material. Finally, however, we reached Mombasa. It was September 16, 1949. It would have been much later, but fortunately Captain Webster decided to bypass Beira, where delays in discharging were the longest. He would stop there on his return voyage to the States.

Vice Consul J. Cudd Brown met the ship, took us directly to a house we had been fortunate enough to rent with Brownie's indispensable help, and generally facilitated our first days in a new environment. Promptly and proudly I assumed charge of the American Consulate at Mombasa, Kenya.

6

Mombasa (1949–1951)

Above all else I remember Mombasa as the birthplace of Deborah Ann Hinton, Angela's and my firstborn child.

The Consulate was small and unimportant, but my consular district was spectacular. On the mainland it included the Kenya Protectorate, legally different from Kenya, a Crown Colony. Nominally the Protectorate was part of the Sultan of Zanzibar's domains. The Sultan's flag flew over the old Portuguese fort of Mombasa and the Government of Kenya paid the Sultan 11,000 pounds sterling a year in "rent." The reality, of course, was that the British ran both the Protectorate, which they called the Coast Province of Kenya, and Zanzibar. Mombasa also had consular jurisdiction over the Seychelles Islands and Mauritius. Zanzibar was added to my consular district shortly after my arrival. Someone in Washington thought it made little sense to divide consular responsibility for the Sultanate between the posts at Dares Salaam and Mombasa. It struck me that while Mombasa itself might not be much, the consular district with Mauritius, the Seychelles, and Zanzibar was unequaled. Much of my professional attention was directed out from Africa toward my far-flung "empire" in the Indian Ocean.

Life in Mombasa was pleasant enough, but hardly stimulating intellectually. Nor, unfortunately, was there a single decent restaurant. "Sundowners," where so called "Europeans," whites in current nomenclature, sipped their Pink Gins or their Pimm's Cups, were the principal and endless form of private entertaining. The Brits, of course, have a genius for club life, which is OK if you haven't anything better. We joined the Mombasa Club as well as the golf and tennis clubs.

Thinking of joining the yacht club, I went sailing with friends in the harbor. Great, I thought, but the very next weekend my friends somehow sailed in front of an incoming freighter. Fortunately all aboard, good swimmers, survived. I, however, thinking of what would have happened to me had I been aboard that weekend, decided to leave sailing for others. Guess I'm risk adverse.

In addition to these clubs, I joined Rotary and was made an honorary member of the Kilindini Shellhole of the Memorable Order of Tin Hats. For better or worse, the Asian social clubs discriminated against Europeans, presumably because Europeans discriminated against Asians, and while I was often invited to speak at their meetings, 1 was barred from membership. I disliked the principle but the result was gratifying. There were no equivalent African clubs. The Mombasa Rotary Club had Asian members; the Nairobi Club did not, but the rules of Rotary meant that an Asian member from Mombasa visiting Nairobi was welcomed at the weekly luncheons. This was a small chink in the armor of the old-line European highlanders. To broaden the salient into racism, I set out with a few kindred liberal spirits to bring an African into the Mombasa Club. It could not be done, or at least my few friends and I could not pull it off in 1950 or 1951. Few Africans even came close to meeting the criteria for Rotarians, and old-line colonial types, including some uncomprehending Asians, blocked our efforts to induct one or two of the few Africans who came close.

On the other hand, the Rotarian charities concentrated on helping Africans, a reflection of paternalism, I suppose. I particularly enjoyed sponsoring a junior football, i.e. soccer, team playing in a league subsidized by our Rotary club. In addition, I represented Rotarians on an oversight committee, where I sat with a government educator as well as representatives of the Referee's Association and the Athletic Association. This effort, said to be a first at promoting inter-school competition, was a marked success.

Angela and I were able to host a very few Africans at our Fourth of July receptions, which provoked many critical reactions and only a few commendations. We did, however, get a commendation in the *Mombasa Times* for our answer to the problem of how to handle hundreds of guests in a very small house: invite people for different times, e.g. six to seven, six-thirty to seven-thirty, etc., and pray it does not rain. It worked; in the crush, only the real souses overstayed their allotted time.

As Angela's pregnancy progressed, we solved the space problem by arranging with the landlord to build an additional bedroom for a nursery and more modest quarters for a prospective nanny.

What we could not solve was the weather problem. In the rainy season, April to October, shoes mildewed overnight and doors and drawers stuck. The heat was not bad as long as the monsoon blew in off the Indian Ocean. However, when the monsoon died, as it did twice each year while shifting from the southeast to the northeast and back again, it was in Angela's words "unpleasant to just plain awful." I did not mind much, but it was terrible for Angela in her "delicate condition."

What bothered Angela even more, if that is possible, were bugs. Bugs in the soup, bugs in bed, bugs everywhere. Neither of us could understand the lack of screening. Without screens, flies, mosquitoes and flying ants became house pets, I mean pests. Cockroaches we had by the hundreds. A few bats we fought off with my squash racket. Still, being awakened by a bat caught in your mosquito netting is an unsettling experience. Then when Deborah arrived we had to set each leg of her crib in a can of water mixed with kerosene. Otherwise the ants would have eaten our baby alive.

We had servants, lots of them: a cook, a laundry boy, a houseboy, a gardener, and Deborah's Ayah, or nanny. Only Mary, the Ayah, and the cook seemed to have a clue about their duties. They, too, however, required close oversight. Supervising this crowd was more demanding than doing it all yourself in the U.S. But they provided laughs and pathos. Also terror, when one tribal zealot tried to put a curse on Mary, an educated (by Kenyan standards) Christian. Educated or not, Mary believed the twigs she found in a pattern before her door inevitably would bring trouble, serious trouble for her. We fired the right individual and convinced a dubious Mary to stay with us. If she had not become deeply attached to Deborah by this time, she surely would have fled to seek a tribal witchdoctor's counter to the curse.

As the Consulate's principal officer, I rated china gold crested with the great seal of the United States. We used it only to entertain. We taught the houseboy to serve with the crest up. We also taught him pie was to be served with the point down. There came a dinner where cook placed the pie on the plates with the point toward the crest. Our house boy sat a piece down in front of the guest of honor, noted the crest was down, so turned the plate around, but then the pie was pointed up. He turned the plate once more. Still didn't work. He was stumped. It was hilarious, if sad, to watch him try his best to do as we had taught him. Unfortunately cook had presented him with an insoluble problem. On another festive occasion, cook served canned peas for dessert. The culture gap was real.

There was a language gap as well as a cultural gap. While I was progressing with Swahili, I had none of even the rudiments of the countless tribal languages. We did understand that as patron and patroness of our staff we were expected to look after them and help in all circumstances. To illustrate what was expected of us, I quote from a letter from Odima, the houseboy, to Angela.

Dear Madam,
    A wonderful great conflagration out broke in my father's village involving 11 ginaries (huts) into complete ruins out of which 5 ginaries were belonging to me.
    My newly built house was completely burnt with everything in it, but only children saved. According to our Native Customary Laws, my wife is now forced by the laws to sleep outside the houses: pending my return home.
    Madam, in the foregoing circumstances, I shall be highly obliged if you will be good enough to... (grant 18 days leave, to secure the permit needed for me to bring my family to the coast, and to lend me fifty Shillings.)
    I am, Madame,
    Your faithful Servant *Odima*

Of course, Odima hired a letter writer to produce his request list. Given our obligations established by British tradition, it worked. Odima got all he asked for and more, although obtaining the travel permit for his family was a bit difficult.

Shortly after our arrival in Mombasa, Consul General Edward Groth summoned me to Nairobi for consultations. I soon decided he was a bit peculiar. He began by telling me he wanted to cap his career by serving as Consul General in Lhasa. He was full of Indian spiritualism. Nothing wrong with that, he was just ahead of his time, but not what I expected from my boss in Nairobi, Kenya. Then, too, he was an overly solicitous host, wanting to verify my bath water was the right temperature. When not talking of India and Tibet, he talked of the approaching re-inauguration of the Hamburg Opera, not of Africa or our responsibilities. Formerly our Consul General in Hamburg, Groth proudly told me his main accomplishment in Germany was patronizing the rebuilding of the Opera House. He had decided he could not afford to fly to attend opening night, but he was trying to arrange through German friends for a short wave broadcast of the initial opera. While I was there he stayed up all night for a test, but only heard static. Next he decided he would listen over a long-distance phone line. Finally as I was leaving to return to my post, he told me he had decided he could only afford to listen to the overture and finale by telephone. Later I learned that did not work very well either. Groth was said to have been desolate.

The next time I visited Nairobi was for a review of my efficiency report at Groth's request. Incredibly, he went through the form asking me what I thought my rating should be for each item. After each of my answers, he would snort or laugh and tell me how he had scored me. It was an exceedingly painful procedure even though he gave me fairly high marks.

Groth loved to travel. However, rather than reporting on economic or political conditions, he wrote at length about such subjects as how many flies there were on his hotel room wall. His love of travel got me crossways with him twice. First, when I drove to a consular conference in Lourenco Marques, he was envious he had not thought to do so. His envy took the form of reaming me for proceeding without his permission, even though I had orders from Washington to go to the conference. On another occasion, he informed Washington he was proceeding to the Seychelles, he would catch the next steamer (almost a month later) to Bombay, and he would take some overdue leave in India before returning to his post via South Africa. I read my copy of this cable with amazement and annoyance since the Seychelles were in my consular district, not his. The consul general supervised me and my office, but he had no authorized jurisdiction for the Seychelles. To my delight and Groth's extreme annoyance, the Department of State, by return cable, instructed him to remain at his post. Groth asked me on the phone if I had had anything to do with his rebuff, which seemed inexplicable to him. I replied, "Nothing, Sir," which was true but less than persuasive to my consul general, who was somewhat paranoid about the incident.

Groth's successor was Angus Ward, also a character, but quite different from Groth. If Groth was seeking salvation in opera and Tibetan spiritualism, Angus Ward was dedicated to the crusade against communism. He had achieved a modicum of fame when he had stood tall while detained for months by the Chinese Communists in Mukden, if my memory is correct. It was also bruited about in Kenya that he was quite unhappy with his assignment as Consul General Nairobi. Too far from the U.S.S.R. Truly too far from the enemy for Ward, but his public statements upon arrival and subsequently could not have pleased the Kenyans more. Angus was a diplomat as well as a Cold War warrior.

I knew things would be different under my new boss from his first message to me about his wishes upon arrival in Mombasa. He did not want to linger. I was to reserve three first class compartments on the overnight train to Nairobi. He, unlike Groth, was a married man. Mrs. Ward, born into Russian nobility, was traveling with a maid. I was to make arrangements to move forty-seven pieces of luggage from the boat to the train. Most important of all, I was repeatedly advised, was that I arrange for the port veterinarian to board the ship promptly and clear two Siberian cats for the onward journey to Nairobi. It was impressed upon me by letter and cable that clearing the cats was top priority. I had discussed this with the port veterinarian several times and been assured he would be there the minute the ship could be boarded.

The ship, the Wards, the luggage, and the cats arrived. When I went aboard I was greeted most kindly, but immediately asked, "Where is the veterinarian?" Exactly what I was wondering. As time passed I faced Ward, an immense man with a red beard, and two of the largest cats I had ever seen, thinking how sad it was my career had been ruined by cats and a wayward veterinarian. The consul general was restrained, but Mrs. Ward was giving me a piece of her mind when, thank God, the Vet arrived and cleared the cats, well documented as they were, for entry into Kenya.

At the station, Ward hoisted two locker trunks and strode down the platform with one on each shoulder. The crowd of Africans stared in utter amazement. Europeans did not carry their own baggage; at least they had never seen Europeans carrying trunks before. I wondered, did consul general Ward carry his trunks in China or did he think Chinese coolies were more reliable than African laborers?

A few days later, to my relief, I received a most gracious note thanking me for my "successful" efforts to get the Wards, cats and all, to Nairobi.

Soon Angela and I were invited to Nairobi as guests of the Wards. We were well treated indeed. The consul general talked to me about my work and African problems, but his heart was not in it. He had tray after tray of vocabulary cards in his office. Noting my puzzled look, he told me he was working on his contribution to victory in the coming war against the U.S.S.R. and the PRC. He would produce a dictionary of Mongolian, Russian, Chinese, and, I suppose, English, although I do not remember his saying so. Mongolia, he assured me, would be the strategic key to winning the war. His dictionary, the only one of its kind, would make the difference. I hope my skepticism did not show.

Our first Christmas in Mombasa was joyous as Tuffy's arrival drew nearer, but not as joyous as we would have hoped. It was deadly hot, too hot to think of Santa and reindeer in the snow. There were no attractive Christmas trees to be had, Angela was suffering from the heat, and expected gifts from home did not arrive in time. Such is life in the Foreign Service.

Tuffy turned out not to be Tuffy, but to be Taffy, arriving early on February 13, 1950. We named her Deborah Ann. I sent off cables to her Grandparents and together with Angela admired our beautiful baby. Angela was taken aback when her British friends asked, "Are you going to feed her?" but thought better of their expression "top and tail time," a euphemism for bath time. Another strictly British idea was to keep mother and child in the nursing home for ten days. That requirement, however, helped assuage my guilt feelings about driving off and leaving Angela to cope with our new family member. That the Zwarts, our best friends in Mombasa, promised to take good care of Angela and Deborah also helped. He was the Holland America Line Representative for Kenya as well as the honorary Dutch consul. Angela understood my desire to see as much of Africa as I could, and, whatever her inner doubts, sent us on our way without objection. I say "us" because the Zwarts' son, Wibor, on his way to a South African university, was to share the driving.

Taffy's arrival was late. Had she delayed another day, I would have had to have canceled my scheduled drive to Lourenco Marques and gone by air instead. As it was, Wibor's and my last calculation convinced us I could arrive in Lourenco Marques in time for the opening of the consular conference. I almost did.

The drive was a fabulous adventure. Spectacular scenery, fascinating people, interesting wild life, and almost impassible roads. It was rainy season in Tanganyika and Northern Rhodesia. No serious problem as far as Dodona, but there we were told the road south was closed. However, the district engineer gave us a permit to proceed rather than impede an American consul traveling on official business. He also told us we would not make it, adding, "When you get stuck, don't worry. A truck will come by late in the day to bring you back here." Fortunately the only time we got stuck was right in the town of Sao Hill, where there were lots of people to help pull us out of mud over our hub caps.

We drove for miles in central Tanganyika without seeing anyone. With one exception, those Africans we did see ignored us. The exception was an old man who came to attention and saluted as we passed. I mentioned my puzzlement at his behavior in the hotel bar that night. Oh, said a Brit, he must go back to the days before World War I when Tanganyika was a German colony. The Germans forced Africans to salute them, and those Africans never forgot!

Floodwaters in the vicinity of Kanana, Northern Rhodesia, delayed us a bit. Reports of these floods upset both Angela and the Zwarts, who feared the worst. They were glad to hear when we reported in from Livingston. Wibor and I took time off from driving to inspect Victoria Falls. To see better, I paid for a light plane to fly me over the falls, an incredible sight. Wibor, who drove like a frustrated NASCAR racer, nevertheless copped out of flying. Strange. Sadly he was killed in an automobile accident in South Africa before he graduated from the university.

We should have had the car serviced and inspected in Livingston while sightseeing, but we didn't. It was quite a shock when our brakes wouldn't work while arriving at the border between the two Rhodesias. As I was downshifting, an alert African policeman raised the bar across the road just in time. We had to have a fluid leak from the main brake cylinder fixed, the springs repaired, and a replacement battery installed. Once on the road again, we also needed new tires, lots of new tires. In Southern Rhodesia roads were partially paved. Two ribbons of concrete, like railway tracks, had been laid. Great, if there were no oncoming traffic, but when there was each driver had to go off the tracks. Since the rains had washed away much of the dirt road, getting back on the tracks risked rubbing the tires against the cement track. Never before or since have I had so many blowouts in one day.

Salisbury looked inviting, but we were behind schedule and so pushed on to Pretoria Kop in Krueger National Park. Dusk and dawn drives gave us fabulous views of countless animals, including magnificent lion prides Wibor and I shot film, but the light was bad and I had little to show for it. Still it reinforced my decision never to use the .303 Savage rifle or the .12 gauge shotgun I had brought from the States for hunting. Rather, I decided to order a movie camera.

The last three hundred miles or so to Lourenco Marques I did on my own, as Wibor headed on to his university on a bus. Arriving in Lourenco Marques, the muffler fell off my trusty Chevy, making my arrival at the Conference a noisy one.

Assistant Secretary George McGhee gave me hell for being half a day late. He also sent me to the code room to help the clerks, who were behind in handing strip cipher traffic. I knew how to push strips, but I did not enjoy it and was glad when McGhee relented, spoke kindly of my adventurous spirit, and let me join the conference. For my part, I was proud of the 3,200-mile drive through Africa in what was said to be the worst rainy season in 8 years. It had taken just over 12 days; my return by air from Johannesburg to Nairobi to Mombasa took just over 8 hours.

The conference was an eye opener. It almost destroyed my faith in the Foreign Service. Many of my senior colleagues, mostly consul generals, literally spoke of Africans as "monkeys in the trees." Almost to a man, they saw no reason or hope for Africans to become free. Nick Feld, Consul in Dar es Salaam, and Margaret Tibbetts, a political officer from Embassy London, were as appalled as I. We wondered if the reason these types were in their posts was because the Service was too short of officers to select them for early retirement. I know not what McGhee thought of the performance of the senior officers, but his exploratory discussion of a possible Zionist homeland in Rhodesia convinced me he still had much to learn about the Middle East, to say nothing of Africa.

My own views of Africa were by now fairly well formed. I agreed with many that the Africans were far from ready for independence, but I favored self-government for dependent areas in an interdependent system, for economic as well as political and social reasons. I argued for an integrated world while opposing the further multiplication of sovereign states. With respect to South Africa, I was horrified by my perception of the Europeans. Their world was accursed. Cape Town and Pretoria were extremely attractive cities, except for the bars on the windows, the locks on the doors, the guns in every European's possession, and the fear of the blacks in their hearts. I concluded an explosion was likely, sooner or later. But somehow, four decades later, there was a peaceful transition from apartheid to a democracy led by President Mandela, an African. One can only hope that tolerance, democracy, and the rule of law will persist, but I worry that the explosion I feared for so long may still come.

Back in Mombasa, I concentrated on getting to know my daughter. She was a delight. So photogenic, too. Angela took the better pictures with her new Rolifex. We could not play enough with Deborah. Yankee and Dixie, our Alsatians inherited from our predecessors, the J. Cudd Browns, loved Deborah also. They guarded her well. Not by coincidence, our firstborn was photographed more than any of our babies that followed.

Consular work at Mombasa was not very demanding, which made it easier for me to spend time at home than it would be with later children. At Damascus, contrary to the practice in the Service now where junior officers almost always start with a heavy dose of consular work, I did so little that I can remember both cases I handled. One was witnessing the marriage of a U.S. citizen; the other, in the absence of the consul at the crash site, I issued a letter of identity to a survivor of a TWA Constellation crash in northern Syria who had lost her passport.

At Mombasa, shipping and seamen, consular invoices, a very few visas, and a couple of estate cases added to my consular experience. I enjoyed dealing with most seamen, although I had a few frights from unruly drunks. I hated the estate case requirements of inventorying all effects of the deceased. I held together the semblance of a softball team, whose only games were against teams from Lykes and Robin Line ships. We never won, partly from lack of practice, partly because many of my team's Brits, brought up on cricket, just did not want to run unless they were certain they would reach base safely! Still we had fun, the sailors appreciated our effort, and we appreciated their beer.

Mombasa provided my first experience with the frustrations of dealing with the Foreign Building Operations of the Department of State. The Government of Kenya, in appreciation for U.S. wartime help, had made available a magnificent property overlooking the entrance to the main harbor. In turn, the United States pledged to construct thereon a consular residence. While I knew I would not be in Mombasa long enough to see construction completed, I nevertheless pushed hard for approval of plans so work could begin. Growing annoyance manifest by the British authorities over lack of any sign of progress spurred me on. All to no avail. I presume we eventually gave back our right to this fabulous property.

F.B.O. did, however, support my move of the Consulate from an inferior facility into the second floor of Barclay's Bank. For this I was grateful.

At Thanksgiving, Angela and I entertained every American citizen registered in the Consular district. Together with my secretary's British husband, Freddy Hills, we numbered sixteen, enough for two tables and two turkeys. I hacked up my turkey and took a long time to do it while Freddy speedily demonstrated surgical mastery at his table. In these few humiliating minutes I would gladly have traded my "big shot" status for the ability to carve.

The Consulate also "facilitated" the efforts of other Americans. Thus, we became good friends with the Al Harrises, anthropologists studying tribal customs, and Ted Munger, a geographer. We also got to know A. Tucker Abbott, a world renowned expert on seashells sent to East Africa by the Smithsonian Institution to collect and ship to Guam a wasp know to be the natural predator of a snail, already ravaging plant life on the island and likely to move on to the Hawaiian Islands sooner or later. Tucker caught hundreds of the desired wasps and I helped stuff them in an official pouch. Despite our cabling transit points claiming diplomatic immunity for our pouches and warning them not to fumigate our wasps, Guam informed us all but one had arrived "moribund." They had died as a result of fumigation. Frustrated, Tucker abandoned the project.

A researcher from the U.S. Department of Agriculture was studying East African fruit flies. To have a steady supply of flies, he contracted with African cucumber growers on the coast to bring rotting cucumbers to the Consulate for onward shipment to his laboratory in Nairobi. My staff and I, holding our noses, pouched the rotting mess, swarming with fruit flies, to Nairobi, until the manager of Barclay's Bank, on the second floor of which the Consulate was located, could take it no longer. Pointing out that we were violating some obscure clause in our lease, he said, "No more rotten cucumbers or out." Barclay Bank's dignity had been impugned. Consequently, the Consulate abandoned its rotten cucumber caper. Thanks to the manager of Barclays, we regained a bit of our own lost dignity. Fortunately for fruit fly research, our expert made other collection arrangements.

Policy was not a staple in the diet of consuls in small African posts. We were seldom asked for our views. I can recall only once in my two years in Mombasa. That was after Secretary George McGhee had given a speech, which was boilerplate. After the requisite praise, I commented that his remarks fell pitifully short of an adequate appraisal of what Europeans were doing to prepare Africans for the future.

Also, from time to time I volunteered my views to the department. My Chicago boy interest in economics led me to take a dim view of British protectionism. Thus, I wrote Washington:

I would urge...deliberately reaffirming to the British that our tacit acceptance of limitations on U.S. trade in East Africa by their exchange control apparatus does not represent default of our treaty rights. We should never allow them to forget it.

On a lesser issue, I criticized both the content and process of our information program. The content of material sent us was undifferentiated by type of audience. It was the same as produced for an audience in the developed world. An error and a waste of money. "I am convinced that the way we talk about communism to the bulk of ignorant and disinterested Africans is more likely to arouse interest than create understanding."

My far-flung consular district beckoned. I sailed for Mauritius, the most important part of my consular district. It was a notable visit for me.

The green sugar fields in the highlands, the climate, and the magnificent beaches of Mauritius reminded me of Hawaii, without the pineapples.

I was the first official American to come to Mauritius after World War II, apart from a Department of Agriculture expert on plant pests who probably contributed far more to the island than I. I was met by British officials at the dock and driven to a comfortable highland hotel free of heat and malaria. This was a kind and welcome start to what became an overwhelming reception. Countless invitations to this and that were waiting for me from British officials, French planters, Hindu merchants, and Chinese traders. I was literally busy morning, noon, and night. Most of these contacts were welcome and facilitated my task of getting a feel for the economic and political situation. But some were troublesome. I was deluged with dinner invitations by individual Chinese and Chinese organizations. I knew these meals would be fantastic. My mouth watered at the thought of Chinese banquets, but I also knew enough to know the American consul should not associate with the Communist Chinese or their sympathizers. But how to tell the Nationalist Chinese, loyal to Chiang Kai-shek, from Mao's sympathizers? In desperation I asked the British for counsel. Colonial Secretary Harford's advice, in this as in other matters, could not have been more helpful.

His office had arranged my program in advance. The schedule, while elaborated largely in accordance with my requests, also struck me as designed to keep me too busy to delve deeply into sensitive political issues. Still, overall it was excellent. While I did not see the point of spending most of a day with the Chief Forestry Officer, I nevertheless thought it best to carry out scheduled visits. To my delight, it turned out that the Forester was a superb conversationalist, most knowledgeable and entertaining about all aspects of life in Mauritius.

Mauritius, while uninhabited when "discovered" early in the sixteenth century by the Portuguese, had been visited in earlier eras by Malay and Arab sailors. The Dutch, however, made the first real effort at colonization. Unfortunately they accomplished little beyond decimating the magnificent ebony forests, totally eliminating the Dodo, a remarkable bird found only in Mauritius, and bringing the first African slaves to the island.

The French did better, taking over in 1715. However, at the end of the Napoleonic wars Mauritius, which a British expedition had seized during the war, was ceded to Britain. Nevertheless, by far the larger percentage of Europeans on the island was of French descent when I visited. There were few English apart from government officials. In fact, I had no sooner arrived at my hotel in Curepipe, in the highlands, than a French leadership group descended upon me to tell me of how they were perpetually wronged by their English masters. Presumably to their annoyance, much of our discussion was in English, since my rudimentary French was not up to their fluency.

The French landowners originally imported slaves from Africa, especially Madagascar, to work their sugar and sisal plantations. When the British undertook first to suppress the slave trade and then to abolish slavery, the resistance of French slave owners was fierce. However, a generous cash settlement paid to the slave owners by London both freed the slaves and largely averted violence. Thereafter the landowners brought in indentured workers from South Asia. By 1861 a clear majority of the population was of Indian origin. This Asian majority was roughly divided four Hindus for every Moslem.

By the time of my visit, the Indians were clearly the future of Mauritius. Some Hindus and a few Moslems had already achieved leadership positions in a number of local government councils. Pressure for universal suffrage had brought a significant expansion of the number of registered voters in 1948, but even so less than 20% of the population of just under half a million persons were qualified voters. If most Indians wanted universal suffrage, the French and Chinese wanted constitutional protection of minority rights, as did the Moslems.

In ten days in a rented car, I took as close a look at and collected as much data as possible about Mauritius and its demographic, economic, and political problems. Upon my return to Mombasa, my conversations, observations, and data gave me material for a number of reports to Washington. One entitled "Parochialism, Politics, and Progress in Mauritius" drew a commendation from Director General Richard Butrick of the Foreign Service. Pleased by his calling my work "an extremely valuable document," I was nevertheless a bit dubious about its practical utility. However, Butrick was right. Our first resident ambassador, Bill Brewer, told me in 1971 that reading my reports had been the best preparation he had had before going to Port Louis. Since Bill was at the time lobbying me for an increase in the sugar quota for Mauritius, I discounted his praise. Nevertheless, it was remarkable, I thought, that my twenty-year-old reports were still available.

I left Mauritius on an Air France flight to Madagascar. I had arrived on the Norwegian M.S. *Thorstrand*. It brought back memories of the Norwegian freighter I had been on at the end of World War II. Same spick and span, but with one memorable difference: no army chow this time, just lots of smoked salmon and lobster salad and rich desserts.

"Madagascar," I wrote home, "is like nothing else on earth. Odd, queer looking people, queerer looking houses. Some resemblance in dress to Mexico." It also provided two fine examples of Foreign Service hospitality to a colleague on leave. Consul General Robert Ferrand put me up and introduced me to a number of his friends. However, apart from being in the same Service we had nothing in common. Ferrand's remarks about Africans had appalled me at the Lourenco Marques Conference. Now, as his guest, I had to restrain myself to avoid reacting to his continually expressed prejudices. Gladys Weintraub, the vice consul's wife, of my generation, was entirely different. We shared somewhat naive liberal views. Fortunately for me, she had time to guide me around Tananarive, including native markets.

Air France was the only airline then serving Mauritius and Madagascar, so when in a hurry one rode "Air Chance." Its reputation in East Africa was hardly that of a careful, conservative carrier. Stories abounded of the pilot and co-pilot leaving their planes on automatic while they caroused with the passengers and stewardesses, especially on southbound equator-crossing ceremonies. Perhaps apocryphal, rumor had it that passengers and crew, being initiated into King Neptune's realm, had to walk the aisles balancing on seat arms while others squirted champagne up, shall we say, their britches. Be that as it may, Air France returned me safely to Nairobi and East African Airways got me the rest of the way home to Mombasa.

Exotic Zanzibar beckoned next. Famous as a base for Arab slave traders in the 19th century, British influence eliminated slavery after a long succession of small steps forward. Here Angela joined me. Thereafter, cloves became the mainstay of the economy. Indeed, at the time of our visit the odor of cloves wafted over most of the island.

Zanzibar had also served as a base for European explorers of the "dark continent." Indeed, one could still visit Dr. David Livingstone's house in the old town. But Arab influences far outweighed European. Carved brass-studded doors to old Arab houses, often almost hidden in narrow alleys, were worth tracking down. The few remaining artisans, whose fathers, grandfathers, and great-grandfathers had crafted these remarkable doors, kept the art alive by producing "Zanzibar chests." We acquired a beauty made of hard wood liberally bossed with brass studs.

A British "protectorate" had been established in 1890 in an imperialist "share-the-African-pie deal" with two other colonial powers, the French and Germans. His Highness Sultan Seyyid Sir Khalifa Bin Harub "reigned" as he had since his accession to the throne in 1911. The sultan could trace his ancestry back to the glory days of Omani rule of much of East Africa. While in the 16th century the Portuguese had controlled Zanzibar, the East African coast, and much of the Persian Gulf, their hold was steadily weakened in the 17th Century. By 1698, the Omanis had taken over north of Mozambique.

Particularly interesting for me, as the modern-day consul, was the historical fact that the United States had been the first country to establish a consulate in Zanzibar in 1837. However, no trace of it remained. At least I could find none.

We were royally entertained, particularly by British colonial officers. The British Resident, Sir Vincent Glenday, and his wife invited us to dinner to be followed by "the theater." He specified tropical formal wear: black tie, but no jacket, for me, a short evening dress for Angela. Peculiar, we thought, but, of course, we complied. After drinks, good conversation, and an excellent dinner, our host invited me to join him "to inspect Africa," a euphemism for "Let's go pee in the garden." Having relieved ourselves we joined the ladies and set off to the theater. We arrived late, entered a dark odoriferous hall, and were shown to our seats. Almost overcome, we watched a simply terrible Indian movie. Finally it ended. The lights went up. We four, in formal wear yet, were seated in the middle of an unwashed, often only partly clothed Arab, African, and Asian audience. With dignity, our host and hostess led us out. With much courtesy, the unwashed stood back so their British "protector" and his guests could exit. The episode illustrated for me in a flash the chutzpah that for so long had helped hold the British Empire together.

Of course, chutzpah was adroitly mixed with an iron hand. For example, in 1896 Seyyid Khaled, an ambitious pretender to Zanzibar's throne, encouraged by the Germans, seized the palace by force. When he rejected a British ultimatum demanding he clear out, British warships firing at point blank range demolished the palace and killed over 500 persons. Belatedly, the pretender fled, taking refuge in the German Consulate. The incident did nothing to reduce British-German tension, but it was not until1917, during World War I, that British forces in the course of overrunning German East Africa finally captured Seyyid Khaled.

Sir Vincent was good enough to present me to the Sultan. He briefed me carefully in advance on what I could and could not discuss with His Highness. The weather was central to the former category. Politics, economics, and foreign policy were subjects reserved for the protecting power. He, Sir Vincent, would be glad to discuss them with me, and did, but for me they were off limits with the sultan. Nevertheless, our meeting went well. I was impressed by the dignity and serenity of the seventy-eight-year-old ruler, who at the time held the distinction of being the world's longest reigning chief of state.

Two days later, Angela and I arranged to take pictures of the sultan and sultana going out in their Red Rolls Royce for their daily drive. We meant to be discrete about it. The sultan, however, spotted us, called us over, introduced his wife, and graciously posed for pictures. I was told later that photos of the sultan and sultana together were exceedingly rare. Mine, it was said, would sell. Somehow, however, my greed was checked by a sixth sense that photo hawking was not an appropriate sideline for an American consul.

We took back to Mombasa wonderful memories as well as a chest, a glance at which still evokes the sultan of Zanzibar--nice ring to that--the scent of cloves, and the twilight of the British Empire.

Immediately before our Zanzibar visit we had entertained Prince Aly Khan, his wife, Rita Hayworth, and his daughter, Jasmine, who shared Taffy's crib for a nap while the rest of us lunched. Aly Khan was visiting the Ismaeli community on the coast, spending

four days with the local leader of the Ismaelis, who just happened
to be our grocer. I had thought the Aly Khans might like a break
from their routine and had heard that, strange as it seemed to me,
the local Europeans, neither official nor private, were going to offer
hospitality. Of course, I also hoped to meet my favorite wartime
pin-up girl. Angela was sure they would not accept our invitation,
but accept they did. Blind racism, horror at interracial marriage,
may have kept the Brits from inviting the Aly Khans to their homes,
but it certainly didn't keep them from calling us trying to wrangle
an invitation once word got out about our luncheon.

We stretched our small house to the limit and had twenty-two
for a buffet lunch. Angela outdid herself with the food. Aly Khan
was exceedingly gracious, skillfully giving the impression there
was nowhere he would rather be than with us and our other guests,
starting with our grocer and his wife. Rita was a bit timid, it seemed
to us, but welcomed, I think, a chance to mingle with some Americans as well as with a selection of the few Brits for whom we had
room, especially the captain of a Robin Line freighter, who was so
excited he stammered when introduced.

A Foreign Service inspector was coming to Mombasa. Anticipation of my first inspection was quite a traumatic experience, especially since the Consulate books did not balance; the accounts
showed us running a small surplus! Better a surplus than a deficit, I thought, but still I was troubled that the accountant could not
find the cause of the imbalance. So two nights before the inspector's
scheduled arrival I stayed in the office late, real late, until I discovered that our windfall profit of a few shillings a month was generated by our system of reimbursement to the office for personal phone
calls. Individuals were paying in slightly more than the Consulate
was being billed. This discovery brought with it a great sense of relief. Our accountant was instructed to make the needed corrections.
All would be well for the arrival of Inspector Lawrence Taylor.

I knew Taylor, since he had been director of my Junior Officers
Course in 1946. It was he who had told us, based on his experience,
that we would not get a responsible job in the Service for at least
fifteen years. What would he think of Hinton, Principal Officer of
a consulate, albeit a small consulate, after less than four years of
experience?

My friend Bob Stookey, stationed in Nairobi, called to say elephants were the key to the inspection. It seemed that despite his
service in Brazzaville Taylor, had never seen an elephant in the

wild. He wanted above all else to fill this void, Stookey told me. Easily done, I declared. You, Bob, drive him from Nairobi to meet me at the Tsavo Park Lodge and I'll show him elephants.

Bob drove Taylor to Tsavo. The three of us dined together. Taylor's excitement about finally seeing elephants was uncontained. At dawn, Stookey set off to return to Nairobi while I drove Taylor and a guide into the bush. During a visit a few weeks earlier I had found the Park overrun with elephants. That, however, was a few weeks earlier. Not while Taylor was seeking elephants. Despite the guide's optimism and mine, we saw lots of game, but no elephants. We came in for a late lunch before putting an unhappy inspector in my car for the long drive to Mombasa.

His disappointment was verbal and loud. I calculated that his dyspeptic attitude would influence his inspection report. I remembered that once I had seen elephant off a bad road, hardly a track. Would that inspector like to risk it when we both knew it would mean night driving later to get to Mombasa. Night driving in Kenya was highly inadvisable, but Taylor said he wanted to pursue any chance to see elephants. So we bounced and bounced down a miserable rut as daylight slipped away. Just as I was about to turn around, as disconsolate about my career prospects as Taylor was about the lack of elephants, there they were, elephants, lots of elephants, baby elephants, mommy elephants, and a big bull elephant with enormous tusks just ahead of us crossing the track, illuminated by my headlights. Taylor's inspection of Mombasa was a foreseeable success! In my imagination, I had gambled my career on there being elephants on that track and won.

The inspection, however, turned up one rough spot I had not anticipated. Provincial Commissioner Mullins, the highest ranking Brit on the Coast, told Taylor I should either be declared or stop spying! As a consul, Mullins asserted, I should stick to my Consular knitting.

When Taylor told me of Mullins' remarks, I understood why some of my sources about the labor situation in the Port of Mombasa had become less forthcoming than previously. Clearly Mullins had told the port superintendent, the police inspectors, and others to limit what they told the Yankee. Earlier I had been regularly shown police intelligence assessments of the situation in the port. No more.

The primary reason for the Consulate in Mombasa was, of course, the port. A magnificent anchorage, it had sheltered over a hundred vessels of the combined British and American Indian Ocean fleets during World War II. British East African Railways terminated in Mombasa, and virtually all imports and exports into Kenya and Uganda passed through the port. Rumors of communist organization efforts among port workers were disturbing. Washington had instructed me to keep a close eye on matters. My British friends, short of Mullins, were cooperative. I reported accurately that while a handful of individuals were a potential threat, they were known and kept under tight surveillance. More important, there were few signs of real labor unrest. Since I was not bribing or paying anyone for my information, Mullins was simply wrong in charging me with spying. I was merely doing what any British consul would have done in comparable circumstances. Fortunately for me, Larry Taylor, he of the elephants, understood and approved of what I had done, as did Consul General Ward.

When I decided it was time for a visit to the Seychelles in 1951, recalling the department's veto of Groth's plans, I waited until after my return to inform Washington by dispatch, thus:

The Honorable
The Secretary of State, Washington.

Sir:

I have the honor to report that I paid an official visit to the Seychelles Islands from....

Respectfully yours,

The British India Line vessel to the Seychelles was comfortable enough but the food was appalling. Even our captain complained, labeling one desert, a tapioca mush with almonds sticking up out of it, "Graveyard Pudding."

The Islands were sensationally beautiful. We had a cottage on a nearly perfect oval bay with a palm-shaded beach. Deborah Ann, who was with Angela and myself, had a tremendous sandbox to play in, to say nothing of the warm water. The Seychelles are famous for seashells, especially cowries, more varieties of which can be found there than anywhere else in the world. We collected some beauties for the fun of it and for my mother's already spectacular shell collection. Deborah, who was then a little over a year old, complains to this day that Mommy and Daddy forced her to ride a large Hawksbill turtle. Does she really remember? or did she invent her story of terror after looking at photos of her gigantic (relative-to-her-size) stead? With few items to buy for gifts for the folks back home, we concentrated on tortoise shell items, imitation butterflies, combs, and cigarette cases. Now, but not then, the purchase or sale of these items is illegal since the tortoises are an endangered species.

I, of course, had to work to justify my passage. However, it was impossible to work very hard in the Seychelles. The total population of the islands was less than thirty-five thousand people. The economy, to say the least, was rudimentary. I collected what statistics were available, mostly about copra exports, and nodded agreement when told the Seychelles had to develop its potential fisheries. For my part, I urged tourism, correctly but quite prematurely, since it was clear to me that the beauty of the islands and the Somerset Maugham atmosphere of the capital, Victoria, would have wide appeal. As the visiting American consul, I called on all the right officials (there were not many) from the governor down, local dignitaries outside the government, including spokesmen for some key religious, educational, commercial, and ethnic groups. Of the latter, the most important was the French community. Interestingly enough, the British had been so impressed by the French governor that even after Napoleon ceded the Seychelles to Britain in the Treaty of Paris of 1814 they retained M. de Quincey in office until his death in 1827. The gesture was not enough. To my amazement, some 140 years later tension persisted between Francophones and Anglophones.

We got to know the Secretary to Government and his wife particularly well. He practically ran the colony, with the governor more figurehead than administrator.

One day the secretary asked me to go on the government's radio station to talk about American foreign policy. There were a handful of privately owned radio receivers, but my main audience, he explained to me, would be gathered before three loudspeakers erected on public squares. A few people with nothing better to do were regular attendees at the nightly outdoor programs. He estimated my potential audience at about a hundred persons, none of whom, I was convinced, gave a damn about American foreign policy. Still, since my friend and the key official of the Seychelles had asked, I duly prepared and delivered an innocuous talk.

Imagine my surprise when the next morning I picked up my

copy of the government's *Bulletin*, delivered daily to our beach bungalow, to face the following headlines: "American Consul Reveals All—Inside Story of MacArthur Firing." The normal press run of the *Bulletin* was some 250 copies in English and about forty in French. Fortunately there was only one copy, mine, of this prankster's edition. Who says the British do not have a sense of humor?

Clearly it was my duty to see as much as possible of the Islands, so Angela and I toured Mahe, the main island. Kind Brits provided transport and served as guides. They were as delighted to meet someone new in their small isolated world as we were to have new friends. But to see the famous Coco de Mer palm trees we had to go by small boat to the Island of Praslin and then hike into the fabulous valley the English traveler, adventurer, and soldier Gordon of Khartoum had argued was the original Garden of Eden. The Coconuts from these unique palm trees resembled female pelvises, complete with pubic hair and vulvas, while the male palms, when it was time for fertilization of female palms, sprouted enormous penises. We brought back some of the Cocos de Mer, but none of the penises. Not surprisingly, when these distinctive Cocos wash up on the shores of India hundreds of miles to the northeast, they are highly valued for their alleged aphrodisiac effects.

We rushed back early to the main island since the local parochial school, run by Swiss Capuchin clergy, was giving a stage show. We had been shown around this school, the best in the Seychelles, by its principal, a French Canadian priest, who was probably the most popular individual in the Islands. To the horror of all, in our absence, our friend, everyone's friend, the priest, had been found dead hanging nude in his room. The show was, of course, canceled. We went sadly over the hill to our bungalow on North West Bay.

The next day three leaders of the French community asked to see me urgently. Murder had been committed, they alleged, and it was all part of a conspiracy to reduce the role of the Catholic Church in the Seychelles and undermine the teaching of French. I listened but allowed that true or not it was not a matter of concern for an American consul. They replied, "But Father X is an American citizen?" And so he was, it turned out. He had been recruited from Canada as a French-speaking priest and had never advertised his American citizenship. This fact, once established, cast matters in a new light. While I thought the charges of "conspiracy" were ridiculous, clearly the American consul could not ignore the allegation of murder of an American citizen.

I went to talk with my friend the Secretary of Government, telling him I would have to report to my government upon my by then imminent return to Mombasa. What could he tell me of the investigation? He said the inquest was proceeding confidentially, but he could categorically assure me there had been no murder. How did he know?, I asked. Father X, he said, had kept a diary. Periodic entries therein made clear what had happened. He promised to send me the report of the inquest.

We returned to Mombasa, I reassured by what I had been told but still puzzled. No sooner were we home than the Catholic Bishop called and asked me to come to tea. He wanted to know what I knew of Father X's death. I told him. He said he understood. It was an old story in the Church, a dangerous method of finding sexual relief from the vows of chastity had gone wrong.

In Mombasa Taffy grew by leaps and bounds. Whatever else was wrong with the town, it was a wonderful place for babies. But for us the continuous heat, day and night, was wearing. I wrote home, "This is the kind of place you have to get away from occasionally or go nuts. The round of sundowners is endless and the conversation truly hopeless."

While most of my travels were official, early in 1951 Angela and I escaped the hottest month the year, when there was no monsoon breeze in Mombasa, to tour much of central Africa in our Chevy. In five weeks we logged over 3,000 miles through Kenya, Uganda, the Belgian Congo, and Ruanda-Urundi. A few highlights of that trip remain in my memory.

In Nairobi, the high commissioner of the Government of India, whom I had entertained in Mombasa and with whom I had shared views about life in Kenya, invited us to dinner. We arrived over an hour late. Inexcusable? Not really, we had been detained by lions! Touring the Nairobi game preserve at sunset with a warden, we encountered a pride of magnificent lions resting smack in the middle of the road. Every so often they would rise, stretch, walk a few yards, and lie down again. I pled with the warden to let us honk a bit and carefully drive through. He told me in no uncertain terms that the rules forbad it. Wild game, perhaps particularly lions, had absolute priority over all, including Indian high commissioners, or perhaps particularly Indian high commissioners.

In Uganda, the Watts, old friends from Mombasa where he had been district commissioner before his transfer to Kisumu on Lake Victoria, arranged for us to see the right things and meet the right people. Impressed by Makerere College and lots of well-educated

Africans in and out of the Government of Uganda, I concluded that, unlike Kenya or Tanganyika, independence for Uganda would work reasonably well. How wrong I was. Later when I read what the British explorer John Speke had had to say some ninety years earlier about the incidence and cruelty of tribal warfare in Uganda, I better understood my misjudgment and the horrors that Idi Amin and others brought to that beautiful land.

On a sunken road in Pare Albert we sat petrified as a herd of elephants thundered overhead. While I took some fairly good home movies of other game and other elephants, I failed to get the lens cap off to take what would have been a fabulous submarine view of the herd.

Arriving in Goma in the Belgian Congo, we learned the narrow road south to Elizabethville was open on Mondays, Wednesdays, and Fridays, but closed to permit northbound on Tuesday, Thursdays, and Saturdays. On Sundays, trusting in God, the road was open both ways! Overwhelmed by the beauty of Lake Kivu, truly one of the most fabulous sights I have ever seen, we nevertheless kept our eyes sufficiently on the road to reach our destination. When I returned twenty-three years later, Elizabethville, renamed Bukavu, was rundown. Even Lake Kivu, which Angela and I had even talked of as a possible retirement refuge, appeared less attractive in the Mobutu era.

Next we headed for Usumburu. Why? I suppose because it was there. Or maybe we wanted to see Lake Tanganyika. In any case, Usumburu was hot, dry, and dusty. Ugh! We had to escape Usumburu. So we had a cool drink and headed for Kigali, a risky venture since we did not know if we could make it before dark. On the road to Kigali, I decided that Belgian road engineers frustrated by the relative flatness of their homeland had simply gone mad twisting and turning the roads in RuandaUrundi every which way. To their credit their road was a good one. The country was lushly green as we climbed into the highlands. And cool. Kigali was a small, unimpressive, but pleasant town. The innkeeper, a priest, and the postmaster assured us all was peaceful. Minor tensions between tribes, nothing else. Certainly I did not foresee that this beautiful country would be cursed, some forty years later, by genocidal war between Hutus and Tutsis. In retrospect, Belgian colonial rule, which at least kept the peace, does not look so bad after all.

Time in East Africa was running out. The good news was I had been accepted for advanced economic training. The State

Department instructed me to report to the Fletcher School of Law and Diplomacy no later than the opening of classes. The bad news was another part of the department instructed me to stay at my post for a full two years or forfeit my leave and pay my own and my family's way home. In vain I pointed out that per the regulations my service in Mombasa, an unhealthful post, would earn me time and a half toward retirement. Why not count time at post the same way so I could start school on time? Why not, indeed? But I had to wait because of the incredible, to me, incapacity of the department to operate with a modicum of common sense. Thus, on September 16, 1951, two years to the day of our arrival in Mombasa, we departed for the States.

In those two years our daughter had gotten off to a great start. We were sad to leave so many good friends and exhausted from so many farewells. My small consulate staff gave us a set of carved ivory elephants, an exquisite and appropriate souvenir of our good years in Mombasa.

Dixie and Yankee, our Alsatians, were put on a freighter in charge of a dog-loving seaman paid to deliver them safely to us in the States. Sadly he had an accident and was hospitalized in Dar es Salaam. By that time, however, our dogs had many friends among crewmembers. Result: they, too, had a university year in Boston.

"Taffy" behaved beautifully on our long airplane ride home. A stopover at 1 a.m. in Khartoum, where the heat was unbearable and the swarms of mosquitoes insufferable, convinced me I would never ask to be assigned to Sudan. On the other hand, an overnight stop in Paris convinced me I was ready to suffer the hardships of safari life along the Seine.

7

Fletcher and Harvard
(1951–1952)

We returned to America from Paris on a Pan American Boeing Stratocruiser, enjoying a bunk for the long flight home. We slept poorly, but for a fifteen hour flight the bunk was a far better deal than sitting up all night. It would be another ten years before jets revolutionized trans-Atlantic flights.

Angela left with Taffy from New York to join her folks in Chicago while I proceeded to Washington, where I was met by my parents. After a weekend reunion with them, I began four days of "consultations" in the department and took my mandatory home leave. Mandatory for the same stupid reasons, rooted in restrictions on how appropriations could be spent, that had decreed we must complete two years at post. Already late for the beginning of classes at the Fletcher School of Law and Diplomacy, I took only one day of leave. So much for the month of leave I had earned in tropical Africa.

That weekend I also bought a secondhand eight-cylinder Buick convertible. I had fallen in love with its appearance, but that car taught me what I should have already known: beware of used car salesmen. While my youthful enthusiasm for a sporty-looking car brought us much pleasure, it also brought expensive problems. The drive shaft broke away from the differential, first in Boston, easy to fix in Boston, and later outside Vézelay, France, where weeks went by before it could be repaired with parts ordered from the States.

My consultations touched lightly on Africa and Mombasa and considerably more on the Foreign Service Institute's rules for FSOs assigned to universities. "As a matter of policy," I was informed, "the Foreign Service Institute does not permit officers assigned to universities to be candidates for advanced degrees." Rather we were encouraged to take a few courses for credit and audit widely. A research paper was required.

I proposed doing a paper on "The Political and Economic Implications of Atomic Energy." My academic supervisor at the Institute somewhat reluctantly agreed, provided I concentrated my efforts on economic issues, since I was supposed to be studying economics. For starters I met with H. Gordon Arensen, the secretary's assistant for atomic affairs. He, too, was skeptical about my proposal, but suggested I talk with a few knowledgeable persons in the Boston area, whose names he gave me.

It did not take me long after a few such meetings and a lot of library research to conclude that my supervisor and Arensen were right. With so much material highly classified, there did not seem to be much I could add to the work of Schurr and Marachak, who had published unclassified articles on the subject. Thinking about it almost fifty years later, the most remarkable thing about the talks I had and the literature I read was the total neglect of environmental problems. Issues about the disposal of radioactive waste were simply ignored. Had I proceeded with my study, given the then hardly challenged consensus that atomic power was great, I, too, presumably would have overlooked a major downside.

Be that as it may, I backed off. Instead I proposed doing my research paper on the European Payments Union. This proposal was accepted enthusiastically by FSI. Better still, carrying it out provided a focus for much of my academic work that year and, as it happened, provided a solid base for my subsequent assignments as a financial-economic specialist at the embassy in Paris and later at United States Mission to the European Communities in Brussels.

My second weekend at home, I drove my cherished convertible to Medford, Massachusetts, where I was fortunate enough, faute de mieux, to be given a tiny basement room in Wilson Hall, a Fletcher School residence, while I looked for family housing.

Newspaper classified sections were filled with "Wanted to Rent" ads. There were no "To Rent" ads. Weeks of searching were finally rewarded when I leased an old house in Newton Center, far away from school. While I had budgeted up to$100.00 a month for housing, I gladly paid $125.00, not including utilities, to have a home for the family. While the academic year would be enormously enriching personally, it was a disaster financially. Moreover, when Angela arrived at the end of October, as glad as she was to have us together, she was appalled at some aspects of the house, specifically the stone sink in an antique kitchen. Listening for months to her continued complaints, however justified, about that kitchen and that sink led me to conclude that never again would I choose our housing.

The five weeks I lived in the dorm gave me an opportunity I otherwise would not have had to get to know my fellow students, all fifty-four of them, outside as well as inside class. Almost a third were foreigners, with some twelve countries represented. With some I was never close; with many I kept in touch for a number of years; with a couple, useful long-lived friendships were formed. David and Helen Ferber, another Foreign Service family, helpful in getting us established despite their own problems with a handicapped child, were particularly close. Irene Meister, later a lobbyist for the American paper industry, bought me countless lunches during and after my days of involvement in trade negotiations. Mike Moynihan, the senator's brother, was a colleague later when he handled public affairs for the Trade Representative. Thirty-five years later in Islamabad I met again with Maqbool Bhatty after his service as Pakistan's ambassador to China.

The Buick helped. Groups of us would go out, just riding, or for this or that. Someone persuaded me to drive several opera-loving students to a memorable performance of *Der Rosenkavalier*. I've been a Richard Strauss devotee ever since.

Angela wrote I should have fun, "but not too much fun." She asked about Tufts girls and wondered if the convertible was attracting them. I replied, "No progress toward feminine companionship. But, if you don't get here soon, something constructive will have to be done. Please hurry."

Before Angela arrived, I screwed up my courage to arrange a date with Marcia Hildreth, a classmate more marked by her intellect than her beauty. Still, with Angela not there, Marcia was growing more attractive with each passing day. I do not know what Marcia's reaction would have been had I made a pass at her in that convertible. But, inhibited as I was by my marital vows and my Puritan upbringing, I behaved properly, enjoying nothing more than her company and conversation.

Marcia visited Angela and me in Paris the following year and we saw a good deal of each other after our return to Washington in the mid-1950s, by which time Marcia was also married and working in the government. We suffered together at an election party in our house the night of Adlai Stevenson's second loss to Ike.

One of the advantages of my assignment to Fletcher was that classes at Harvard were also open to me. Thus, in addition to economic courses with Charlie Kindleberger and George Halm at Fletcher, I studied with Alvin Hansen, John Williams, and others at Harvard. Halm was by far the best teacher, systematic and clear in his explanations. Kindleberger was by far the most fun; in class, when he would tie himself up trying to explain the effects of differing income elasticities on exchange rates; and out of class, talking of life. Charlie became a friend, sharing my interest to economics as a tool for dealing with real world problems. Haberler at Harvard, like Halm, was too theoretical for me. Hansen actually taught little, bringing in guest lecturers to his seminar. Anyway he was a Keynesian. My Chicago school favorite, Henry Simons, had skewered him years before in his review article, "Hansen on Fiscal Policy." John Williams also applied economic theory to real world problems. Working at the New York Fed and advising Treasury, he still had time to help me with my E.P.U. project. His common-sense approach to economic problems reminded me of Ted Schultz, a professor of mine at Chicago, and, years later, George Shultz reminded me of John Williams. Williams, Kindleberger, Schultz, and Shultz shared a down-to-earth quality that made economics useful and understandable.

While I concentrated on economics, I audited other subjects. Leo Gross on international law—dull, I thought. The law, not Leo. Alex Inkles at Harvard on Soviet affairs. Art Maas, also at Harvard, was superb on government administration and public policy. Maas provided my first experience with case studies, including one I found particularly fascinating about how the Foreign Service Act of 1946 came into being. The case approach wowed me. The cases themselves, several of which suggested Corps of Engineers lobbying was too successful for the overall good of the nation, as well as the classroom discussions they provoked, were an eye-opening look into how government really works. What I learned from Maas helped me immeasurably in my endless bureaucratic struggles in later years.

Angela and I also renewed old friendships, with Jerry Kahl, studying sociology at Harvard, David Mark, like me a FSO on a university assignment, studying Soviet issues at Harvard, and Gordon Tullock, who after obtaining an advanced degree at Chicago came into the Foreign Service with a record score on the written exam. Now he struggled to learn Chinese at Yale. My former chief in

Damascus, Minister Hugh Keeley, was also at Fletcher that year, on the faculty. His seminar on development issues was great fun. His imitations of various national diplomatic types, Russian, French, Arab, what have you, were both hilarious and valid teaching tools.

With a baby girl at home, Angela and I were unable to enjoy much of the cultural life Boston offers. Incredibly, we never got to Fenway Park. I nevertheless found time to supplement my studies in various ways. For example, by writing a letter to the editor of *The Foreign Service Journal* expressing alarm at some personnel policies, especially large scale lateral entry, and urging more recruiting of new blood at the bottom of the Service. I spoke at other colleges about the Service as part of a belated recruiting drive and contributed a small sum to the Foreign Service Defense Fund, which was aiding FSOs under attack by Senator McCarthy. I also submitted several book reviews to the *Journal*. I naively thought it was an independent publication, as it later became. In one case I learned better. My review of a United Nations report on *Measures for the Economic Development of Under-Developed Countries*, one of the authors of which was my former University of Chicago professor Theodore W. Schultz, was passed to a department officer, who took issue with it since I had not pointed out U.S. opposition to creation of an International Development Authority. I regret to say I complied with the suggestions for changes, but also resolved to submit no further reviews to the *FSJ*.

A quote that sounded like pure Schultz to me survived in my review. Since in my view it makes a critically important point, and one I thereafter tried constantly to bear in mind when later I served as an AID director and otherwise was involved in development assistance policy, I repeat it here:

> There is a sense in which rapid economic progress is impossible without painful readjustments. Ancient philosophies have to be scrapped; old social institutions have to disintegrate; bonds of caste, creed, and race have to be burst....Few communities are willing to pay the full price of economic progress.

In October Dixie and Yankee, our Alsatians, were scheduled to arrive on a Robin Line freighter. I had paid a sailor to care for them on the voyage from Mombasa to the States, but had since learned he had been hospitalized in Dar es Salaam. As I drove to Portland,

Maine, to meet the ship, I wondered how our dogs had fared. Couldn't have been better. The entire crew took over their care and feeding. Never had they eaten so well with us. Nevertheless, they were bounding with joy to see me. After a short discussion with a Customs officer, the dogs and I headed back to Boston.

Soon thereafter I received an indignant letter from the Collector of Customs in Portland. Dixie and Yankee had not been properly cleared for entry, he asserted. An FSO returning to the States after an overseas assignment was indeed entitled to free entry of his personal effects, including dogs, but to effect a delayed free entry he had to produce a certified copy of a customs declaration made at the time of the original entry. I had failed to do so. Serious business, I was told. After some back and forth, including a humble apology from me for overlooking the applicable regulation, this imbroglio was settled. To close the matter out, I sent the Collector of Customs a check for all of one dollar and fifty cents!

Angela and I wondered if it had been worth it when one night in Newton Center Dixie and Yankee retreated to the house after a losing encounter with a skunk. Me oh my, bathing two dogs stinking violently of skunk spray was a nightmarish experience.

Working hard on my study of the E.P.U., while on consultation in Washington I talked to many concerned U.S. officials, including my old friend Judd Polk at the Treasury. Judd had been stationed in Cairo as Treasury Attaché for the Middle East when I had served in Damascus. Our discussions of the E.P.U. and related international financial issues led to a suggestion for an exchange program between State and Treasury. I was most interested and Judd thought he could convince his bosses, but State personnel procrastinated. Only years later did State come to see the value for the U.S. Government, especially State, of such exchange programs. Treasury was even slower in accepting such exchanges.

Shortly after returning to Fletcher, Bill Bosworth, a senior officer in Personnel whom I hardly knew, telephoned me. His question astounded and delighted me. "Would I rather be assigned to Stockholm or Paris? There are financial analyst positions open at both posts." I knew the answer was Paris, but as a dutiful husband, I replied I would consult my wife and call him back. I was right. Angela, too, thought Paris was for us. Never before nor in the next forty years of my service was I offered a choice of posts as an ongoing assignment.

As time ran out I had to finish my E.P.U. study, complete a course evaluation for FSI, and make travel plans.

Without undue modesty, I believe my E.P.U. paper is probably still the best single study of the subject in English. John Williams and Charlie Kindleberger both praised it. As I glance through it again, almost fifty years later, I am amazed I had so much energy to dig so deep and pleased the paper reflects well the bureaucratic struggles about E.P.U. waged within the U.S. Government between the nondiscriminatory multilateralists and those who saw, correctly in my view, that a discriminatory regional approach was a necessary step toward an eventual convertible multilateral world. My academic consideration of this profound policy issue was a solid introduction to my future work on the process toward European unity.

I concluded my study thus:

> The cooperation of lesser units within the overall framework of the "Free World", such as the European Army within NATO, the "Schuman Plan" within the OEEC, and EPU within the IMF, is desirable only to the extent that it does not obscure the larger issues. We must, therefore, constantly ask: "What do we mean by integration? Will this proposed measure promote a desirable form of integration? Will it fit in the larger pattern?"

My evaluation of my academic year was overwhelmingly positive. To live again in an American community, free of operational responsibilities such as budget administration or reporting schedules, combined with the incredible intellectual challenge of two great universities, was simply a wonderful and worthwhile experience. Critically, I thought it would be better if FSI followed the military practice of having their students work for advanced degrees. (This policy change was adopted a year or so later.) I also pointed out that "the unsupplemented salary of a junior FSO is scarcely sufficient to cope with the high cost of living in an American city. While I would have assumed even a greater financial burden for the year's experience, that year was nevertheless a financial disaster.

Once my assignment to Paris was confirmed, I wrote the traditional letter to my future chief, telling him a bit about Angela, daughter Deborah, and myself, expressing our delight at the prospect of serving under him, and offering to be of any desired help in the States. In due course, Ambassador Jimmy Dunn replied with a warm letter of welcome. Not surprisingly, he did not take us up on our offer of assistance. However, proper form had been observed. Now I could get on with attaining updated passports, arranging for leave in Chicago with Angela's folks and in Channelside with my folks, obtaining our tickets, booking the dogs, arranging for our Buick to be on the same ship as we, insuring our effects, and so forth. Al Peyraud, my father-in -law, somehow arranged for me to attend a day of the Republican National Convention in Chicago. Former President Herbert Hoover spoke, but he was not the highlight of the day. The vibrancy and enthusiasm of the delegates impressed me far more. Our time with my folks was spent at Channelside, the waterfront home they had purchased in tidewater Virginia. What a wonderful place. Sadly, they sold it later to move to outside Washington to be nearer their grandchildren and me.

On August 1, 1952, we sailed on the S.S. *United States.* The world's fastest ship got us to Le Havre in 4 days, 7 hours, and 43 minutes. Or so showed the log abstract circulated to passengers. In any case, we debarked safely after bidding farewell to Dixie and Yankee, destined to wait in a kennel until we found housing. On the road to Paris on a sunny day, we kept the convertible top down. When we found an attractive bistro in a small town, we introduced Taffy to diluted wine. We were in France. The good life was ours for the taking.

8

Paris (1952–1955)

Paris, for me, is memorable largely for three things. First, Chris, our long hoped for son, was born there. Second, professionally, I had made it to the big leagues. I was still a rookie, but I was playing in France, a critical Marshall Plan participant, a NATO member, and a leader in the search for European Unity. Third, Paris and France were as unforgettable as writers and lyricists have long proclaimed.

But our beginning in Paris was rather shaky. The embassy had reserved a room for us in the dreary Hotel Malesherbes. The best that could be said for it was that we were sheltered from the rain and were within easy walking distance of the Embassy.

It helped that Dan and Dania Brewster, the same Brewsters who had met us in Beirut, were also camping in a hotel, looking for housing. On the upside, we did weekend excursions together; on the downside, we consoled each other about the lack of suitable housing.

I walked to the Embassy the morning after our arrival, located the personnel officer, and told him I was ready to go to work. He said, "Come back tomorrow." So I did, and the same thing happened. The third morning I asked what the hell was going on.

He said, "You think you are going to work in the Combined Finance Section."

"Yes," I said, "that is what I was told in Washington."

"Well," he said, "no one works there without being vetted by Graham Martin and he's out of town."

Graham Martin, much later our last ambassador to Vietnam, was then Counselor of Embassy for Administration. He wanted to check me out because he had committed himself not to let any "turkeys" slip into the Combined Finance Group in which State, Mutual Security Agency (MSA), and Treasury worked as a team under the direction of the senior treasury attaché, the legendary William "Tommy" Tomlinson.

Tomlinson was just in his mid-thirties, but his job titles encompassed the waterfront of U.S. efforts in Western Europe. Senior Treasury Attaché at Embassy Paris made him the chief financial advisor to the ambassador to France and to the director of the Marshall Plan Mission. In addition, he was Treasury Advisor to Averill Harriman, the President's Special Representative in Europe for Marshall Plan coordination and NATO. If this were not enough, he was Acting United States Representative to the European Coal and Steel Community and Deputy United States Observer to the proposed European Defense Community.

Already Tommy had had an enormous positive impact on our relations with France. Beyond that, he had been a key influence on a critical overall foreign policy decision. With Ambassador David Bruce, he had won Washington support for the Schuman Plan for a European Coal and Steel Community. As there was intense bureaucratic opposition in Washington to a "cartel" as well as policy opposition from Atlanticists, what Bruce and Tomlinson accomplished in reversing Dean Acheson's initial opposition and putting the United States firmly behind the Schuman Plan was no small matter.

The secret to Tommy's success, besides intellectual brilliance, hard work, and a strong supporting staff, was the relationship he had developed with Jean Monnet. When Tommy arrived in Paris, Monnet was head of the French Investment Plan, aptly named "The Monnet Plan." Tommy used his influence in Washington to swing aid allocations to support the investment priorities of the Monnet Plan, and in Paris he helped Monnet win internal French policy debates over priorities. Together Monnet and Tommy held off pressures for more investment in social projects, such as housing, and stuck with Monnet's thesis that productive industry came first.

Monnet, concerned about French-German relations, foreseeable tensions over the Saar, and a sense of drift toward war in East-West relations, reshaped one of his old ideas and sold the concept of a pooling of European coal and steel resources first to Robert Schuman, then Foreign Minister of France, and thereby to the French cabinet. Recognizing the importance of American support for a startling, indeed revolutionary, initiative and trusting his friends, Monnet told David Bruce and Tommy what was coming before Foreign Minister Schuman on May 9, 1950, made his historic proposal for a European Coal and Steel Community.

When I was told in Washington that my new position in Paris was in the Combined Finance Group, I was delighted. My academic year and particularly my study of the E.P.U. had prepared me. As I heard stories about Tomlinson and learned that, strange as it sounded, the Treasury attaché was responsible for U.S. relations with the European integration process, I could not have imagined an assignment more to my liking.

Paris turned out to be a great assignment, but not for the reasons I had imagined in my fantasy about working on European integration. At just about the time of my arrival in Paris, the "Bruce Mission" was created, apart from the embassy, apart from the NATO and OEEC Missions, and apart from Harriman's oversight as Special Representative Europe. Bruce was to conduct U.S. relations with the six-country Coal and Steel Community and, more importantly, with those Europeans in the six charged with negotiating a treaty to create a European Army. The Combined Finance Group was being split; some officers went to the Bruce Mission, some stayed. Tommy, of course, kept his feet well planted in both operations. I inherited Art Hartman's desk in the embassy; he joined the Bruce Mission.

My direct boss was Donald J. McGrew, the assistant Treasury attaché, known behind his back as "Dangerous Dan." In our first conversation, after Graham Martin had okayed my assignment, McGrew laid it on the line. "If you cannot conduct business in French within six weeks, you are out of here." Don's French was grammatically impeccable, but his accent was pure Ohio. To help me understand the importance of speaking French, he observed that while the FSOs in the political section, about some of whom he spoke with contempt, hobnobbed with the English speakers of the Foreign Ministry, we economic types worked with the technical ministries. English might get you by at the Quai d'Orsay, France's Foreign Ministry, but at the Rue de Rivoli, that part of the Louvre where the Ministry of Finance was located, French was essential. Don also assigned me responsibility for following, analyzing, and reporting on French monetary and fiscal policy. He left no doubt in my mind as to what I had to do. First of all, I had to learn oral French.

In 1952, the embassy had no language classes. I was on my own. Fortunately, I was able to hire, at what for me was considerable expense, a competent young lady who from 7 to 8 a.m., five days a week, drilled me in French. Although my language aptitude was far from what I would have liked, the incentive to avoid dismissal by Don spurred me on. About six weeks later, I conducted a conversation about French defense expenditures, using NATO definitions, with French technicians. Don was pleased but with his urging I kept up my lessons. Finally, to thank my tutor, I invited her to dinner. To my surprise, she insisted on showing me where she worked as a doctor's receptionist when she was not tutoring. How naive I was! Only later did it dawn on me why she had shown me an office suite with a comfortable sofa. At the time, I was simply puzzled. However, we did have an excellent dinner.

Many of my embassy colleagues helped ease our way in Paris by inviting us around. Bill Miller, whose French was fluent, and his French wife, Francine, were particularly kind. That Francine was a marvelous cook made their invitations doubly inviting. Bill and Odette Toomey, Bob and Nellie Miner, as well as Art and Donna Hartman were others who became longtime friends.

Later Warren Baum, who had backstopped the Marshall Plan Mission, came to Paris to write a book about the French economy. I think we stimulated each other's thinking about French problems. He and Jessie, his wife, became good friends of ours. Years later when he had become a big-shot vice president of the World Bank our relation lapsed.

Official social life for us, as I was a relatively junior FSO, was limited. We were guests but had assigned duties at the ambassador's Fourth of July receptions held in the garden of the residence on Faubourg Saint-Honoré. Only once were we invited as non-working guests at the ambassador's residence. Ambassador Dunn invited us and all other new FSO arrivals and their wives to one of his regular large receptions. We were lost in a sea of diplomats and high ranking French officials. Douglas MacArthur II, then political advisor to the Supreme NATO Commander and "Wahwee," his wife, saw Angela's and my distress, took us in tow, and with a few perspicacious introductions turned our evening from one of torture into a most enjoyable time.

Paris was our first encounter with a Marine Corps ball. We had not had Marine security guards in Damascus, where they would have helped, nor in Mombasa, where they were not needed. The Marine Ball, given each year in November to celebrate the anniversary of the founding of the Corps, is the high point of the social season for most embassy personnel. In Paris, however, officers of my status, instead of attending, volunteered to stand watch for a Marine so he could attend his ball. (For security reasons this practice was ended sometime in the 1970s when it was ordered that only Marines could stand duty. Now nearby posts try to schedule the balls on different nights, so that Marines, from say Managua, can free Marines in San Jose to attend their ball and vice versa.)

Social invitations from the French were few and far between. We rationalized that since life in postwar France was still difficult, our poorly paid French contacts, whom we would entertain at home and in restaurants, could not afford to reciprocate. One French couple, Pierre and Christane Nacivet, were a wonderful exception. Happily, we saw more of them years later in Brussels.

One memorable social event was a reception given by the Prefet de la Seine. I might not stand high on the Diplomatic List, but as a consul I rated with the municipal and provincial authorities. Climbing impressive broad stairs to the prefectural ballroom between uniformed *cuissars*, swords drawn, provided a vision of past French splendors.

My biggest disappointment in Paris involved my University of Chicago French friend, Bertrand Dreyfus. We had been, I thought, close. From the moment I knew I was going to Paris, I looked forward to renewing my friendship with Bertrand. When I finally located him, not easy, we had dinner together. We talked from time to time and had another meal downtown. Once established in our second house, Angela and I had Bertrand out for dinner. After dinner, I was driving him back to the center of Paris when he informed me that he was terribly sorry, but we would not meet again. My efforts to get an explanation were unrewarded. So I said an uncomprehending "Goodbye." I could not believe that this break was Bertrand's independent decision. I speculated that Bertrand, working on the French atomic program, had been told to end all contacts with foreigners. I also wondered if his patrician Jewish family had forbade further contact with that American, recalling that Bertrand had earlier apologized for not being able to invite me to his home, implying it was a family matter. Whatever the explanation, Bertrand's action hurt; indeed it still hurts.

As the annual December NATO Ministerial meeting approached, Tomlinson assigned me as an additional staff aide to Secretary of the Treasury Donald W. Snyder. At this meeting, the ministers adopted ambitious force goals, which in practice were never reached. The secretary asked me to prepare for him one-page summaries of the documentation to be considered by ministers. An absurd assignment. Imagine trying to sum up in one page NATO

Strategic Doctrine, Projected Alliance Force Levels, the NATO Common Infrastructure Program, and a half dozen other long, top-secret documents. Well, I did my best, learning a good deal about NATO in the process, and earned a warm commendation from the secretary (presumably written by another staff aid). Nevertheless, it was fortunate indeed that Secretary Snyder did not need to speak to these issues on the basis of my summaries.

The biggest stir caused by Secretary Snyder arose when his tuxedo was not to be found in his hotel room. What ensued impressed me. Urgent cables were sent in all directions and searches instituted wherever there was the remotest chance of finding the missing tux. It eventually turned up in Istanbul (someone had failed to pack it after a dinner there) and was flown to Paris, where my boss Don McGrew was ordered to meet the special flight. It was, however, too late. Despite the forces mobilized to find the errant tux, the secretary had to rent another for the NATO Ministers' black tie dinner.

While I struggled with French and the intricacies of the economy, Angela was house-hunting. Life in a hotel room with Taffy was hard, even after we got somewhat more space, including a primitive kitchen that helped greatly since we no longer had to eat all of our meals out. We wanted desperately to get into a house, but almost nothing was available. Apartments there were, not many, but some, but houses... With our Alsatians, Dixie and Yankee, waiting in a kennel, we thought it better to continue the search than to move two large dogs into an apartment.

Eventually, Angela located, for an exorbitant rent, the lower two floors of a Maison Particulier, which had a small gravel garden onto which opened French doors from the living room. So 66 Rue Singer in the snotty XVIth arrondisement became our Paris home. If not too spacious, it met our minimum needs. Well located, it was close to fabulous bakeries as well as mouth-watering cheese, wine, fruit, vegetable, and butcher shops. The metro, which I rode to work at the embassy, was also close at hand. For Taffy, there was a wonderful park just minutes away. Dixie and Yankee had the yard for daytime use. At night I walked them. This led to some interesting, and once or twice bloody, encounters with other dogs. One night I opened the gate just as a lady with two Boxers walked by. Boxers don't like Alsatians and Alsatians don't like Boxers. Somehow, however, I eventually got my dogs back into the yard. The lady, fortunately, understood dogs. We exchanged apologies. She went her way; I went mine. Never again, however, did I see her Boxers on Rue Singer.

Our landlord was Madam Helene Mamoulaichvili, a Georgian exile, who lived with her sister and brother, a onetime Colonel of Czarist cavalry. They were friendly enough; indeed Benny Boitelle, a Dutch girl we hired to help with Taffy and housework, thought the Colonel was too friendly. Today we would say he engaged in sexual harassment. Then we simply objected when he chased Benny around the house, as he did rather persistently. Calvary tactics, no doubt. While Dutch resistance proved stronger than Georgian persistence, the continuing skirmish was one more reason beyond the financial drain for seeking to move.

Late in 1953, Angela was again pregnant, reason for rejoicing, but it was a difficult pregnancy, with Angela bedridden for weeks at a time. Benny took great care of her and Taffy. Fortunately it ended well. On March 26, 1954, "Tufty," our son Christopher Roesch, was born. "Tufty" had joined "Taffy," but somehow the name "Tufty" did not take. Chris it was, and is.

In the meantime, we had found a larger house with a good garden for less money. Location was the explanation. We moved from the fanciest part of Paris to Maison Alfort, a communist-dominated industrial suburb. One day talking to an acquaintance at the Quai d'Orsay, he asked where I lived. When I replied "Maison Alfort," astonished, he exclaimed, "No diplomat lives in Maison Alfort." Tactless snobbery, that.

Our new house, built at one end of a shut-down perfume factory, had been the owner-manager's house until he died. His widow, Madame Lasegue, was more than happy to rent to us. To our surprise and delight, our new Commie neighbors were far friendlier than the elite of the XVIth Arrondisement. The downside was commuting time for me. Our house was a long walk from the nearest Metro station. I had to cross the Seine on the Charenton bridge, then walk more than a mile. OK in good weather, but awful in bad. Taking the car was generally better, but rush hour traffic through the center of Paris and then out of town was murderous. All in all, though, we were much better off; more room, bigger garden, and we could pay the rent without borrowing more money.

Part of moving into a rented house was to establish Un Etat de Lieux, or an agreed detailed inventory, and I do mean detailed, down to the last scratch on a chair. Moving out, this document was closely checked. The tenant was dunned for new scratches as well as for any missing items. We found the procedure painful, but there was no avoiding it.

At home, my folks were also on the move. As much as they

(and I) loved Channelside, they had to admit farming it was too much. Since they wanted to be near where their grandchildren were likely to spend time, their search for another home centered around Washington. Finally they bought land at Manor Club on the northeastern fringe of the metropolitan area, hired an architect, and built a house on Great Oak Road. Included was an apartment for Grandma Roesch, who patently could no longer go it alone in Chicago. She helped finance the house, paying for her part and an extra lot with lots of pines and oaks that she looked out upon from her porch. A year later she gave mother and mother's brother a considerable sum in bonds. Mother lamented that had she had the money earlier the house could have been closer to her ideal. Another observation that makes me think it would be well to pass on as much as reasonable earlier rather than later. Something similar happened in my case. Money inherited from mother would have meant a great deal more to me earlier. When mother died, Miren, my beloved Chilean-born second wife, had not much more than a year to live herself. Understandably, with alimony and child support to pay, we had always been strapped for money. My inheritance came too late to permit Miren to enjoy an easier life style. Moreover, her dream house, the one she had wanted me to buy in Washington, but for which, at the time, I could not find financing, had long since been sold.

As Dad was abandoning farming, in April 1953 I was discharged from the U.S. Army Reserve. I just could not see my way clear to accepting an indefinite appointment. A Foreign Service career and a family seemed to leave insufficient time for training with the reserve.

My work at the embassy was quite different from what I had done at Damascus and Mombasa. No more a political pundit or a consular team manager, I was now part of a team of specialists analyzing the French economy. I had to master details about the French tax system and how to measure the growth of the money supply by adjusting and combining what little data the French made available publicly.

The Combined Finance Group produced a comprehensive annual *Briefing Book on France*, Donald J. McGrew as editor. The coverage was comprehensive. To see what we did, I have appended the table of contents of the 1953 *Book*. The United States was providing hundreds of millions of dollars in aid to France each year. There was intense congressional and public interest in the program. That is why the briefing book was prepared and why we were staffed as we were. The Finance Group had a national accounts expert, Harold Lubell. He also played the cello. Our balance of payments expert was Carter Ide. Bill Miller watched the press for both the Finance Group and the Bruce Mission. Bill, Carter, and Harold were MSA employees. I was from State. Don McGrew from Treasury oversaw our efforts. We were supported by a staff of French nationals who collected and massaged statistics. Without their contribution, notably that of Fred Lowensohn and Jackie Lluillier, we would have been far less efficient.

The critical role of local employees in the Foreign Service, who contribute so much, is all too often overlooked. It should not be. I had had excellent support from locals in both of my previous posts, as I would in my future posts, but for skill and dedication no one equaled Fred and Jackie.

Toward the end of my assignment, in July 1955, Robert Marjolin published an eleven-part analysis of the French economy in *Paris-Presse*. I reported his views, enthusiastically endorsing most of them. I was especially taken by his advocacy of a European Customs Union and for the need for timely exchange rate adjustments. This former secretary general of the OEEC, one time deputy to Jean Monnet at the Plan, and a future vice president of the European Commission, where I would get to know him, presaged the launching of the European Economic Community, the so-called Common Market. It was probably not a coincidence that the Messina Conference of the Foreign Ministers of the Six, which would eventually prepare the Treaties establishing the European Atomic Energy Community (Euratom) and the Economic Community, was just getting under way.

The election of 1952 brought Dwight Eisenhower to the presidency and a fierce attack on what was alleged to be a mismanaged and bloated aid program. Harold Stassen took over and "Stassenation" began as he personally culled assistance staffs.

A reduction in force (RIF) was also mandated. It affected our French employees and some American Foreign Service Staff Officers, who had always assumed their jobs were safe since only FSOs were subject to promotion up or out. Ben Cramer, 48 years old, with a wife and four children, was RIFed after fifteen years of service. I thought it was outrageous and wrote a letter of protest to the director general of the Foreign Service. Bob Miner, way senior to me and a friend of DG Gerald Drew, improved my draft and forwarded it over his signature. Among other points, we argued that to provide for no consideration of a longtime employee's dependents was "heartless." Maybe so, but Ben was forced out of the Service.

The change of administrations in Washington provoked the following anonymous doggerel about the Foreign Service:

These are the boys who make the place run. They have little
publicity and none of the fun. They loiter behind, and pick
up the pieces, And cling to the rather discredited theses
That you need a trained staff to backup the new men, So
they don't repeat errors again and again.
No matter how sharp the political schism, The Service keeps
working with patriotism.

By 1952 the French Republic was secure, but when McGrew had arrived in Paris in 1948, it was touch and go as to whether or not France would survive as a free world democracy. The Communist Party was strong and widespread labor agitation threatened the government. Don told us of how there had been tanks in the Place de la Concorde in those troubled times.

Four years later the major issues we faced were the push for a European Defense Community (EDC), viewed in part as a way to get a German military contribution for the NATO alliance without permitting a German national army, and French efforts to hold on to Indochina.

The Bruce Mission had responsibility for the EDC. Bruce and Tommy, always the activist, worked without letup to shape the EDC and the European Political Community, which was envisaged as exercising democratic political control of the EDC in a way that would win the support of the French Assembly. Tommy was so convinced the votes were there, if only the Treaty could be brought to a vote, that he bet a case of champagne with Prime Minister Pierre Mendès-France on the outcome. The prime minister, never an enthusiast for European integration, made a show of trying to improve chances by seeking, with some success, new understandings with France's partners in the Six and far more critically a commitment to membership by the UK. When Churchill turned Mendès down, the die was cast. Mendès brought the Treaty to the floor, where after a passionate debate it was rejected. Tommy paid his bet.

Sadly, Tommy shortly thereafter suffered a stroke which left him greatly curtailed until his premature death months later. I had never worked closely with Tommy, but my admiration for him was unbounded. I do recall, however, a poignant conversation with him one night when, while apparently recovering, he wandered into his embassy office. He wondered aloud if he had been right to work both himself and his staff so hard. His doubts surprised and saddened me. After his death, Monnet was the driving force behind the creation by the Bank of France of a trust fund for the education of Tommy's children. Moreover, Phyllis, his wife, obtained employment at the Community's Washington office. Thus the appreciation for Tommy by Monnet and Tommy's many other French friends was made tangible.

Paradoxically, the defeat of EDC, coupled with the manifest need to raise more European divisions to deter the Soviets, provoked irresistible pressure on France to agree to German rearmament as a NATO ally. In the end, the opponents of EDC brought about what they had said they feared the most: a German national army. Not the first nor the last time the French outsmarted themselves.

The doomed French effort to hold on to Indochina posed serious policy problems for the United States. Our anti-colonialist bias conflicted with our desire to stand together with a key NATO ally. The Atlantacists won, up to a point. It was decided to support France financially. For me, this meant marginal involvement in the decisions as to how much assistance to provide and how to avoid its misuse. Even on the margin, I was excited to participate in policy meetings chaired by Henry Labouisse, the head of the MSA Mission to France.

Labouisse was a gentleman of the old school. Courteous but firm in his views, I found him enormously impressive. His deputy, Benson Lane Timmons, was the bad cop. Egotistical and driven, sharp elbows extended, Lane hardly ever let a document drafted in the Finance Group go forward without making some kind of change. Then he added his initials in the drafting block!

The Indochina exercise generated my first working relation with E. J. Beigel, an extraordinarily able civil servant who handled the economic side of our relations with France in Washington. E. J. traveled to Paris a number of times while arguments raged about Indochina and our aid program. He was a delight to work with.

To justify our continued assistance, the French shared with us their top secret "Navarre Plan." They expressed confidence that implementing their plan would bring victory. Some of us were skeptical, but our job was to work out the details of needed external assistance. Others could discuss military strategy and tactics. Ambassador C. Douglas Dillon must have decided the plan was dull reading. His copy was found by one of his staff aides in a toilet stall! Fortunately, the Plan was not compromised

Dillon impressed me as extremely bright and poised, but apparently he was also a bit absentminded. Embassy Marines found lots of security violations in the ambassador's office. Embarrassed, Dillon came up with a foolproof solution.

He called in the Gunnery Sergeant who was the Marine Security Detachment Commander, and instructed, i.e. ordered, "the Gunny" to sweep his office whenever he, the ambassador, left it. Any violations found thereafter would be charged to the Gunny.

Most of the rest of us lived in terror that the Marines would find unsecured classified material in our offices and charge us with" Security Violations." If one had enough violations, it went into your personnel file for consideration along with everything else at promotion time. Even so, one individual at Embassy Paris defied the Marines and the system.

From time to time, he would hide classified material and leave a note for the Marines, challenging them to find what he had hidden. The Marines would tear his office apart, without always finding what was said to be hidden. While I did not think this was an appropriate response to the annoying security checks, I did admire the chutzpah of my colleague, whose name sadly has now slipped from my memory.

Agreement having been reached with the French, the ambassador and Labouisse presented the French Treasury with the largest check I had ever seen, four hundred million dollars, if memory serves me right. We were not going to let France blame defeat on a lack of American financing, but wisely when defeat came at Dien Bien Phu, President Eisenhower declined to provide American military force to extract the French and redress the situation.

While the struggle continued, however, the embassy Treasury attaché, Don McGrew, collected thousands of "fiches" (a form of receipt or voucher), each one presumably justifying an expenditure of our funds. Happily for me, I was not involved in this auditing process.

Rather, day in and day out, I analyzed French fiscal and

monetary policy. The pace picked up when new data became available. The annual budget and then the seemingly inevitable supplementary budgets required much study and rearrangement into a less esoteric presentation than used by French governments. Bank of France balance sheets, published weekly, also required careful scrutiny and data manipulation. Beyond these challenges was the entire question of the French tax system. Tax reform was a vital necessity, but excruciatingly difficult to achieve. Tax evasion, patriotic during the Nazi occupation, was a way of life. Since no one, or almost no one, submitted honest income declarations, the French devised a system of taxing "external signs of richness." Thus, if the tax collector learned one had an apartment on the Riviera or a yacht or both, the tax bill was adjusted upwards. Clumsy, but up to a point an effective way to raise revenue.

Responsible for reporting on tax issues, I made the acquaintance of Simon Nora, an *inspecteur de finance* who then headed the tax reform effort of the Finance Ministry. He, with lots of support, was fighting to install a tax on value added. Nora argued its main advantage would be to spur investment by eliminating the pyramiding effect of a simple sales tax applied to successive transactions. In addition, a value added tax made it easier to catch businessmen who collected sales tax but did not remit all of the proceeds to the Treasury. Nora and his minister prevailed. France became one of the first countries in the world to have a value added tax. They still have it and its efficiency has made it widely copied, especially in Europe.

When in June 1954 Pierre Mendès-France became prime minister, my acquaintance joined the premier's staff in the Matignon, the official residence and office of the prime minister, where Nora was his deputy chef du cabinet. Building on my having worked with Nora when he was reforming taxes, I invited him to lunch.

To Don McGrew's delight, both because he thought economic officers could also do political reporting and because he liked to tweak political officer noses, the resulting Memcon received high praise from the minister and the political counselor. Personal contacts with Mendès' staff were few and I had learned much of interest to the political types as well as getting a better understanding of Mendès' economic program. Although I also made the arguments for the European Army, Nora, out of conviction or from loyalty to his boss, was not buying.

During the three years I served in Paris, the United States and

France were negotiating a Status of Forces (SOF) Agreement to govern the rights and immunities of our armed forces in Morocco. The pace of the negotiations would ebb and flow, but inevitably some roadblock was encountered to prevent final agreement. Mac Godley, a senior political officer and an ambassador to be, headed our team, which included military and Pentagon civilians. Don and I handled financial issues. My particular responsibility was, of all things, the Moroccan dog tax. The Moroccan Government taxed dogs. Many of our servicemen were fond of dogs, but obviously not of the tax. As a government we argued to the French that the standard exemptions from taxation of the property of servicemen exempted our men from the dog tax. The French argued that for the Moroccans the dog tax had religious significance since the Koran declares dogs to be unclean animals. When pushed hard, the French negotiators would fall back to saying the tax could only be waived by His Sharifian Majesty, the Sultan of Morocco. We should talk to the Moroccan government. Eventually it was decided this and a number of other issues also allegedly needing His Majesty's attention and hopefully his accord required a trip to Rabat, capital of Morocco, for resolution on the spot.

Thus it was that I first visited Morocco, but precious little of Morocco did we see. Our team flew on an Air Force plane, upon arrival we were bused to a meeting room, and after a day of "negotiations" met briefly with Bill Porter, our consul general, before being bused back to the airport, and hence flown back to Paris. Our "negotiations" were no more successful than our sight-seeing. The Moroccan government officials, mostly French, whom I tried to convince that a GI defending Morocco against the infidel communists should not be taxed on his best friend, his dog, were, up to a point, diplomatically sympathetic, but their bottom line was that France as the "protecting power" had the power of decision. So we returned empty handed and frustrated by this manufactured "catch-22" situation. My impression is that when years later we withdrew our forces, mainly long range bombers, from Morocco, the argument over the dog tax was still unresolved and we were still without a SOF Agreement.

While my work, which fascinated me, even the details of tax issues, was demanding, and while Angela was mighty busy with children and housekeeping, we fortunately still had time to explore Paris and France. There is no way I can do justice to the pleasure we derived from taking Taffy to play in the Jardin de Luxembourg, the

Bois de Boulogne, and countless other parks, from walks along the quays to Notre Dame and Sainte Chappelle, from visits to the flea market, from excursions to Versailles, Rambouillet, and so many other chateaux for Sunday picnics. And did I mention the restaurants? And the wines! Art Buchwald, who became one of America's foremost humorists, was then reporting on Paris restaurants for the *Herald Tribune*. For the provinces, the *Bouquet de France* was a wonderful guide to both the sights and the restaurants. We followed their recommendations religiously and never regretted it.

There was so much to do and see in and around Paris that we delayed taking overnight trips. However, for our anniversary in 1953 we drove in the Buick to Saulieu to enjoy a fabulous meal in a Michelin three star restaurant and then on to Vezelay. The Romanesque abbey in Vezelay is still one of my favorite spots in France; I have returned there time and time again. Headed back to Paris, the drive shaft of the Buick broke, as it had in Boston, but in France there were no parts. Far from spoiling the trip, the breakdown introduced us to French bus service. We learned that contrary to bus or metro riders in Paris, bus riders in the provinces were a friendly, helpful lot.

With the Buick out of action for we didn't know how long, we decided to buy a second car, a Simca. So small compared to the Buick, it was much better suited to Paris traffic, if not to touring. Angela learned to drive it and got her first driver's license there in Paris after having successfully negotiated rush hour traffic in the Place de l'Etoile. Her folks were astonished and so proud, as was I.

Trips were easier now, although Angela complained I did not let her drive often enough. We had gorgeous visits to the Loire chateaux and to Provence. I even won a small sum at roulette in Monte Carlo.

When in late summer of 1953 Bettie and Al Peyraud came to visit us, Angela unfortunately was bed ridden, expecting Chris, but I drove them into Alsace and then south into Switzerland to an alpine village from which Grandpa Peyraud, the landscape painter, had ventured forth to the new world to make his fortune. My folks came the following year after Chris's arrival. Angela still could not travel, so I put the Buick, back in action, on the cross-channel ferry and drove to meet Dad and Mom in London. Dad's main interest was to spend some time with his wartime buddies from SHAEF, British Colonels M. D. Molloy and G. H. Winterburn, reminiscing about the war they had helped win. Mother's interest was in gardens, of which England seems to have an inexhaustible supply. Kew Garden and Hampton Court were all right, even interesting, but the endless others.... Oh well, mother enjoyed herself. Then to Paris to see their new grandson, Taffy, and Angela.

Mother's visit put an end for a while to her seemingly endless complaints, mainly justified, about a lack of letters from Angela or me. Being there, she understood better the pressures on Angela, not in robust health, with two children and a house to run in a working class neighborhood of a foreign country.

In 1953, Angela and Taffy had gotten away from the early summer heat in Paris, joining Dania Brewster and her boys at Montreux, Switzerland. Dan and I exploited their absence to see some girlie shows at night spots. Actually, we did not need to wait for the ladies to be out of town; we were given dispensation from time to time to ogle, provided we did not touch.

After Christmas of 1954, the Brewsters and we, leaving Chris with Benny, traveled by train to a U.S. Army recreation facility at Garmisch-Partenkirchen, a famous Alpine resort. There we tried, largely unsuccessfully, to learn to ski. Brewster and I were considered by the Army to be the equivalent of field grade officers, although it seemed they must have thought we were general officers. The Army of Occupation put a car and driver at our disposal and quartered us in a chalet, complete with servants, for our exclusive use. The victors, nine years after the end of the war, were living high on the hog, while the defeated were still clearing bomb damaged buildings around the railway station in Munich.

As 1955 rolled around, my thoughts were on "Where next?". I evinced interest in Morocco. Bill Porter wanted me, but it was not to be. After three overseas assignments, Washington was much in order. I reverted to my idea of taking an assignment in Treasury. By now I was well known to senior Treasury officials, especially to George Willis, Director of the Office of International Finance. I thought George would swing it. How wrong I was. The old fuddy duddy ruled me out, apparently fearing I might compromise some of Treasury's secrets.

Disappointment followed disappointment. When my orders came I was to report to the Bureau of Intelligence Research where I would head the French Benelux Division. I had been Wristonized!

Walter Wriston's report on the functioning of the Department of State had recommended incorporating many Civil Service positions into the Foreign Service.

As individuals moved out, these positions were then to be filled by FSOs. I was one of the first FSOs assigned to INA, which until Wriston shook things up had been almost completely staffed by Civil Service analysts, many of them holdovers from the wartime Office of Strategic Services (OSS) analytical corps.

Not surprisingly, most of the civil servants being pressed into the Foreign Service were unhappy to pull up long-established Washington roots. While they read foreign languages they often did not speak them well. They might know a great deal about Europe, but they had earlier consciously chosen not to live there. Moreover, many of them looked askance at the Foreign Service.

As for me and my fellow FSOs, we had no desire to serve in the passive roles of INR analysts.

Ambassador Dillon, saying he wanted to say adieu in person, asked me to come to his office before my departure from Paris. Standing at his high desk, used because his back problems would not permit him to sit for long, he suggested I get in touch with Robert Amory and Jim Hunt of the C.I.A., to whom he had recommended me. I much appreciated the ambassador's desire to help, but decided that as little as I was looking forward to INR, I was even less interested in the C.I.A.

So we sold the Buick and the Simca to our friendly communist "garagista," and after a round of farewell parties, we sailed home on October 7, 1955. Sadly Benny decided not to accompany us. Fortunately, after visiting Al and Bettie Peyraud in Chicago, we had a comfortable base for house hunting while living with my folks in their new home just outside Washington.

9

INR – Washington
(1955–1958)

House hunting led us to a small white rambler at 6615 Rannock Road, just beyond the end of Massachusetts Avenue in Bethesda, Maryland. The yard behind the house backed up into a forest, through which Debi, Angela, and I would walk to reach the Merrimack Park Community Swimming Pool. We and our dogs were happy in the first ever home of our own. Work was another story, but frustration there was more than compensated for by our domestic situation, which improved wondrously, first when on May 13, 1956, Jeffrey Joe joined our family, followed on July 2, 1957, by Joanna. As delighted as we were with their arrival, a small house with four young children was extremely taxing for Angela.

When I reported to the Department of State for my new job in the Bureau of Intelligence Analysis and Research (INA), my assignment was as division chief for Western Europe (DRW) in the Office of European Research. Clinton Knox, holder of a Ph.D. from the Sorbonne, was the office director. Soft spoken, erudite, but firm in his views, he seemed to understand my unhappiness with the job, while making it clear I had to make the Division a productive contributor to "independent research." The Foreign Service had not yet begun to place emphasis on "management skills," but Clint Knox did. What I learned from him stood me in good stead later in my career.

My staff was sizable, divided into those concentrating on current analysis and those writing chapters for the National Intelligence Survey (NIS). The division had a quota of NIS chapters to be finished each quarter. Those who ground out these dull surveys were generally academics who had stayed in government after the war. Some were knowledgeable, some were not; some could write, some could not; some were quite intelligent, some were not. More below about the managerial problem posed by one of these "scholars."

The current analysts were a livelier lot, some exceedingly talented. There was a plethora of talent concentrated on France: Sue Hadzel, Edith Scott, Anton de Porte. Elsewhere in the Office, Tom Fina, at times persona non grata at our embassy in Rome because of his alleged "leftist sympathies," produced biting analysis of the Italian political scene. We became lifelong friends. While DRW was also responsible for analysis of the Benelux Countries, apart from NIS chapters we produced little. Our attention was focused on France, where some thought there was still a potential for a communist takeover.

Work conditions on the seventh floor of the converted apartment building occupied by INR, State Annex A, were deplorable. Crowding was bad enough. No air conditioning and an antique heating system made matters worse. In winter if there was enough snow and in summer if the thermometer rose enough, we were released from work early.

DRW had an "editor" who reviewed all output. At first I was annoyed when the editor rewrote material I had approved, and in some cases written. Soon, however, I learned to appreciate the advantages of his sharp eye and stylistic skill. He, too, suffered mightily trying to rework poorly drafted NIS chapters. That he helped me bear that cross was much appreciated.

It was dogma in INA that intelligence analysis had to be uncontaminated by contact with policy makers. My inherited deputy, Walker Givans, lectured me on the absolute need for INR analysts to guard their "independence." He was outraged when I looked up E.J. Beigel, the economist on the French desk with whom I had worked closely the preceding three years, and then went on to establish personal links with some FSOs in the Bureau of European Affairs. These FSOs were "colleagues" to me, "false sirens" to Walker. I wanted my people to work on problems of relevance to policy makers, not just pontificate from an Ivory Tower. Walker argued so doing would destroy our objectivity. Walker's argument was not entirely without merit. There was a danger that in working too closely with the policy side, analysts might not accurately appraise threats to the policy or spot false assumptions underlying the policy. On the other hand, I've seen cases where analysts opposed to a policy lost all sense of objective analysis, grossly exaggerating negative factors influencing a situation. To conclude, it seems to me that objectivity resides in the individual analyst, who in a given case may or may not be unduly influenced by others.

Our boss, Clint Knox, had always done it Walker's way, but he recognized the Wriston Report was changing not only the mix of Foreign Service and Civil Service personnel, but also the work environment as well. He gave me a cautious green light to work with operational people in Main State.

Tension between Walker and myself, which complicated the management of DRW, was probably accentuated by the fact that he was as bitter about having been pressed into the Foreign Service as I was about being assigned to a former Civil Service job in INA. He was now subject to selection out in the Foreign Service's "up or out" promotion system. Even worse from his standpoint, he had to give up a comfortable lifestyle in Washington to move his family overseas. Moreover, he would face new moves every three years or so. If this were not enough, Walker clearly resented that a younger man had come in from the outside to occupy a position to which he had aspired. We had no choice, however, but to work together as best we could until he left for overseas.

That first year in INR, my work won mild praise in my efficiency report, prepared by Al Irving, the deputy office director, but my attitude was noted, correctly, as less than enthusiastic. Clint Knox, the reviewing officer, told me that while I showed talent, I had better stop grousing. He suggested a different boss might have reacted much more strongly to my conduct. That efficiency report was the worst I would receive in almost fifty years in the Service. It was also the most helpful. I took Knox's advice to heart. In due course, he rewarded my new attitude.

Irving, a veteran analyst of Britain and newly minted FSO, was soon assigned to London. Fred Sanderson, the able economist who had been running the Division of Regional Analysis, moved up. Knox, who knew of my deep interest in European integration, asked me to add the Regional Division to my responsibilities.

In Europe after the disaster of the European Army, the supporters of integration had maneuvered to convoke the 1955 Messina Conference. As a rather unexpected result, "Europe was re-launched." Negotiations for creation of both an Atomic Energy Community, "Euratom," and of an Economic Community, the so-called "Common Market," were initiated. Paul Henri Spaak of

Belgium, a convinced Europeanist, was in the chair. To the surprise of many, formidable political, economic, and technical obstacles were overcome. In 1957 the Treaties of Rome were signed and ratified by the six member governments.

The United States favored this process and closely followed the negotiations. Somehow virtually all Conference documents reached us. The officers in the Bureau of European Affairs could not find time to read the mass of documentation nor to analyze nuances behind frequent changes in Treaty articles. With Knox's approval, my people and I endeavored to screen and highlight important points for the operators. We made, I think, a minor contribution.

Another offbeat task arose when J. Robert Schaetzel, then, if memory serves me right, working with Under Secretary for Economics George Ball, told me Jean Monnet, who was using his incredible connections to push the negotiations from the outside, needed an analysis of the legislative history of some articles in the U.S. Atomic Energy Act. Monnet wanted to know how a number of issues, particularly public ownership of nuclear fuel, had been dealt with. And why. After much work I provided a paper, which was said to have been helpful. Whether it was or not, I felt good about doing research with the promise of making a positive contribution to the future of U.S. relations with Euratom. The purist would object that we in INA were not there to research American legislative history. Pragmatists would applaud.

Then, my people and I got more directly into the policy process.

As prospects brightened for establishment of a European Common Market, in 1956 the Council on Foreign Economic Policy (CFEP), a body that in the Eisenhower administration weakly paralleled the National Security Council, launched a review of U.S. policy toward European Integration. Numerous papers were prepared by interagency subcommittees. Leadership in State came from Isaiah Frank in the Bureau of Economic Affairs and Stan Cleveland in the Bureau of European Affairs. RPE (Regional Political Economic Affairs) participated actively. It was a welcome introduction to policy analysis and bureaucratic skirmishing. Bob Yost, Bob Brungart, and I, with close oversight by Fred Sanderson, did much of the basic drafting, especially of the papers reviewing the history of United States policy toward European integration, the European Movement itself, economic cooperation in the Organization for European Economic Cooperation (OEEC), the Benelux, and the European Coal and Steel Community (CSC). I wrote a paper entitled "The Political Significance of the CSC," which to my regret was not included in the final report, but to my satisfaction was drawn on in the subcommittee report on United States policy.

My paper reviewed the basic arguments for U.S. support of European Integration, from *realpolitik* considerations of the need for strength through unity in the face of the threat of Soviet communism to recognition that a bold political concept was essential, if the entrenched power of restrictionist interests was to be overcome and the economies of the European nation states freed from suffocation within narrow markets. The integration of Germany within a wide framework both freed Germany to contribute to Western strength and reassured many, most prominently Frenchmen, who feared a revival of German militarism. Jean Monnet may have exaggerated when he argued that the CSC had made war between France and Germany "not only unthinkable, but materially impossible," but so far he has not been proven wrong. I thought then, and I think now, that the integration movement, perhaps above all promised to restore the self-confidence needed for Europe to play a constructive world role.

This was fairly standard fare and only indirectly would I maintain that it affected policy. In fact, while in many ways Eisenhower appointees tried to differentiate Ike's administration from Truman's, American support for European integration was a dear exception. Neither Ike nor John Foster Dulles nor other senior policy makers needed the CFEP study. But there were many GATT purists, agricultural experts, those who insisted currency convertibility should come first, and others within the U.S. Government opposed to U.S. support of European integration. The CNEP study gave these opponents of the policy a forum in which to make their arguments. It gave those of us in RPE, together with our colleagues in the operational bureaus, an opportunity to counter objections and hone argumentative skills not normally associated with intelligence analysis.

To my regret, one part of my paper did not show up in the final documents of the CFEP. I had tried to spotlight the importance of the "Action Committee for a United States of Europe." This high-powered group, organized by Jean Monnet, was to play a substantial role in winning approval of Euratom and the Common Market. Monnet used the political connections he had built through a long lifetime of high-level government and international service to rally support first for completion of the negotiations and then for ratification of the Treaties of Rome. The committee membership included the leaders of the socialist and Catholic parties in each of the six CSC member countries as well as leaders of key liberal parties and the Free Trade Unions. Monnet was a lobbyist *sans pareil*. He must have run up enormous telephone bills in advancing and negotiating draft after draft of Declarations of the Action Committee. His efforts paid off, as the committee's consensus carried real weight.

In 1957 Sputnik flashed across space, touching off alarms in Washington that the Soviets were ahead in the race for technological dominance. A task force was assembled with the mandate to produce ideas to strengthen the NATO alliance. For once, contributions from INA were said to be welcome. After much thought and drafting all of one night, I submitted a proposal for an approach to economic union, starting with an Atlantic free trade area. I recognized that a successful Atlantic free trade area would be devastating to European integration. As a believer, this bothered me. On the other hand, however, I argued such a free trade regime would give a solid economic underpinning to the alliance. My concern over the proposal's impact on the European movement was not why my proposal received short shift. Bob McBride of the Bureau of European Affairs, who chaired the mid-level review panel charged with vetting proposals prior to high level consideration, told me later my paper, while the most interesting of those reviewed, was just too far reaching. Rather, as usual the powers that be came up with a menu of not very imaginative NATO-specific improvements.

While I intensely disliked work on the National Intelligence Survey (NIS), National Intelligence Estimates (NIE) were exciting. One thought, for example, that the NIE on France, on which I worked as the State/INA representative, might even be read by the President. Trying to predict the future course of events was a real intellectual challenge. The process was dominated by C.I.A. experts, but the rest of us had a voice. From time to time our voice was persuasive. At other times our view could only be dropped or, at best, preserved in a footnote. Sherman Kent, an imposing, intellectually sharp character, ran C.I.A.'s estimate operation. He knew all the nuances of judging an event as "remotely possible" to "almost certain." Himself an experienced analyst of France, he was obsessed with General de Gaulle. He was right about the General's eventual return to power, but wrong about the timing and provoking events, i.e. the Algerian rebellion. Actually, in many cases future events can be predicted with a high degree of probability.

Seldom, however, can anyone accurately judge in advance the timing, say, of revolutions or the acquisition of nuclear weapons.

I didn't know Sherman Kent well enough to wager with him about the future, but with Clint Knox I could and did. Kent was a conservative, convinced de Gaulle would soon return to power. Knox was a liberal, similarly convinced Pierre Mendès-France would soon return to power. I bet him a lunch, "$2 minimum," that he was wrong. When June 30, 1957, arrived with PMF still in the political wilderness, Clint paid. To my embarrassment and I'm sure to Knox's deep resentment, when we lunched together, as we did regularly, it was invariably in the State Department cafeteria. To America's shame, most Washington restaurants would not serve a black in the 1950s.

If working on an NIE was stimulating, working on NISs was mind numbing. As the division chief, I was responsible for submitting on-time studies programmed by a committee somewhere in C.I.A. Most of my analysts turned in tolerably decent work, but one was hopeless. When submitted for review, his turgid prose was largely irrelevant to the assigned topic. I could see no way to meet our required output with him as an analyst. First I explored possibilities of switching him to another division or office of INA. No way; his reputation, like that of a quarterback who throws almost as many interceptions as completions, was well known. So I researched how one fired a civil servant. Then the office editor, who suffered with me, and I carefully documented a solid case for dismissal: disregard of schedules, disregard of specific written instructions, failure to observe work hours, and so forth. I gave notice. Hardly fazed my man. He simply appealed to the Civil Service Commission. After a few weeks of back and forth about the case, my boss, Clint Knox, called me in to his office. "Deane, I agree that your analyst is worthless. We have a choice, however. We can get on with our other work, or you and I and others can spend days and weeks tied up in the bureaucratic proceedings of the Civil Service." After some discussion, I gave in. I would withdraw the charges. Knox volunteered to try to help solve my problems. To my relief, shortly thereafter my analyst departed and DRW's production schedule was cut back. How he did it, I do not know, but I do know I never again contemplated firing a civil servant. P.S. Years later, the analyst in question approached me in the East Gallery of the National Art Gallery, where we had a brief but pleasant chat without reference to our clash of some thirty-five years earlier.

One afternoon I took all of the French analysts to the movies. Queried by my puzzled superiors about our mass absence, I told them I had concluded that to better understand France and the French we had to see Brigitte Bardot in *...And God Created Woman*.

Speaking engagements provided another welcome break from the office. I spoke at the John Hopkins School of Advanced International Studies on "Euratom," at the Industrial College of the Armed Forces on "European Economic Capabilities," at Brandeis University on "France," and on similar topics elsewhere. Good experience.

It helped me overcome my fear that talks, like babies, are easy to conceive but hard to deliver. This was good since a compliant FSO needs to be able to talk persuasively to the public.

In early 1958 with my three-year assignment to INA coming to an end, I was wondering what was next when Stan Cleveland called and informed me I was headed to Brussels to work under Ambassador Walt Butterworth. I was surprised, but happily so. Stan, who knew me from his days at the Bruce Mission while I was in the embassy in Paris and from our contacts in Washington, took credit for persuading Butterworth, about to add accreditation to Euratom and the Common Market to his role as U.S. Ambassador to the Coal and Steel Community, that I should be his economic-financial officer. Angela was delighted at the prospect of civilized Belgium and the prospect of competent help with our four kids.

For this assignment, I was for once well prepared. Already quite knowledgeable about Europe, I spoke French and , had time to talk to a variety of officials about their interests in and views of the Communities before leaving. In the course of these "briefings" I learned Treasury was miffed about my assignment, since some there held the view that the financial job should be held by a Treasury attaché. (Some years after my departure, it was.) Miffed or not, many Treasury officials helpfully laid out quite a list of subjects in which they were interested. A central concern of Treasury was the perceived danger the Common Market, in a foreign exchange crisis, would impose quantitative restrictions on trade in a discriminatory fashion, exempting Community member countries. On the other hand, John Leddy in State, then assistant to Under Secretary C. Douglas Dillon, was hopeful the Community would move forward toward a common currency. He urged me to monitor closely efforts at financial coordination, a necessary precondition for eventual financial integration. When Dillon went to Treasury as Secretary, he named John Leddy as assistant secretary for international finance.

How John reconciled his new responsibilities with his interest in financial integration, which ipso facto would create the kind of discrimination his staff had warned me against, I do not know. In any case, the process of moving to a common European currency became a matter of decades. As far as I can recall, not once in those decades did the Community apply discriminatory quantitative restrictions for balance of payments reasons.

10

USEC – Brussels
(1958–1961)

Angela and I were excited about going to Brussels. Western European posts promise a good bit of the good life. I was thrilled I was to be a charter member of the United States Mission to the European Communities (USEC). When I was assigned to Paris in 1952 I had been led to expect I would be working primarily with Europeans trying to unify the old world, but my hopes had been disappointed. What I had been told in Washington was changed by senior officers in Paris. The result, not all that bad, was I learned a good deal about financial analysis and, more important, the French, while concentrating on bilateral problems. France, after all, was a key player in the drive to integrate Europe. This time, however, it was for real.

Brussels was to fulfill our personal and professional expectations. Indeed, more than fulfill them since to our surprise, initial concern, and ultimate delight Veronica Jean joined the family in 1960.

Before reaching Brussels, however, we had a scare. Just days before our scheduled departure from Washington, Dad had a heart attack. Fortunately, his attack came when he was driving near Fort Meade. Mother got him to the emergency room of the post hospital. When we saw him, the doctors said he would recover and he told us not to change our departure plans. A few months later he wrote he had lost nearly twenty pounds, was now walking the golf course eighteen rather than riding a cart, and felt better than ever. He lived for almost another thirty years. One might conclude surviving a heart attack, with its warning about diet and weight, is good for you.

After an enjoyable sea voyage and a leisurely drive from Le Havre, once in Brussels we had a rough transition and considerable difficulty in finding adequate housing. We had reservations at an attractive pension on the outskirts of town with a wonderful garden, where I enjoyed playing boliches and the children could romp. But 1958 was the year of the Brussels World Fair and our pension limited stays to two weeks. Thus we had to find other temporary housing at a time when there was hardly any available due to the influx of visitors to the Exposition. As a result, we had to move repeatedly from one miserable boarding house to another. It would not have been bad for just Angela and me, but with four energetic youngsters it was hard going. Nor was permanent housing easily available. The establishment of the headquarters of the Common Market and Euratom in Brussels translated into the nearly simultaneous arrival of more than a thousand European Community employees looking for housing. Fortunately, we finally found a tolerable house at 331 Avenue Baron d'Huart in Crainhem, a suburb on the eastern fringe of Brussels. No stone sink this time, but instead of central hot water heaters we struggled with devilish and dangerous European devices, individual *chauff-bains*. One of the better things about the house was that it was but a short walk to the Tervuren tram line that took me right to my new office. Having a house also made it possible to reunite the family. Dad shipped our beloved Yankee to us. A heavy expense for us, but worth it. Unfortunately the government does not finance the travel of pets. Dixie, old and feeble, stayed behind, enjoying the good dog life on a farm.

Even with the tram, I yearned for my own car. Finally I decided on an almost affordable Morris Minor convertible. Lovely car, especially when Belgian rain let up and the top came down. The first week I had it, I parked it a long block from the USEC office building near Exposition Park. To my horror, when I went to drive home I discovered someone had rammed my new car. Whoever did it did not bother to leave a note. Unfortunately, however, for the Belgian count who was the guilty party, a lady in a nearby apartment had seen the incident and taken down the culprit's license number. She gave it to me. The police dealt with the count, a most apologetic count, who paid for repairs to my car.

The chief of mission of USEC was Ambassador W. Walton Butterworth. "Walt," an outstanding, savvy career diplomat, was by background a China expert. Foreign Service China experts, including Butterworth, unfairly and unfortunately were attacked during the political furor over "Who Lost China?" essentially for having been right about the corrupt Chiang Kai-shek regime and for having foreseen the success of Mao's Communist revolution. While Butterworth was not driven from the Service unlike some other old China hands, he and the State Department's leadership were aware the Senate would not confirm him as an ambassador. To his credit, Secretary of State Dulles found a partial remedy for this by having Walt appointed as the United States Representative to the European Coal and Steel Community in Luxembourg. This ambassadorial level post did not then require Senate confirmation. Originally it also looked like a dead end job, but Butterworth came into his own as the Treaties of Rome creating the Common Market and Euratom were negotiated, ratified, and put into effect. His well-deserved reward was to be named to head the new U.S. Mission to all three Communities.

Jean Monnet, after France's rejection of the European Defense Community, had seen in nuclear energy a sexy way to reinvigorate the European integration process. At the same time, he underestimated the possibilities of moving forward on a broad economic front, as was, in fact, done with the Common Market. While the U.S. was more hopeful than he for the Economic Community, Monnet used his great influence with U.S. policy makers to get commitments for U.S. assistance to Euratom even before the Treaty entered into effect. Thus the prospect was for a joint power reactor program supplemented by a joint research program. When the French, however, acted to minimize Euratom's potential and opposed the incremental construction of U.S. light water reactors beyond the SENN project to advance their nuclear weapons program and their own power reactor designs, the handwriting was on the wall. Euratom had a limited future. Nevertheless, the joint research program delivered valuable, if unspectacular, results.

American support for the Economic Community was wholehearted, recognizing both its political potential and its likely overall growth-stimulating effect. We were not blind, however, either to the political split developing between the Common Market countries and European states that had opted not to join, led by the United Kingdom, or to the economic risks involved for our interests.

My job at USEC left me far away from the central issues of European policy, but I kept up with whatever cable traffic was in the USEC reading folder, and when I began to attend the debates of the European Parliament I heard a great deal from the viewpoint of Community parliamentarians.

The British had, of course, missed the boat when the Coal and

Steel Community was established. Their reluctance, to put it mildly, to support the European Defense Community contributed to its demise. Their decision not to join the Economic Community was an even bigger blunder. The British, genuinely concerned at the trade diversion potential of the Community, made a bad situation worse by proposing to deal with this problem by establishing a European Free Trade Area. The six members of the Communities were not having any of this. They viewed the Communities as part of a political process aimed at the eventual integration of Europe. They saw British proposals as fatally designed to weaken their efforts. For our part, we concluded that if the British scheme were put into effect the impact on our trade would be serious without the mitigating political advantages we saw in the Communities.

When it became clear to London that a broad European Free Trade Area was not in the cards, the British persuaded other non-Community states to form a small free trade area among themselves. Thus developed the so-called problem of the Six and the Seven. To the dismay, even non-comprehension, of the Seven, the United States opposed their efforts. Our policy of support for the Communities was steadfast despite the political pain of a split with our British ally and other NATO members. Immense pressure both domestically and internationally was brought to bear on us to change our approach. President Eisenhower, Secretary Dulles, and later Secretary Herter held firm. This issue is a good example of what a policy requires to be successful. We understood the importance of the eventual achievement of a united Europe and would not abandon our long range objective under the pressure of transitory events. The British and other EFTA members were consistently told that in our view the answer to their trade problems was either to join the Six or participate in a major round of multilateral trade negotiations with us and every other country in the GATT.

If we were firm on the policy, we also recognized the damage being done to Free World unity by the quarrel between the Seven and Six. The situation called for constructive initiatives on our part. One was to propose with the Canadians that we both join the OEEC (Organization for European Economic Cooperation) and renegotiate its mandate with new emphasis on worldwide development. Another was to press ever harder for multilateral trade negotiations in GATT. This policy stance led to the OECD (Organization for Economic Cooperation and Development) and the Kennedy Round of trade negotiations.

From the outset, the United States, while broadly supporting the Six, articulated three economic concerns. First was the danger that development of the promised common agricultural policy would harm American agricultural exports. Second, we opposed what we viewed as GATT illegal preferences granted by the Community to Associated States in Africa, the Caribbean, and elsewhere. Third, we made clear our opposition to the imposition of Community-wide quotas as a potential remedy for a national balance of payments problem.

Each of these points was a specific application of an overall concern, much debated by theoretical economists, that the Common Market might be more trade diverting than trade creating. For political reasons, including the perceived strength a united Europe added to the West, the United States would accept some trade diversion. Nevertheless, some particular cases of potential damage to our trading interests were far less acceptable than others. Our belief that overall the growth inducing role of the Community would outweigh negative effects on trade, especially our trade, while an important consideration in our policy of support for the Community was less so than the political arguments.

The Associated States, so recognized in the Treaties of Rome, were, of course, in almost all cases former or actual European colonies. One acute American concern about the preferences given imports into the Common Market from Associates related to bananas. American banana companies had a large stake in Latin American production, particularly in Central America. Then, as now, they were not shy about advancing their views.

While the Eisenhower administration made our concerns known, it was the Kennedy administration that first pushed hard to achieve better access to the European market for the bananas of U.S. companies. Under Secretary of State George Ball, a solid advocate of American partnership with the European Communities as well as a close collaborator of Jean Monnet, nevertheless was an eloquent exponent of American opposition to Europe discrimination in favor of bananas from the Caribbean and Somalia. Cynics might note that Ball had represented the United Fruit Company in private law practice before joining the Kennedy administration.

Our third concern was more a theoretical concept. Purists, particularly in Treasury, feared that once a member country of the Community got in balance of payments difficulties, not only might it impose quantitative restrictions to right its ship, but also the Community as such might impose them, much as the common external tariff was applied. Such a major action discriminating against outsiders would be bound to be highly disruptive of world commerce. Fortunately, such fears have until now proven to be unfounded. Still with the evolution of the EURO common currency area, Union wide quotas might be justifiable were the European Union as a whole to fall into a serious balance of payments crisis.

Ambassador Butterworth elected to organize his Mission so that most staff related to one of the Communities. Thus Carl D. Corse, a veteran trade negotiator and authority on GATT who had come into the Foreign Service via the Wriston program, was Deputy Representative for Economic Community Affairs, usually called Common Market Affairs; Lou Boochever, stationed in Luxembourg, was Deputy Representative for Coal and Steel Community Affairs; and Amasas Bishop, a distinguished nuclear physicist from the Atomic Energy Commission, was Deputy Representative for Euratom Affairs.

Of these three outstanding deputies, Am Bishop was by far the most impressive. Brilliant and personable, already the author of a book on the subject of controlled fusion, he assured me the terrifying force of thermonuclear weapons was close to being tamed for the peaceful purpose of generating electricity. However, after later heading the controlled fusion program of the United States for almost ten years, he joined the United Nations Economic Commission for Europe where he worked on environmental problems of all things! Today controlled fusion appears to remain a distant dream.

I was fortunate to be assigned to the Office of the Ambassador. My first official title in the mission was "Attaché for Financial Affairs." Since I would have to deal with all three Communities, as well as with such separate institutions as the European Bank and the Economic and Social Council, I reported to the ambassador through the DCM. Best of all, I enjoyed great freedom in choosing on what to work. Of course, when the mission was engaged in active negotiations, for example with Euratom on the Joint Program, the financial aspects of such negotiations, including Export-Import Bank "Buy American" requirements, became a priority for me. Normally, however, my priority was to comprehend and report on significant financial problems. To do this I had to follow the general economic and financial situation of the European Community, including Community relations with the Associated Overseas Territories. When appropriate, I presented the views of the United States Government to the relevant European officials.

"Contacts" are important in all aspects of life, but for a diplomatic observer in a foreign country or in a six country Community they are critical. My success at USEC, and a success it was judging from Washington appreciation of my reporting even or especially at Treasury and the Fed, was based on good relations with a wide number of key European officials. That many Europeans dedicated to the integration process also recognized and appreciated the supportive role the United States was playing certainly facilitated contacts.

Of course, the fact that I was a Foreign Service officer, not a Treasury attaché, handicapped me to some extents. Eventually (but not until recognition in Washington dawned of the importance of the Monetary Committee in particular and EC efforts at economic coordination in general), I was kept as closely informed of American thinking concerning the IMF and European financial problems as were Treasury attachés in Europe. Having official, often sensitive, information to share when authorized to do so furthered my efforts to collect information of interest to Washington. It also helped me prioritize my reporting.

I was particularly proud of the success I had in keeping track of developments in the Monetary Committee. Much that went on in the Communities was reported generally accurately in *Europe*, a newsletter edited by a remarkable Italian, Emmanuele Gazzo. This was not true of the Monetary Committee, where a serious and generally successful effort was made to keep discussions confidential. While everyone seemed to leak about Commission and Council of Minister meetings, this simply was not the case in the monetary field. The sensitivity of discussions bearing on exchange rates was recognized and protected. Even so, I had a number of contracts, both in the Commission and in the national delegations, that kept me well informed. Indeed, thanks to a couple of key contacts I regularly forwarded Committee documents, passed to me under the table, to Washington.

Robert Marjolin was a vice president of the European Commission. Under Commission President Walter Hallstein, Marjolin was charged with economic and financial matters, including the objective, established in the Treaties of Rome, of freeing capital movements within the Community. Marjolin, I recalled, had written about a common European currency when I had been at the embassy in Paris. Quite properly, contacts at the commissioner level were handled by Ambassador Butterworth, so only on rare occasions did I see Marjolin. However, I was on good terms with his director general, Franco Bobba, and most of his key people. Also Robert Triffin, an advisor to Marjolin, and I met regularly when he was in Brussels. Triffin was pushing the Community to harmonize economic and monetary and tax policies, all seen correctly as prior requirements if the goal of a common currency were someday to be achieved. Progress was slow, but the effort was advanced with persistence by Marjolin and others.

One meeting on economic policy coordination, where progress was expected, backfired when Bobba, a womanizer, kept an assignation rather than chairing the meeting.

Never mind, the ground was recovered later.

In December of 1958, Under Secretary of State C. Douglas Dillon chaired an Economic Officers' Conference in Paris of over thirty participants. Big shots from Washington, including John Leddy and Jack Tuthill, accompanied Dillon. All European posts were represented. To my delight, along with Carl Corse I attended as a USEC representative. I recall virtually nothing of the discussions, but have a vivid recollection of having had a new sense of importance, even if I were seated in the back row, removed from the conference table. A buffet dinner at Ambassador to NATO Burgess's residence and a reception by Jacques Reinstein, economic minister in Paris, provided welcome opportunities to get to know colleagues laboring in the European economic vineyard.

In later years I attended many more such meeting and too many similar receptions. Indeed in the mid-1960s I organized and was a major participant in such events. But nothing replaced the thrill of the first.

Unlike the African Consular Conference I had attended in Mozambique in 1950, the quality of the participants in Paris was impressively high. Talented officers were scarce in Africa but abundant in Europe.

Butterworth shared my view that I should have a broader mandate than finance or even economics. As a result, I often joined my old buddy from Paris days, Bill Miller, the ambassador's special assistant, in reporting on the debates in the European Parliament.

While the Parliament had little power, it provided an important sounding board. Moreover, it was predictable that if the Communities flourished, the influence of this representative body would increase and its powers would be expanded. And so it has transpired, although at the start of a new century the process of endowing an elected European Parliament with decisive power has yet to be completed.

Observing and reporting on the Parliament's work gave me new insights into the philosophies and programs of the major political parties, except the Communists, who originally were not represented, in the member states of the Communities. It was a wonderful opportunity to get to know "comers" on the European political scene and to enjoy, on per diem, delights we could seldom afford at home in Brussels. The Parliament generally met in Strasbourg, the restaurants of which rivaled those of Brussels. There are no smells in the world charged with more memories than the *pissoirs* of Strasbourg restaurants during asparagus season. Even better, about sixty kilometers south of Strasbourg is my favorite restaurant in the world, L'Auberge de L'Ill. In addition to many visits during my two assignments to USEC, I have returned to L'Auberge while traveling on leave from other posts and in retirement. Just the *soufflé de saumon "vaut le voyage"* (is worth the trip), as the French say. The authoritative Michelin guide still gives L'Auberge three stars.

It was while at Strasbourg in November of 1959 that Bill and I saw the magnetism of General Charles de Gaulle. He not only wowed the Alsatians, he also wowed us. Despite our dislike for his policies, we could not help but be impressed by his presence and eloquence as he spoke to an overflowing crowd before the Hotel de Ville.

In 1959 my mother inadvertently triggered one of those magic moments that will live in one's memory forever. It happened like this. Grandma Roesch, whom I loved as I did my mother, passed away months after our departure for Europe. Sad as death is, it nevertheless liberated Grandma from suffering and freed my folks to travel. On the way to see us and their grandchildren, Dad wanted first to show mother where he had served in and near London during the war and introduce her to some of his old British buddies from SHAEF days. I was to take our car on the Ostend ferry to England, meet them in London for a few days, and drive us all back to Brussels.

After fulfilling Dad's agenda, Mother wanted above all to see English gardens. Finally after almost a day at Kew Gardens and another day visiting the gardens of Windsor Palace and various lesser gardens, we set out for Brussels. Mother wasn't feeling too good, worn down in part by horticultural extravaganza, I suppose. So while heading down the highway to Brussels, with our objective, our house in Crainhem, just two hours away, she said we had to find a hotel for the night. Naturally, I pulled off at the next highway outlet and found in the rain a good-looking hotel, where mother rested while Dad and I dined quite well, as usual in Belgium.

After dinner I walked out for a bit of fresh air. To my utter amazement, shining through the light rain and fog was a fairy city. Truly a magical moment. I wandered enchanted through the misty evening, wondering at having been somehow transported back many centuries to an illuminated medieval town. I had, of course, stumbled on Bruges. I have returned many times, always enjoying the city, but it is the thrill of that surprising first discovery in the mist that lives in my memory. Bruges is a remarkable reminder of days gone by, when the merchants of Bruges were known the world over. Fortunately, they invested their trading profits in splendid buildings. Even better, the tides of war that have so often rolled over Belgium spared Bruges.

A second magical moment came in early 1960. While attending the European Parliament in Strasbourg I was informed that Clarence Birgfeld, the USEC deputy chief of mission, and his wife would visit Strasbourg. It was my job to make their visit professionally profitable and personally enjoyable. The professional part was easy. With the help of friendly staffers at the Parliament, I introduced the DCM to the right people and arranged for him to listen to a rather duller than usual debate. Also I scheduled a visit to the world famous cathedral and a walk around the more picturesque parts of the city. But what to do in the evening?

Strolling around town before their arrival, I spotted an advertisement for a recital by Edith Piaf. I bought three tickets, even though I knew little of Piaf, ignorant fellow that I was. When after dinner in a modest restaurant, Birgfeld having resisted the idea of a fancy meal I had hoped he would finance, we tramped through the snow to the concert, where we were ushered into a hardly heated gymnasium and shown to cold metal chairs. Boy, I thought, I've blown it this time. But, of course, I hadn't blown it. Once Edith came on stage and began to sing, we were completely captivated, the cold and the uncomfortable chairs forgotten. Her presence, standing dead still before the microphone in what I learned later was her trademark simple black dress, enrapturing the audience with "Mon Dieu," "Je ne Regret Rien," "Mi Lord," and countless ballads such as "Le Vieux Piano," was astonishing. Before her passing I heard Edith Piaf, "the sparrow," sing twice more, once in Paris and once in Brussels, both times in proper sold out theaters. However, nothing could match the surprise, the magic of that first concert. Today I have a dozen or so Piaf CDs, which I love. Sadly, my children, for the most part, especially sons Sebastian and Akbar, allege they cannot stand Piaf. It's their loss!

A few months later I was again in Strasbourg when word came that I should urgently return to Brussels and then proceed directly to Washington. At the December 1959 NATO Ministerial Meeting, Secretary Herter had launched a long-term planning exercise in the NATO Council. Almost simultaneously he had asked Bob Bowie, who had served in Europe as Legal Advisor to John McCloy, our High Commissioner in the German Federal Republic, to prepare a report on initiatives we might take in the Council and issues likely to arise in the planning effort. I was assigned to work with him and his team. I was also told that since 1960 was an election year our review of policy toward NATO and Europe would help guide the next administration. Heady stuff.

I was thrilled by the prospect of helping shape policy in a team established by Secretary Herter and headed by a man who enjoyed an outstanding reputation. My ego soared when I was informed my presence in Washington was required "immediately." The earliest flight was British. The aircraft was a converted bomber, which shook and groaned for nearly sixteen hours crossing the Atlantic. When I eventually returned to Brussels, what a delight it was to do so in a Boeing 707, so smooth, so fast. The contrast between the propeller and jet ages was incredible.

Of course, as so often happens, my flight to Washington proved to be another case of hurry up and wait. Moreover, while it was highly educational for me to work with outstanding colleagues and be challenged by Bowie, who had both a pleasant personality and a brilliant inquiring mind, I soon came to wonder if we would make much policy difference. Formally we were all assigned to the Office of the Secretary, but I never saw Secretary Herter. Nor, as far as I could see, did Bowie meet often with Herter. Worse, what was originally said to be a brief period of temporary duty at the department lengthened into several months as Bowie backed and filled. After seemingly interminable discussions, Bob asked for papers on this and that and then for rewrite after rewrite All our work fit within the broad framework established early on by Bowie, but he also sent us to work on ideas hardly central to our task.

Soon I and the other Task Force members, drawn mainly from think tanks like the RAND Corporation, began referring to the operation as "Bowie's Seminar." Bob believed in the Socratic Method. Every morning before we drafted anything we were subjected to endless probing questions, starting with absolutely basic points. For example, we discussed for days what justification there was for economic assistance. Could aid programs be warranted as a moral imperative? Was there a moral reason for rich nations to help poorer nations? If so, which, in what circumstances? Or rather had there to be a strategic interest to justify economic assistance? Should aid be given to countries that needed it or be reserved for those that would make good use of it? Fascinating questions on which, as on questions of nuclear strategy and containment of the Soviet Union, among others, Bowie showed the searchlight of his intelligence, trying to guide us to a significant report.

Trouble was, as July turned into August there appeared to be no way to bring the discussions to a conclusion. Bob's deputy, Francis Williamson, a delightful, portly, fairly senior Foreign Service Officer, finally solved this problem. When he concluded Bowie would never be satisfied and the report would never be finished, he began one by one, on various pretexts, to send task force members back to their normal pursuits. Thanks to Francis, who also kindly commended my work, I returned to USEC and my family before the birth of Veronica Jean on September 14, 1960.

Angela, pregnant and over-taxed by four vigorous children, was not amused by my extended absence. Besides frantically calling for my return she kept me informed of Brussels gossip, of how much rain had fallen, lots, and of how the kids were doing. She also asked me to bring various things with me when I returned. Apparently she had not asked for a tent, since when I told her I had bought one she replied, "I was nearly as happy about the tent as I would have been had you purchased mountain climbing equipment...Maybe next spring I'll feel differently (Maybe not too!)" She did; we had a wonderful camping trip through Norway, a bit of Sweden, and Denmark. However, when I told her I had a chance to be assigned to Leopoldville, just then enveloped in the chaos of the Congo's drive for independence, she vetoed that possible move in a flat, uncompromising manner.

What did I do under Bowie's direction other than learn in his seminar?

I wrote papers.

Bowie clearly and correctly thought developing a strategic doctrine to replace the Dulles idea of "massive retaliation" was a critical priority. He also favored a NATO, not just a U.S. or UK, nuclear deterrent for which Europeans would share responsibility. But his mandate was a much broader one. Bowie was yet another admirer of Jean Monnet and had long been a steadfast supporter of NATO and European integration. Nevertheless he wanted to reexamine the assumptions underlying our policies toward the Communities, NATO, and the OEEC-OECD.

So I wrote a study of "Fundamental Assumptions Regarding Western Europe in the 1960s."

Another paper looked at the process, by then nearly complete, of turning the OEEC (Organization for European Economic Cooperation) into the OECD (Organization for Economic Cooperation and Development). The United States and Canada were joining the organization originally established to help allocate Marshall Plan assistance. In doing so, the focus of the organization was changing. In this context I wrote about the pros and cons of the U.S. joining the European Monetary Arrangement. We should not have, and we didn't. To my amazement, since I was certainly not qualified to do so, I was also asked to write about Atlantic scientific cooperation. While examining, in passing, science and monetary relations as possible foci for the OECD, Bowie clearly wanted the new organization to concentrate on coordinating macroeconomic policy and providing development assistance. Had he had his way, the Development Assistance Committee of the OECD would have been a leader in the entire assistance effort.

One of the few personal comments of approbation I earned from Bowie came for my observation that the key problem in coordinating economic policy in the OECD was that the U.S. Treasury and the Federal Reserve Board did not want to consult with anyone about our policies. I'm reasonably sure a strong recommendation that they do so was part of the final report.

Challenged by Bowie, I wrote a far-out paper proposing "a Supranational Development Authority" to be financed by a tax on electricity generation.

Bowie insisted, rightly, that any effective long-term planning exercise had to establish clear and realistic long-term objectives. His objectives were to contain Communism, integrate Western Europe, and modernize the less-developed world. In each case, he wanted in depth analysis of capabilities in order to be certain the stated goals could be achieved.

"The Challenge of the 1960s," written largely by Francis Williamson but in accord with an overall report outline Bowie formulated, was largely, but not entirely, defined as how to deal with the Soviet Union. Thus there was to be a chapter on the Communist threat, another on Western defense, and yet another on the responsibilities of the Atlantic nations in less developed areas. There were experts on our team for each of these subjects. The report saw Soviet activities in the Near East, the Congo, Laos, and Cuba as a new dimension of the threat Western countries had to counter. From his seminar comments and questions, I think Bowie understood the importance of the modernization process in the developing world, quite apart from the Soviet threat, but it was the Soviet dimension that provided much of the rationale for his decision to make Western assistance for development one of the three major challenges on which he focused.

As directed, I wrote a first draft of a paper on "The Capability of Atlantic and European Institutions to Meet the Challenge." Once again the issue of a possible Atlantic Free Trade Area arose, only this time I was an opponent, not a proponent. I successfully argued against on the ground that proposing such an arrangement, by antagonizing the six Community members would do more to split the West than to unite it. Since it was also clear American public opinion was not ready for such a step, the report merely mentioned an Atlantic Community as a possible long-range development.

I also did countless drafts of a paper on "Political Requirements for an Effective Response." The key point: the West had the capability to do the job, but had to muster the will.

My work with the group was certainly stimulating, but what did it contribute? Bowie, for his part, arranged for a writer to pull together an overall draft after his seminarists had departed. C[name] did not know much about the subject(s), but he had a fine literary style. So he and Bowie put together a final draft. Secretary Herter made if "close hold." Then the election of John F. Kennedy rather than Richard Nixon drastically discounted the significance of Bowie's effort. I do not know if the new Democratic administration even reviewed the Bowie Report. My own, not too persistent, attempt to obtain a copy of the final report failed. In writing to Henry Owen of the Policy Planning Staff in State, I complained that the secretary's decision to restrict circulation was "unfair to disorganized labor." More seriously it kept me from fulfilling a commitment to Ambassador Butterworth to get him a copy.

Someday I should read it.

Thinking about this exercise now, two things strike me.

The development problem was badly analyzed. The modernization process is much more complicated than we then realized. Bowie was right, however, to emphasize its importance. Vietnam, of course, took the wind out of American efforts to lead worldwide economic development efforts. Sadly, as I write the development problem is more critical to world stability and individual welfare than ever.

Bowie and the rest of us missed a politically astute presentation of Atlantic relations adopted by President Kennedy. "Partnership" between the European Community and the United States was a formulation with a public relations kick, notwithstanding the fact that Europe was far from capable of being a full partner. Moreover, the concept met Bowie's desire for a sound long range goal. Too bad we didn't come up with that one. Monnet had been urging it for some time. We were asleep.

When I finally returned to Brussels, Butterworth exploited my seminar training by having me write a speech about our European policy. He wanted to cover all the bases when talking to the International Business Conference. Consequently, the draft was longer than I thought it should be. Naturally the ambassador prevailed, but when delivered it became apparent to Walt that I had been right. He made cuts as he went along.

One day the ambassador called me into his office and to my consternation told me I was now USEC "protocol officer." The night before Hans Krekler, the Euratom Commissioner from Germany, had been offended by Butterworth's seating arrangement and had walked out of the ambassador's dinner. It struck me as good riddance of a pompous, bad-mannered man, but Butterworth was concerned. Henceforth I would prepare the seating plans for his dinners.

The rules of protocol, while scoffed at by many, are designed to facilitate relations between and within nations. When rules establishing relative rank among attendees are accepted and observed, for example at an international conference or dinner, social conversation and resolution of problems are facilitated.

Not knowing much about protocol, I consulted the embassy protocol officer and acquired the official Belgian government protocol list. My problem, however, was that not only did the three European Communities not fit in the Belgian scheme of things, but neither did NATO. By this time there were three American ambassadors stationed in Brussels heading three separate diplomatic missions. Matters were relatively simple if the U.S. ambassador to Belgium were hosting only Belgians, but what if European and NATO officials were also attending. What rules applied to a Belgian holding high rank in the Communities, for example Jean Frere, Secretary General of the European Bank? Eventually I worked out a chart resolving the obvious problems to my satisfaction. Apparently it also pleased Butterworth. At least no one thereafter walked out of his dinners in a huff.

I had nothing to do with it, but could not help being amused by reports from Washington that Commission President Hallstein's chief of staff, temporarily in Washington advancing an official visit by Hallstein, had proposed that when Hallstein drove to the White House to call on President Eisenhower his car should fly the flags of all six member states. I'm not sure, but I think our rejection of this absurd proposal hastened the decision to adopt a European Community flag.

Knowing my assignment to USEC was coming to an end, I prepared my 1960 Office Preference Report with more care than usual. After all there was some chance it might influence my future, although until then that had not happened. I still was fascinated by Africa and Angela was resigned, so I indicated interest in next serving there in a "program direction" position, with either State or the International Cooperation Administration (ICA). By 1963 I hoped to attend the National War College. Thereafter, I suggested I should be DCM of an embassy in Europe, the Near East, or Africa.

When my orders came I was to report to the National War College. I was delighted; Angela was ecstatic.

With the advent of the Kennedy administration in Washington, members of the new team began to visit. Among them was W. Michael Blumenthal, a dynamic and ambitious political appointee. He was assigned as a deputy assistant secretary of state in the Economics Bureau. When he visited USEC his interest was mainly in trade relations between the Common Market and the Associated States, an interest that fell in my area of responsibilities at USEC. At his request I provided him a paper and took him calling on the right European officials. He pushed hard for free non-discriminatory entry into Europe of tropical products, especially bananas. The expressed rationale was expanded trade as a means of helping developing economies. The American interest in selling bananas produced by our companies was not overlooked, but Mike downplayed it. He did not have much success in several visits to Brussels, but he was impressing senior people in Washington. President Kennedy had called for a new emphasis on the commodity trade of developing countries and soon Mike Blumenthal was negotiating an International Coffee Agreement. That our working relation might have something to do with my future never occurred to me.

Before heading off to the War College, a project I had carefully nurtured with the ambassador's approval moved to a decisive
stage. I had long advocated joint U.S.-European Community aid
projects. A proposal for extending the Transcameroun Railway
from Yaoundé to N'Gaoundéré, supported both by the French government and the European Commission but short of financing, was
brought to my attention by the Commission staff, as I recall it by my
good friend Jacques Van der Lee, a director for Overseas Development. To my gratification, our embassy in Yaoundé welcomed my
proposal that we help, Washington bought the idea, the Cameroun
government convened a mid-June negotiating session in Paris, and
I was ordered to join the U.S. delegation. Even better, as it happened I headed the delegation until the designated head of our delegation, a senior ICA official from Washington, belatedly arrived
in time to sign the completed agreement. There was, however, one
fly in the ointment. Even with each delegation stretching the limits
of its authorization to contribute, there was not enough funding.
Nevertheless, we decided to recommend to our governments that
we should do what we could. Thus, we produced an agreement for
extending the rail line to end in what a Cameroun official told us
was a swamp. To those who questioned our judgment, we replied
that inevitably, in a year or so our governments would recognize
the imperative need to complete the line. And so it happened.

Maybe my reporting on financial matters was more important,
but I drew immense satisfaction from having led our delegation
and from having stimulated a tri-part assistance effort. Lunch given
by Prime Minister Charles Assalé of the Cameroun Republic and
an exceptionally generous letter of appreciation of my efforts from
Ambassador Leland Barrows in Yaoundé were, for me, icing on the
cake.

I have only one regret about this project. The Transcameroun
Railway was famous for its dining car. Trust the French. Several
years later other official business precluded me from riding on the
inaugural train, where I'm told the French chef outdid himself.

USEC Brussels had been an ideal assignment. Our family had
grown with the arrival of Veronica; Joanna was happy in preschool;
and Deborah, Christopher, and Joe had been admitted to and benefited from the rigors of the European School, a remarkable joint
effort of the member states of the Communities. Angela had had
good help, at least most of the time. Indeed, Angela arranged for
her final helper, Helena Pitkanen, a fine Finnish lady, to join us in

Washington, assuming we could obtain a visa for her. When eventually the visa was approved, Nelson Sievering, a helpful atomic expert, arranged her travel on the *Nieuw Amsterdam* and we met her in Hoboken. Helena made life more or less bearable for Angela for the next few years. Eventually she married and became a U.S. citizen.

11

The National War College
(1961–1962)

The academic year I spent as a "student" at the National War College (NWC) was exhilarating, not demanding. In every sense it was a refreshing break from Foreign Service work.

The mission of the National War College is to "prepare future leaders of the Armed Forces, State Department, and other civilian agencies for high-level policy, command, and staff responsibilities by conducting a senior level course in the study of national security strategy."

Lt. General Francis Griswold, commandant of the War College, assured us early on that getting to know our colleagues in other services was also an important part of the year. He predicted we would make many lasting friendships and useful professional contacts. To a limited degree he was right.

To this end we were forced into making the acquaintance of each and every class member. The military, as the military is wont to do, organized everything. Maybe over-organized our activities. In any case, each month we were shifted into a different discussion group. Periodically we were expected to host a social get together of our group members and their wives. On balance this was a good thing, but the transitory nature of the relations developed each month and over the year as a whole did not really promote many lasting friendships. In later years as I toiled in the economic fields, encounters with military colleagues whose acquaintance I had made at the NWC were few and far between.

Nevertheless, whatever I learned about national strategy paled beside what I learned of our military colleagues. They, like the Foreign and Civil Service civilians in attendance, were generally outstanding individuals. Of course, as in any group of over two hundred persons, there were goof-offs, dumbbells, and clowns. By and large, however, the class, chosen from officers considered likely to reach flag rank, was impressive.

Particularly impressive for me were many of the Naval officers in the class. Perhaps I judged them as I did because I am an introverted, analytical type. I concluded that where it existed, the intellectual superiority of sailors was attributable to the fact that they had lots of time at sea to read widely. In any case, as we argued about issues in the discussion groups they struck me as more thoughtful and better informed on average than our Army, and especially our Air Force types. That Jim Holloway and Bud Zumwalt rose to the top of the Navy as chiefs of naval operations and Jim Calvert became commandant at Annapolis tends to support my judgment.

Naturally I knew more of the civilians and had more to do with them afterwards. Except for one business conversation in 1980, I think, with Admiral Zumwalt on a subject I can no longer recall, and participation in the mid-1970s in a NATO war game at Garmisch-Partenkirchen with General Lou Wilson, the class' sole Medal of Honor holder, I can recall no official relations with any of my Armed Service colleagues after our class disbanded. Attempts to keep up by exchanging Christmas greetings and attending NWC lunches at the Ft. McNair Officers' Club bit by bit became rarer and rarer.

That said, I think close exposure to our military helped me deal with various senior officers in later days when I served as an ambassador. Certainly my credentials as a War College graduate did not hurt my standing in the eyes of the generals and admirals with whom I dealt.

Home from Brussels, for once we had a fairly extensive home leave before reporting for duty. We moved in with my folks, who when they had built their house in Manor Club outside of Washington had provided lots of room for us and their grandchildren. It was an ideal base for house-hunting which was our initial major preoccupation, since our house on Rannock Road was by now nowhere near large enough for our family. The search was time consuming and frustrating, but one Sunday we saw a house at 6025 on Dellwood Place in Bethesda with a tennis court in the next lot that looked like it would do nicely. However, it was way above our budget. By coincidence, Howard and Gail Furnas, old friends from Paris days, lived on the same block. Howard encouraged us to make an offer, pointing out that the tennis court owner was a good guy who welcomed his neighbors using his court. So we took the plunge. How could I resist a tennis court? To our surprise, our not-too-generous offer was accepted, probably because the house had been on the market a long time. Moreover, fall was upon us; with winter coming up, not the best time to sell a house. We never had occasion to regret our good fortune. Stanley and Judy Frosh, owners of the tennis court, are good friends to this day. Howard decided he would rather play tennis and ski than continue working at the State Department, so he and Gail Furnas retired early and went on to New England. We kept in touch for years, but sadly no longer.

At the NWC I was one of the younger class members. To my recollection, none of the military class members and only Arv Kramish of the Defense Department and Ed Strait of the Bureau of the Budget were younger than I. I still see Arv, who now lives in Chapel Hill, and Ed was a friendly colleague during my White House years. In my class I had one old friend, Herman Klein, with whom I roomed on trips until his snoring became unbearable. Herman had been a back stopper to those of us who worked on French economic problems during my days in Paris. Later he was a most helpful friend in many roles in AID, rising to a top job as coordinator for the Alliance for Progress. Others in the class whom I knew, if not well, from previous assignments included: Tom Dunnigan, a German expert whom I had known when we were both in the Junior Officer training program in 1946; Findley Bums, an ace administrator who retired as an ambassador; and Hermann Eilts, whom I had known as an Arab language student studying in Beirut with my esteemed friend Fergie Ferguson, and who would go on to be an outstanding ambassador to Egypt and authority on the Middle East as a professor at Boston University. Classmates of whom I saw a fair amount in later years included: Ed Nickel and Dan Oleksiw of USIA; Bob Simpson from Commerce; Dick Sneider, a Japan expert who was a key negotiator of the arrangement that returned Okinawa to Japan and with whom I worked in 1972 on Japanese economic problems; John Stutesman, who was occasionally helpful to me during his service on the executive Secretariat of the Department of State; Bob Stevenson, who turned up again as an ambassadorial colleague in Africa; and Frank Devine, who as a former ambassador to El Salvador gave me good advice before I went to his old job.

Life at the NWC was mostly relaxed. Competitive sports, our class members vs. the class members of the Industrial War College, were taken as seriously as anything. Assigned reading lists were substantial, but nothing like at the Fletcher School or the University of Chicago. I enjoyed reading--far beyond the assigned material. It was great to have the time to do so. A typical day started with a lecture by an academic authority or senior member of the administration, followed by a break for athletics, either inter-school competition or friendly games of touch football, softball, volleyball, golf, or bowling, then lunch, sometimes with the morning1ecturer and discussion group session in the afternoon, finishing in time to go to the Officers' Club for a drink or go home early. Each of us was expected to do a research paper for the year. Only in bowling, where I won a couple of trophies, did I excel.

I have virtually no memories of our lectures. I do recall that quite understandably, with President Kennedy facing off with Khrushchev and the Cold War appearing to be warming up, our readings and lectures concentrated on communism and the Sino-Soviet bloc. There were a few hints that maybe there were important differences between the Soviets and the Chinese, but these were only passing bows to that possibility. Henry Kissinger lectured and the pre-lecture buzz was to the effect that he was terrific. However, he talked so fast and with such a heavy German accent that I gave up and tuned him out early on: so much for my first exposure to Henry.

The program also provided for much travel, for example to Fort Bragg to observe a parachute attack, to Camp Lejeune to watch a landing by Marines, to air bases in the West, and to a carrier task force at sea. While in the hands of the Air Force in Omaha we were scheduled to see missile silos, but someone goofed and when our bus arrived out in the boonies there were no missiles, only an electrical generator. Our Air Force colleagues never quite recovered from the ribbing they took about that generator!

The most eagerly awaited and memorable travel was a three-week overseas area familiarization trip. Since I had never been to the Far East, I asked for and was assigned to that tour: Washington - Honolulu - Sydney, Australia - Canberra, Australia - Darwin, Australia - Rangoon, Burma - Bangkok, Thailand - Saigon, Vietnam - Manila, The Philippines - Taipei, Formosa – Okinawa - British Hong Kong - Seoul, Korea - Tokyo, Japan - Anchorage, Alaska - Washington. On March 22 we flew to Hawaii. A long haul to Sydney, Australia, was next.

Everywhere we were exposed to excruciating briefings about the organization of the host nation's armed forces. It was a problem to stay awake, but we were expected to be intensely interested.

Maybe some of us were, but if so they were few indeed. Our leader, a one-star general, had a major on his staff whose assignment was to poke him in the ribs when he started to nod off--fairly frequent--or when it came his time to reply with effusive appreciation for "the outstanding briefing."

Apart from the briefings we had a marvelous time. Hospitality never failed; at times such as a dinner at the Taiwanese Defense College it was dangerous, involving as it did endless toasts, *Gam Beis*, with a potent brew. Whoever was toasted had to stand and drink "bottoms up." Clearly our hosts, who outnumbered us about nine to three per table, were going to knock some of us out of action. At my table my classmates and I devised a counterstrategy. We concentrated our Gam Beis on a couple of older Chinese officers. They amazed us with their resistance, but eventually, before any of us passed out, we had scored two decisive wins. Our honor was preserved!

Australia and the exuberant Aussies made our visit particularly pleasant.

Rangoon was next. Run down and dirty, redeemed only by beautiful Buddhist pagodas, it was the only city on our itinerary to which I have no desire to return. Some of my colleagues were enchanted by the Burmese women and the spell of Kipling, but not me. The Mongolian stew pot dinner served was not an appetizing meal by my standards. Then I had a memorable haircut in the Imperial Hotel. As the barber finished, without warning me or asking, he twisted my head violently first one way then the other. Somehow no lasting damage was done, but I resolved then and there never to return to Rangoon. That resolve was fortified the next day. We were told early in the day no one had signed up for a swim sponsored by the Burmese Army in their Olympic pool, of which they were exceedingly proud, and that volunteers were needed or U.S.-Burmese relations would suffer grievous damage. Out of patriotism or sheer stupidity I joined Marine Colonel Gordon West in volunteering. We arrived about midday to find our hosts seated in the shade of the grandstand. However, they showed us where we could change and urged us to enjoy ourselves in their "Olympic Pool." Gordon and I, suffering from heat of over a hundred degrees Fahrenheit, dove in only to discover the water was too warm to be refreshing and the peculiar floats we had seen in the water were turds. We paddled a bit, had a fruit juice with our hosts, complimented them on their pool, declined lunch, and got the hell out of there. The rest of our class enjoyed a picnic on the green grass at a yacht club on a pretty lake, where, we were told, the girl-watching was incredible.

We were flying in a 707 air to air tanker converted with enough canvas seats for the passenger list. As a result, while we went places we could not see a thing from the air. Going into Bangkok, we sensed we were slowing on final approach when suddenly our pilot poured on full power and yanked the plane up. Unnerving. However, we went around and landed safely. We were told a Thai fighter had cut in under us to land ahead, but had we not gone around our plane would have overtaken the fighter on the runway with deadly results. Once down, we discovered Bangkok was a beautiful and fascinating city. The Royal Palace compound, the canals, the markets teeming with life, the food all made the boring briefings bearable. Also, under peer pressure I discovered something new to a boy brought up with Puritanical values. I went with my buddies to a massage parlor, where at least sexual release was safe. But my conscience troubled me. Not enough, however, to tell Angela about the experience.

Saigon was next. Fascinating place, bustling with life and the ranch influence still evident in some architecture, some food, and many chic young Vietnamese. Here the briefings were given mainly by the U.S. Mil Group. They sounded confident and gung ho about the war. I with some others volunteered for an observation flight over part of the highlands and much of the delta. From our old Douglas DC-3 we saw miles and miles of green rice paddies. Although we flew low, we drew no fire. Still it was clear that if the Viet Cong were hiding below us, they would be mighty hard to root out.

Taiwan, site of the memorable dinner with our hard drinking Chinese hosts, followed. Part of our visit involved a flight to Quemoy, of Quemoy Matsu fame from the Nixon-Kennedy debates and many exchanges of artillery fire with the mainland. Here, in addition to observing the fortifications I got my first glimpse of Communist China.

Okinawa, still occupied by U.S. forces, was next. From here I took away lots of stamps, but missed one that became a rarity. Maybe someday I'll find it at an affordable price.

From Okinawa we flew to Hong Kong, naturally for shopping, as well as for a first rate briefing by the American consul general, our number one China watcher.

Then Seoul, where I was fortunate enough to have dinner at

Political Counselor Phil Habib's residence. Phil also had a fine selection of up and coming Koreans as guests. They added spice to
the evening, but getting to know him was the real treat. I'll have
more to say about experiences with Phil in later years, but for now
let me just note he was an exceptionally able Foreign Service officer
who made a great contribution to our country.

After Seoul we visited Tokyo. And then stopped in Anchorage,
Alaska, where we had a fabulous meal at the air base Officers' Club
of fresh salmon, crab legs, and wild game of all sorts: bear, moose,
elk, duck, goose; you name it, it was available. The next day, April
14, we were back home.

With the Asian trip behind me, it was time to turn to two priority projects. The War College expected me to write a research paper
and I expected a good assignment. Silly boy that I was, I focused
both efforts on Africa. The subject of my paper, duly approved by
the NWC faculty, was "The Strategic and Political Importance of
West Africa and United States Policy Relating Thereto." My efforts toward getting a "career enhancing" onward assignment, also
driven by my unredeemed interest in Africa, no doubt enhanced
by President Kennedy's policy decision to give Africa more importance in our foreign policy, got me what I thought was a lock on the
DCM position in Mogadishu, Somalia, and a reasonable chance at
DCM in Algiers, Algeria.

It was not to be. Mike Blumenthal was looking for staff to help
him invigorate commodity policy. He not only maneuvered my assignment to his part of the Bureau of Economic Affairs, but he also
broke me out of the NWC before graduation. I was furious at not
being able to graduate with my War College colleagues. Worse, I
actually cried when I was informed of my future role as "Chief of
the Commodity Policy Division." Once again, however, the system,
such as it was, had done me a favor. The commodity job under Blumenthal was challenging and important. It also proved to be more
"career enhancing" than any job in Africa would have been. Moreover, the trip I was to make with Willard Cochrane, the Department
of Agriculture's head agricultural economist, besides taking me to
Rome, Athens, Paris, and London, where we were treated as V.I.P.s,
placed me close to the center of the agricultural policy issues that
were to so complicate the Kennedy Round of Multilateral Trade
Negotiations.

The summary of my research paper answered the question:
"What is the strategic importance of West Africa?" as follows: "Not

much, relative to other areas, e.g. Europe and the Middle East, particularly in an era of thermonuclear weapons." I saw some "political importance" to an area containing eighteen U.N. members. However, I noted these states "are artificial, inchoate, noncohesive, basically tribal societies suffering from intense transitional instabilities induced by urbanization, commercialization, and technological change." As for policy prescriptions, I stressed that while we should aim to help develop stable, effective, and democratic societies, we would not reach these objectives "in this century." Forty years later, that judgment stands up. Nevertheless, I argued for "an effective American presence and growing economic assistance, aimed both at "nation building" and at U.S. political influence." However, "we must encourage the French, the British, and the European Economic Community to strengthen their presently paramount position."

Clearly, I thought an activist role was appropriate for U.S. officials. I wrote:

> What is needed now and will be needed for a considerable time to come is a U.S. capability to intervene without the appearance of intervention. Indeed, perhaps the most compelling reason for U.S. economic assistance in West Africa will prove to be the entree and leverage which it can give the astute American diplomat.

While "nation building" is currently out of favor, I remain convinced that I was right in my views, both about its importance in the developing world and the necessity for U.S. diplomats to have the tools for astute quiet influence on the process.

12

Commodity Policy (1962–1963)

The Kennedy administration gave a new prominence to economic development. Whether from its philosophical links to liberal idealism or from a realistic concern to strengthen the Western Hemisphere against the lure and subversive activism of Cuba's Fidel Castro—probably a bit of both—the proclamation of the Alliance for Progress put development issues front and center. With the Alliance came a strikingly new commitment to reduce the ravages of unfavorable terms of trade in Latin America, often traceable to undue dependence on volatile exports of primary commodities. Chief among these was, of course, coffee. Coffee prices were critical to the economies of Brazil, Colombia, and the Central American countries.

If coffee, the second most widely traded world commodity after petroleum, was key to the Kennedy administration's approach to try to stabilize commodity earnings, the new administration's commodity policy also concerned itself with problems, each and every one different, in the cocoa, tin, rubber, tea, oil seed, and banana markets. In a broader approach, it also pushed for a compensatory financing scheme in the International Monetary Fund. The latter initiative, which made more sense and had fewer problems than traditional commodity agreements, albeit not problem free, yielded results a few years down the pike.

Placed in day to day charge of this effort to help Latin America and developing countries in general was Deputy Assistant Secretary of State Mike Blumenthal. Aggressive, dynamic, and highly ambitious, Mike set out to make a name for himself. His first priority was to negotiate an International Coffee Agreement. Indeed by the time I was pressed onto his team, he was close to success with coffee. I was to work on other commodities. In fact, his successful effort to spring me from the War College before my graduation was based on his desire to involve me in the GATT work on tropical products. After a baptism of fire during four days in Geneva, I was sent to represent the State Department on the Cochrane Mission, tasked to study the effect of the European Common Market's emerging agricultural policy on American agricultural interests.

Membership in Cochrane's Mission was a splendid introduction to world agricultural trade problems. Ironically, during my three years at our Mission to the European Communities the only subject I did not work on was agriculture. It was in the capable hands of Oscar Zaglitz, whom I would soon be consulting regularly.

Willard Cochrane, a University of Minnesota professor before he joined the Kennedy administration in a senior job with Secretary Orville Freeman in the Department of Agriculture, was a superb teacher. He knew how to pose the right questions to our interlocutors wherever we went. Moreover, he encouraged his team members to participate in the discussions. If this were not enough, the Mission, which had already visited Paris, Brussels, and Geneva, also gave me a chance to enjoy the sights and restaurants of Rome, Athens, and London while partaking, such as it was, of the wisdom of our hosts, who memorably included Papandreou in Athens and a host of knowledgeable experts at the Food and Agricultural Organization (FAO) in Rome. I also got to know Les Brown, then agricultural attaché in Rome, later world famous for his study of environmental dangers, and his helpful secretary, as well as my after-hours tour guide, Mollie Iler

Papandreou, then minister of planning in the Greek government, had been a professor at UCLA and would eventually become a rabidly anti-American leftist prime minister of Greece. I found him impressive. I might have thought otherwise of him had we discussed politics, East-West issues, or NATO, but we didn't. He concealed his anti-Americanism from us. His leftist views concerning agriculture did not shock. Willard was a believer himself in a state managed farm policy. Moreover, for better or worse all of the major powers pursued, and still pursue, highly interventionist government support policies for their agricultural sectors. There are bad reasons for this: politics. There are also good economic reasons having to do with price elasticities and price inelasticities. Unfortunately, with many primary commodities production responses to market changes are slow to take place. Critically, a surplus in the market pushes prices down much more rapidly than consumption increases. Hence the popularity of price support schemes.

Cochrane was an extreme advocate of government market intervention. He was the prime architect of Kennedy administration proposals to Congress for new agricultural legislation. They were being debated as we toured Europe. To his great distress, many of his ideas were rejected. It was clear to me that soon he would return to academia, but first I enjoyed his company and probed his wisdom. Clearly he was leading our Mission to conclude that a worldwide grains agreement was needed if our wheat and feed grain exports were not to suffer grievously from the emerging Common Agricultural Policy of the European Community. And clearly the key provisions in such an agreement would relate to price.

Before joining the Cochrane Mission I had had my baptism in multilateral diplomacy at the meeting in Geneva of the "Special Group on Tropical Products." I was excited and proud to represent the United States, but destined for frustration and disappointment. To my amazement, positions were all over the map with few signs of constructive results likely to emerge. The Nigerians were at least straightforward, calling for elimination of all restrictions on trade in tropical products. Unfortunately their proposal had about as much chance of success as the proverbial snowball in hell. As it became clearer that agreement was nowhere near, the Special Group resorted to a dodge familiar to more experienced negotiators, but one I viewed as pointless. We agreed to form a working party! Then the Group broke apart over the working party's terms of reference. One issue: per my instructions I sought to include bananas in the list of products to be considered. The French, British, and Italians objected. Compromise: delete the product list, leaving the U.S. free to pursue bananas and others free to say they had not agreed!

A major motivation of the United States in its attempts to liberalize trade in tropical products was our concern over likely adverse effects on Latin American producers of preferential trading relations enshrined in the European Communities' Agreements with its Associated Countries and Territories and, as the United Kingdom negotiated for entry into the Common Market, fear that Imperial Preferences would be merged in the Community system. That the UK negotiations were ongoing and the Community was in the process of renegotiating its agreements lent urgency to our efforts while making it much harder to achieve results.

As we were nearing the end of the Special Group session, one meeting illustrated the complexity and difficulty of the entire effort. M. Janton, the senior French representative, purported to support the idea, but observed it was the firm policy of his government not to engage in any activity that conceivably could compromise the ongoing EEC-AOC negotiations. Herr Schoeller of the European Commission also purported to like the idea, but thought the Commission was too short of competent people to participate. Mr. Rich from the UK Foreign Office agreed careful preparatory work would be needed, since the Working Group would include the Indians, Ceylonese, Nigerians, and Indonesians, to say nothing of the Brazilians, all of whom he thought had so far contributed little other than confusion. The British almost always welcome consultation, especially if the U.S. seeks it, but that does not mean they will support our substantive views. Finally, I talked at length with Finn Gundelach, the deputy executive secretary of GATT, who had a vested interest in progress, and showed it. Eric Wyndham White, the astute Executive Secretary of GATT, totally immersed in preparations for a multilateral round of trade negotiations, had delegated responsibility for tropical products, a side show in the bigger effort, to Finn. Sadly, despite his and my continuing efforts almost nothing came of them.

Back in Washington, preparations for what came to be known as the Kennedy Round of trade negotiations were heating up. The Department of Agriculture (USDA) had circulated a tariff quota proposal. I was asked to analyze it. I declared it simply was" not feasible." Although if achieved it would have benefited U.S. farmers, it had less chance of being negotiated than the Nigerian proposal I had dealt with in Geneva. USDA proposed to negotiate import entitlements for third countries into EC member states. Not only would such member state import obligations be the total antithesis of the concept of a unified European Community, but to make quotas effective in Germany, for example, U.S. wheat would enjoy a price preference compared to French wheat!

USDA's ideas quite properly horrified Under Secretary George Ball and Assistant Secretary for Economics Griffith Johnson. Their strongly expressed political view won for State the first of many skirmishes over agricultural policy in the Kennedy Round.

It was easy enough to shoot holes in USDA's ideas, but an alternative approach was needed. I argued price was the key to market access in Europe. I wrote, "Reasonable grain prices mean a difficult situation." High EC prices mean "an almost impossible situation of rapidly contracting markets."

"A low wheat price" would restrain an increase in European production, while a "low feed grain/wheat price ratio" would maximize the market for U.S. coarse grains. The analysis was, I was sure from my talks with Willard Cochrane, correct. Could we, however, find an effective way to negotiate prices? Would we be prepared to put U.S. support prices on the table? I was not certain, but I argued we should explore the "oft-expressed French interest in a world grains agreement."

George Ball agreed in talks with Australia's prime minister Robert Menzies to explore "commodity arrangements." On June 26, 1962, he instructed Blumenthal "to give the highest priority to establishing a dear-cut U.S. proposal." I chaired a three man task force trying to respond. The more we dug into the matter, the more complicated it became, but we came up with an agreed proposal commended by our leaders and we were in business. Ball had what he needed to initiate talks with Secretary of Agriculture Freeman and Under Secretary Murphy. Willard Cochrane, kept informed by me, could be counted upon, within limits, to help.

Mike instructed me to press forward with discussions, really negotiations, with key staff in the Department of Agriculture. Irwin Hedges, a tough, knowledgeable, if overly emotional, agricultural economist was named to head the USDA team. We did remarkably well, and the resulting "Hedges-Hinton Agreement On Grains" became the starting point for unending future arguments over agriculture in the Kennedy Round of trade negotiations.

The agreed statement of "Objectives" made clear our political interests as well as our trade interests. We were "To preserve, insofar as possible, access for traditional Free World supplies of grains to the enlarged EEC market" and "To facilitate U.K. entry into the EEC on reasonable terms." Also we were "To facilitate Commonwealth acquiescence in U.K. entry into the EEC by focusing attention of all third world countries on satisfactory long run access arrangements" while protecting "specific United States agricultural export interests."

The magic formula to accomplish all this was succinctly stated in Para II: "Means: Achievement of low EEC domestic price policies (intervention prices) is the key to both interim and long-range access to the EEC market by grain exporters."

There was much more, including a number of technical points where either Irwin or I reserved our respective positions. As we will see, it mattered not; the EEC would dominate the course of negotiations, basically stalling us, while doing what the Member

States believed was necessary to promote political unification by establishment of a common agricultural policy.

Nevertheless, with basic State-Agriculture agreement achieved, Mike decided to send me to head a U.S. Observer Delegation to a meeting in Lagos, Nigeria, of the Economic Commission for Africa, a United Nations institution, on commodity price stabilization. Whether this was to compensate for his having frustrated my desire to return to Africa or, as he said, because he attached importance to having our perspective on commodity problems explained to African countries, I do not know. But I welcomed the assignment despite my suspicion the players were not all that influential. In fact, some invited member countries of the Commission did not show, and South Africa, despised in "Black Africa" for its apartheid policies, was not invited despite being a Commission member.

Whatever the case, I had a ball, marred considerably when Pan American misdirected my suitcase, leaving me in steaming Lagos for several days before I had a chance to buy a clean shirt. The meeting gave me an opportunity to see teeming, stinking Lagos, breakfast with Ambassador Joseph Palmer, and, at the invitation of the other member of my delegation, Agricultural Attaché John A. Wenmohs, visit Ibadan, the new capital of Nigeria. The trip impressed me primarily with the incredible number of wrecks along the road from Lagos to Ibadan, powerful evidence of reckless driving habits by Nigerians.

The Conference itself provided some insights into African thinking and relations with European countries, some of which, together with the European Commission, were also observers or even present as members of African delegations. Indeed Uganda and Kenya were represented only by Europeans.

Discussion of existing commodity marketing boards and Caisses de Stabilization was of high quality. However, when UN and FAO officials outlined plans for an international compensatory finance mechanism, African Conference participants, invited to react, were literally speechless. This as well as some ill-informed hostility toward American proposals in GATT concerning tropical products led me to conclude that once all others had had their say I should make a statement outlining our commodity policies. It was well received, but naturally had no impact on history. Still I was proud to be able to speak about United States policy. I was more successful privately in inspiring the deletion of some nonsense in the Conference final report, not that that mattered either. Both in my statement and privately I tried, pursuant to my written instruction, "to win support, particularly among those African states associated with the European Economic Community, for the development of positive alternatives, which would include price stabilization measures, to the system of EEC-AOC preferential trading." My audience was interested in what I had to say, but I won no new converts to the cause.

On the way home, I had an unscheduled bus tour of Accra, Ghana while our Pan Am pilots personally repaired a faulty hydraulic line. Then I spent two interesting days in Dakar exploring Senegalese thinking about an African Ground Nuts (peanuts in our terminology) Council backed by Nigeria, intended to exercise supranational authority over export quantities and prices. Apart from obvious political difficulties, it struck me that the plan had little future given the high degree of substitutability in vegetable oil markets.

Peanuts in the United States, of course, were highly subsidized and our market was protected by import quotas. It still is! Thus our drive for free trade in tropical products was marred by considerable hypocrisy on our part.

Back in Washington I was submerged in a mishmash of odd jobs mostly related to preparations for what became the Kennedy Round of Trade Negotiations. Examples:

At Mike Blumenthal's request, I spent some time reviewing the status of British efforts to negotiate membership in the EEC, writing a memorandum for him on the subject.

A briefing paper for Secretary of State Dean Rusk, recognizing that countries in the French franc area often judged our proposals as an attack on the alleged advantages they enjoyed as the result of preferential tariffs, provided arguments intended to counter this view, including the promise that adjustment measures to provide at least equivalent benefits should accompany the phasing out of preferences. This argument, pursued subsequently and consistently by many American administrations, was a hard sell.

I did a letter delivered by our embassy in Dakar to the senior official responsible for Senegal's agricultural marketing efforts commenting on the evident infeasibility, to the U.S. at least, of his proposal for a multi-commodity compensation scheme and trying nevertheless to engage his help with his government's attitude toward our efforts in the GATT.

Another memo advanced ideas about a possible International Cocoa Agreement.

Drafts Mike considerably improved turned into Blumenthal speeches on commodity policy given to the U.N. Committee on Commodity Trade and business groups.

I wrote a memo requested by another deputy assistant secretary for economics on the likely effects of the European Common Market on a range of agricultural products including grains, cotton, wool, and soy beans.

Various of my seniors, principally Isaiah Frank, involved me in preparations for the upcoming U.N. Trade and Development Conference, including the drafting of some instructions, which meant I got to know an expanded list of individuals, notably including Lincoln Gordon.

My central concerns remained, however, grains and tropical products. In both cases, preparations for negotiations were partly in and partly out of the GATT.

Since the rationale for eliminating restrictions on trade in tropical products was to assist developing countries, it was decided to raise the issue in the Development Assistance Committee of the OECD. Accordingly, I drafted a statement for our representative, Frank Coffin, calling inter alia for OECD support for GATT efforts to expand developing country export earnings. This simple and sensible proposal ran into a buzz saw of opposition. While the GATT secretary general, Wyndham White, paid lip service to the idea, as did senior officials of the OECD, their staffs, certainly with the knowledge of their bosses, blocked almost all efforts. Finn Gundelach, Wyndham White's deputy, at least was clear that he did not want the OECD mucking about in trade issues. In Paris, there were similar fears GATT would move further into issues involving development assistance. Bureaucratic turf protection was more important to many than helping the least developed countries (LDCs). The thought that the two secretariats might cooperate at least to prepare country studies that would highlight the importance for many LDCs of trade in tropical products was consistently pushed by U.S. representatives in Geneva, Paris, and concerned capitals, but results were hardly perceptible. GATT did do a few country studies, but cooperation with the OECD was minimal.

Under Secretary Ball wanted, nevertheless, to pursue the idea of synergy between trade and aid. Consequently, as the annual OECD Ministerial Meeting approached, I and a cast including members of State's Policy Planning Staff and officials of the Council of Economic Advisors, Treasury, Commerce, and Agriculture developed a proposal on the relation of trade, aid, and economic growth. An OECD Ministerial communiqué incorporated some results, but in language so general as to be nothing more than rhetorical exhortation.

Having reached agreement with the Department of Agriculture on a basic starting position, the next step was to try to work out a consensus with other major producers of grains. Mike sent me to Ottawa, heading, in effect, a seven man delegation including individuals from our Bureau of European Affairs, other parts of the Bureau of Economic Affairs, and members of our embassy. The U.S. Department of Agriculture was represented by their attaché in Ottawa, a sign perhaps that USDA did not attach much importance to the talks. The Canadians did. They fielded a large, strong team, sixteen officials in all, and including Jake Warren, Swartzmann, their economic minister in Washington, and Simon Reisman, whom I would get to know well in the years to come.

The Canadians while indicating a desire to work out a common exporter position were hardnosed about the details, asserting rightly that Canada was the biggest economic supplier to the European market. They were skeptical about commodity agreements in general, dug in deeply in opposition to market-sharing provisions although agreeing producer prices were critical , and were worried by our tentative ideas about surplus disposal. Clearly Canada's basic approach was far different from that of Australia.

Bilaterals with Argentina, handled by Mike, followed. They were much more supportive of our ideas provided we would help them maintain access to the European market for meat.

Next I was sent to represent the U.S. at the GATT Subgroup on Tropical Products, enjoying consultations in London, Paris, and Brussels (with the EEC) en route. As a bonus, I watched Ball speak to the OECD Ministerial. I was fascinated to note that, entirely without staff preparation, he added to his cleared remarks comments on the prospective U.N. Development Conference, suggesting investment guarantees be considered. Oh, with cabinet or sub-cabinet rank one can do so much more!

Agriculture Secretary Orville Freeman, speaking to an OECD meeting of his colleagues, had also used his Cabinet level prerogatives to blast the Common Agriculture policy of the European Community. He thought it was all illegal: contrary to GATT rules. My interlocutors were almost as strident in pointing out that he risked both driving the Community away from a willingness to negotiate and further complicating EEC-UK negotiations, a

Kennedy administration priority. Freeman's remarks played well to our domestic farm community, but at their worst, hinting at broad scale retaliation against the EEC, they threatened to torpedo chances for the administration to liberalize trade as envisaged by the Trade Expansion Act. George Ball, back in Washington, advised Agriculture that except where we were on strong legal grounds, specifically GATT Article XXIII cases, talk of retaliation was self-defeating.

I made virtually no progress at the three day GATT subgroup meeting on tropical products since the EEC reserved its position on all points, citing continuing negotiations with Associated Overseas Countries as well as the absence of representatives of the latter. It was tentatively agreed to try again in early 1963.

Grains were front and center back in Washington. Jake Warren led a Canadian delegation; Mike chaired our team. The Canadians had largely listened in Ottawa; this time they presented their considered ideas and we largely listened. While they now seemed favorably disposed to a global agreement and agreed to efforts to reach a common exporter position, they also urged pushing for an interim agreement possibly including an EEC price freeze, no new measures impairing imports, and quantitative remedies.

Agriculture lost no time in letting us know they liked the Canadian ideas about "interim" measures. At the same time, the new Special Trade Representative's Office (STR) was coming to life, led by ex-Secretary of State Christian Herter. Herter's deputy, William Gossett, echoed Agriculture's hard line about the EU's Common Agricultural Policy (CAP). The Washington negotiation over what positions to take with the EEC was taking a new turn, one that I found discouraging.

Joe Greenwald, our economic minister in London, who had accompanied me to my consultations with the British, wrote perplexed to ask what was going on. Since it was hard, if not impossible, to send agreed instructions while arguments raged in Washington, I wrote Joe that we "have had to give ground on the substance of our position in exchange for Agriculture's hard won agreement not to declare war on the EEC about gains until after the (GATT) Ministerial".

In the circumstances, cooperating with Hedges I drafted a "Joint State-Agriculture" telegram to our posts asking a lot of questions. We in State thought we knew the answers, but Agriculture was not prepared to accept our answers. After analysis, the replies helped underpin a meeting to sort matters out between Governor Herter, Secretary Freeman, and George Ball. They decided not to call for a meeting of the GATT Cereals Group before the scheduled May GATT Ministerial. They also agreed we should proceed promptly to a multilateral exporters' meeting. Accordingly, I drafted and circulated to STR and Agriculture the "United States Proposal to Argentina, Australia, and Canada for a Concerted Exporter Position on Grains." Basically, it was the same proposal for a grains agreement we in State had been backing for months, but with some tactical add-ons flowing from previous rounds of consultations and the guidance of our leaders.

On a lighter note, or as I called it in a memo, a "ridiculous" note, some bureaucrat for the nth time rejected my position description, demanding a rewrite to excise a sentence that had survived three previous reviews! Mike had assured me my job would involve "commodity policy" as it did, in fact, but those in charge of titles correctly had pointed out there were already many parts of State, starting with the Policy Planning Staff, using the term "policy." OK, we could not argue with that. To describe my small unit we came up with the meaningless term "Commodity Programming Division," not that we programmed any commodities. This designation was accepted upstairs, but then the anonymous reviewers of position descriptions quibbled over this and that. Exasperated, I urged our senior administrative officer, the famous Frances Wilson, either to submit it once again unchanged or rewrite it any way she wished that would satisfy the position clerks. It had taken over six months, but I heard no more about this bureaucratic foolishness.

Instead I was sent to represent the Economic Bureau at a meeting of our Central American chiefs of mission in San Salvador. My friend from touch football days in Paris, Ed Martin, now assistant secretary of state for Latin America, had called the meeting to prepare for President Kennedy's scheduled visit to Central America. This welcome break from grains and position descriptions required me to get up to date on other issues, particularly compensatory finance and coffee. It also introduced me to many officers who would become good friends and colleagues in later years, principally Ray Sternfeld and Olie Sause. I enjoyed myself and was impressed by the personal warmth of those Salvadorans I met, including one who showed me the city and took me to his humble home for a coffee. It never occurred to me that eighteen years later during a horrific civil war I would return to serve as ambassador to El Salvador.

The 1963 promotion list buoyed my morale. Not yet forty years old, I was promoted to FS0-2, a senior grade. An extra bonus that year was that President John F. Kennedy received all promotees in the Rose Garden. His remarks made us all feel even better about the Foreign Service.

While I remained a division chief working on commodity problems, at least they had become hot button issues. Ed Fried and John Pincus of State's Policy Planning Council were pushing hard for adoption of "irrational" methods to increase developing country foreign exchange receipts. With the U.N. Conference on Trade and Development looming, they and Jack Tuthill, our ambassador to the OECD, argued that the mere willingness of the United States to negotiate "fairer" commodity prices would pay substantial political dividends. Analytical work was stepped up on coffee, cocoa, and tea and expanded to include studies of sugar, cotton, as well as some metals, and new impetus was given to compensatory finance. Eventually the IMF adopted a compensatory scheme; otherwise, nothing much came of all this. Even with a coffee agreement in place, opposition among producers to mechanisms to restrict supply in order to raise prices, to say nothing of American coffee consuming interests, was fierce. "Irrational" measures simply have little appeal once they are subject to intense scrutiny.

In late February of 1963, the Special Trade Representative circulated a "Position Paper on Basic Issues Concerning Tariff Negotiations." I was appalled by parts of it and prepared a critique, stressing that we had to conduct *trade* negotiations, not just *tariff* negotiations. I argued this was so because of the non-tariff aspects of Europe's common agricultural policy and because for LDCs, quantitative restrictions and internal taxes are often more significant trade problems than tariffs.

The conclusions reached at the meeting of major grain and meat exporters in early March reinforced the case for trade, not just tariff, negotiations. Not much more was heard of this, but tensions were growing between "GATT traditionalists" and those of us with a more pragmatic view. So was discontent with Bill Gossett, Governor Herter's deputy at STR. Mike Blumenthal was busy maneuvering with George Ball and others for changes. They came.

Gossett either tired of the bureaucratic battles or was pushed out of his job. I knew not which. In his place, Governor Herter named two new deputies. Bill Matson Roth became the senior deputy, charged with coordination of the interagency process in Washington. Mike Blumenthal was to be our field negotiator, resident in Geneva. Mike was ecstatic.

To my delight, I was informed that I was to replace Stan Cleveland as director of the Office of Atlantic Political Economic Affairs (APE) in the Bureau of European Affairs. My good friend Joe Greenwald was called back from London to head the Office of Trade Affairs (OT), replacing the overly combative Len Weiss. Joe knew trade issues and GATT, but unlike Len he agreed with the reasons for U.S. backing of European integration. In fact, he thought the UK should join the Community.

When the dust had settled, Assistant Secretary Johnson surprised me by saying he had reluctantly decided I was not experienced enough to head his trade office. If he thought I would be miffed at being passed over for OT he was wrong. I preferred APE to OT. Moreover, I recognized Joe was better qualified for OT than I. Joe and I were instructed that friction between EURIAPE and ECON/OT was to be minimized. We were to work together to make a success of the Kennedy Round. We could and we did.

I had to wait months before I could take over APE since Stan was in no hurry to get to his new assignment as economic minister in Paris, but Joe replaced Len Weiss fairly promptly. Blumenthal also brought in Fred Sanderson, my good friend and former boss in INA days, to take over agricultural trade issues other than tropical products and commodity agreements, including grains, which remained my responsibility until I moved to EUR.

Angela thought I was traveling too much of the time, viewing my trips to Central America, London, Brussels, and Geneva as plots to avoid her and our five hyped, if wonderful, children. It was no plot, but it was true I was out of town more than in. So much so that I resigned from my early morning Spanish class, for which I had signed up in a burst of enthusiasm after my jaunt to Central America. Four years later I would be back as a serious student of Spanish.

Mike was our representative to the 1963 Meeting in New York of the Commission on International Commodity Trade, an arm of the Economic and Social Council of the United Nations. He named me as delegation vice chairman. This meant he returned to Washington after giving a policy statement to the Commission, leaving me and a much too large delegation in New York to see what could be accomplished. Nothing could be. The U.N. bureaucracy frustrated me and my delegation. Even our commonsense proposal to abolish some useless, totally non-productive subgroups stirred up outraged protests from professional meeting attendees, who otherwise seemed to care not a whit about commodity issues.

My main achievement during my week as U.S. Representative came when despite having to fight our way out of a bar or two, the Australian Representative and I made it safely back to our uptown hotel. My friend decided as we left a reception in the Village that he wanted to buy me a beer, "an Aussie beer." We went from bar to bar, sampling various brews, but without finding one from Australia. "Fosters" may be well known in the U.S. these days, but in 1963 it could not be found. My friend became outraged at this failure of New York bars to stock his country's good stuff. My suggestions that we just go back to our hotel were rejected out of hand. We had to check every bar between Washington Square and our hotel, some fifty blocks! I had learned to admire Australian (and New Zealander) capacity for drink during my days in Mombasa, but this fellow could outdrink them all. Unfortunately, however, he became more belligerent at each stop. Twice it took force to escape bar men and patrons outraged by my friend's outrage safely, but somehow we made it. Neither of us was too lively at the next days' Commission meetings. Fortunately it did not matter.

Some travel seemed to be paying dividends. It appeared after the GATT Tropical Products subgroup meeting in late March that apart from bananas, we were finally making progress. The EEC had announced a willingness to suspend duties on tea and tropical woods provided the UK did the same. In addition, straws in the wind seemed to indicate that by the May GATT Ministerial Meeting agreement for removal of duties on cocoa and semi-processed cocoa products might also be achieved. It was not to be. The Ministers essentially put tropical products aside to concentrate on the much larger issues of how to cut developed country tariffs. Mike knew I was distressed. Indeed, he apologized to me for not having advanced the ball he had originally placed in my hands, but clearly he had moved on to new interests. He now thought "tariff disparities" were the critical trade issue and he almost knotted up the Ministerial in an attempt to win concessions from the European Community beyond the concept of linear cuts, with exceptions. The idea of a commodity agreement for grains did not fare much better, but at least with establishment of a GATT Cereals Group it was not as dead as my tropical project.

In my last days working for Mike, I was placed in the middle of another "can of worms" or, more accurately, a chicken stew.

After reviewing the situation in late May of 1963, I pointed out, correctly, that EC inaction on our legitimate complaints, mutual recrimination, and possible US retaliation posed dangers for the larger purposes of the Atlantic Partnership, including, of course, general trade negotiations. Given the understandably vociferous nature of the poultry lobby, early rulings of STR's Gossett that we had to have satisfaction from the Community or we would retaliate, and the eventual personal involvement of President Kennedy, the "Chicken War" became one of my less pleasant responsibilities in my new role as director of Atlantic Regional Political Economic Affairs.

13

Atlantic Political Economic Affairs (1963–1967)

As director of RPE, the Office of Atlantic Political Economic Affairs in the Bureau of European Affairs, I had new, quite different, and highly challenging responsibilities. In one sense, I felt like a small fish in a large sea. In another sense, I marveled at how I had a hold, sometimes tiny, sometimes crucial, on important issues, not only in Europe but also in the rest of the world. I was no longer an analyst or reporter; I had become a manager. I had long thought the first rule for a successful manager was to get good people. Though most of my staff was already there, the second rule, use your staff well, still applied.

John Renner was the deputy office director. A careful and meticulous officer, he was far more knowledgeable about OECD than I. Working with Ruth Phillips, the division chief, he would continue to oversee the widespread US-OECD relations, constantly dunning individuals throughout our government to answer their mail and form appropriate delegations to the endless meetings in Paris. One of their continuing problems was getting top administration officials such as the chairman of the Council of Economic Advisors to represent the United States at high-level OECD committee meetings and limit the number of lower-level officials seeking a free trip to Paris. John knew his business and did it well. I helped when he asked me to do so. Only for the annual ministerial meeting and on some major issues, usually involving trade matters that might impact the Kennedy Round, would I take a more active role.

Dick Vine had done a superb job as chief of the division dealing with the European Communities, and hence the Kennedy Round, but he was on his way back overseas. His replacement was one Tom Enders, a relatively untried junior "water walker" recruited from

Embassy Stockholm for fulltime trade work. Dick assured me I had nothing to worry about.

I was skeptical, but Dick was right. Tom was impressively tall, exceptionally intelligent, hardworking, and prepared to tell you about his family's achievements: an uncle had won a Nobel Prize and made the cover of *Time* magazine. Tom and his vivacious wife, Gaetana, bought not one but two houses in Georgetown, which they joined into one for their family. Soon they were recognized figures in Washington society.

President Kennedy had defined Atlantic partnership between the United States and a united Europe as a cornerstone of his foreign policy. Support for European integration and our membership in the North Atlantic Treaty Organization (NATO) were fundamental elements of this partnership. A sister office, the Office of Atlantic Political-Military Affairs (RPM), handled political-military relations, mainly NATO affairs. Day to day implementation of partnership policy with the European Communities was the responsibility of the division of my office that backstopped USEC, our mission to the European Communities. Another division backstopped the emerging Organization for Economic Cooperation and Development (OECD), which had grown out of the Marshall Plan's Organization for European Economic Cooperation (OEEC). The OECD's Development Assistance Committee tried to coordinate worldwide economic assistance efforts. Thus, when the United States wanted to assist India, Yugoslavia, or Latin America, my office had a role to play. The third division of RPE handled a hodgepodge of issues, including economic discussions in NATO, those arising in the Coordinating Committee for Multilateral Export Controls (COCOM), an intergovernmental group aimed at restricting trade in critical strategic items sought by the Soviet Bloc, and our participation in the Economic Commission for Europe (ECE), a United Nations body with both Eastern and Western European members and the United States.

To the considerable extent that policy is made in cables within the constraints of the main lines laid down by the president, the secretary of state, and other top-ranking officials, my staff and I made policy. Day in and day out, we shaped the implementation of the overarching visions of our leaders. We did so in a complex web of the State Department bureaucracy and in an even more complex web of other departments and agencies. Control of communications was and is critical in government operations. Most of the time, RPE controlled cable traffic to our missions to the European Communities, the OECD, and the ECE. Basically, RPE cleared all official instructions to these three missions. RPE's influence, one might say power, came from its right to clear or not clear instructions. Before authorizing a cable of instructions to be sent, it was incumbent upon us to make certain other parts of the government with a legitimate interest in the subject also agreed. All hell could break loose if we failed to get appropriate clearances. Similarly, we in RPE expected to be included in the clearance process of cables relevant to our responsibilities authorized by other parts of the government. If this was not done, due to oversight or deliberately, we, too, raised hell.

By and large this complicated process worked smoothly if all too often slowly. Much negotiation was required, but the generally concerned officers wanted to get the job done and quickly worked out reasonable compromises. However, when serious disagreements arose resolution required kicking departmental issues upstairs to the assistant secretaries, the under secretary, or the secretary of state, or, in the case of interagency disputes, into meetings of the principals in the concerned departments or agencies, or, as a last resort, to the president.

It would be too much for me to go into detail about my day-to-day role in what came to be known as the Kennedy Round, but perhaps a few memories of personal high points are in order. Tom Enders took hold and early on began to contribute significantly to our analysis of European negotiating objectives. He wrote outstanding papers on agricultural issues and the congressional politics of the negotiations. Early on I sent him to Brussels and Geneva to get to know our people working the problems in the field. He hit it off with Ambassador Mike Blumenthal, the president's deputy special representative for trade negotiations.

Negotiators from the European Economic Community (EEC) were hitting hard on ASP, the American Selling Price, a system Customs used to value chemical imports. In practice it meant there were almost no imports. The Europeans had a point and made resolution of the issue a condition for concluding the talks. Our problem was we did not see how to resolve the issue in a way that might gain industry acquiescence, if not agreement. Tom developed a way and was making progress when one day I received a phone call from Bill Roth, the deputy special trade representative. Bill was upset, but nowhere near as upset as he said his boss, former Massachusetts governor Christian A. Herter, was. Bill alleged Tom had been disrespectful to the governor. Consequently, Bill said Tom was no longer welcome at the Special Trade Representative (STR) office or at meetings concerning the negotiations.

It was hard to believe a Foreign Service officer would be disrespectful to a distinguished former secretary of state, but Tom admitted to me he had spoken too sharply. I instructed him to seek an appointment with Governor Herter "to apologize." He did, and fortunately the governor, a gentleman of the old school, rescinded the ban. It was well that he did, because Tom would make an important contribution to the success of the Kennedy Round.

Meanwhile, European measures overly protecting their market for chickens and parts thereof and the increasingly strident U.S. reaction cast a pall not only on trade negotiations in Geneva, but on Atlantic political relations as well. As the controversy escalated, I was spending more and more time in staff-level discussions about what could be done. One day Under Secretary George Ball asked me, "as an expert," to accompany him to a meeting with the president. Never having met a president or even been inside the White House, I was excited. However, Ball left me to wait in the Roosevelt Room while senior policy makers, who I had to admit did not need my "expertise," decided on our next move. I'm not certain, but perhaps this was the meeting that led to President Kennedy's controversial letter provoking Chancellor Konrad Adenauer of Germany to exclaim he could not have imagined the president of the United States would write to him about "chickens."

As the Europeans showed no sign of easing their restrictive practices, pressure for retaliation grew, fanned by the political clout of our chicken producers and led within the government by the Department of Agriculture under Secretary Orville L. Freeman.

One of my major responsibilities as director of RPE was to keep our ambassador to the EEC in Brussels, Jack Tuthill, closely informed of major developments affecting our relations with the European Communities. Jack was trying to convince the Commission that the need for an agreed solution to the chicken situation was critical but was having difficulty conveying the urgency of the matter. When, however, I informed him that unilateral retaliation was likely in a matter of hours, he called back to urge me to somehow delay the planned Short-Term Arrangement announcement for another twenty-four hours, promising good news if I did so.

Joe Greenwald and I were scheduled to meet with Bill Roth in his office, ostensibly to touch up and sign off on an agreed telegram announcing our decision. Joe agreed we should try to stall. We did. Finally Bill even brought in drinks and around 9 p.m. agreed to wait overnight. In the morning Tuthill's cable arrived reporting that Jean Rey had agreed on behalf of the Community to the formation of a GATT panel to determine the amount of damage done to our producers and set the level of approved retaliation. We eventually retaliated, not unilaterally but as agreed internationally, thereby avoiding a likely cycle of retaliation and counter-retaliation.

My boss, J. Robert Schaetzel, credited me with the idea of a GATT panel in evaluating my performance that year. I didn't argue, though he may have stretched the truth. But I do claim frivolously that I served as chief of staff for the "Chicken War."

Next, after the interagency process decided on our list of products I called in the economic counselors of Community countries in Washington to give them the news. Unfortunately, tensions over chickens continued for years longer and still do with many of our other trading partners around the world.

"President Kennedy has been shot." That announcement on a TV in the crowded, smoky dining room of Kitty and Al's, a beer-and-sandwich joint close to the State Department, devastated a relaxed lunch. Stunned, we waited for confirmation of our worst fears. It came all too soon.

As world leaders flew to Washington for a state funeral, I was assigned as escort officer for Jean Monnet, a French political economist and diplomat often credited with being one of the chief architects of the European Union. My first task was to greet him when he arrived at Dulles Airport and escort him to his limousine while a junior officer took care of his baggage.

Later I met Monnet again, greeting him when he arrived at the State Department for President Johnson's reception for foreign visitors. My job this time was to meet him at the entrance and escort him to an express elevator to the eighth floor. How I would have loved to join that reception!

Even though my role was limited to a protocol responsibility, meeting Monnet, the catalyst for European integration, was a thrilling experience.

***

In the meantime, Bob Schaetzel pushed Atlantic affairs in every way possible. His ideas about training Atlantic affairs specialists and establishing a special system for Atlantic assignments collapsed, as they should have, when he was no longer in Washington to push for it. The training made sense, but a narrow cone of political, economic, and military officers in a service priding itself on worldwide availability did not.

Nonetheless, Bob's ability to persuade the powers that be to support his ideas was phenomenal. Particularly useful, many of us thought, was his success in securing ample funding for regular meetings on Atlantic affairs in Washington and Europe. These meetings became a crucial coordinating mechanism for withstanding de Gaulle's assault on NATO and advancing our Kennedy Round objectives.

One of the early Atlantic affairs meetings proved to be painful for me. Mike Blumenthal had raised an issue about the so-called tariff disparities at the ministerial meeting where the round was formally launched. He developed the argument and pushed it hard, as hard chargers do. But a lot of us thought he was overdoing it and producing a needless political backlash in Europe. Our analysis indicated the problem was not as serious as Mike was alleging. It fell to me to outline our view. The cold water I threw on Mike's approach infuriated him. After the meeting he ran up to me screaming, "You have betrayed me." I was appalled, not having viewed the matter as involving personal relations. Our relations were never again as warm as they had been for the previous three years, but when Mike calmed down and thought it over he handled the issue in a much more balanced way.

Ministers had agreed to exchange exception lists on November 16, 1964, but it was clear the Community, engaged in almost perpetual internal negotiations about the Common Agriculture Policy, would not meet the target date. Our draft list was pretty good, I thought, although it seemed too heavy on wool textiles. The issue, however, was what to do in the absence of a European list. At senior staff level we agreed to proceed, but Governor Herter overruled not only Greenwald and myself, but also Bill Roth, his deputy, and Frances Bator, who handled economic issues on the National Security Council (NSC). In a backchannel letter to Ambassador Tuthill I noted, "Agriculture is becoming more concerned with the protection of the American farmer and of our domestic policies than with trying to hold on to the European market."

Subsequently, the grapevine indicated President Johnson was unhappy and did not want a crisis in the negotiations. In late October during a tense discussion in preparation for putting the issue to the president, National Security Advisor McGeorge Bundy told Freeman he sounded as though he did not want the overall negotiations to succeed. That did it. Freeman abandoned his attempt to obtain substantive advantages from the rules negotiations, indicating he was satisfied provided future negotiating objectives were not abandoned. The next day Herter approved a cable saying, "We want to put the onus on de Gaulle for any further delay . . . and to minimize French opportunities to assert that U.S. agricultural demands have made progress on the Kennedy Round impossible."

The United States got credit for having made an important contribution to the negotiations. I particularly enjoyed congratulating Jacques Kosciusco-Morizet, the French economic counselor, "on the success of French diplomacy, which forced us to make a major concession."

In December the EEC reached a grain price decision. The levels approved represented a serious threat to our exports, but otherwise opened the way for progress in the Kennedy Round.

Yet as the outlook for U.S. wheat and food grain exports to Europe dimmed, , I suggested in a private conversation with European Commissioner for Agriculture Sicco L. Mansholt that it would be extremely helpful if the Community would favor a food aid plan. I do not know whether I can rightly claim credit for the World Food Program that eventually came into being, but I can recall no previous discussion of the concept.

Then, in early 1965 it appeared the Community was planning to adopt regulations for fruits and vegetables that would once again seriously impact our trade. After interagency discussions, I drafted a cable instructing our ambassador or a senior economic officer in each of the capitals of the six member states to deliver a note stressing that the United States expects "unimpaired maintenance of EEC bindings on U.S. exports." I also called in the economic and agriculture attachés to reinforce the message. These efforts paid off and our bindings were respected.

Tensions within the Community were driven by de Gaulle's desire to check Commission leadership in pushing supranational aspects of the EEC, which were incompatible with his vision for

France. But the Commission had fairly wide support among other member states. Thus, these tensions culminated on July 2, 1965, in a French walkout from a Council of Ministers meeting. While personified by the pretensions of Commission president Walter Hallstein, the issues were broader and more fundamental. The resulting Community crisis was the most serious it ever faced.

Our top policy makers immediately indicated we would have "no comment" on an internal EEC matter. Subsequently, however, Under Secretary George Ball informed Dutch Foreign Minister Joseph Luns that there should be "no question about the U.S. position on European integration."

What did the French walkout mean for the Kennedy Round? Early on there was a widespread view that we should merely wait it out since the EEC was clearly in no position to negotiate. I opposed this, arguing we should proceed on schedule and submit our agricultural offers on September 16, thereby putting the onus for any Kennedy Round negotiating failure clearly on the French.

Joe Greenwald shared this view. We argued the case in a joint memorandum to Under Secretary Ball and Under Secretary Thomas C. Mann through Assistant Secretary John Leddy (EUR) and Assistant Secretary Anthony Solomon (E). Since Secretary Freeman was dead set against proceeding, Joe and I noted a presidential decision would be necessary. Ball, Herter, and Freeman met with the president on August 18. LBJ decided we should table offers on time. The community crisis continued into early 1966. It was resolved by important concessions by the Five to the French, limiting majority voting and increasing the role of the Council of Ministers vis-à-vis the Commission. The roadblock to concluding the Kennedy Round was now gone.

Governor Herter resigned in early 1967. I was genuinely sorry to see him go. Joe Greenwald and I sent a memo to Secretary Rusk asking him to urge the president at their next regular luncheon meeting to name Bill Roth to succeed Herter. It probably happened because it was the sensible thing to do, not because Joe and I favored Roth.

Herter had at times given me heartburn. Understandably given his frustration with the EEC's Common Agriculture Policy, he toyed with a bad idea that the Germans might reach a bilateral grains agreement with us. He also thought, contrary to U.S. policy, that he could perhaps enlist the members of the European Free Trade Association (EFTA), dominated by the U.K., to put pressure on the

EEC for us. He initially supported Secretary Freeman, but came to see that Freeman's approach could kill the Kennedy Round. He became, at my urging, an advocate of food aid. He was accessible. Indeed he sought the views of mid-level officials like myself. Once he sent me a pretty terrible draft speech asking for comments and I sent back a three-page critique. He called to thank me, compliment me on a "meticulous" memo, and say he had adopted 98 percent of my suggestions. It made my day.

Then, early in 1967 agreement was reached to conclude the Kennedy Round, if at all possible by May 14. Bill Roth, now STR, went to Geneva with full authority to reach agreement. An executive committee was formed in Washington to help him. As only one representative from each department was to sit on it, Joe Greenwald, now deputy assistant secretary of state for trade, was the logical choice. I was disappointed but recognized Joe was the man for the job.

After the Round concluded, Bill Roth, heir to the Matson steamship fortune, invited everyone in the government who had participated to a marvelous party on a chartered tour boat on the Potomac. It was a splendid way to conclude a five-year effort.

In May of 1967 as I was counting the days before moving on to my next assignment, Egyptian president Gamal Abdel Nasser threw the United Nations Emergency Force (UNEF) out of Sinai, moved Egyptian forces to Sharm al-Sheikh, and announced the closure of the Straits of Tiran, thereby denying Israeli ships passage into the Gulf of Aqaba. Israel, having a legal right to free passage, quite correctly viewed these Egyptian actions as a major threat to its existence. The cabinet began debating the pros and cons of military action. The United States wanted to do what it could to avoid conflict. At the time it had little leverage on Egypt but much more on Israel as its most powerful friend.

Normally these developments would not have involved me. But to my amazement I was summoned to Under Secretary Eugene Rostow's office and told I was in charge of lining up support for a maritime declaration drafted by our lawyers. For a number of frantic days I had fun sending instructions to posts, some far outside my normal concentration on European posts, monitoring the count of supporters, sitting in on many of Rostow's meetings with ambassadors, and recording what transpired in MemCons (memoranda of conversation).

Initially, it looked as though we would have widespread agreement among developed countries, and someone decided not to even try to get the support of the least developed countries (LDCs). But as the implications of participating in what was widely viewed as a pro-Israeli, blockade-breaking effort began to sink in, support rapidly dropped off. The French, as usual, were obstreperous, but soon even the British and Canadians had second thoughts about the so-called Red Sea Regatta.

Rostow fascinated me. Highly articulate, if too obviously pro-Israel, and given, I thought, to stretching the truth, he was committed to averting war. But just as Secretary Rusk was having problems lining up congressional support for enforcement of a maritime declaration, the number of countries willing to sign dwindled to a handful. Worse, only the Netherlands and Australia were willing to provide ships for a blockade-breaking effort.

Rostow, however, was determined to press ahead. He instructed me to draft a cable to The Hague making clear that running the blockade together with U.S. ships meant the Dutch should be prepared for war. I did so. Rostow approved the draft and told me to send it to his brother, National Security Advisor Walt Rostow. Walt asked that I obtain the approval of Secretary Rusk. By this time it was late, so I had a courier take the cable out to the secretary at his residence. I was told, "The secretary wants to sleep on it."

So home I went. At about 2 a.m. the Operations Center called to tell me Israel had attacked Egypt and I should come in. "No way," I replied, "I was supposed to prevent it. I'm going back to sleep."

Ever since, I have wondered if the secretary knew an Israeli strike had been scheduled. Frankly, I doubt it, but he clearly knew the overall situation was extremely dicey and, from the Israeli point of view, eroding rapidly. Bearing in mind the Tonkin Resolution and subsequent events in Vietnam, he also must have been aware that the threat of war without congressional support was not sensible policy.

That's the story of how I failed to avert the Six-Day War. Bill Baracloough of my staff in RPE helped me throughout this crisis. He and I then wrote a history of the Maritime Declaration, which must be somewhere in the Archives.

The war provoked an oil embargo by Arab states. To try to develop a shortfall sharing mechanism, I was sent to Paris to push for a coordinated Atlantic countries response at OECD. My efforts ran into stubborn French objections. My mission, nevertheless, made limited progress, although considerably less than we had hoped for.

To cap it off, some of my remarks came to the attention of General de Gaulle, who was not pleased and let Washington know it. When Assistant Secretary John Leddy told me of this, he also praised my handling of the fracas. I felt mighty good; it's not every day that a mid-level official is criticized by a chief of state. Even less often does he get praise from his own government for doing so. With this adventure my four years in the European Bureau came to an end.

14

Guatemala (1967–1969)

In late 1966, I was advised that I was to replace Leroy Wehrle in Saigon as financial advisor to Ambassador Henry Cabot Lodge, Jr. In effect, Wehrle had become the wartime economic czar for Vietnam. While flattered the system had that much confidence in me, I was not looking forward to separation from my family (in 1966 family members were not allowed at post there). Moreover, the medical director of the Foreign Service had concluded it was important that my eldest son, Christopher, who was under the care of a psychologist, not be separated from his father; but this was not likely to stop my assignment. Vietnam was priority number one and the financial advisor job had to be filled, and filled well. Thus, I began reading books about wartime economics, especially about problems of inflation control. But although the Foreign Service may have thought I should go to Saigon, Ambassador Lodge liked Wehrle and knew he could handle the job. So to keep Wehrle, he changed the family rule. With his wife coming to Saigon, Wehrle extended. I was free after almost six years in Washington to seek another assignment.

Having devoted fifteen years to Europe, I decided it was time for a change. Once again, the lure of the developing world called to me. I was well and favorably known not only on the European circuit but elsewhere as well, since in part of my job backstopping the Development Assistance Committee of the OECD I had often worked closely with the Agency for International Development (AID) and on many developing country issues, especially in South Asia and Latin America. I soon discovered personnel officers in other parts of the world were seeking to fill vacancies with officers who had experience in their area. But I persisted in my view, even as I rejected in turn offers to be economic minister in Paris, Bonn, and Rome. Most of my colleagues thought I was nuts. There was an opening as consul general in Calcutta. I talked about that job with Gordon Mattison, my boss in Damascus, since he had been consul general. He encouraged me, but an officer with area experience got the assignment. Jack Tuthill, now ambassador to Brazil, suggested I be his DCM, A great idea, I thought, but needless to say the office director of Brazilian affairs thought differently. I was also recommended to Ambassador Phil Talbot in Athens, but another officer got the DCM's job there. Still, I kept telling anyone who would listen that I wanted a change. Then I was asked if I would like to be deputy aid director for Turkey. I was intrigued; after all, I had sought an assignment to Turkey when I entered the service. Still I observed that a deputy was supposed to know the aid business. A director need not necessarily know the details, but a deputy should. Regrettably, I declined the offer. Oliver Covey, our ambassador to Colombia, briefly encouraged me to think I might go to Bogotá as his DCM, but he eventually concluded, not to my surprise, that my lack of Spanish disqualified me.

Then one day my phone rang. Don Palmer, a senior economic officer for Latin America and a tennis buddy of mine, asked if I would be interested in being the AID director in Guatemala. Without hesitation I replied, "Yes, that would be great." Fortunately, Angela was as pleased with the idea as I was. Clearly I had the right qualifications. I did not speak Spanish. I was not an AID officer. I had never had an assignment in Latin America.

Nevertheless the assignment held up, in part because Bob Sayre, temporarily in charge of the Bureau of Latin American Affairs, supported my candidacy. Another hurdle was that President Lyndon B. Johnson personally interviewed candidates for directorships at major posts.[1] In my case, for this less important post I was vetted at the White House by Special Assistant to the President Marvin Watson. After a challenging conversation, he wished me well on the job. At a late hour, John Leddy called to ask me to be economic minister in London. That was the one economic job in Europe I would have jumped at, but by the time John called I was already committed to Guatemala.

On his first day in charge of Alliance for Progress efforts throughout the hemisphere, Jim Fowler could not have been warmer when he swore me in as AID director for Guatemala as one of his new duties. Months later, Bill Turnage, his special assistant, told me that when Jim looked at my record before the ceremony he swore like a trooper. "How in the hell, had this blankety blank stripped pants diplomat from Europe been chosen for a top AID job? There are lots of deserving, far better qualified AID officers." Fortunately for me, it was too late for Jim to change the assignment.

AID was about to have an in-depth review of the Guatemala program. With the approval of our ambassador, John Gordon Mein, I accompanied the Washington contingent to Guatemala. It was an ideal way to learn more about the program and the people involved, including key Washington back-stoppers. Acquiring a feel for what were considered program weaknesses was particularly useful. The rigorous process of examining field actions, proposals, and thinking based on tough-minded analysis was quite unlike anything I had seen in the Department of State. Our analysis of trade and balance of payments issues resembled it but differed in that Washington's vigorous confrontation of field thinking was far more systematic in the AID process. I was impressed.

Another impressive aspect of my new situation was the admirable relationship between State and AID. In those days personnel in the Bureau of American Republic Affairs and AID's Alliance for Progress staff were integrated. A mix of AID and State officers staffed the Guatemala desk. Sitting side-by-side, political types got input from economic development types and vice versa. When I joined it the Office of Central American Affairs was led by a long-serving FSO, Ambassador Charles R. Burrows. Upon his retirement, an AID officer, Dick Breen, became the new office director. In my view, the subsequent breakup of this system was a sad mistake.

My visit to Guatemala with the Washington AID contingent also gave me the chance after calling on Ambassador Mein, who warmly welcomed me to his team, to check out school prospects to inspect the AID director's residence. After I had twenty years of service Uncle Sam would provide living quarters while I was overseas. This simplified life. In Guatemala, to my delight, the house was large enough for our family and had a garden for Balthazar, our black Labrador. While comfortable, the house was furnished in a strictly government-issue sort of way. When the government provides furnished quarters, it also reduces one's shipping allowance for household effects, limiting what personal items one can bring to make a house a home. However, unimaginative furnishings were more than offset by the fact that the house was beautifully sited, overlooking Plaza Berlin at the southern end of Guatemala City with a spectacular view of the Pacaya volcano. When Pacaya erupted, as it regularly did, there was no better view to be had.

In the family, Deborah was off to attend Mills College in

California, chosen in part, I thought, to maximize the distance from parental oversight. Chris and Joe enthusiastically encouraged my idea that we three drive to Guatemala, while Angela bravely oversaw the finishing touches to packing and awaited word that we had arrived safely so she, Joanna, and Veronica could fly down to join us. It was a memorable trip; almost forty years later, Chris and Joe still enthuse over it. The stunning, world-class anthropological National Museum of Anthropology in Mexico City, the Toltec pyramids, and the Monte Albán Zapotec ruins at Oaxaca were unforgettable high points of the trip. The boys' only regret was that they were not in Washington to meet our new tenant, Scott Carpenter the astronaut.

Guatemala is a fabulously beautiful country, endowed with magnificent lakes, fiery volcanoes, strikingly green mountain valleys, and lush tropical forests. Indeed, Saint Peter is said to have complained to God that Guatemala was being endowed with more than its fair share of beauty, to which God reputedly replied, "I'll balance it out. Wait until you see the inhabitants."

In addition to touring the country, we enjoyed two fabulous vacations on a deserted key in the Caribbean. Together we and other families chartered a tug in Puerto Barrios to take us out and pick us up. With no water on the key, we carried drinks and ice as well as food. Sunsetters in eleven-ounce cans, mostly filled with rum and fruit juice added to taste, made for good sleeping. Amazingly, on the key seashells came to me. As I sat by the campfire at night, hermit crabs crawled up, making shell collecting ridiculously easy. My mother, a serious shell collector, was enchanted with the take.

Actually, almost half of the population is Indian, descendants of the Mayans. Tikal, once a large city, the major temple of which remained the tallest building in the Western Hemisphere until the late 1900s, is evidence the Mayans were once powerful and enormously talented. However, when we served in Guatemala the Indian population was—and, I assume, still is—marked by poverty, illiteracy, use of Quiche and other Indian languages, not Spanish, and a communal, as opposed to national, outlook. The Ladino majority spoke Spanish and the wealthy among them, in alliance with the army, ran the country. Strikingly, some twenty extended families owned over 80 percent of the land. Guatemalan democracy was and is largely nominal. It is severely flawed despite regular elections.

My overwhelming impression of Guatemala is of a violent society, nothing like Montgomery County, Maryland. Violence was a way of life for the *guatemaltecos*. A Guatemalan I got to know early on was shot down in front of his house a week or so later. I asked why? No one was certain, but it was thought to be the result of an argument he had had some ten years before. The president of the Congress invited the ambassador and senior embassy officers to his *finca* for a dinner dance to say thank you for a trip to the States Ambassador Mein had arranged for Guatemalan legislators. To my utter amazement, every Guatemalan male at the party carried a weapon. They danced with their sidearms in their holsters. When I entertained, I insisted that guns be left on the fireplace mantel. My guests always accepted this practice in good grace. What would I have done, had it been resisted?

AID had a small rural development program in the province of Zacapa, an area where a rebellion had flared in the early 1960s. I thought I'd have a look but was told I would need an escort. What an escort it turned out to be. Colonel Carlos Manuel Arana Osorio, then a senior army officer and later president of Guatemala, told me we should meet at 6 a.m. at the airport. When I arrived, he and his bodyguards were heavily armed. Once in Zacapa, Arana kept a sub-machine gun on his lap as he drove me around in a jeep surrounded by a large military escort. I was far more concerned by this friendly firepower than by any guerrilla threat. He was probably staging a show. Never again did I have or think I needed an armed escort in Zacapa. Moreover, Angela visited the province regularly to help with a woman's self-help group. Still, Arana impressed me, though not entirely favorably although he was an affable host.

Further, from time to time there were firefights in the city between rebels and security forces. One day, to my surprise, a stray round came into my ninth floor office. Far, far worse, driving home for lunch I passed the bullet-riddled vehicle in which Col. John D. Webber, the U.S. Military Group commander, and Lt. Commander Ernest A. Munro of the U.S. Navy had been killed, and their driver badly wounded. Also, an AID officer was kidnapped, driven around for a day in the trunk of a car, and then, most fortunately, freed. But to our horror, Ambassador Mein, who once assured me, "No Latin would ever kill an American ambassador," was assassinated. When his limousine was cut off and armed men wanted to take him prisoner, he bolted for cover. "*Mateselo!*" the guerrilla leader shouted, and our ambassador was gunned down. Presumably, the gunmen hoped to use Ambassador Mein as a hostage to trade for the freedom of companions held by the government. He was the first U.S. ambassador killed by terrorists, but, sad to say, far from the last.

Standing my turn at casket watch, I was moved by the endless lines of ordinary Guatemalans who passed by to pay their respects to a good man most of them had not known. Yet the turnout, from the president on down, seemed to me an expression of profound shame at what Guatemalans had done. The guilty gunmen were, it turned out, members of a revolutionary group linked to Fidel Castro. Even so, it was noteworthy that the guerrilla newspaper, *No Nos Tiente*[2], concentrated its fire on *la epoca, la jodida* (government abuses) of Guatemalans—of which there were far too many—while containing nothing particularly anti-Gringo.

When asked by Max Krebs, who became chargé upon the ambassador's death, to add bodyguards for my protection, I stupidly refused. Max, just as stupidly, did not insist. He merely informed Washington of my rejection of bodyguards. There was no objection from Washington either. How different things are today. Silly boy that I was, I rationalized my decision in terms of "I'm here helping Guatemala; no one would harm me." How foolish! I did, however, listen carefully to security briefings and thereafter took a serious interest in looking for surveillance. One day I spotted new individuals across the street from my residence. Instead of driving to work, I called the Embassy Police, who promptly arrived. As it turned out, my suspiciously behaving individuals were workers waiting to start constructing a new house!

Just before Christmas of 1968, my son Chris, with Mark Bell, the son of another embassy officer, and a Guatemalan friend of Chris' did not answer when called for lunch. Soon we were badly worried. Then the Guatemalan boy arrived in tatters. He told us the three boys had been kidnapped and the kidnappers wanted $20 and a pair of shoes as ransom. I was so thankful and so agitated that I not only gave him the twenty, but also my best pair of shoes to take back. An old pair would have served just as well. A tense hour or so later, the three boys arrived in rags and barefoot. Despite having been told many times not to do it, they had gone down into a *barranca*, a deep gorge in which slum dwellers lived, where teenagers who wanted something for Christmas had seized them. These poor Guatemalans had no idea whom they were holding or the ransom would have been much greater. As it was, I was glad they had shoes and clothes, and so much gladder our son had safely returned to us.

After I left Guatemala, German ambassador Karl von Spreti,

who had been my next-door neighbor, was kidnapped, tortured, and killed. His children and mine had been great friends, which made the sad news even sadder.

Time, in addition to violence, distinguished Guatemala from Bethesda. When Angela and I moved in, our neighbors invited us to lunch at 1 p.m. We arrived on time but there was no one to greet us. A surprised maid asked us to sit and offered coffee. Hours went by. Eventually another guest arrived, and sometime after 4 p.m. our host and hostess showed up. The "lunch" ended around midnight. Latin concepts of time are just different from ours, although bit by bit this is changing. Now, retired in Costa Rica, if my dentist gives me an appointment for 11 a.m. I'll be in the chair within five minutes of 11 a.m. In Guatemala I would regularly wait for about thirty minutes to see my dentist. Finally I complained. He told me he had started on me at the time shown on his clock. It just happened that his clock was thirty minutes behind the one his receptionist used to make appointments. With this information, I rarely waited thereafter. I, like other patients, merely arrived thirty minutes late.

Politicians everywhere like to inaugurate public works of benefit to their constituents. Guatemalan politicos outdo themselves in this respect. An inauguration is a time for a fiesta. It is also a time to invite foreign guests, especially if they have somehow contributed to the project, as was often the case with USAID. After the requisite speeches, the drinking and eating begin. But it is not like a political event in the United States. Only the big shot invitees eat and drink. Indians and *campesinos* stand around and watch, often, say, outside a fence around a new two-room school.

While I deplored the segregation of the poor, whom the project was generally intended to help, overall these fiesta-inaugurations were great fun. They were also chaotic, at least after the initial takeoff, especially if a couple of locations were involved. At the airport early in the day, all guests were advised as to how they were to get from the landing area to the initial inauguration site. Thereafter it was everyone on his own; at least that is how it seemed. But I didn't mind; I was there for the adventure. One day, after the speeches I could not find my designated vehicle or any other. So I started to walk. Not certain as to where I was walking, I was delighted when a jeep pulled over and its driver asked me to join him. It turned out he had his own helicopter. Off we went, with me trying to point out to him various obstacles such as a radio tower as we circled above the next event site. We made it down safely and were waiting to greet President Montenegro and Ambassador Mein when they arrived by road, my ambassador being duly astonished to see me in the welcoming party. Later I learned my new friend had just bought his helicopter and had had far fewer hours with an instructor than would have been required to pilot it solo in the States.

Another day after an interminable lunch in the steamy lowlands near Lake Isabel, reached after more than two dusty, bumpy hours on the road, I accepted with alacrity an invitation to fly back to the capital. To my horror, once in the air the pilot took a slug of whiskey and passed the bottle back. I and the other two passengers drank, in my case at least to keep it away from the pilot. Fortunately our polluted pilot somehow landed us safely. I, however, could hardly walk away from the plane. A few weeks later the press reported our pilot had been killed in an "accident." Seems he flew into a cloud-covered volcano!

By and large, my new colleagues were a friendly, competent group. I cannot imagine how much more difficult my new job would have been without the unstinted support of Ed and Kay Marasciulo. While they wanted to return home, Ed had nevertheless agreed to stay on a bit longer as deputy director. From correcting my Spanish—accent, grammar, and vocabulary—to guiding me through the endless paperwork associated with AID projects, to helping me answer GAO criticisms of the alleged errors of my predecessors, to assessing staff strengths and weaknesses, to briefing me on Guatemalan individuals and institutions with which we dealt, Ed provided invaluable assistance. Similarly, Kay immeasurably helped Angela adjust to a new life, a new language, and a new culture.

I did, however, clash over issues with two of my new colleagues. Nestor Sanchez[3] was a good friend, but we disagreed over embassy—not AID—program priorities. When I objected to wasting resources on coastal patrol boats, Ambassador Mein overruled me. Maurice Hawes, a fine fellow with whom I shared an enjoyment of poker, was economic counselor. He seemed dedicated to arguing against almost all proposed AID expenditures. This meant far too many issues had to be resolved by the ambassador, who invariably supported my view. Eventually, with Maury due for transfer, Ambassador Mein accepted my proposed remedy for these time-consuming and sterile bureaucratic arguments: when my poker-playing friend moved on, I became economic counselor as well as AID director.

My AID responsibilities put me in touch with a wide variety of individuals whom I would have been unlikely to meet otherwise. Three reverberate in my memory.

Dr. Carroll Behrnhorst ran a clinic in Chimaltenango, a small village inhabited mainly by Mayan Indians. He was indefatigable in administering care to his "seventy-six patients in forty-eight beds."

Sam Green, a bridge partner in town, had accomplished late in his life not one, but two, of the things I had long before decided would make for a successful life.[4] He had invented an institution, the Centavo Foundation, which made small loans to Indians. The theory was the borrowers would repay the foundation one centavo each week. The scheme worked. It helped improve the lot of the poorest of the poor, for example, by financing a pedal-operated sewing machine. AID supplemented Sam's initiative, originally self-financed, by providing a small amount of capital. This meant AID auditors, which meant trouble for Sam because his books, when they existed at all, were not well kept. I told the auditors to go after him and I told Sam to shape up. He did. His books and finances were found to be OK in the next audit.

Second, having been inspired by *The Story of San Michele*, I thought it would be great to have a fabulous house. Sam occupied such a house at Lake Atitla.[5] His dock, reachable by boat from the main hotel on the lake, was at the foot of stairs leading steeply upward to the house. The view from the house across one of the more beautiful lakes in the world was simply breathtaking. Angela, our children, and I never tired of visiting Sam.

Dr. Imrich Fischmann, a Czech refugee, ran a successful plastics factory long before Dustin Hoffman in *The Graduate* was pointed to the future in plastics. Imrich was an entrepreneur with a social conscience. He became the source for me of sound judgments about many of the Guatemalans trying to get something or other out of AID.

In mid-1968, I participated as a bit player during my first presidential visit, far simpler in those days than now. President Johnson had met with the Central American presidents in San Salvador, following which he flew the other four visiting presidents to their respective capitals. LBJ's stop in Guatemala was brief, but the image of my president towering over President Méndez Montenegro remains with me.

Our next important visitor was Nelson Rockefeller, named

by newly elected President Nixon to review policy toward Latin America. My memory of that visit is that the governor sent ahead a case of his favorite sherry. Apparently he did not drink anything else. I saw him at a reception the ambassador gave where he was sipping his sherry but had no substantive talk with his host, as far as I can remember.

The heads of state of the Alliance for Progress countries, meeting that summer in Punta del Este, had agreed emphasis in development programs should be on agriculture and education. Jim Fowler let me know in unmistakable terms that this meant I was to put together education and agriculture loan programs as well as move ahead on a number of smaller loans already under discussion. I was also to negotiate significant Guatemalan contributions to these programs. Overall, I was to somehow find a way to increase Guatemalan savings as a percentage of GNP. Yeah, sure. This challenge would have been nearly hopeless had it not been for two outstanding members of the government who, within limits, agreed with the objective. They were the minister of finance, Alberto Fuentes Mohr[6], and his number one assistant, Gert Rosenthal. Gert and I along with Diego Aria, the representative of the Inter-American Development Bank (IADB), worked together professionally and, together with our wives, became good personal friends.

Before I left Guatemala, Ambassador Nathaniel Davis and I signed an education loan. Chuck Connolly, the mission loan officer, slogged through the seemingly endless paperwork requirements of AID Washington. Peter Wright, a locally hired AID contractor who had studied Guatemala's floundering school system as an anthropologist, provided key conceptual ideas. His ideas, however, were often too radical for Minister of Education Martinez Duran. Indeed, Ambassador Mein had predicted Duran would never agree to spend loan funds to benefit illiterate adults. He was right that the minister would delay and complicate achievement of a sound loan, but wrong about the ultimate outcome. In the final stages of the negotiation, the Guatemalan government agreed to raise modest additional tax resources for incremental investment in education.

Diego Aria and I agreed, as did Gert tacitly, that we should insist on significant Guatemalan self-help efforts. We also agreed not to relax performance requirements embedded in existing loans. One day, however, Diego told me he could no longer carry out his commitments. He was sorry, but the annual IADB meeting was to be held in Guatemala and the Bank's president, Felipe Herrera, wanted to sign a number of loans on the margin of the meeting.

Not only did he do so, largely without self-help commitments, but he also wore out those of us attending the plenary meetings with a three hour-long speech. I was turned off by Felipe Herrera.

For my part, at times I was perhaps too tough. During discussion of a small, low-priority loan to support social projects, I blew my stack when the Guatemalans, seeking funding for rural health clinics, indicated they had no plan to staff the clinics with trained personnel. Transparently we were being asked to finance clinics their politicians would inaugurate and forget. I also clashed with the minister of public works over the government's desire to draw down an existing loan to finance a contract for a water project awarded, I was convinced, to the wrong bidder. The minister of defense, a real power in Guatemala, intervened. I could see I was outgunned, so I briefed Ambassador Davis, fairly new at the time, telling him President Montenegro would soon ask him to overrule AID. I hoped that he would support us. He asked for the voluminous file about the case. After reviewing it, he assured me he agreed with me. The president did ask him to act and Nat Davis did tell him AID was right. My ambassador impressed me. Thereafter, agreement was reached on a new study of the situation, and eventually the project proceeded.

On another occasion, I was distressed when the ambassador asked me to reconsider proceeding against the bishop of Zacapa. AID supplied grain through the Catholic Relief Services to make tortillas or bread for school lunches. The bishop was selling this grain on the market. Nat did not tell me to ease off; he just made it clear that in his judgment it would be politically better to do so. The archbishop of Guatemala had asked him to intercede, arguing only a technical violation of our grant terms had occurred, since our food met a low-priority need and the bishop used sale proceeds for higher-priority projects. The archbishop assured the ambassador that were grain again made available, the bishop of Zacapa would scrupulously use it only as intended. I backed off.

In addition to trying to advance my loan priorities, namely, agriculture and education, I was supervising over two hundred American and Guatemalan employees, overseeing an existing loan pipeline of slightly more than $20 million, and managing a considerable technical assistance (TA) program. Some parts of the TA program, such as leadership training at Rafael Landívar University, made eminent sense to me. The leadership program recruited Indians and *campesinos*, largely from rural communities, for up to six weeks of training in leadership skills. In rural communities, lethargy prevails all too often. No one believes anything he or she can do will make a difference. Thus, the training was intended to persuade the participants they could make a difference if they tried.[7] I found the program to be impressive and well run.

Other elements of AID's program, such as public safety, meaning cooperation with the police, provided countless headaches. The U.S. military ran a civic action program with AID support[8], the activity that had led me to visit Zacapa with Colonel Arana. To assist Guatemala in overall development planning as well as in specific project preparation and implementation struck me as useful but hardly excited me. On the other hand, I found family planning efforts exciting.

In fact, I doubt I made much personal impact on our technical assistance projects, with two exceptions. AID had resources that could be used, with the ambassador's approval and after review by an embassy committee, to support small projects. Early on, with Ambassador Mein's approval they were used to provide help, including mattresses, to victims of a large fire in a Guatemala slum. More often, though, we would finance a well or cooperative. Small projects made sense to me, but good small projects. Those where there would be follow-through and a significant local contribution were in surprisingly short supply.

An obvious answer occurred to me: have Peace Corps volunteers submit projects and oversee their implementation. I proposed this to the Peace Corps director, who categorically turned me down. My idea, he said, would compromise the independence of the Peace Corps. His volunteers did not want to be contaminated by working in any way with the embassy or AID. Damn foolishness, I thought, but there was nothing for me to do but accept his view. Fortunately, the next Peace Corps director shared my interest. His volunteers had projects but few or no resources. AID had resources but few viable small projects. A Peace Corps volunteer, Dick Burke[9], joined my staff. We provided him a Chevrolet Suburban, "The White Monster," in which he visited volunteers all over the country, studying project possibilities on the spot. Dick lost the Monster one day, unadvisedly fording a fast-flowing river. Otherwise the joint program was an enormous success. I think, but am not certain, that Guatemala's was the first such joint PC-AID effort in the world. Some years later such collaborative efforts were common wherever Peace Corps and AID missions operated.

The other technical assistance area where I made an impact, although there is some uncertainty about whether it was positive or negative, was family planning. The Guatemalan government, heavily influenced by Catholic doctrine, was not interested. Indeed, to my amazement the then director of national planning had flatly turned down a United Nations offer of demographic training for his economists. AID supported a modest program of private health clinics, *Asociación Pro-Bienestar de la Familia de Guatemala*, where family planning advice and assistance were available. The AID advisor to this program was an exceptional individual, Dr. Donald MacCorquodale, who also oversaw the leadership program at Rafael Landívar University. Impressed as I was by Don, he easily stimulated my belief that population pressure was a major constraint on development. The more I learned, the more passionate I became in discussing the problem with anyone who would listen. Not entirely serendipitously, the Guatemala branch of the Society for International Development, of which I was a member, invited me to give a talk on population issues. I was well aware the subject was a contentious one, particularly in Catholic Guatemala. Accordingly I proceeded with caution. I drew heavily on material in United Nations, Ford Foundation, and United States government publications, wrote and rewrote, and fairly widely circulated my drafts for comment, including to Guatemalan experts and the minister of health.

My talk was well received by the audience and stimulated a generally temperate discussion; but it also provoked some criticism in the press, from church spokesmen and from my then boss, Ambassador Davis. Incredibly, in retrospect, I had neither cleared my talk with him nor informed him of my intentions. He quite correctly chewed me out for this, but we differed on one key point. He thought a U.S. official should not tread on such thin ice. I thought the AID director should address it precisely because the subject was so central to development. I feared indifference more than controversy. My respect and admiration for Nat, who five years later arranged my first ambassadorial posting, is boundless. Nevertheless, I never learned to avoid controversial speeches.

My initial public remarks in Guatemala, made to the American Chamber of Commerce and entitled "What AID Is All About," were anodyne boilerplate. But I was surprised to note, reading them over thirty years later, a concluding forecast of "the formation of an integrated Latin American common market of continental scale."

Certainly, at that point I was more influenced by European thinking than by Bill Clinton. Maybe, however, Bill stole the idea from me. Just kidding.

There were two AID missions in Guatemala City, one bilateral, the other regional. The United States backed a Central American Common Market (CACM), which I thought was a good idea. However, Central America had no Jean Monnet. Nor was Oliver Sause, the director of the Regional Office for Central America and Panama (ROCAP), in the same league as David Bruce of the Bruce Mission to Monnet's Europe or Walt Butterworth of USEC. Far worse was the inward-looking orientation of the CACM. One concept was to "rationalize" industry by designating which corporation in which country would supply the entire Central American market. This idea of officially endorsing monopolies is the antithesis of a competitive system. Carlos Manual Castillo, head of the South Central Chapter of the International Erosion Control Association (SCIECA), modeled on the lines of the European Commission, was a tireless, dynamic leader. Unfortunately, however, he devoted more effort to setting quota levels than to reducing trade barriers. In contrast, the regional financial institutions made sense to me, concentrated as they were on financing the establishment of badly needed infrastructure.

In any case, the dream of Central American integration suffered an almost fatal setback in 1969 when two member countries, El Salvador and Honduras, waged the so-called "Soccer War." Hostilities were sparked by a rough soccer match between the two national teams, but tensions over Salvadorian migrants illegally occupying land in Honduras and provoking persecution thereby underlay the outbreak of the conflict. As tension mounted, I read the cabled reports from our embassies in Tegucigalpa and San Salvador with more amusement than concern. It had been clear to me two members of a "common market" would not go to war. How wrong I was! The lesson I learned was never to underestimate the irrationality of man. Fortunately, neither country had armed forces capable of decisively defeating the other. Private planes of Salvadoran air club members dropping bombs on the Honduran capital made for great stories as the pilots returned to their home fields, but were otherwise a ludicrous exercise. El Salvador occupied some of Honduras, the Organization of the American States (OAS) called for a ceasefire, the United States weighed in on the side of sanity, and after a few days the war ended. Unfortunately, some ill feeling persists to this day, even though the International Court of Justice in The Hague eventually settled residual disputes over the frontier.

Then in the summer of 1969, I was unexpectedly summoned to Washington for a lunch with Robert Ellsworth, ambassador-designate to NATO. He was considering me as his potential DCM and I was flattered the personnel system thought that well of me. Although tempted by Europe and a job central to U.S. foreign policy, I was honest enough to tell Ambassador Ellsworth he needed someone better qualified than I on European defense issues. I recommended for the job, as I presume others must have also, George Vest, who had worked for years on NATO issues. He got this prize job, moving from DCM at USEC in Brussels to DCM at NATO in Brussels. I got an excellent lunch and a chance to spend time with my parents.

It is not much of an exaggeration to say that agriculture in Guatemala was essentially of two kinds. There were small plots owned or farmed by Indians and poor *campesinos,* and there were large *fincas* owned by rich Guatemalans. Workers on the *fincas* often lived in almost feudal conditions. AID wanted to help the little fellows. The government, dominated by rich landowners, wanted assistance chiefly for large landowners. The minister of agriculture, Montenegro Giron, had reluctantly conceded that his government would accept a U.S. loan, but under no circumstances would it contribute its own resources. Instead, he repeatedly urged me to finance high-quality breeding cattle. He and his friends would no doubt have made good use of such animals and, indeed, were privately improving their livestock herds. When I countered that improving corn production would help far more individuals, the minister mumbled a go-ahead, provided the government would not contribute incremental financing. He did, however, designate his much more liberal vice minister to head the government's negotiating team. Under the influence of Fuentes Mohr, the vice minister worked with me to advance the project. We were ambitious. We wanted to have a positive impact on as much of the rural economy as possible. Thus we aimed for a comprehensive rural development loan.

To improve chances for success, I had AID contract with Iowa State University for technical advice and organized an in-country seminar, the like of which Guatemala had never before seen. Every government agency related to rural development and agriculture participated. Interestingly, many of the participants had never met before, much less participated in an open discussion of rural problems, needs, and possible solutions. The vice minister found this discussion as useful as I. To keep myself focused on what mattered, I read and reread Theodore Schultz's *Agriculture in an Unstable Economy*. That book, by my former professor at the University of Chicago, together with Ragnar Nurkse's *Problems of Capital Formation in Underdeveloped Countries*, served me well during my years with AID and in subsequent work on economic development.

Skeptics told me the descendants of the Mayans, who had raised maize in the highland for over a thousand years, would not change their ways. Better seed and fertilizers, better planting techniques, rural extension services, and credit facilities would, the skeptics insisted, make no impact. I argued that if productivity could be improved by such measures, the Indians would adopt them. I pointed to the rapid adjustment of these Indians to raising flowers. Once a foreign entrepreneur had started to grow and export flowers, the Indians quickly recognized a cash crop. In almost no time, small plots of colorful flowers were all over the highlands. The Mayan Indian might be illiterate, but he was not dumb.

The seminar made progress. Mindful of my instructions, I noted additional Guatemalan resources would also be needed. Perhaps, I mused, resources could be raised with new taxes? What happened then was repeated several times, as if it were choreographed. The vice minister, having reported to his minister, would telephone me to say no further discussions would be possible. My mention of a Guatemalan contribution was the problem. A day or two later I would call on the minister and eventually extract his permission to resume.

When I left the country the question of a Guatemalan contribution was still pending. The loan negotiations were carried forward, led largely by Morey Bell, an FSO assigned as an economic officer but co-opted by me as my deputy for the rural sector loan negotiations. With much help from Gert Rosenthal and Fuentes Mohr, he and my AID deputy, Richard Kaegi, somehow won a financial commitment from the Guatemalan government. Mohr and Rosenthal, however, lost their positions when in an electoral surprise, Colonel Arana, who had shown me around Zacapa two years before, was elected president. The new government as one of its first acts singed the Rural Development Loan. In Washington it was said to be the best such loan developed pursuant to the mandate from the Heads of Government Meeting in Uruguay in 1967.

At the urging of my Iowa State team of advisors, I also led a group of about fifteen to see the Rockefeller Foundation's Pueblo Project, an outstanding maize improvement program in Mexico. It was a good idea, not only to learn more about how to improve maize yields but also to further cement the kind of relations we were contributing to among Guatemalans participating in the discussion of the proposed loan. I think the trip was a success, but it proved to be my swan song in Guatemala.

Jim Fowler asked me to take over the AID program in Chile. His endorsement of my efforts in Guatemala, bearing in mind his initial prejudice against "a striped pants diplomat," was and is a source of immense pride for me—of even more pride than the Superior Service Medal I received for my years at the head of EUR/RPE. The Chile program was one of the larger and more important in Latin America. Moreover, I knew Santiago would be a wonderful posting.[10]

While we had thoroughly enjoyed Guatemala and overall had had a marvelous time there, family problems, in particular differences with Angela over how to react to crises brought on largely by our children, were increasingly becoming an emotional drain.

On her vacations from Mills, Deborah started an affair with a slick Guatemalan who promised eternal love, but meant it not. She resented my warnings about Latin gigolos. Angela was appalled, but her counsel had no more effect than mine. Deborah, already in revolt against U.S. policies in Vietnam and unable to focus on her academic work, decided to go to England. The trust fund provided by my mother for her education allowed her to live as she wished and study at Kent University there.

Chris and, to a lesser extent, Joe began experimenting with drugs. Unfortunately, the school they attended in Guatemala hardly even tried to deal with drug issues. The 1960s were not an easy period for teenagers at home either. In Guatemala, however, pot and more potent drugs were easily and cheaply available. At one party for our kids and their friends at our house, several guests were so high I literally threw them out. Chris was not amused. Angela thought I had overreacted, as perhaps I had, but I was not as permissive as she. We did agree thereafter that Chris should be placed in a private school in the States. After consulting educational counselors, Chris was enrolled in Oakwood School in the Hudson valley. Run by Quakers, it had an excellent reputation, but sadly it, too, failed to control drug use. A letter my father wrote to the boys telling them when they came home they should not have long hair did not help matters. He overdid it, writing that their reaction to his and my mother's wishes would be a test of whether or not they respected their grandparents. While I was not enamored of my sons' sloppy appearance, I was with them on this one. I wrote to Dad, "There are more important things in relations between people than the length of their hair, or at least there should be."

Not all family matters were tense. The visit of Angela's parents had been a great success, both in showing Bettie and Al the sights, including Antigua, Chichicastenango, and Sam Green's house on Lake Atitlan, and in their bonding with their grandchildren. "Daman" and "Tata," as our kids called them, were great favorites. Perhaps my mother's frail health, which unfortunately led them to cancel their planned visit, somehow influenced the sad tenor of our exchange over hair length.

During the team visit to Mexico I thought much about the family situation. Upon arrival in Washington, I talked matters over with Stan Frosh,[1] a good friend and the Bethesda neighbor on whose tennis court I had so enjoyed playing. At my request, he agreed to lunch with Angela to explore her thoughts about the family situation. I explicitly asked him to find out if she still loved me. Her answer was "No."

As a consequence and after confirming this answer with her, I told her I wanted a divorce. She reluctantly agreed. After painful discussions with and without our lawyers, the court decreed separation. Angela was awarded custody of Deborah, Joe, Joanna, and Veronica. She insisted I take custody of Christopher. We split our equity in the Dellwood house. With her share Angela acquired a new home in Kensington. I guaranteed the mortgage. We returned separately to Guatemala, amicably divided our possessions, and said our goodbyes. Angela returned to Washington. I proceeded to Chile.

The process was terribly hard on us, and more so, I fear, on our children. In a memo to myself written in October 1969, I noted our mutual recognition of our incompatibility and expressed anguish over the possible impact of divorce on our children, but concluded it was better than raising them in an atmosphere of bitter parental rancor. Bettie and Al stopped speaking to me, which I suppose is understandable, but it hurt nevertheless. My folks were upset; they did not approve of divorce. Still they provided us board and room, and, more important, psychological support. Angela and I agreed on one point: divorce imposes immense financial strain on each of the parties.

Ambassador Nat Davis in a personal note to me had reacted to the news of my impending divorce by telling me "I had rocks in my head." Before leaving Guatemala, though, he cheered me up somewhat by giving me a rave efficiency report. I would have gladly traded it for peace in a unified family.

Notes

1 Indeed, LBJ's practice, whatever its merits, had resulted in a number of long delays in getting qualified officers into key jobs, such as AID director in Santo Domingo.
2 This paper, which came out irregularly, called the epoch in which we were living "the most fucked up." Not too far wrong there. The paper's title translates roughly as "Don't Touch Us." At about the same time Reader's Digest published an article, "Nightmare in Guatemala," also not too far wrong.
3 Nestor and I worked together on El Salvador and Panama years later. We generally disagreed.
4 Sam apparently had made a small fortune in the textile business in New York before deciding to retire in Guatemala.
5 I write "occupied" since I think Sam's title to the property, if he had one, as he said he did, was of dubious validity, given that Guatemalan law prohibits the ownership of waterfront property by foreigners.
6 Fuentes Mohr was later minister of foreign affairs and still later was killed by a rightist hit squad. Although it certainly was not the case, many thought he was a communist or at least a socialist, given his liberal thinking, which was quite radical for Guatemala. Gert Rosenthal later headed the Planning Bureau, and still later fled the country with his family in face of death threats. I intervened successfully to have him named a fellow at the Adlai Stevenson Institute. Years later, we met again when he visited San Salvador as secretary general of the UN Economic Commission for Latin America.
7 Sadly, I understand that many of the trainees, precisely because

they became social activists, were killed in the horrible years of systematic repression, particularly in the 1980s.

[8] Major Fred Woerner headed the Civic Action Section of the Military Group in the embassy. He and I became good friends. Later he was to be enormously helpful to me in El Salvador. He retired with four stars as CINC South, where we overlapped, in part, during my ambassadorship to Costa Rica.

[9] Dick went on to have an AID career himself. Sadly, cancer killed him in his prime.

[10] How could I forget what my Italian truck driver friend had told me in Panama nearly thirty years before about the delights of Chile and of his regret about having moved on toward the United States? It has struck me as an incredible coincidence that the two countries, Guatemala and Chile, I had long desired to know better were precisely those of my first two posts south of the border.

[11] Stan Frosh, later Judge Frosh, represented me.

15

Chile (1969–1971)

John Hannah, the AID administrator, hosted my swearing in. Jim Fowler did the deed, this time with no regrets or private curses. Joe, Joanna, and Veronica attended and were photographed with Hannah, their dad, and Ambassador Korry. The three of them later joined me at the Ford offices in Washington, where Veronica insisted the Cougar I was ordering be orange. Distinctive, if undesirable from the security standpoint, there would be nothing else like it in Chile. Orange was not my preference, but how could I reject Wonky's advice?

Soon thereafter I was back off to Guatemala, where Angela and I said our goodbyes and Ambassador Nat Davis gave us a great *despedida*, despite his expressed view that "You have rocks in your head to divorce."

After departing Guatemala, I made a shopping stop in Panama and then headed on south. All the while, I was excited by memories of what my Italian friend in Panama had told me about Chile years before. I made several stops along the way in Guayaquil, Lima, and Antofagasta, the dry desolation of which made me briefly wonder why I was in Chile. And then finally, Santiago. Ray Harkins, my new deputy, and his wife, Sue, met me at the airport. Hernan, my new chauffeur, drove me—much too fast—to the director's residence. The house was considerably more pretentious than the one in Guatemala, English Tudor style but without the view of a volcano. From the rather large garden containing a sizable fish pond, I spied a hint of snow-covered Andes, so close to Santiago one could be on the ski slopes in an hour or so.

The residence came complete with a staff: Salome, the cook, Amelia, the maid, and Gonzalo, the waiter. Sidney Weintraub, my predecessor, and his wife, Gladys, had spoken highly of the first two but less enthusiastically about Gonzalo. The staff was put to the test almost immediately by my desire to hold an AID mission Christmas party. My worries about this plan partially vanished when three mission officers and their wives offered to help with the party. It was a great success but resulted in the disruption of the residence staff. Gonzalo got stinking drunk, so I fired him. The next day Amelia phoned me in hysterics. I couldn't grasp what she was sobbing about; but shortly thereafter Don Jaime called from General Services to say he had gone to the house to reclaim embassy glassware used in the party only to find a drunken Amelia asleep in my locked and unclean bedroom. He had fired her. Salome verified Don Jaime's account of events, hinting that Amelia and Gonzalo had been having an affair. I was encouraged to conclude his departure had led to her disgraceful resort to the bottle. After pondering the situation, I ruled that if Gonzalo ever returned, he was not to be let in, but that Amelia might return "on probation." These traumatic events along with my realization that Salome wanted only to cook, not handle money and buy food, led me to hire Esther Levy as housekeeper.

Over my first weekend, in the absence of the ambassador I paid a duty call on Chargé Harry Shlaudeman, who with his wife, Carol, became a good friend of mine. I also enjoyed the warm hospitality of Ray and Sue Harkins as well as their three small children. The evening was marred only by his insistence that I study the briefing book the mission had prepared for me.

I had been in Chile for about a month when in early January, to my amazed dismay, I received an "Eyes Only" cable notifying me I had been picked to be ambassador to Togo. Incredibly, it was not sent to Santiago but addressed to and forwarded from Guatemala. Not a bad country as African countries go, but ... Presumably the personnel people, who did not even know where I was currently serving, cleared this idea with the Africa Bureau but somehow failed to consult my bosses, either at AID or at the Bureau of Latin American Affairs. The director general of the Foreign Service retracted this proposal when confronted with objections from John Hannah, Jim Fowler, and Charlie Meyer, as well as my reply to the effect that I would be honored to be ambassador to Togo but preferred to stay where I was. Being AID director was a less prestigious job but entailed responsibilities I considered far greater.

The program I inherited was large and complicated. The U.S. government, through AID and in support of the Alliance for

Progress, had devoted over $500 million to development in Chile. Per capita assistance to Chile was almost the highest in the world. My predecessor, Sidney Weintraub, in his *Reflections on Foreign Assistance* argued for the program in terms of results obtained. Among other achievements, Sidney cited hundreds of thousands of children fed under the Food for Peace program, construction, largely U.S.-financed, of the main airport, roads, a seaport, machinery imports, reductions in the cost of tractors and fertilizer, and rural electric cooperatives stimulated by U.S. initiatives.

My new staff of over fifty Americans was more than twice my staff in Guatemala. Capable junior officers had been drawn to Chile so the level of competence was way above an average mission. I was enormously impressed by Robert Maushammer, Jerry Hirsch, Andre Colpitts, and Judd Kessler, to mention just a few. To maintain an outstanding staff was a priority concern of mine. Starting with the recruitment of Brian Bosworth as the new program officer and Jim Dean to the economic section, I think staff quality held up.

Further, as I worked my way through my briefings and took in the work atmosphere I noted significant differences from Guatemala. Early on I had a painful learning experience. I inadvertently insulted a little boy. It turned out that an affectionate phrase commonly used in Guatemala had a pejorative meaning in Chile. Indeed, throughout Latin America the Spanish vocabulary used, especially slang, varies widely. Somehow I had not fully appreciated this before my blunder.

Moreover, while Chile had a much larger middle class than Guatemala, wealth was similarly concentrated and distressing poverty was evident in the slums of Santiago and the countryside. With foreign assistance, President Eduardo Frei Montalva had attacked these problems, instituting agrarian reform and low-cost housing programs. He had made progress but it was far from sufficient. Also, catering to nationalist sentiment he negotiated a government takeover of majority interests in U.S. copper companies. He understood, however, the critical contribution American capital and know-how made to the Chilean economy and left the companies with a 49 percent ownership interest.

Moreover, negotiating with Chileans was quite different from what I had to put up with in the ministries of education and agriculture in Guatemala. By and large, Chilean ministers and officials were well qualified for their jobs. They knew what they were doing. They understood our concerns and usually reacted rationally to them. Even so, some of these Chileans did not seem to attach too much importance to written loan commitments. Problem loans, therefore, were more of a concern than they had been in Guatemala. Interestingly, however, on my first expedition to check into a problem loan, one to finance improved grain handling facilities at the port of San Antonio, I learned the problem was mainly our fault. "Efficient" American business firms had fallen behind in their equipment delivery schedules.

Nonetheless, Chilean responsibility and screw-ups were apparent at Valparaiso. Washington wanted me to deobligate a large port improvement loan unless I could promptly straighten matters out. It was not easy. Rather, it was a complicated mess involving technical engineering problems, alternative pier designs, differing ways of calculating fill, varying payment and certification procedures, and the interrelationships between AID, the Port Authority, contractors, consulting engineers, the Ministry of Public Works, and the Chilean controller general. Despite knowing little or nothing of these matters, I made considerable progress and kept the project alive. Yet I shocked the minister of agriculture, whose ministry had fallen way behind on commitments, by refusing after a long review session to agree to further disbursements until he corrected key deficiencies.

Unlike in Guatemala, the press and public generally did not devote much attention to the activities of American representatives. It seemed there was, however, a more widespread undercurrent of anti-Americanism. Despite this, there was no anti-American violence—nothing like the killings and kidnappings I had known in Guatemala. Indeed, except from the Left there was little overt hostility and less pandering. For this I credit Chilean democracy, permitting all parties from Communist to Fascist to legally exist and freely compete in elections. Another difference was a more sophisticated citizenry, which focused on things other than the activities of the gringos. The American presence and role in Guatemala had been predominant to the almost complete exclusion of other countries. It was not so in Chile, where ties to Europe, culturally and in political philosophy, were more important. For me, this was a welcome change.

Another welcome difference became apparent when I accompanied Chile's Cardinal Silva Henriquez south to a ceremony where titles to church-owned land were distributed to *campesinos*. Everyone joined in singing the Chilean national anthem. The speeches were short and sincere. The titles were real ones. Moreover, at lunch, unlike my experiences in Guatemala, the *campesinos* ate with the big shots.

No difference, however, was greater than the fact that I was a bachelor. My children were elsewhere and I tried to keep in touch as best I could. I would write long letters to each in turn with carbon copies to the others. Years later I learned this practice annoyed some of them, maybe all, but it seemed then, and still does, better than the alternatives. Unfortunately, computers were not available then. When replies arrived, as they did fairly regularly, it was a great day. Assurances of love and promises to visit me immeasurably improved my morale. Letters from Dad and Mother after initial promises to visit reported my mother's health was deteriorating. Arthritis and back pains made their visit unlikely.

Word from Deborah that she had visited Brussels with David, a boyfriend, upset my parents. I was not enthused by this development either. Nevertheless, I recognized different generations have different behavior patterns.

Far more disturbing were reports from Oakwood School about Chris. He was a rebel and was eventually expelled. The school cited "irresponsible" behavior, failure to keep appointments with his psychiatrist, "fireworks, smoke bomb throwing, absence from study hall," and, far more serious, drug use. Angela and I had thought Oakwood would at least keep its students away from drugs. We were wrong. My letters requesting an explanation of what Oakwood had or had not done drew no meaningful response. Since it had always been our intention that he would join me for summer vacation, I asked that he come down immediately, even as I worried about how I would handle him. Angela then made a mistake. She agreed to send him to me, but via Guatemala, where he was to stay with our good friends the Bells. She generously gave him extra funds for his trip. He used the funds to buy LSD, some of which he distributed to girlfriends. Indignant parents complained to Morey Bell, who phoned and told me, quite reasonably, that he was putting Chris on the first flight to Santiago. I was no longer to be without company.

When he arrived Chris was quite contrite. We had long heart-to-heart talks. He acknowledged his errors but I concluded he needed professional help. It appeared to me he lived most of the time in a dream world, unable to estimate in advance the consequences of his foolish acts. Yet he had remarkable insights into his own character and the reasons he had slipped. But he rejected the idea of rules, structure, and discipline, insisting he must be allowed to do exactly what he wanted. I tried to impress upon him that neither I nor the world in general would permit that.

We then began to work hard on improving matters. He needed lots of love, at all times, solid support when he tried to do well, and firm guidance when he strayed. I tried to follow this recipe.

For once, Chris approved of the psychiatrist I hired. Dr. Raphael Drullinsky had an extremely positive effect on Chris before he immigrated to Israel. What to do about further schooling was another worry. Fortunately we found a solution. Pat Larson, the wife of the Braniff agent in Santiago, undertook to tutor him. She, too, was a positive influence on Chris. Still, given a chance he would relapse; occasionally I would find he had been smoking marijuana at home, but I thought this was happening less and less. Hence, I was furious when one night at a fishing camp the wife of my legal advisor invited him to smoke dope with her. On balance, however, Chris and his behavior improved much. I valued my time with him, but my job kept me from spending as much time with him as I would have wished. With this in mind and Christmas coming, I proposed that we make a long car trip together into Argentina and back.

We drove south for three days to the beautiful Lago Todos los Santos, fished fruitlessly, and then went on to fabulous Lake Bariloche in Argentina, where we celebrated a rainy Christmas. The drive through the Andes was a beautiful and memorable adventure. In 1970, the route was not well traveled. Lost, we asked for directions. Trusting our informant, we turned downhill at a sign toward a lake. When we stopped at the shore there was no one in sight and no conceivable way to get my Cougar back up the hill to the road. Since there was nothing else to do, we sat there and waited. Eventually we saw a makeshift ferry approaching; a more welcome sight I could not imagine. Somehow we got the car aboard, then off across the lake, then onto another ferry, then off, and so forth. At each of five embarkations and landings I feared my car would end up in the lake. It's an easy trip today, I am told. It used to be fabulous then, but not easy. After Bariloche we took a decent, far less challenging northern road home.

Chile was everything I expected and more.

What I had expected was a challenging job in a beautiful country filled with attractive ladies and great wines. This Chile provided. More than that, Salvador Allende's election as president gave me a ringside seat to a peaceful Marxist revolution.

To top it off, Chile was where I would fall in love with Miren. With the demands of my job and the warm hospitality of my new colleagues, I had little time to be lonely. Moreover, I was so inexperienced at the dating game that I was getting advice by letter from Debi in London. After being stood up a time or two and after concluding that other relations, one with an art professor at a university, were not right for me (too much culture), I lucked out on a blind date.

When our cultural attaché gave me four tickets to "Holiday on Ice," I asked Fred Schieck, the AID mission loan officer, if he and his wife, Sarah, would join me and bring along another lady. Sarah, herself Bolivian, persuaded a reluctant Miren Arrivillaga to join us. Reluctant because she was depressed by a devastating marriage and had no interest in meeting another man, much less an American. Nevertheless, Sarah somehow convinced her the ice show would be fun and I might not be too bad. As it happened, the show was terrific, although not as terrific as competing Soviet cultural offerings, including the Moscow Circus and Symphony Orchestra, both top-flight.

Our date got off to a weak start. Miren spoke no English and my Spanish was still not what it should have been. Worse, I was exhausted from a hard week. The effort of trying to converse with her wore me down further. Consequently, after the show, as fascinated as I was by the lovely lady, instead of doing the town we said our goodnights.

Yet I wanted to see more of Miren, to meet with her alone. She, however, had disappeared, gone south, I was told. Someone added, "No, I do not know when she will return to Santiago." It was frustrating, but for weeks I persisted. Finally she returned to town. We talked. I called for her at 11 p.m. at her brother's house. Once there, I met Kepa, her brother, who mixed me a drink and then disappeared. Restless, I waited. Eventually Miren appeared. She knew an excellent restaurant and, for fun, a club where students sang leftist, often anti-American songs. We had a great time together.

From then on, my life improved. Life in Chile, particularly once I met Miren, was fabulous. I enjoyed interesting and stimulating work in an exciting political setting and played tennis almost every day at a fine club. I also played a poor second base on an AID softball team. Nevertheless, we won the championship, beating both a

U.S. military and an embassy team. The city has great restaurants and nightclubs, and vineyards near enough for weekend expeditions to taste and buy. Also, Santiago is one of only a few cities in the world where you can drive to ski slopes in the morning and beautiful beaches, with great girl-watching, in the afternoon. For most, however, the water, chilled by the Humboldt Current off Antarctica, is too cold for swimming.

Soon Miren had her own apartment, where I met three of her children: Miren, 12, known as Michu, Maria Luisa, 9, known as Coca, and Juan Jose, 5, known as Juanjo. Her two older boys, Pedro and Guillermo, known as Mincho, had opted to stay with their father, who was resisting Miren's efforts to win an annulment. In Catholic Chile there was then no divorce. Miren's accounts of her battles in and out of court were almost unbelievable to me. The contrast with my own divorce proceedings could not have been greater. Only when Miren's family paid a substantial sum to her husband, one Guillermo Arrivillaga, was it established without challenge that an address on their marriage license had been incorrect! With this devastating error revealed, the judge granted an annulment. Not a divorce, but an annulment, allegedly because of a clerical error, after years of marriage and six children, one of whom had died from cancer as a small boy.

Joe, Joanna, and Veronica's visit that summer was the highpoint of my year. They wanted to ski, so we went to Farellones with Miren and her three youngest. Everyone got along famously well. Veronica, in particular, had a great time with Juanjo. Younger than she, for the first time in her life there was someone she could help take care of, to say nothing of boss around.

We did the sights in Santiago, including a splendid concert by the Moscow Symphony Orchestra—lots of Soviet interest in Chile in 1970—then headed north. Our first stop was Portillo. With a "beginners" ski slope far beyond our poor capacity for skiing, we concentrated on eating. Thereafter, as we drove north I told my trusting but gullible offspring about the incredible "bacon trees" we would see in the Atacama Desert. What we did see, at the end of the line, was a small Catholic mission with a smaller museum, containing, amongst other items, mummified remains of individuals who lived long before the Spanish conquest of Chile. Their remains had deteriorated, but not too much since the Atacama is one of the driest parts of the world, going years without rain. On the way back to Santiago, Joe having asked to visit a copper mine, we visited Chuquicamata, the world's largest open pit mine. It was spectacular. For me, however, the best of it on a hot, dusty day were the Pisco Sours served at the Anaconda Company's rest house.

It was a sad day for Chris and me when we bid his siblings farewell. Their trip home, thankfully, was uneventful; not like the trip down, when they had to overnight in La Paz, Bolivia, after aircraft trouble. The altitude, over 12,000 feet at the airport, gave my tired children headaches. Joanna advised me never to be assigned to Bolivia. I tried to comfort them by pointing out that they had been to a country I had yet to visit.

As my courtship picked up speed, Miren asked me to accompany her to family functions. Glad as I was to be with her, I was confused by the overwhelming number of cousins, aunts, and uncles. In Chile the extended family is a reality. Her father, Don Pedro de Aretxabala, the family patriarch, had me around. He also asked me—a good sign, I thought—to bring him a freezer of meat from Mendoza, where Miren and I journeyed several times, in an effort to beat the *veda*, which limited meat purchases in Chile to once a week. I began to think seriously about a future together with Miren. However, rather than approaching Don Pedro I decided to sound out Kepa regarding the family's reaction to me and to my relationship with Miren. I broached the subject at lunch at the Union Club. Kepa encouraged me to think Miren and I had a future together. He said, "There is only one problem. Miren is too good a person for her own good." He was right; she was like an angel on earth.

Other remembrances of Chile center on two striking personalities: Ambassador Edward M. Korry and Don Salvador Allende.

Korry was self-centered and domineering. When he returned to town from a visit to Washington, I naturally called on him. He warmly welcomed me to his embassy and instantly put me to work commenting on his draft of what became "The Korry Report" concerning U.S. economic assistance programs. Having just run a fairly successful one in Guatemala, I thought I would help my new boss with a serious critique. He thanked me for the fourteen-page critique and changed not a word in his draft.

Mrs. Korry was no less egotistical and dominating. During my initial call she reproached me for not having informed her my wife would not accompany me to Chile. Had she known I would be alone, she said, she would have vetoed my assignment. Apart from the reproach, she was charming. Later she perhaps came to like me and I her, at least most of the time. In any case, at residence dances she would order me to dance with her, which reminded me of the redoubtable "Wahwee" MacArthur, who had similarly summoned me to dance in Brussels.

Mrs. Korry, "to build morale," liked to have mission ladies to tea. AID wives, not as well housebroken as Foreign Service wives, did not consider her invitations to be command performances. Thus, as regular as clockwork, the day after several AID wives had not shown my phone would ring. Mrs. Korry would tell me how upset she was with so-and-so and ask, "What are you going to do about it?" What the hell could I do? To appease her I would promise to speak to the husbands of the errant ladies. I did so and hated myself for not having told her to get lost. A year or so later, a reform, long overdue and greatly welcomed, ended the command authority of ambassadorial spouses.

The ambassador himself amazed me with his cable output. A former newspaper reporter, and by reputation a good one, he reported at length. Different cables would have varied predictions. By covering many bases, he later could, and did, report, "as foreseen in my telegram of such and such a date." At rare country team meetings we would be subjected to monologues, sometimes lasting over two hours. In a letter from Guatemala Morey Bell commented to me that Korry's yearend wrap-up cable, sent to every post in the Hemisphere, "was not excessively brilliant, but rather brilliantly excessive." Amen!

President Eduardo Frei Montalva was coming to the end of his term when I arrived in Santiago, and political life was dominated by election campaigns. Running for president were Salvador Allende, a Socialist with Communist support, Jorge Alessandri, a former president and candidate of the right wing National Party, and Radomiro Tomic of Frei's Christian Democratic Party. Frei appeared to give lukewarm support to Tomic, who foolishly tried to outflank Allende on the left. I watched the speeches on television and decided a drooling 74-year-old Alessandri would leave voters cold. I expressed this opinion in a meeting, only to be told by the ambassador that I just did not understand Chilean politics. Chilean voters, he asserted, would go for a "father figure." I attended, inconspicuously, a large Allende rally and watched when TV stations reported his speeches. I was impressed by his dynamism and particularly by his analysis of Chile's economic and social problems. He stressed the need to reduce large income disparities, promote land reform, improve education, and reduce child mortality. He also advocated nationalization of foreign investments, particularly those controlling copper and other Chilean mineral resources. The AID mission operated on the basis of a similar analysis, except that, needless to add, AID did not advocate nationalization of foreign assets. In this regard, AID's proposed remedies and Allende's Marxist program could not have been more different.

To my amazement, Korry forbade his staff from any contact with Allende or his people. Thus, DCM Harry Shlaudeman and Political Counselor John Karkashian, both outstanding officers, were essentially handcuffed. And as far as I could judge, so were C.I.A. personnel. My staff, however, had long had fairly good professional relations with pro-Allende professors at several universities and with Marxists working at ECLA, the United Nations Economic Commission for Latin America. Program Officer Hank Johnson and AID economist John Sprott had excellent contacts with pro-Allende economists and introduced me to many of them. Korry, fortunately, was oblivious of this or, more likely, could not be concerned with what we economic types were doing. In any case, after discussions with these individuals and studying what Allende was proposing I sent Washington my analysis of Allende's program. I concluded it would produce economic disaster. Inflation, already a concern, would explode were his proposals put into effect. And as it would turn out, I was right.

But the more I observed the political scene, the more convinced I became that unless the opposition to Allende cut a deal he would win the election. At a staff meeting in Washington, when Charlie Meyer, assistant secretary for Latin American affairs, asked for my views, I predicted Allende's victory. Ambassador Korry, confident Alessandri would win, was not pleased with my prediction or me.

Clearly the subsequent Chilean tragedy was due in large measure to the failure of the Nationalists and Christian Democrats to compromise before the election and deny a plurality to a Marxist. Allende polled 36.2 percent of the vote, Alessandri, 34.9 percent, and Tomic, 27.8 percent. Allende's plurality made him the likely president when pursuant to the Constitution, Congress would meet to choose the new president from the top two vote-getters. So although the combined vote of the democratic parties won over 60 percent, Allende became president.

Time magazine put him on its cover, a totally red cover. Concern that Allende would inevitably be followed by a communist takeover was widespread. President Nixon and Henry Kissinger, we now know, decided to try to deny Allende the presidency, fearing both a communist contagion in the hemisphere and a political backlash at home about "who lost Chile." However, Rube Goldberg efforts to somehow block Allende's election in Congress failed. To my amazement and unease, Korry, who under instructions was trying to manipulate the situation, talked to me at great length and with pride about his instructions and the covert monies made available to him. To his credit, he did seem remorseful and taken aback when the attempted kidnapping of General René Schneider resulted in the general's violent death. It appears the United States tried, but failed to abort that nutty scheme.

In January 1971, Joseph Kraft wrote in *The New Yorker*:

> After the election, the Ambassador apparently thought highly of the scheme to keep Allende out of office by having the Congress elect Alessandri and having Alessandri force a new election by resigning. He [Ambassador Korry] now talks of Chile in a tone suggesting that since the Chileans didn't take his advice, they are doomed.

Many well-to-do Chileans feared a repeat of Cuba was in the cards. Conversation was virtually limited to politics, the Communist threat, Fidel Castro, and the risks involved. Allende's inauguration provoked even more discussion of the pros and cons of leaving while the going was good, or of waiting it out and hoping for the best. Many prominent conservatives, including a number of friends I had gotten to know through Miren, sold out and left for the States. Suddenly, the newspapers were filled with auction announcements. Had I had any spare funds, I could have bought treasures for a song. As it was, Miren and I attended many auctions just to window shop. Twice, however, I could not resist bidding: once for a superb set of the eleventh edition of the *Encyclopedia Britannica*, another time for a striking colonial-era painting of Saint Augustine. The *Britannica* went to another bidder for far less than its value but for more than I could afford. The painting became mine. A European banker who doubtless could better afford it than I dropped out of the bidding somewhere above the limit I had set for myself before the stimulation of the occasion got the better of my judgment. Would that all of my misjudgments had turned out so well. I have never regretted acquiring that magnificent Saint Augustine.

***

Apart from the fascination of my courtship of Miren and the excitement of the electoral campaign, I was busy running a large AID program, greatly missing and worrying about my children, trying to manage a bachelor's household, and enjoying a beautiful country.

In April 1970 two events impacted me, one positive and the other negative. First, Pablo Neruda gave a reading of his poetry. I had already read his *Veinte Poemas de Amor y Una Canción Desesperada*, but hearing him recite favorites of mine such as *Poema 20*, which starts, "*Puedo escribir los versos más tristes esta noche*," was a rare treat. It was sad to note that, in addition to having won a Nobel Prize for Literature, Neruda was a convinced, active Communist. On the negative side, that night robbers made quite a haul at my residence. It was too bad about the government's replaceable sterling table service; but I mourned the tragic loss of the three irreplaceable ivory elephants given to me as a farewell gift by friends in Mombasa.

Then in September I received congratulations from the director general of the Foreign Service on becoming a member of "an elite group of some 400 Foreign Service officers" who had attained advanced competence in at least two foreign languages. It had taken almost three years of hard work since my language aptitude is limited. Knowing full well there is no substitute for language competency in a foreign country, I was particularly proud of my achievement.

One of the better aspects of being AID director was the access it gave me to an eclectic group of fascinating people. This included Dr. Elda Fagetti, an oceanographer at the University of Chile; Terrence Cardinal Cook, who was in Chile to check up on Catholic Relief Services; Padre Luis Ramallo, the Jesuit head of the Latin America Center for Sociology; astronauts Conrad, Gordon, and Bean of Apollo XII; Adrian Dufflocq, fisherman extraordinaire; Dr. Fernando Mankelberg, world famous Chilean nutritionist; and many more, to say nothing of President Frei, ministers, bureaucrats, and a steady stream of U.S. government visitors.

Opportunities to travel within Chile, to Argentina (Mendoza, Bariloche, and Buenos Aires) and to Rio de Janeiro came my way. By coincidence, I was in Rio attending a conference on population problems during the 1970 World Cup games in Mexico City. It was a unique experience. On game day, the city literally shut down at 3 p.m. so everyone could be home for the 7 p.m. start of the semi-final between Brazil and Uruguay. Not a person, not one, was on the street. Ten million or so Brazilians were at their TVs or radios. When Brazil scored, millions surged outside, screamed, shot off barrages of fireworks, and quickly ran back in. After victory, millions celebrated with street dancing, sambas, and congas. It was just as I had imagined Carnival. I have never seen a more relaxed, fun-loving people.

On November 4, 1970, Salvador Allende was inaugurated as president of Chile. Earlier, his coalition of supporters, led by the Communist Party, had proclaimed that while "foreign capital" might be acceptable in some circumstances, "imperialist capital" was not wanted under any. The nationalization of the American copper companies was proclaimed immediately. Managers of smaller U.S. firms were harassed by their employees. Factories were sometimes seized by their workers while the government did nothing. Key economic ministries—finance, labor, and public works—were now headed by Communists. The minister of economy was an avowed Marxist, although not affiliated with the Communist Party. Cuban "advisors" were arriving in force.

"Democracy" was established in the universities. In the case of the University of Chile, everyone—students, professors, janitors—was given an equal vote on any and all issues. AID had a tiny project to finance the publication of research papers of the university's oceanographic institute. After the project was denounced, an overwhelming majority of the thousands now eligible to vote rejected further U.S. funding. It mattered not that this miniscule American effort was totally nonpolitical. What did matter, for the future of Chile, was that entrance requirements to the university, including to its graduate schools, were abolished. Thousands of would-be doctors enrolled in the University of Chile Medical School. The "revolution" was off to what looked to me to be a self-defeating start.

Ambassador Korry, under instructions from Washington, told me I was to drastically cut back the AID program. In his regular meeting with American businessmen he told them I was out of the AID business and they were to look to me as economic counselor for assistance with their now endless problems. Up to a point, I welcomed his charge; but I often found there was little I could do to help beyond handholding.

Korry further instructed me not to proceed with the supplementary education agreement I had negotiated with the minister of finance, Andrés Zaldívar. Its intent was to help finance key aspects of elementary education. Trying to keep alive one of our better assistance efforts, even though I knew it was probably a hopeless cause, I fired off a dissent cable. I argued improvement in education was critical for Chile's future, Marxists or no Marxists. Zaldívar and I were particularly proud of our planned effort to counter the Communist domination of the preparation of teachers in normal schools. My dissent was, of course, in vain. In any case, the ambassador was probably right, since the Allende regime would have found a way to frustrate our kind of educational improvement.

One evening in January of 1971 while I was sitting in my office admiring the sunset on the Andes and thinking how lucky I was to be in Chile, the phone rang. Calling from Washington, my friend in the under secretary's office, Arthur Hartman, told me I was to get the earliest possible flight out of Chile. Upon my protests and demands for an explanation, he added I would be given further instructions when I reported to the under secretary's office in the State Department. Neither Miren nor I liked the sound of it, but off I went.

In Washington I was given a roundtrip ticket to Chicago and told to be at the residence of one Peter G. Peterson in Lake Forest at 6:30 p.m. the following day. Peterson, I was informed, would soon be named by President Nixon as special assistant to the president for international economic policy. He wanted to check out possible staff members. State was clearly trying to insert me into the new mechanism. Yet my personal interest was different from the department's. As Marxist control tightened, Chile was getting more interesting by the day. I had often hoped to serve in a Marxist state; to be in delightful Chile and have Marxism come to me was fabulous. More important, I did not think courting Miren by mail would be much fun. In fact, I feared it might fail. So I resolved to convince this Peterson character I was not who he needed in the White House.

In fact, death almost spared me from him. There was a blizzard in Chicago. Arriving in a taxi at the large, well-lit Peterson residence, I walked to the door and rang the bell. I rang and rang and got no response apart from a dog barking. In subzero temperatures with a gale blowing off of Lake Michigan and wearing a light coat, suitable for a less cold Chile, I recognized I had to quickly seek refuge elsewhere. Houses are far apart in Lake Forest. I saw a light. Freezing, I walked to it. Again, there was no one home. In desperation, I went as fast as I could through snow drifts to another house. Fortunately, the owner opened the door, saw my condition, dragged me in to his fire, and produced warm toddy. He probably saved my life.

He was not surprised Peterson was not home. "Pete is rarely on time for anything," he remarked. We left a message on Peterson's answering machine. In due course, with profuse apologies Peterson picked me up and took me to his home. There, his delightful wife prepared us hamburgers while Pete and I talked at length. He was thrilled by his new responsibilities and wanted me to join the staff of what was to be the Council on International Economic Policy. Quite mistakenly, he said it would be equivalent to the National Security Council. Sadly I failed to dissuade him and so he arranged for me to report to him in Washington in a few weeks.

Thus, I returned to Chile to say my goodbyes. Chris was to finish his school year, staying with the Larsons, before joining me in Washington. Miren bravely promised to come up "as soon as possible."

16

Council on International
Economic Policy (1971–1974)

Reluctantly leaving Chris and Miren in Chile, I flew to Washington, D.C., and checked into the Francis Scott Key Hotel. The next morning, March 1, 1971, I walked to the Executive Office Building to report to Pete Peterson. To my surprise, I found him in the same office—then in the State Department—in which I had reported to the Syria desk officer twenty-five years before.

He welcomed me and immediately put me to work. I was to collect data and available charts on the American economy, particularly on its international standing. A C.I.A. analyst would be my staff. Without any explanation as to why he wanted these statistics, I was summarily dismissed. My vision of economic policymaking in the White House had been deflated. In fact, I wondered if Peterson was entirely sane.

A day later he instructed me to look into a Department of Agriculture demand that we respond to the European Community's latest "egregious" behavior. So, it was back to discussing a trade problem, this time involving grains and the United Kingdom, with my friend Ray Ioannes, head of the Foreign Agricultural Service. He was his old self–"We must retaliate." However, I soon discovered the facts were not what Agriculture was alleging. This explained why Carl Gilbert, then the special trade representative, was hesitant to act. His skepticism, I thought, had led Agriculture to appeal to Peterson, the new decision maker on the block. I acquainted Peterson with my conclusions. Unfortunately, the political climate in Washington called for us to get tough. Worse, Peterson appeared to want to prove he could make firm decisions. But as he explored matters further, he soon recognized a key point. "Deane," he told me, "if we retaliate with weak justification, the Europeans will retaliate in turn. We'll have a trade war." He turned Agriculture down and explained how they should handle the public relations aspect of the situation. Ioannes fumed and his department ignored Peterson's marketing directive.

This incident, even while I continued to collect statistics, gave me a feel for Pete—as I was now asked to call him. I learned something basic about him. He was intelligent. He might start wrong but would chew matters over and end up right. Working for him was incredibly demanding. I wrote Chris, "I've hardly had time to turn around....Thursday was the worst: 8 in the morning until midnight. Your Dad is too old for this kind of foolishness." Yet I would go on, with little letup, for three more years.

Fortunately there were many rewards, starting with awe at being on the White House staff, close to power. During the first week, Pete took me to a late night get-acquainted meeting with Kissinger. Henry, as I expected, not only had a razor sharp mind, but, to my surprise, also had us breaking up with laughter. He recruited Pete then and there as a friend and as a bureaucratic ally.

That alliance proved to be crucial much later in blunting Treasury Secretary John Connally's hard line. It eventually helped terminate the import tariff surcharge established by an August presidential decision. It also slightly softened Connally's blunderbuss policy preference for dealing with foreign expropriations of American-owned investments.

Shortly thereafter, Pete made what I came to view as a major blunder. He asserted his jurisdiction over the preparation of pending sugar legislation. He assigned me to chair an interagency group tasked to produce a new Sugar Act. I doubt he knew what a can of worms he was getting CIEP into. Did he know sugar was as highly protected and politically charged as any trade issue? U.S. consumers had to pay up to 100 percent more than the world price. This hurt the little man. However, as long as competing large commercial users pay the same price, which they then passed on to consumers, their interest in assured supply overrode cost concerns.

When word of my assignment leaked, I learned quickly about lobbyists: those of cane growers, beet growers, refiners, foreign country quota holders, and those seeking quotas, tax breaks, or other advantages from sugar, to say nothing of those hoping to get cheaper sugar or reduce the budgetary drain of the program. My phone rang incessantly and my secretary noted countless attractive invitations. Within twenty-four hours I concluded I should have no contact with anyone concerned with sugar outside of government. Soon, however, I had to add some individuals from government, such as U.S. ambassadors to countries seeking quotas or larger quotas.

With help from departmental experts, all with their own axes to grind, I put together an options paper for the president, which Pete then worked over at considerable length. It came back with some notations from Nixon; he was not interested in reforming the system. He thought we should stay as close to existing quotas as possible, with one exception. He asked that we arrange a larger quota for Panama—he wanted something for Omar Efraín Torrijos Herrera. He had recently met the Panamanian leader and the administration was contemplating negotiations over the Panama Canal. He also urged us to consult with specified individuals.

With presidential guidance, my task became much easier, although a complicated excise tax issue still took considerable sorting out. I talked further to key congressmen, but, to my relief, others largely took over the legislative battle. I had, however, learned that sugar was another word for politics. Damn little economic policy involved.

Pete needed more staff, starting with a deputy. Others in the White House virtually forced Richard V. Allen on him. Allen was a conservative Republican who knew little about economics and seemed to care even less. I found him courteous but difficult. His peculiarity as a boss was exemplified by the sandbox in his office and by his obsessive note-taking. Before he moved on after the 1972 elections, Peterson apologized to me for Allen, not that he had much choice in the matter.

I, too, needed staff and did much better than Pete. When I contacted Bob Morris, an FSO who had long impressed me, Bob gave up a prize school assignment to join the White House staff. Bringing him on board was my single most important contribution to CIEP. For a secretary, I lucked out with Lori Bider. She was efficient, tireless, and a temperamental character with a sharp sense of humor. When not threatening to quit, she took devoted care of me.

I needed it. Not only was I working killing hours, as did Lori, but personal concerns were overwhelming. Hopes of Miren's joining me faded as months went by without resolution of her annulment case. I missed her enormously, as I did Chris. Miren and I wrote regularly. Still, trying to sort out our future by mail was highly unsatisfactory. She, too, was frustrated. At one point she suggested that she and her smaller children would somehow just slip out of Chile and join me. As much as I wanted to be with her, I did not think well of exposing her to charges of child kidnapping. Moreover, while my parents were pleased with my intentions, once Angela learned I intended to marry again she complicated matters by reopening our agreement and upping the money ante. Questions of where we would live, where Miren's children would go to school, Chris' future, and what furniture to buy and/or ship also weighed upon us.

I was still spending much time on my initial assignment. Now, however, Pete let us know the president had asked him to prepare an analysis of our changing position in the world economy. With this explanation, our project no longer struck me as insane. Indeed, as Pete shaped the data into charts for presentation to the president, always asking for more and constantly reworking both his charts and his talking points, I came to share his enthusiasm.

On April 8, 1971, Pete presented his charts and analyses to the president and some cabinet members while I sat at the back of the Cabinet Room. Thrilled to be there, I was impressed both by Pete's presentation skills and by most of the president's remarks.

The president opened the meeting, noting CIEP owed its existence to the Ash Committee and particularly to the leadership of Secretary John Connally. Thereafter, Nixon frequently intervened in the discussion. Among other points, he asked for a breakout of the Soviet share in the chart of world GNP and an early council discussion of East-West trade. He and Secretary of State William Rogers stressed the importance of antitrust issues (a new subject for me). He also noted labor union opposition to corporations' exporting jobs and thought investment in breeder reactors needed consideration. Additionally, he suggested Pete do a study of the movie industry's contribution to the U.S. economy and the nontariff barriers it faced. It was, I thought, a good beginning, but I was puzzled by Nixon's skeptical remarks about foreign investment.

In August after five months on the job, Peterson named me assistant director for trade and development. To my delight, with the title came White House mess privileges—a prestigious eatery with better strip steaks and hot fudge sundaes than any I had ever before enjoyed.

As his assistant for trade, I pushed Pete to back a proposal advanced by Ambassador Joe Greenwald for a high-level OECD trade group to examine the possibility of new multilateral negotiations; and eventually the Rey Group came into being. It took its name from its chairman, Jean Rey, the European commissioner who had helped bring the Kennedy Round of trade negotiations to a successful conclusion.

Around the same time, concern arose in the administration that Carl Gilbert, the special trade representative, needed to be replaced. As momentum was building for the activist, highly protectionist monetary and trade policies the president had adopted at the August 15 Camp David meeting, it was announced that William D. Eberle would replace Gilbert.

I suppose Eberle's political connections must have been decisive, since he knew nothing of trade problems and even less about the monetary issues stirred up by U.S. actions on August 15. Moreover, the September 15, 1971, issue of *Forbes* reported he had left behind a "shambles" at American Standard Inc. when he resigned as CEO. If not politics and availability, why else make Eberle STR? Nonetheless, he was to be our representative on the Rey Group, every other member of which had deep experience with international economic questions. Peterson named me his advisor, an assignment I welcomed but which provoked an angry letter from Miren. She did not want me traveling to Paris every month or so. Fortunately, she soon came to accept that some travel came with my job.

On the personal side, Eberle could not have been more pleasant. Working with him, however, was both a joy and a source of immense frustration. Joy, because he used well the initial talking points I prepared for him before each meeting. Frustration, because once questions and comments arose he had little idea as to what to say next about trade, monetary equilibrium, adjustment, or growth issues. Worse, his pride kept him from being cautious when out of his depth. Late in 1971 I accompanied him to New York, where he was the featured speaker on trade issues at a session of the Council on Foreign Relations. Afterwards, Mike Blumenthal, our Kennedy Round negotiator, took me aside and said, "He doesn't know what he is talking about." All I could say in reply was, "I know."

Although each representative on the Rey Group was said to be serving in his personal capacity, thus avoiding any commitment by governments, the exchanges did reflect national positions. At its July 14, 1972, meeting, the group adopted its report. Bill Eberle signed, but later provided a stringent commentary taking issue with many points. Mostly he was on target, having learned a good deal in his first ten months on the job. I think, however, that a different American representative—one more experienced, more diplomatic—could have worked many of Eberle's concluding objections into the report itself. Some members wanted to reply to Eberle's blast, but Chairman Rey persuaded them not to reopen discussions.

It didn't matter because the first recommendation of the group was: "The effort to improve international economic relations and to liberalize trade must be resolutely pursued." The Rey Group had created momentum for a new round of trade negotiations. And on that point Eberle was solidly on board. Soon, ministers agreed to launch a new negotiating round, scheduled to begin in late 1972.

Meanwhile, Peterson wanted to move forward with legislation. He wanted input from experienced trade types, so he asked me to develop a list of people to be invited to the Roosevelt Room to discuss how to proceed. Naturally, my list, as would any list of leading trade experts, included Democrats, for example DeVier Pierson, who had handled trade matters in the White House for LBJ, and Robert McNeil, who had been in Commerce during the Kennedy administration. Apart from the Republicans on my list, not one participant had visited the White House since Nixon became president. Rumor soon had it that Pete was in trouble for consorting with the enemy; using my list perhaps cost him his job. In the new administration he was kicked upstairs to become Secretary of Commerce. Peter M. Flanigan, a blue-blooded Nixon supporter and aide who had ably handled a number of special projects for the president, replaced Pete as special assistant to the president for international economic policy.

Flanigan, while properly demanding, was much easier to work for than Pete. He was not as frenetic as Pete. Though perhaps not as brilliant, he had, I thought, more common sense. Efficient good work was the goal, not perfection. Lori, now spared Pete's often needless rewrites, also appreciated Flanigan. It did not hurt that one of his first acts was to ease Richard Allen out, followed not long after by naming me his deputy. To cap it off, Flanigan and his wife Brigitt were delightful personally. Pete was 100 percent business; Flanigan worked hard, but he also enjoyed life. Maybe this reflects the difference between a rich, established Irishman and a wealthy, ambitious Greek.

As time went on, tension had been increasing between Eberle and Peterson. It would be even worse with Flanigan. Eberle resented first Pete's then Flanigan's oversight of trade issues. He began to play destructive bureaucratic games, trying quite unsuccessfully to sideline Bob Morris and me when preparing the legislation needed for another round of multilateral trade negotiations. Tension persisted even after the president on December 1, 1972, named Secretary of the Treasury George Shultz chairman of a new Council on Economic Policy. This gave Shultz control of domestic and international economic policy. Efforts at monetary and trade reform were united. CIEP became in effect a staff agency for Shultz. Eberle found himself one more layer removed from the president.

Flanigan suggested combining STR and CIEP, but here Eberle's resistance carried the day. Bill Pearce, Eberle's deputy, was designated to work with Congress to pass trade legislation. I was confirmed to continue as chairman of the Legislation Working Group. A cabinet-level group under Shultz would review our proposals and decide policy. At most meetings of this political group I was the only career participant.

As the Watergate scandal unfolded, George Shultz became, in effect, president for economic affairs. He was the most impressive leader I ever served under. Capable of anger, he was normally even-tempered. He was a Chicago School economist, guided by principle and leavened with wide experience in government.

Twice he and I had rough exchanges. First, on the legislation for renewed multilateral trade negotiations he opposed trade-related adjustment assistance, arguing such assistance should be available to anyone unemployed. In principle, I agreed with him. Nevertheless, having advanced a proposal for extensive adjustment assistance a year before only to be frustrated by the Domestic Council, I thought it too late to try again. But provisions for such assistance were essential in the trade bill if it were to pass. Pearce, who was handling congressional liaison, argued the Ways and Means Committee would not even report on a trade bill without adjustment assistance. I agreed, but to no avail. Shultz kept the concept out of the administration's proposal but promised a separate bill with benefits for all unemployed workers. The Ways and Means Committee, with Pearce dutifully opposing, nevertheless wrote trade adjustment assistance into the bill reported to the floor.

I also had a small group working on highly sensitive antitrust issues. Unfortunately, someone leaked and *The Journal of Commerce* ran a fairly accurate story on the very day the cabinet-level group was to consider the issue. Shultz was furious, as was I. However, I viewed leaks as inevitable, to be lived with. Shultz, overreacting, instructed me to stop holding meetings of my working group. I told him I could not meet the deadline he had imposed if I could not meet with experts. And about a week later he relented.

Unable to move Treasury staff to change our antidumping and countervailing duty procedures, I asked William Simon, deputy treasury secretary, to meet with his staff and me to review the arguments. To my satisfaction, he ruled partly in my favor but not enough to call the changes a breakthrough. Still, the 1973 Act set a precedent in that for the first time it provided authority to negotiate these issues as well as other nontariff barriers such as American Selling Price (ASP).

Another important issue was whether to include authority for Most Favored Nation (MFN) treatment for imports from communist countries. Henry Kissinger wanted the authority but preferred a separate bill to approve the U.S.-Soviet Commercial Agreement already negotiated. He ceded only when it became clear every other concerned cabinet member wanted a comprehensive bill. Thus, on April 10, 1973, the president sent to Congress the 150-page Trade Reform Act of 1973.

For several years, Bob Morris and I had written countless papers about trade issues and on the reasons for moving ahead with legislation. Once the president's proposals were sent to Congress, we used these papers to draft a statement for Flanigan to use at a White House press conference. Later we contributed to the May 9 testimonies of Secretaries Rogers and Shultz and of Flanigan before the Ways and Means Committee. This Act was my most important and most satisfying White House achievement.

My most regrettable failure occurred in June of that year. I failed to argue convincingly enough to stop the administration from imposing an export embargo on soybeans. That shortsighted action, reversed in September, immediately cost us agricultural exports and our long-run reputation as a "reliable supplier." Even George Shultz, normally a leave-it-to-the-market advocate, pressured by the Cost of Living Council overreacted to the intense burst of inflation triggered by the Middle East war and the OPEC oil embargo.

In October the Ways and Means Committee reported out a much-amended, yet, most of us thought satisfactory trade bill.

However, the congressional amendment known as Jackson-Vanik provoked a major battle. Senator Henry "Scoop" Jackson vigorously opposed the administration's policy of détente with the Soviets. Representative Charles Vanik, concerned mainly about human rights, wanted the Soviets to free up emigration. After intense pressure, particularly from the pro-Israel lobby, and over vociferous administration objections, Jackson-Vanik passed. The amendment required that before a nonmarket economy could receive MFN treatment, the president had to determine the country in question did not deny "its citizens the right or opportunity to emigrate." This provision in effect killed the commercial agreement with the Soviet Union along with a negotiated Lend-Lease settlement. In so doing, it also endangered the process of détente. The Soviets viewed the amendment as unacceptable interference in their emigration policy. In retrospect, it is clear Jackson-Vanik also would have killed Kissinger's proposed separate bill. Interestingly, however, the intense debate on this issue took some of the heat off of other controversial parts of the bill, notably provisions for some tariff preferences for less developed countries (LDCs).

In June of 1971, Chris joined me in Washington, having, with Pat Larson's help, completed high school by correspondence. I was mighty glad to have him back but knew I could not spend as much time with him as he needed.

In July, Miren, still without her annulment, came "to visit her sister, Begonia." Pete chose the weekend of her arrival to call a Camp David meeting at the under secretary level. It was great to be at the president's weekend retreat, but why when Miren was finally arriving?

Even so, as wonderful as it was to see her, I pondered how to renew our intimacy without being crude. It was not possible in a small apartment, shared with Chris, nor at Begonia's, nor in a Volkswagen Beetle. Miren, bless her, took the initiative, asking, "Don't they have motels in Washington?" Before she returned to Chile, we agreed that when married we would move into the Dellwood house. Although it was inappropriate in some respects, Bethesda's good public schools for her three children were a decisive consideration.

In August, once annulment was finally granted I immediately applied to the State Department to marry Miren. She filled out forms for essential security and medical clearances. Once permission was granted, she came to Washington and lived with her sister while we waited for my divorce. We saw much of each other, especially on weekends. Each weekday she slaved away at a combined naturalization-English course.

After some last-minute complications, a court issued my divorce. Finally, we could marry! On December 6, 1971, Miren and I were married in a small civil ceremony. Pete, all heart, gave me that Friday off. Even so, shortly after arriving at our new home he called and said he needed me at work. For once, I told him, "No." Later we drove through a blizzard to Annapolis, where we celebrated, I happier than I had ever been.

Michu, Coca, and Juanjo, after more difficulties generated by their father, arrived in the late summer of the following year just in time for school. Together with Chris we were a family. I proposed adopting Miren's three youngest. However, Guillermo Arrivillaga would not agree to adoption without one more payoff. I could not afford it, and neither Miren nor I wanted to ask her family to bail us out once again. Indeed, except for their keeping the Arrivillaga surname it mattered not. Soon Mincho and Pedro, Miren's big boys who had opted to stay with their father, proposed to visit. Miren feared their father was trying to offload them on us. In fact, we could not afford providing for them long. Nevertheless, we approved a short visit.

Money was a problem. But we scraped by, largely because Miren, whose improving English now supplemented her fluent Spanish and French, worked in fancy retail stores. The girls, inwardly concerned at finding themselves in a new environment, nevertheless adapted well to their new schools and language. Juanjo did have problems. His behavior led to his being moved about before being sent to a special class in yet a third school. School officials wanted to treat him with Ritalin for attention deficit syndrome. Miren categorically refused; and she was right. He gradually adjusted and calmed down.

Chris, wonderful to be with when he was in a positive mood, increasingly became another problem. He grew more rebellious, refused to see a shrink, reverted to smoking pot, and was suspended from George Washington University. Once he went wild at dinner, grabbing my African spear, running around the table, threatening me, but eventually subsiding. I still wonder what Miren's children made of that episode. Another night after midnight, I was called by the Fairfax, Virginia, police. They were holding Chris but were willing to release him to me. When I arrived he was filthy, incoherent, and restrained in a strait jacket. LSD, the police said. Somehow I got him home. Miren helped strip him, put him in the shower, wash him, put him to bed, and clean up the mess. I was amazed at how calmly she handled the situation. More proof, if any was needed, of how lucky I was to be married to her. For her part, if she at that point regretted getting involved with me and Chris—as would have been reasonable–she never let it show.

Miren was in the States on a tourist visa. To stay for eventual naturalization she needed an immigrant visa. Normally, one has to be in their country of citizenship to obtain an immigrant visa. However, invoking an exception, I wrote to ask the consul general in Toronto if he would issue the visa. He replied that once the paperwork was in order and whenever Miren appeared in person, she would have her visa. So, I took a few days leave and we drove to Toronto, returning to Washington with Miren having immigrant status. When I was later assigned as an ambassador she qualified for expedited naturalization. She took and passed the requisite examination. Proudly, I watched her take the Oath of Allegiance to the United States of America and become a citizen. At that point, Michu, Coca, and Juanjo also became citizens.

While my main objective from early 1971 had been to contribute to a new round of multilateral trade negotiations, I had some interesting experiences with other trade issues as well.

In late August 1971, Pete Peterson and I flew with others to the Western White House for an NSC meeting devoted to strategy toward Japan. While I did not see the president, it was still exciting to be there. Kissinger presided, but the star performer for me was Alex Johnson, an FSO with great experience in Japan.

On the flight west, a Colonel Alexander Haig went out of his way to introduce himself. It was an appreciated gesture. I did not know it then, but we would see much of each other in coming years.

Additionally, Pete, well aware of the president's and Henry's interest in East-West economic issues, became host to a Soviet delegation. To my amazement, when with little warning he took the senior Soviet minister to see the president, I found myself chairing a meeting with the rest of the delegation. No harm was done. The meeting involved lots of posturing by the Soviets, followed eventually by generalities from both sides about the need for and promise of improved relations.

Later as a Moscow Summit loomed, Peter Flanigan had CIEP working on various ideas; but Kissinger was the dominant player. He was issuing lots of National Security Study Memoranda (NS-SMs), tasking different departments to study this and that. Martin

Hillenbrand, then assistant secretary of state for European affairs, asked me to stop in for a chat. He wanted to know, "What is going on?" Incredible! A senior officer, responsible to the secretary of state for Soviet affairs, asking me that question! I told him what I knew, which wasn't much, and that I thought some of the NSSMs were deliberately meant to obscure Henry's and the president's intentions.

At least we were seeing all of this material, or thought we were. Finally, since so much of the material being studied was economic, Flanigan decided to call for a CIEP meeting on the economic issues to be discussed during the summit. After obtaining the president's approval, he asked me to see Henry and tell him. When Henry received me, he asked what was on my mind but continued shuffling his papers. Then it registered on him. Flanigan was calling a cabinet-level meeting on summit preparations. He jumped from his chair, ran out of his office to Flanigan's with me trailing, blew in, and slammed the door behind him. All I could hear was yelling. When Henry exited, he looked at me and said, "Hinton, if you worked for me, you would be on your knees, crawling." I was mighty glad I didn't work for him. Henry won. There was no CIEP meeting.

Yet to my delight, I was on the list of people accompanying the president to Moscow. I did not fly with the president but on a backup presidential aircraft. In Moscow, thanks to Peter, I was invited to the dinner in the Kremlin Brezhnev gave for the president. In the Soviet receiving line I met every member of the Politburo. American Soviet specialists with years of experience rarely ever met a Politburo member, much less all of them. It was a rich dinner: many courses, many toasts, and a magnificent setting. It was a truly memorable evening.

My assigned role for the summit was to negotiate establishment of a Joint U.S.–U.S.S.R. Commercial Commission. Yet, I knew the negotiation was fixed. It was hard to miss this one.

When I sat down at the table with Alexi N. Manzhulo, deputy minister of foreign trade, I was offered a cigar; a Cuban cigar to be precise. The Soviets knew my weakness. We talked for over an hour as I raised objections to the Soviet draft. The next day, another cigar, more objections, but when I returned to the Rossiya Hotel I found Peter and Secretary Rogers baffled and a bit upset that agreement had not been reached. So the following day Alexi and I speedily reached agreement. A glitch about translation arose but was worked out.

The agreement was announced at a press conference by Ron Ziegler, Nixon's press secretary, and explained by Peter Flanigan. Peter also took questions; but stumped by one in Spanish, he turned to me. Consequently, I, too, answered a question at the summit, assuring the world improvements in U.S. trade relations with the Soviet Union would also improve prospects for Latin American economies.

Inexplicably, the press gave more coverage to the Strategic Arms Limitation Agreement, announced that night, than to my view of the Joint Commercial Agreement.

As I left Moscow, Alexi sent me a box of Cubans. Sadly, as a good citizen I declared them. U.S. Customs confiscated them, of course. But I suspect the Customs agents enjoyed them almost as much as I would have.

Moscow was a fabulous trip, but it was not the most enjoyable. My most enjoyable trip I owed to George Shultz. He knew Miren was from Chile and thoughtfully included me in the delegation to the Inter-American Development Bank's 1973 annual meeting in Santiago. Better still, he invited Miren and me to fly with him in an Air Force 707. So we saw Caracas, Brasilia, and Rio in addition to returning to Santiago. While I pretended to work during bank sessions, Miren spent much time with her extensive family. We both enjoyed Santiago's night life with her father and brother, Shultz having excused me from the endless receptions and official dinners. I did, however, have to listen to speeches by him, Chilean dictator Augusto Pinochet, and others. Pinochet, on good behavior before his guests, would be a hard man to get to like.

Another memorable trip was a trans-Pacific jaunt to Japan for a cabinet-level meeting of the Joint Committee on Trade and Economic Affairs. My role, a futile one, was to convince the Japanese to let in more American agricultural products: oranges, orange juice, apples, and beef. For me, the high point of the trip was playing nonstop in-flight bridge with Bill Rogers, then the secretary of state, as he shared with us a kilo of Iranian caviar, a gift from the shah's ambassador to President Nixon.

Other side benefits of my White House job that I shared with Miren included two state dinners, a "Musical Evening with Roberta Peters," occasional tickets to Kennedy Center concerts, several gala balls and dinners in connection with Nixon's second inauguration, and a trip to the Kennedy Space Center to watch the thunderous launch of Apollo XVII. Miren and I were also able to take our children, to their delight, on a Christmas candlelight tour of the White House.

***

While trade issues were my central concern, they were far from my only concern. As early as June of 1971, a CIEP study memorandum focused on U.S. policy in expropriation cases. It was but the first of several CIEP/NSC studies of investment issues.

Expropriation cases were active in Bolivia, Peru, Guyana, and Allende's Chile. The basic U.S. response was to insist on "prompt, adequate, and effective compensation." Congress, convinced these words were not an effective policy even with the Hickenlooper Amendment, was determined to force the administration to be tougher and passed the Gonzalez Amendment to do so. Not that Nixon or Treasury Secretary John Connally needed much pushing.

Efforts to evolve a tougher, more effective policy clearly involved political, economic, and legal considerations. Generally the NSC and CIEP were thus both involved. In practice, this meant I worked closely with Robert Hormats, who had replaced Fred Bergsten as Henry's economic watchdog. We tried to be honest brokers between State—with predominately foreign policy concerns—and Treasury—with financial and legal concerns. The policy issues were complicated and the bureaucratic in-fighting was fierce. A presidential decision memo issued in October 1971 leaned toward the Treasury view and temporarily established a fairly tough policy. I say "temporarily" because in Washington such battles between powerful departments defending legitimate points of view never end.

And as fascinated as I was watching the policy issues play out, I was more interested in finding a way to solve some of the problems, not just flex Uncle Sam's muscles with bilateral aid cutoffs and negative votes in multilateral institutions, notably the IMF, the IADB, and the World Bank.

Peter Flanigan, a banker in private life, agreed we should seek a negotiated settlement with Peru. The outstanding issues were many, including what was probably our most vexing case—the 1968 seizure of the International Petroleum Company (IPC) by the Revolutionary Government of the Armed Forces of Peru, headed by President Juan Velasco. We thought a special presidential envoy, negotiating in secret, might work. Peter drew on his connections in Manufacture's Hanover Trust Bank to recruit a senior vice president, James Greene, for the job. It was an inspired choice. I called on John Crimmins, then handling Latin American issues in State, to explain what was going on. He didn't like it, but beyond asking me to let him know when Greene was to arrive in Lima, he had no choice but to agree to the plan.

Bearing a letter from President Nixon to President Velasco, Greene was received coldly. Velasco made it clear he would not change his mind about IPC; Peru would not pay compensation for its expropriation. He argued IPC had exploited Peru's natural resources for years. In fact, he asserted that IPC owed Peru for having cheated on what should have been paid.

Although I sat in on strategy sessions with Peter and Jim, my contribution to the strategy they devised was minimal. On February 19, 1974, after six months of negotiations our efforts brought success. Peru was hurting from our aid cutoff, our veto of IADB loans, and our opposition to lending to Peru at the IMF and International Bank for Reconstruction and Development (IBRD). Some cabinet members wanted a settlement. Once the fact of negotiations leaked, we approved some lending as evidence that we were serious and a settlement would be rewarded. Peru also made concessions on some issues. Velasco, however, was adamant about IPC. Jim hammered away and found an ingenious, diplomatic solution to which Velasco, under pressure from his cabinet, acquiesced.

Peru would both directly settle some outstanding claims and pay the United States government $76 million, agreeing that "the distribution of this sum falls within the exclusive competence of the Government of the United States without any responsibility arising therefrom on the part of the Government of Peru." Thus, Peru was able to claim nothing had been paid to IPC. We knew, as did a few knowledgeable Peruvians who were careful not to say, that after the secretary of state's decision concerning the distribution of the money among valid claimants Standard Oil of New Jersey would receive compensation for IPC.

Peter and Jim traveled to Lima to complete the agreement, working with Ambassador Taylor Belcher. For my part, a few minutes after it was signed I briefed on it in the White House press room, ducking and weaving with care.

Besides Peru, I had other involvement with investment issues as well. By this time, political pressure to curb inbound foreign investment, an issue that still arises fairly regularly, was mounting. After a CIEP-led interagency study, Peter testified before a House committee on February 5, 1974, in opposition to new restrictions. Later in February I followed up before a Senate subcommittee.

Supported by representatives of Treasury, State, Commerce, and the Securities and Exchange Commission, I gave the lead testimony for the administration.

In April in a speech to a Canadian business forum, I outlined U.S. thinking on investment issues. With the Canadian government opting for a number of new restrictions on investment in Canada by U.S. companies, I implicitly criticized their actions by stressing our openness and provision of national treatment to foreign investments. Press treatment of my remarks was balanced; editorial treatment mirrored the pro or anti Trudeau government policies of the paper in question.

Peter Flanigan's naming me his deputy was great, but it was not without its downside. It made me a manager. Thus, while involving me in some fascinating activities, it also exposed me to unwelcome political pressure. Asked to answer expected phone calls following a Nixon speech, I told Peter that since I had accepted a political position, I would help answer the phones; but I protested that as a professional, I did not like it. He instantly arranged an exemption for me.

In August 1973, Peter left me in charge of CIEP when he took a two-week vacation in Europe. In my "Welcome Home" memo to Peter, I described my experience as "busy, fascinating, frustrating, and, in some cases, rewarding."

Al Haig, then the president's chief of staff, told me that in Peter's absence I should attend the morning White House meetings. That was fascinating. Subjects in my areas of responsibility seldom came up, but the glimpses I got of the administration struggling with the fallout from Watergate were memorable.

To say the least, I was frustrated in trying to stop Henry, now both secretary of state and NSC advisor, from proceeding with an NSSM on agricultural policy without a bow to CIEP. Chuck Cooper, Henry's new economist—who would eventually replace me at CIEP—explained it was to appease the French by developing a commodity agreement approach. Brent Scowcroft, then the deputy assistant to the president for national security affairs, suggested Henry wanted to get hold of the export control problem. Whatever was behind Henry's machinations, I did not enjoy being run over.

More rewarding was working directly with the cabinet and key subcabinet members. Planning a White House export promotion conference involved me with Secretary Frederick Dent at Commerce.

Trying to head off further export controls while inflation raged, I worked with Secretary Earl Butz at Agriculture. I was already well acquainted with Under Secretary Paul Volcker at Treasury and William Casey, under secretary of state for economics, which made it easier to reach agreement on how to handle some tricky issues with Canada.

I also dealt with the Tariff Commission, chaired a meeting to set policy concerning mushrooms (!), worked with Scowcroft to formulate our approach to issues in U.S.-Belgian commercial air relations, and struggled as energy issues came to the fore with a largely new cast of characters, including John Sawhill. Not the least difficult of these concerned nuclear facilities. I was busy and was glad to see Peter return to work.

By 1974, CIEP had grown. I was managing, or rather trying to manage, a staff of twenty-nine permanent employees, twelve on detail from other agencies, eight consultants, and four part-time messengers. I was also bird-dogging half a dozen interagency studies initiated by our office.

Pete Peterson's 1971 report "The United States in the Changing World Economy" and his many presentations had impressed many, including those in Congress. In approving CIEP as a permanent government body in 1972, Congress also mandated that it prepare each year an "International Economic Report of the President." In addition to my other responsibilities, I read and edited drafts; others did most of the analysis and writing.

One day in March 1974, I was told President Nixon wanted to meet those who had worked on "his" report. Peter was away so I led the CIEP staff to the meeting. Nixon seemed appreciative of our efforts. He gave me the pen with which he signed the transmittal letter to Congress. I still have it. Not known for his interest in economics, could it be that he wanted to show that he was carrying on routine activities without concern for the political firestorm surrounding him? Be that as it may, we were delighted with the meeting. I treasure my souvenir photo of the president with the CIEP staff.

Secretary Rogers wanted me to become ambassador to the OECD. It was flattering, but I did not want the job. I knew well that the more important OECD work was handled by visiting Washington officials. Then Secretary Kissinger, also through the director general of the Foreign Service, asked me to be ambassador to Panama. With negotiations pending to redo the Canal Treaty, I welcomed the proposal. My friend from Guatemala, Morey Bell, was now Panama desk officer. He arranged a small get-acquainted session for me, including with Ellsworth Bunker, the White House negotiator whose deputy I expected to be. Then, to my consternation, just before my nomination was to be announced, Henry changed his mind. At the time, I was both annoyed and baffled. I now know that Panamanian president Torrijos asked Henry to send him William Jordan, an NSC staffer whom he knew.

Instead of Panama, I was offered Costa Rica. I told the director general, "Sorry, I am too young to retire on the job." There matters stood, until one day Director General Nat Davis called to ask if I would like to go to Zaire. It was the fifth time I had been offered an ambassadorship. And with Miren's enthusiastic agreement, I accepted.

PART THREE

Ambassadorial Years

17

Zaire (1974–1975)

Soon the president submitted to the Senate my nomination to be ambassador to Zaire. To assume my post, I needed to be confirmed. State's Bureau of Congressional Relations (H) advised me that my hearings would be easy, since, they said, it would be the last time Senator Fulbright would chair the Foreign Relations Committee. He would not be interested, I was told, in complicating his swan song.

How wrong H was! Fulbright wanted to go out with a bang. He attacked, saying our relatively small military assistance program was a mistake. Moreover, he asserted, our overall presence in Zaire was much too big. His lecture was interlarded with detailed questions.

I knew the basics. Our Foreign Military Sales program was budgeted at $3.5 million. Asked how many American officials were in Zaire, I cited the figures on which I had been briefed. Fulbright alleged there were more. At this point, Senator Mansfield came to my rescue, suggesting I check the facts and send the data to the committee by letter. I promised to do so. The storm passed. I provided the facts. Thereafter, as I recall it, the Committee reported my nomination to the full Senate unanimously. In any case, I was confirmed by the Senate.

Shortly thereafter, with eight of our children watching along with a few friends and Ambassador Mbeka Makosso of Zaire, I was sworn in by Deputy Under Secretary of State Ingersoll, Miren holding her bible. After almost twenty-eight years in the Foreign Service, I was an ambassador.

Bob Strand, the Zaire desk officer, organized my consultations. In fact, he over organized them, scheduling me for fourteen days of meetings in Washington as well as four and a half days with businessmen in New York. From this I learned how not to do it, were I ever again to be an ambassador. Too many of the meetings were a waste of time, at least to me.

Of course, some were of marginal utility and some were important. The latter category included my talks with Don Easum, assistant secretary for African affairs, with Congressman Charles Diggs, head of the African subcommittee of the House Foreign Affairs Committee, with Dr. Samuel Adams, Jr., assistant administrator for AID/AFR, and with Director William Colby of C.I.A. and Stu Methven, my future station chief. None of these key players had I known before. On the other hand, Bill Casey, president of the Export-Import Bank, and I had worked together when he was under secretary of state for economics. The Bank had a fairly large exposure in Zaire, about which Bill was rightly worried. My first solid warning of the economic mess I was to encounter came from him. Still I encouraged him, as DCM Mike Newlin had urged me by letter to do, to keep an open mind about future lending. There were many large scale mining projects (copper, uranium, cobalt) seeking financing.

In New York, sessions with First National City Bank, holder of some loans to Zaire on which payment was overdue and with Pan American Airways, the American carrier flying to Kinshasa that also had a contract to help the Zairian National Air Line, were helpful. Even more useful was lunch with Maurice Tempelsman, an astute investor in diamond and copper mines in Zaire. Sessions with representatives of the Ford Foundation and Catholic Relief Services gave me a needed sense of the work of nongovernmental organizations (NGOs) in Zaire.

In retrospect, the amazing thing about these extensive consultations is they failed to tell me what I needed most to know. Only my dinner with my predecessor, Ambassador Sheldon Vance, came close to revealing how different the pattern of thought of Zaïrois, starting with President Mobutu, was from what I was familiar with from my time in Europe, the Middle East, Latin America, and Washington. But even Sheldon's stories of Mobutu's eccentric behavior while visiting New York or sending his dogs in a DC-7 while he traveled separately in a 747 fell far short of what I needed to know about a radically different culture and a devious egocentric dictator. A solid in-depth psychological study of Mobutu was called for, but did not exist.

Had I read V. S. Naipaul's *A Bend in The River,* I would have been far better prepared. He got it right. Indeed, I think works of fiction, including plays, often provide valuable insights into foreign cultures. Unfortunately for me, Naipaul did not write his novel until I was gone from Zaire. Joseph Conrad's *Heart of Darkness*, which I did read before serving in Kinshasa, was illuminating on the past, but I did not think it highly relevant to my mission in 1974.

I did understand that resentment about past Belgian exploitation was basic. Indeed, I thought colonialism in Zaire and elsewhere had left millions of Africans with an acute "inferiority complex." Mobutu's stress on "authenticity" was up to a point an understandable reaction. Nor did I doubt Mobutu shared the goals for southern Africa of the so-called Lusaka Manifesto. Neighboring Angola, however, was by far his top concern. He not only wanted the Portuguese out, but his own influence firmly established. But knowing this much was not enough for me to understand Mobutu well enough to avoid his declaring me "persona non grata." I would leave in haste after less than a fascinating, if frustrating, year.

Before heading for Kinshasa, I worked hard on a crucial staffing problem. I needed a first rate economic counselor. Solving this problem was doubly important since I was being pressured to name a poorly qualified but politically well-connected individual as AID director. Eventually I concurred, having first won AID's agreement to beef up their mission economic staff.

I gave Personnel a list of eight officers, any one of whom I thought would be a fine economic counselor. Personnel struck out. It's not easy to recruit competent people for a Central African post. Finally I turned to Lannon Walker, who I knew could do the job, but not surprisingly he declined. So I promised him that if he would serve, he would be my DCM when Newlin moved on. In the meantime, he would be both economic counselor and assistant director of the AID mission. This attractive package brought him on board.

Miren, too, had briefings. One about our Kinshasa residence was helpful; another about security, well, it was about security, important but boring; a third left Miren fuming, close to tears. The snob running the Art in Embassies program clearly thought Kinshasa, and perhaps Miren as well, were not worthy of much of her time or art.

Nominated, confirmed, and briefed, it was time to travel. I scheduled a stop in Lisbon, given that Angola was the central foreign policy concern of Mobutu. To my amazement, Embassy Lisbon seemed totally relaxed about an alleged communist threat and largely uninterested in my interest in Portuguese policy toward

Africa, especially Angola. Or did I just talk to the wrong people? The charge was away at a horse show somewhere.

After Lisbon we stopped in Morocco, driving from Casablanca to Marrakech. All of us were impressed by the setting, the people, and the souks. Juan Jose, Miren's youngest, watched belly dancers pop-eyed. In Rabat, Morocco's capital, we paid our respects to an old acquaintance, Ambassador Bob Neumann.

We landed in Dakar, Senegal, staying with Ambassador Rudy Aggrey at his residence. He also took us to Gorée, the island where millions of slaves tragically had been imprisoned before being shipped to the Western Hemisphere. Then on August 9 in the wee hours of the morning, Rudy and I listened to the moving farewell speech of President Nixon. Our country's Watergate nightmare was over, but would the country recover under our new president? Rudy and I also wondered if my credentials as ambassador to Zaire, signed by President Nixon, would be accepted by Mobutu.

After a brief stop in Monrovia, the rundown capital of Liberia, we arrived in Kinshasa. At the Ndjili airport we were welcomed by Mike Newlin, the senior officers of the country team, and a Zaïrois protocol officer. Then a long drive in the ambassadorial Cadillac, a vehicle much exclaimed over by Juanjo. As we drove into and through the city, peering avidly at our new surroundings, we saw everywhere slums, scurrying multitudes, and large billboards of Mobutu. A personality cult was alive and well in Zaire.

Our new home was in an upscale neighborhood. The American "Residence" was spacious, attractive, and had a large swimming pool, important for Miren and the kids, but no tennis court, something I determined then and there to remedy. Our new home stood on the bank of the fabled Congo. Mobutu, of course, had renamed both the river and the country Zaire.

That evening we were dinner guests of the Newlins.

Miren and I took an instant liking to Milena, Mike's wife of Czech origin. The two expatriate ladies would become the best of friends, greatly aiding our adaptation to a new world.

The comfortable DCM residence was something else. It had been a brothel in colonial days. The swimming pool was raised and had below-water windows provided for patrons to choose from the naked swimming beauties. For Mike, it was a wonderful conversation breaker.

The Embassy Chancery was in town, somewhat dilapidated, undistinguished in appearance, and crowded. Senator Fulbright was right, in part; there were too many employees for the available space. While I pondered the future, Mike went to work to try to arrange for me to present my credentials. Until that was done I would not be entitled to conduct diplomatic business.

Mike quickly overcame my first concern, winning assent to my presenting President Nixon's letters of recall of my predecessor and my letter of accreditation. This moved me into line for the ceremony behind ambassadors from the United Kingdom, Canada, and the Congo.

Nothing in Zaire seemed to run on time. Credential ceremonies, however, were an exception since Mobutu had decreed the precise form and time the ceremony was to take.

None of my six presentation ceremonies impressed me nearly as much as this one. It was, of course, a first.

Also it was impressive.

I was driven in a Continental convertible, escorted by a colorful motorcycle escort to the presidency, located on what once was Mont Stanley, now renamed Mont Ngaliema. Upon arrival, the president's chief of protocol and I walked through an honor guard toward a grass-roofed *paillette*. Halfway there, a mandatory stop, a band fanfare, our national anthem, and a first mandatory bow toward where Mobutu waited. At his office door, another mandatory bow. Then inside, a third bow, a handshake from Mobutu, an exchange of *mots classique* about the friendship between our two countries. The president introduced me to his chief of staff, Citoyen Bisingemana, and his foreign minister, Citoyen Umba Di Lutate. I presented my senior staff to him. Then Mobutu motioned for me to sit with him. My staff withdrew. I was invited to have either palm wine or pineapple juice. Having been warned about palm wine, I opted for pineapple juice, as did Mobutu, but Umba was stuck with palm wine, there being no other choice when it was his turn. Before drinking we went outside and poured a bit on the ground to honor Mobutu's African ancestors. Then indoors a few sips and the ten minute *causerie* with Mobutu, which I reported to my kids went well, even if nothing of any significance was said by either of us. Back outside for photos, a look at his leopards, word of his lioness having given birth, a good omen, signature of the *Livre d'Or*, then leave taking exactly thirty minutes after the ceremony began.

That night after a long delay "for technical reasons" and after we watched Mobutu descending through the clouds, as he did every night on TV, Kinshasa television carried the entire two hours of the ceremonies for the four newly accredited ambassadors. Hardly lively programming, but Miren, Michu, Coca, and Juanjo saw what I had lived. They seemed not to be too bored even as the Canadian anthem went on and on.

Ten days later, I and other ambassadors were summoned to the Ndjili airport to join in greeting President Gaafar Mohamed el-Nimeiri of the Sudan. Precise timing no longer applied. We waited and waited in the heat while twenty or so fat Zairian *citoyennes* swirled hips moving in time to a sort of jungle drum beat. The name for this "entertainment" was "animation." It was a constant at ceremonies where Mobutu would arrive sooner or later.

I also received an engraved invitation to a 7 p.m. "diner de gala" from

Le Président Fondateur du M.P.R.
Président de la Republique
Le Citoyen Mobutu Sese Seko Kuku Ngendu
Wa Za Banga

The dinner was, I learned, to honor President Nimeiri, but he was not mentioned on my invitation. I was told, however, in small print, that *"les invités doivent occuper leur place une heure avant."* I decided this injunction to arrive early did not apply to ambassadors.

When I did arrive, I was astonished to see numerous North Korean officers. To the best of my recollection, no one in Washington or in my embassy had mentioned to me that North Koreans, at Mobutu's invitation, were now training his army. Offended by something, Mobutu had abruptly dismissed an Israeli mission. Big mistake. His forces needed good trainers. They were routed when they encountered Cubans in Angola two years later. Not surprising since there were few Koreans who spoke French, to say nothing of Lingala, the language of most Zairian officers and men. Nor were tactics appropriate for the Korean peninsula easily transferable to tropical jungles.

For months Mobutu had been seeking M-16 rifles. In Washington it had been decided to provide them shortly after my arrival. The thinking was that the rifles would help establish me with the *citoyen* president.

When the cable came authorizing me to tell Mobutu the good news, my first problem was getting an appointment. The telephone system did not work well. When I did get through, whoever answered seemed to have no interest in connecting me to the president or to Bisingemana, his chief of staff. Dialing and dialing and then dialing some more, I wore out both my index finger and my patience. Eventually Mary Pollock, my highly competent secretary inherited from Ambassador Vance, got Bisingemana on the line. He arranged for me to see Mobutu. The meeting, however, did not go as envisaged by Washington nor as I had hoped it might.

When I told Mobutu the news, he nodded, then without any sign of appreciation he asked me to arrange for the supply of numerous other goodies. Promising to convey his requests to my government, I left his office puzzled and disappointed.

American relations with Mobutu from the time the C.I.A.'s Larry Devlin helped him take power had often been conducted more by the Agency station chief than by the ambassador. I was determined to change the pattern, even knowing Mobutu liked it. When Stu Methven, the new station chief, arrived, I explained my view that there could only be one ambassador. He was not to seek a meeting with the president, even if instructed to do so by his agency. Relations with Mobutu were to be my responsibility. His were spy operations and liaison with Mobutu's intelligence services. However, give long standing practice and Mobutu's pride, I agreed Stu could not refuse a Mobutu request to meet with him. However, were Mobutu to ask to see him, he was to inform me before the meeting if at all possible and fully afterwards. These arrangements worked to the satisfaction of both of us.

As I was getting to know the small American business community and finishing my list of mandatory calls on senior government officials and other ambassadors, I decided I would both start to travel and seek to broaden America's contacts with significant Zaïrois. I discovered problems with each of these ideas. Travel beyond a narrow area around Kinshasa required prior approval by the Foreign Ministry. Approval was rarely refused, but it was often delayed.

When my colleagues in the embassy heard I was thinking of calling on Cardinal Malula, they advised me not to do so. Mobutu, I was told, considered the cardinal to be an opponent of his regime. He would not like the American ambassador meeting with him.

After some consideration, I nevertheless sought and received an appointment for an afternoon call. It had long been my view that American diplomats should know and, if possible, develop good relations with significant members of host country society, including opposition leaders. While Mobutu might not approve, I found it hard to believe he would be seriously offended.

How wrong I was. The day following my totally innocent non-political discussion over tea with his Eminence, Stu Methven came to see me with word passed to him by General Sethi, the head of Zaire's intelligence service, that Mobutu was furious. I was in the doghouse and should watch my step or I might be denied access to the president.

Belatedly, I recognized my error. I had misjudged how strongly Mobutu would react. Obviously for my mission to succeed, access to Mobutu was far more important than my desire for relations with other significant members of Zaire's society. I had simply not appreciated how strongly Mobutu would react.

Miren had asked repeatedly, without a response, to call on Mama Mobutu, the president's wife. Apparently the freeze was being applied to her also. When months later Miren was invited to meet Mama Mobutu, I was told the invitation also meant I was out of the doghouse.

The Belgians did practically nothing to prepare the Congo for independence, having every intention of staying for decades. However, when troubles arose they calculated that an effort to suppress the growing unrest would be more expensive than their potential commercial gains. Accordingly, with startling speed they changed course. On June 30, 1960, the Congo became an independent state.

To exploit the riches of the Congo, the Belgians had developed an infrastructure. However, the newly independent government did virtually nothing to maintain it. By the time of my arrival, roads had deteriorated steadily for years. Fortunately for me, given the tremendous size of Zaire, the sad state of its roads, and our far-flung offices, the embassy had a U.S. Air Force C-12, a two-engine aircraft, and pilots to fly it. The aircraft was available to the ambassador and his wife for official travel.

Colonel Grow, the defense attaché, was an excellent pilot but politically illiterate. At an early country team meeting, he told the gathering of attachés where he had met a North Korean officer he intended to cultivate. When I vetoed any invitations from him to North Koreans, he objected that he could not do his job of learning what they were up to without building good relations. I told him about the policy of the United States. He argued, so I ruled that he and I would each of us put the issue to Washington through our respective channels. We did. My view was affirmed by State and the Pentagon straightened him out.

My first business trip was to Lubumbashi, the capital of the mineral rich Katanga Province. Our consul general, Ed Marks, and his Iranian-born wife, Aida, quite correctly exploited our visit to strengthen their already deep ties to the local community. Miren and I were happily astonished to see how easily individuals of all races and backgrounds, including government officials, mingled socially. In his capital, Mobutu often nixed his officials mixing with foreigners. Consequently, our social life in Kinshasa was largely restricted to the diplomatic corps, not a lively group, and to expatriates in the private sector, a more interesting group. In my almost fifty years in the Foreign Service, Kinshasa was the only post where I was unable to make good friends with local citizens.

Ed also arranged some private meetings for me with officials and friends, including some Americans, who regaled me with Mobutu stories. Crawford Young, a distinguished American scholar, a genuine Africa expert, told me most of his students at the university, while woefully unprepared for higher education, were eager to learn. He also told me of the president's arbitrary decision to have Zaire's fledgling universities concentrate: one on social sciences, another on humanities, another on science, and so on. In itself, not too bad an idea, but Mobutu also directed that university libraries similarly concentrate. Sadly, the process of trying to carry out his order resulted in great disarray and the loss of many books in transit.

Our next visit was to Bukavu, where we arrived with a bang, literally. A tire blew out on landing. Our pilot skillfully brought the plane to a halt just off the runway. He told us that in over 6,000 hours of flying he had never before had a blowout.

In Bukavu, the United States had a two-man consulate, noteworthy as one of a few posts with a launch. Unfortunately, it was almost always in need of repair. Lake Kivu was as beautiful as I remembered it from a quarter century earlier, but Bukavu had grown and deteriorated. Maintenance was not as high a priority for the Zaïrois as for Belgians.

After calling on local dignitaries, visiting with Peace Corps volunteers, who loved life in the Kivu region, and inspecting the nonfunctioning launch, we had a rare treat on the third day of our stay. Consul Loving had arranged an expedition to see gorillas in their native habitat. For this, my friend Ambassador to Burundi David Mark and his wife joined us. They also brought us a replacement tire flown from Kinshasa to Usumburu.

Enjoined repeatedly by Alain Deschnijver, our guide, in silence we first walked, then crawled, then tiptoed until suddenly there they were, a gorilla family, not a half dozen yards in front of us. Alain "talked" to Kasimir, the alpha male. What a thrilling moment! My memory of it is still sharp. I also still recall that for days after we nursed scratches and insect bites. Never, however, was I bitten for a better cause.

Our representation in Kisangani was one American information officer and numerous Peace Corps volunteers. Visiting, we discovered the volunteers had a hard time in Kisangani, a sweltering town, much run down. In the early 1960s just after independence, there had been horrific violence, including massacres of Europeans followed by an airborne U.S.-Belgian rescue mission. Nevertheless, the enthusiasm and work ethic of the volunteers was infectious. Young people can handle a lot.

The Congo River is navigable from Kinshasa up to Kisangani. Indeed, river steamers are the principal form of transportation. Above Kisangani the Tshopo Falls prevent further navigation. Hard for commerce, but for a visitor the Wagenia fishermen, dangling from frail perches over rapids, are a sight that rivals gorillas.

That November, Miren and I flew Air Zaire to Lubumbashi, then drove to Lusaka, Zambia, to attend a Chiefs of Mission Conference, the highlight of which for me was an oatmeal breakfast with President Kaunda. After all the talk, Miren and I had a short vacation. We visited the Victoria Falls. Then in Botswana we rented a car to tour the Chobe Game Reserve. We took great pictures of elephants but missed one of a cobra. It had reared up right outside my window. Frightened, without thinking I put our car in gear and left. Should have taken a picture; cobras can't strike through glass.

Other notable trips included a visit to the massive Inga Dam, participation in the inauguration of the Inga-Shaba high tension power line, and remarks at the dedication of a missionary hospital in Kasai. But none was more memorable than a trip in a Gulf Oil chartered plane and helicopter to an impressive offshore oil rig.

Heading back to Kinshasa, I was in the copilot seat listening to the pilot's exchanges with the Kinshasa tower when dead ahead loomed towering black storm clouds. I knew we should turn back, but the young Belgian pilot, new to Zaire, flew right into the weather. Instantly we were tossed every which way. The pilot dived, escaping the worst of the turbulence, but soon thereafter told the tower, "I'm lost."

However, I spotted a rail line. Since I knew it had to go to

Brazzaville, across the river from Kinshasa, I signaled to the pilot to follow it. He ignored me. Fortunately, when my gestures alerted him to the need to switch fuel tanks, he responded. But when he saw a road I heard him tell the tower he'd had enough. He would land! The tower said, "No, don't panic, climb." He circled once for a better look at the road, then told the tower he was landing. As he made his final approach, I feared the worst. That rain-swept road, straight for a bit, veered right over a ridge long before our plane could stop. There was no way we could land safely. At the last moment, the pilot reached the same conclusion. He pulled up from his approach and climbed. In a few more minutes, the storm broke, the clouds cleared, and there right below us was the Ndjili airport.

We landed safely even though the pilot not only had lost his nerve, he had messed his pants. The following day the aeronautic authorities, having reviewed the taped conversations, expelled him. For my part, the image of that short, rain-swept road is engraved forever on my memory.

Intercepts of cable traffic between the National Bank of Zaire and the Bank of International Settlements (B.I.S.) in Switzerland in October 1974 suggested a criminal plot to divert much of Zaire's gold reserves. I discussed my concerns with Assistant Secretary Don Easum. He agreed I should alert the president. The opportunity to do so arose when Mobutu invited us to lunch with him in Lubumbashi. Never before had I flown 1,500 miles for lunch!

When Don asked me to explain the delicate matter to the president, Mobutu listened thoughtfully. He expressed gratitude for the information. He asked that we, on his authority, tell the B.I.S. not to proceed. We did so and that was that. Only it wasn't.

Great acting! I now know Mobutu was himself the key conspirator, intending to enrich himself further by having the diverted gold processed into coins to commemorate the upcoming Foreman-Ali fight. The coins would have been sold for many times their value in gold. Guess I should have recognized that the national bank president must have been acting at Mobutu's direction. Result: we frustrated a Mobutu scheme to enrich himself with state resources. Presumably, in his eyes, another strike against me.

Among many memorable events during our stay in Kinshasa, nothing was more memorable than "The Rumble in the Jungle." Mobutu intended the fight and related concerts to draw attention to Zaire and, of course, to Mobutu. To this end, he provided large financial guarantees to the fighters, without which Don King, the lead promoter, would not have brought George Foreman, the reigning world heavyweight champion to Zaire, to defend his title against Muhammad Ali. Mobutu also helped finance the concerts, starring James Brown, B.B. King, Miriam Makeba, the Spinners, and others.

Yet, as the *Washington Post*'s David Ottway reported, "The Zairian government was simply not ready for the onslaught of free-wheeling Western journalists that befell this inexperienced African country. The result was massive confusion, a telecommunications nightmare, and verbal bouts between journalists and Zairian officials." Nevertheless, in the end the fight and its coverage were magnificent.

When Foreman suffered a cut in action with a sparring partner, the fight had to be delayed six weeks. The music festival, however, could not be postponed; the artists and their sound equipment were already in Zaire. Unfortunately most foreigners who were coming to see the fight and might have attended rescheduled their visit. Maybe a thousand, including Miren, Miren's father and stepmother, Don Pedro and Nellie, and I paid to see the festival. Only on the third night when admission was free did the stadium, seating 100,000, fill with ordinary Zaïrois.

Rolling Stone cited the lack of paying patrons among grave problems with the effort "to tie in the beat and the rhythm of black American music with its roots." Nevertheless, its reporter concluded, "What the hell, the festival did get off the ground; it sputtered, it foundered, and it closed. But it was unique and historic."

What, if anything, did the American ambassador have to do with these spectacles? Not much. Miren and I had some notables, including Don King, to lunch. We proposed to Don that we host a reception for Foreman and Ali. He vetoed, explaining he could not take the chance of a premature battle. So we held one large reception for other notables, including many of the singers.

I cherish photos taken during visits to each of the fighter's training camps. Mine with Ali is special; it includes Juanjo and Miren. Asked by a journalist who would win, I got it right, boldly predicting victory for "an American black."

State, somewhat reluctantly, finally authorized purchase of a ringside seat for me but would not do so for Miren. When Don King heard she would not attend, he sent me two tickets. His thoughtfulness saved Uncle Sam $250 while assuring Miren and I both saw the epic "Rumble in the Jungle."

The year before "The Rumble," Mobutu had expropriated most foreign-owned firms, turning many over to well-connected but generally incompetent Zaïrois. It was a disaster. Many of the new owners just sold off inventory and equipment. They had no idea of how to run a business.

Mobutu reversed course eventually, but much damage had been done. If Mobutu's understanding of economics was limited, his political talents were impressive. He played challengers to his authority off against each other, took credit for "nationalizing" already state-owned enterprises, brainwashed and hoodwinked his populace, and to his credit held Zaire together, mostly in peace, for thirty-two years.

Once in a conversation with him, I remarked that with appropriate price incentives he could greatly increase agricultural production. He replied that if he wanted more corn he would order more townspeople to work in the fields. This exchange epitomized his approach to economics.

Faced with a collapsing economy, hastened downhill be falling copper prices, and growing popular discontent, Mobutu announced a new program, "Revolutionizing the Revolution." Perhaps his early December visit to Mao and Mao's "Cultural Revolution" gave him the idea. This time political measures predominated. Changes in MRP party hierarchy, the cabinet, and even military command were decreed.

Government came close to a stop. The foreign ministry sent embassies a circular note saying that except for emergencies they would be open for business only on Wednesdays! Other days, all ministry personnel would be engaged in MRP party activities.

Ignoring Zaire's new revolution and the problems it posed for me, Washington continued to instruct me to see the new foreign minister, Mandungu Bula Nyati. He was accessible, on his time schedule. I had gotten to know Bula in his role as a facilitator of the Foreman-Ali "Fight of the Century." Then when a Portuguese-Zaire understanding about the future of Angola was announced, I was amazed to see Bula in the photos. He had used his frequent trips to the States on fight preparations to stop in Lisbon for negotiations. Then Mobutu named him as the new foreign minister. When I asked to see him, after apologizing because he was busy promoting the "Revolution," he would invite me to meet him on the Foreign Ministry roof at 2 a.m.!

An embassy officer trying to arrange an appointment for me to call on municipal officials found the municipality deserted. A notice tacked on the door said all employees were engaged in *Salongo*, Mobutu's word for work details. Until the radicalization of the revolution, most people engaged in Salongo, e.g. cleaning up garbage one day a week, a practice I found admirable. But six or seven days a week of Salongo and nothing but Salongo was a bit much.

The diplomatic corps was expected to attend Mobutu speeches. I always went, of course, but it was not a pleasure. After long preliminaries featuring "animation," Mobutu spoke for hours, mostly in Lingala, to the hundred thousand or so assembled in the "Sports Stadium" under a tropical sun. My first speech was exceptionally painful. Later, I knew to bring a thermos with lemonade, or martinis, and an umbrella. Not understanding Lingala did not help, but I did want to know what he was saying. I could read an account later in the press. However, since the press omitted much apparently intended only for illiterates, I had local employees of the embassy interpret. Mobutu's performances amazed me.

In one speech he called for discipline, unconditional fidelity, and obedience to the "Guide"; self-sufficiency in agriculture; all high school graduates to do civic duty, to include agricultural work, political, and military training; soldiers also to work in the fields; all students studying abroad to return to Zaire at end of their current school term; religious education in schools to be replaced by civism and political orientation courses; henceforth the President's birthday to be "Youth Day"; and a new Department of Social Affairs to be headed by Mama Mobutu Sese Seko. Comparing the role of his imposed doctrine of "Mobutism" to Christianity, he once spoke of himself as Christ and his political commissars as his disciples. There was more, much more, some of which made sense to me: foreign investment under the Investment Code was not to be affected, "Zaire will keep its word," and "enterprises taken over under Zairization to be returned to their owners." The latter directive was too late, but better late than never.

Of course, there was a wide gap between Mobutu's words and implementation of his ideas. Only once, to my recollection, did he seem to acknowledge criticism. After some static about one aspect of his lavish lifestyle, specifically that in each provincial capital the best residences were his and were seldom used, he invoked the prerogatives of tribal chiefs, telling the crowd he was certain they would not want their paramount chief not to have the town's best accommodation on arrival. The crowd cheered.

In January of 1975, the African-American Institute together with the School of Advanced International Studies of Johns Hopkins University held a conference in Kinshasa bringing together delegates from all over Africa. Officials of South Africa and Portugal were not invited, but leaders of revolutionary movements in South Africa, Namibia, Southern Rhodesia, Guinea-Bissau, and Angola attended. Representative Charles Diggs headed a sizable U.S. congressional delegation, including Andrew Young and John Anderson. I was invited as an observer. Outgoing Assistant Secretary Don Easum attended as a delegate.

Secretary Kissinger, under pressure from the right, had decided to kick Don upstairs, sending him as ambassador to Nigeria, Africa's largest country. Don had been less than a year in the job. His sin: while on a tour of African countries, he had not expressed sufficient support for the apartheid government of South Africa. Don told me Henry treated him like a mushroom: "I was kept in the dark, shat on, and then canned."

Henry's candidate to replace Don was another friend of mine, Nathaniel Davis. His nomination was strongly opposed by the Black Caucus, with whom Don was popular. In addition, unwarranted suspicion of Nat's role in the overthrow of Salvador Allende in Chile was voiced by a number of administration critics.

Mobutu spoke, this time in French, to the conference. After a few words of appreciation for "the generous assistance of the United States Government," he added, "We are obliged to speak frankly about your great country's policy toward Africa," or lack thereof. Then he praised Don Easum as one who understood "the problems of decolonialization and apartheid." He added, "Our surprise was great, not only when we learned of his dismissal, but also when we learned he is being replaced by the person who was American ambassador to Chile at the time of the death of President Allende."

This struck me as blatant interference in our internal affairs. It is one thing to attack our substantive policies, as he did later in his remarks, but quite another to publicly comment critically on a personnel issue before the U.S. Senate. I mentioned to Bisingemana my astonishment at Mobutu's intervention in our internal affairs.

The next day Don told me I would not be ambassador much longer. Mobutu, he said, was furious I had criticized him, even in private.

As the conference wound down, Congressman Diggs furiously complained to me that Dick Berg, my counselor for administration, had turned down his request to convert his leftover zaires into dollars. Berg was right to do so; the regulations were clear. However, Diggs indignantly insisted he had never been refused elsewhere. Maybe not, but we held firm.

Larry Devlin arrived that year in Kinshasa as the representative of Maurice Tempelsman, the American entrepreneur with large interests in diamonds and minerals. Larry was a friend from our poker-playing days together in Brussels. More significantly, he was the Larry Devlin who as C.I.A. station chief had brought Mobutu to power. Tempelsman knew what he was doing. No one had better access to Mobutu than Larry. I had enough problems without facing competition for Mobutu's ear from Larry. Stu Methven, my station chief, was even more concerned.

Having pondered Mobutu's request for more equipment than M-16s, I suggested that a U.S. military mission visit to assess Zaire's needs. Headed by Brigadier General Rockwell, his six-man group did good work, getting on well with their counterparts. As their effort wound down, I proposed Mobutu might like to hear its conclusions. Word came back that the president would receive the mission, but the ambassador should not attend. I was back in the president's doghouse. To this direct challenge to my role as ambassador, I replied that unless I was present the mission would not meet with the president. To my relief, Mobutu caved. To my regret and General Rockwell's, nothing came of his report.

Suddenly, out of nowhere came word that Mobutu, piqued by something a Peace Corps volunteer had reportedly done or said, had decided to expel all volunteers from Zaire. After much effort, I finally got the president on the phone. He confirmed his decision. Then, for once he listened to my arguments to the effect that the volunteers were a valuable asset for Zaire. Finally he agreed they should stay, but warned that next time he would not be so forgiving. It was the one and only time I had a significant effect on Mobutu.

Mobutu had long focused on Angola, important to him for many reasons. Among them were the long common frontier, his desire for worldwide recognition as a powerbroker, and the economic importance to him of Angola. The Benguela railroad, running from Lusaka, Zambia, across part of Zaire to the port of Benguela in Angola, carried about half of Zaire's exports from mineral-rich Katanga.

Mobutu skillfully negotiated with Lisbon and established an Africa-wide leadership role, all the while consistently maneuvering to strengthen Holden Roberto and the FNLA, based in Kinshasa. The FNLA "Liberation Army," drawn from the Bakongo tribe, was strong in northern Angola, where for years it had fought the Portuguese; but other groups, other tribes, and other leaders were dominant elsewhere: the MPLA led by Agostinho Neto, a Mbundu, in Luanda and central Angola; UNITA, led by Savimbi, onetime foreign minister of the FLNA before he split from Roberto, an Ovimbundu, Angola's largest ethnic group in the south. Frankly, despite trying I never understood the intricacies of these groups, nor of other groups, for example, in Cabinda, to say nothing of the conflicts, splits, and shifting alliances among and within the main groups. I did think, however, that chaos was a more likely outcome in Angola than a smooth transfer of power from Portugal to any of these groups or to them collectively, as envisaged by the Alvor accords signed by the Portuguese and the three Liberation movements.

Early in 1975, I sought and was granted permission to visit Luanda. Long talks with Consul General Tom Killoran and personal observation were not reassuring. A side benefit on the trip was watching a fisherman fighting a tarpon. Decided right then that if I ever had the chance I'd try my luck with tarpon.

In the spring of 1975, I noted a few intelligence reports indicating Cuban forces were in or expected in Angola once the Portuguese departed. Frankly, I did not believe them. How wrong I was. Like others, I did not recognize Fidel Castro's audacity. I was, however, worried about the evolving situation.

I knew Holden Roberto. While I was not overly impressed by him, he struck me as the most moderate of the contenders for power in Luanda. Moreover, he was Mobutu's man. Given Moscow's backing of Neto's MPLA, I concluded nonmilitary support for the FNLA would be in our interest. I proposed a significant humanitarian aid program to supply the FNLA with all kinds of equipment, other than weapons.

Nat Davis, finally confirmed as assistant secretary for Africa, advised me that he doubted Henry would agree.

After I was no longer involved in Zaire, I learned that Henry, concerned by Soviet activities and evidence of Cuban intervention, had decided to provide "covert" military assistance to both the FNLA and UNITA. South Africa also would help UNITA. To restore "good relations" with Zaire, after my ouster he promised Mobutu financial help.

Nat opposed the secretary's plan, was overruled, resigned, and was sent to Switzerland as ambassador.

Nat was right. Neither the extra aid for Zaire nor our "covert" intervention in Angola paid off.

While I had my problems, Miren and the kids flourished. Kinshasa was a lot easier on them than Washington, where Miren had had to work to make ends meet on my income. In Kinshasa, she studied art at the university, made good friends, even enthused over her official duties, and enjoyed our swimming pool, as did our kids. Our worries about schools turned out to have been misplaced; our girls did well in the Kinshasa International School, Juanjo in a British school.

We had a housekeeper, Madame Despino, a difficult Greek lady who sometimes handled the staff roughly and always insisted she was right. Mostly she did the shopping, since she spoke Lingala, but Miren often went with her to buy meat and produce. We inherited a fairly competent household staff and an incompetent guard force. Once the guards discovered they would be rewarded for dead snakes, we were deluged as it seemed they brought them to us from all over town. They also drank on duty if they had a chance. Turnover among guards was high.

What we did not have was a tennis court. There was, however, room for one in back of the pool. I proposed to remove some trees to build it there. Miren would not let me touch those trees. Then on Good Friday of 1975, a tremendous tropical storm blew down nine trees where I wanted a tennis court. Clearly, divine intervention! Sadly, I never played on the court. But my successors enjoy it.

Michu attracted a boyfriend, Zohair, whose delightful Lebanese mother, somewhat to our embarrassment, deluged us with tasty dishes she had cooked. A good person and a good friend, obviously fond of Michu, she even persuaded Miren to allow Michu to visit her (and Zohair) in Lebanon in the fall.

Zohair's dad was a self-confessed murderer and a fascinating human. As a young man in Lebanon, he had killed in "self-defense." Escaping arrest, he joined the French Foreign Legion. During the war he had been wounded repeatedly, but survived to win the Medaille Militaire at Bir Hakeim. His import-export business in Kinshasa had made him a wealthy man. Somehow, he found ways to continue doing business even as Mobutu was expropriating foreign "exploiters." Well connected, his observations about Zaire helped me immeasurably to understand what was what. He also had a sense of humor. Once invited to dinner at his house, I was introduced to Fidel Castro's ambassador. Our host, Mr. Attoue, was highly amused by our surprise and reactions: polite, but cold.

As 1975 progressed, copper and cobalt prices continued to fall and Mobutu ignored advice provided by the IMF. Default on Ex-Im Bank loans looked increasingly likely. Washington wanted me to turn Mobutu around.

When I finally reached him by phone, to my surprise he invited me to breakfast, an honor I had had only once previously. Maybe I was out of his doghouse or maybe he wanted something from Uncle Sam.

I talked over with my economic counselor, Lannon Walker, how I should handle the meeting. We agreed I should be fairly blunt. Accordingly, at a one on one breakfast I told Mobutu his economy was "sick." He should administer it the medicine of a good doctor, the IMF. I also suggested some cosmetic changes he could make that would help convince the world he was serious about economic reform. He visibly did not like my message. If I had ever been out of his doghouse, I feared I was back in it.

In May 1975, four Stanford students were kidnapped in Tanzania. When a Dutch girl was released to convey the demands of "The People's Liberation Army" to their families and the authorities, we learned the three Americans were being held in Zaire. I and our consular representatives in eastern Zaire did what we could. For once, the government, including Mobutu, cooperated, or seemed to cooperate. But what could they or we do? The Americans were being held somewhere in an immense area, much of it covered by jungle. No one even seemed to know who the kidnappers were

"*Un coup d'état manqué?*" was the headline in a special edition of *Elima*, Kinshasa's leading paper, on June 15, 1975. The United States had reportedly financed a "tribal movement" to overthrow Mobutu. Such a story could only appear with Mobutu's approval; indeed, I thought he had instigated it.

I told Miren across the breakfast table, "I'm afraid we will soon be leaving."

Two days later, Mobutu publicly asserted "a great power" was behind the failed "Machiavellian plot." The arrest of a number of army officers was announced. Rumor had it I had imported a sniper rifle in the diplomatic pouch. Allegedly I planned to have Mobutu assassinated. Mobutu himself publicly spoke of special rifles equipped with telescopic sights and silencers. He intimated the United States was behind the plot. Later, asked about this by a newsman, I replied, "If I had been out to assassinate Mobutu, he would be dead." The rumors were, of course, absurd.

My final days in Kinshasa were tense. I was worried about my likely expulsion and deeply engaged in futile efforts to free the kidnapped Americans. Then Ed Marks called me from Lubumbashi to report that Colonel Grow and his crew had been arrested. They had landed without permission at an airport listed as restricted by Zaire. Once again the colonel had shown terrible judgment. Never mind, Ed and I had to do all we could to have them freed.

After a few days during which I tried to stay focused on my job, wrote efficiency reports, and played some tennis for relaxation, I was summoned to the ministry by the *commissaire* for foreign affairs, Mandungu Bula. This time I was shown to his office, not to the roof, and at 4:30 p.m., not after midnight.

He wasted no time in telling me I was persona non grata. Why, I asked. You know, he replied. I had, he said, forty-eight hours to leave the country. I asked if my wife might stay longer to pack. He said, "Yes, but without diplomatic immunity." In that case, I said, we will all leave together. And we did, fifty-two hours later on an Iberia flight to Madrid.

I was depressed. I thought my Foreign Service career was at an end. In my mind, career officers were not supposed to be declared persona non grata. I was so down that when Dick Berg asked me to a farewell party the embassy staff wanted to give us, I declined. Then Miren told me we had to go. We did, and I was glad she had changed my mind. The turnout was total and, for me, most moving.

Miren also accepted a late dinner invitation from Mami Thome, her best friend in Kinshasa. Mami and Jacques gave me far more to drink than was good for me, but I saw no reason not to indulge. Then their phone rang. It was for me, which amazed me, since I could not recall having told anyone where we were going. My amazement grew greater when Walt Cutler, the office director who backstopped me in Washington, told me he was calling at the secretary of state's request. I was not to worry. I would have a future in the Foreign Service.

The lights of Kinshasa spread out below us twinkled brighter with that reassuring news. Henceforth I told his detractors Henry Kissinger had a heart!

Initially, I thought the charge that the United States was plotting a coup and that I planned his assassination was a Mobutu invention to justify throwing me out. After reflection, however, I think there was a plot. I doubt even Mobutu would have general officers arrested, summarily tried, and then executed just for show. Perhaps Mobutu, in dealing with the plot, decided to get rid of me, i.e., kill two birds with one stone.

And perhaps not. Mobutu suffered from paranoia. He never forgot how he arrived in power. Moreover, he knew he was not endearing himself to us with his policies, to say nothing of his corrupt exploitation of Zaire's mineral riches.

In his letter of June 16 to "Elima," he wrote:

> Certain backward, reactionary, colonialist, imperialist circles as well as their puppets, will never forgive me for having committed my people ... to dignity, total independence, and mental cleansing.

He cited as "never to be forgiven" his break in relations with Israel, his policies of Zairization, his speech to the African-American Institute, and his friendship with China and North Korea.

Not mentioned publicly, but probably in his mind, was a recognition that he had broken his personal pledge to Henry that he would not recognize the Khmer Rouge regime in Cambodia. That pledge had been given after he established diplomatic relations with North Vietnam as well as South Vietnam.

My predecessor, Ambassador Vance, and Walt Cutler, my successor-to-be, visiting Mobutu after my departure, were surprised by how persistently Mobutu insisted on the existence of an American plot. Was he just acting or did he believe it?

There is no definite answer. I do not believe records exist of Mobutu's policy deliberations with his closest advisors.

18

Washington (E) (1975–1976)

PNG'd, sadly we said farewells at the airport before flying Iberia to Madrid, taking Salongo, the stray dog Miren had adopted, with us. Met by media upon arrival, I opined that Mobutu was moving hard left. Three days later, Under Secretary Joe Sisco tracked me down to tell me Henry wanted me to shut up. Not difficult, since it was a long time before any journalist again wanted to know what I thought about anything. This chat was my first intimation that Kissinger had decided to get closer to Mobutu. Angola, I guessed, was behind my gag order.

Amazing, I thought, to have a policeman tap me on the shoulder in a shoe store to tell me to telephone Sisco. Miren and the girls, after a year of no shoe shopping, were happily trying on one pair after another. Credit the Spanish police for having efficiently located a car rented in Madrid, spoken at the car to Joe and Mincho, and divined that I'd be in one of many nearby San Sebastian shoe stores.

We were to visit Jose Maria and Mirentxu Bilbao, longtime close friends of Don Pedro Aretxabala. They lived in Anglet, a small town above Biarritz. Miren traced her origins to a village we would visit higher up in the French Pyrenees. In a lovely old cemetery, graves of her family moved Miren to tears.

The Bilbao hospitality was fabulous. Great food and drink, lots of terrific wines, and a chance to catch up on sleep. Also time to reflect that our sudden ouster had two advantages: no stream of farewell parties and someone else to do most of the packing.

Back in Washington, we stayed with my parents while we looked for a place of our own, having decided that since our stay was likely to be a short one, we should not dislodge the renters of our Dellwood house. Eventually we found a house, more or less in our old neighborhood, suitable for camping.

For the first time in thirty years I was without a job.

Worse, apart from a few old friends, no one seemed to want to have anything to do with me.

One exception was Assistant Secretary Nat Davis, who was interested in my views. He tasked me to write a memo assessing how long Mobutu would last. I had long argued he would survive indefinitely. Now, noting Mobutu's arrest and torture of widely respected officers and dismissal and arrest of a dozen general officers, I thought that in reaction he might be thrown out "at any moment."

Wrong, once again! However, I also observed, "We don't know enough about how Zaire's society works to be able to predict with full confidence."

My morale got a needed boost when my promotion to Career Minister was announced on July 15.

Then, Under Secretary for Economic Affairs Charles Robinson, with whom I was acquainted from my days dealing with Peru, recruited me as a senior member of his staff to represent him on the Economic Policy Committee, now chaired by the secretary of the treasury. The plus of the position was that it was a job; the minus, it was not a very responsible one. I tasked line officers in the Bureau of Economic and Business Affairs to prepare briefs on subjects on the agenda of the Economic Policy Council, where I represented State. Most of the issues were domestic. When important international economic issues were to be discussed, more often than not Robinson also attended. I had far less of a policy role than I had had in my CIEP days. Even worse, I found myself in the middle of a nasty bureaucratic battle between my old buddy Tom Enders, now assistant secretary for economics, and Robinson, my boss and Tom's nominal chief.

While I was acquainted with "Chuck" from my CIEP days working on Peru expropriation problems, I now got to know him quite well. He was a dynamo in incredible physical shape. Every time he was driven into the State Department basement he ran up the stairs to his seventh floor office. While a delight to be with, to me, his judgment was suspect. He had decided to work closely with the French in dealing with developing country pressures to create "A New World Economic Order." Foolish and naive, I thought. However, unless asked I kept my views to myself. Once asked about a French ploy, I spoke candidly. I was never again asked about such an issue. Dealing with his French counterpart on the phone, Chuck cut out Enders and others working the same problems. I was happy not to be involved.

In early August, Chuck called me into his office. The secretary, he said, wants you to figure out how to barter U.S. wheat for Soviet oil. He told me Kissinger thought we could use Soviet interest in buying our grain to obtain an oil supply commitment from them that would marginally weaken OPEC. He added that I was to work in complete secrecy developing a barter agreement.

I started with only limited knowledge of the issues. From listening to discussions in the Economic Policy Board, I was aware of concerns that Soviet purchases of U.S. grains might produce a repeat of the "1992-93 Great Soviet Grain Robbery." Secretary of Labor John Dunlop, I had learned, was particularly outspoken about the dangers of large purchases heightening already serious inflationary pressures. I also knew Secretary Butz had announced a "temporary" suspension of grain sales to the Soviet Union.

I welcomed this substantive assignment, but the idea of a "barter agreement" struck me as nonsense. Economists seldom think well of barter. In this case, the two economies operated differently, completely differently. Ours was market oriented and largely private. The "Marxist" Soviet economy was run by a government bureaucracy. Pondering the differences, I soon concluded the U.S. government would have to go into the grain export business if the "barter concept" was to be implemented.

Not likely, I thought. Indeed, I was right about this and soon had a green light to outline a somewhat different concept. I proposed negotiation of "three interrelated Government to Government agreements." One would provide for long-term (five years) Soviet purchases of perhaps five million tons of U.S. grains per year; a second would contain Soviet assurances of a long-term supply to us of "at least 200 tbd [thousand barrels a day] of oil for five years"; the third would improve an existing shipping agreement the Soviets had so exploited that U.S. unions were refusing to load grain for the U.S.S.R.

My concept paper was approved with one key difference.

Kissinger insisted Soviet oil be overtly priced below the OPEC price. I thought this would be hard for the Soviets to swallow. I favored a firm quantity commitment (standard practice in Soviet commercial agreements), but also suggested in my paper that we might "hide a small price discount in the shipping agreement or in financial arrangements." I was overruled. In the end, this meant that there would be grain and shipping agreements but no oil agreement.

As time passed, our negotiating position deteriorated. If the Soviets ever would have traded an overt oil price deal for a grain deal, they eventually figured out it would not be necessary. They could see that grain farmers, the Farm Bureau, other interest groups, and many politicians wanted to end the "embargo" on Soviet sales.

As I worked on a detailed negotiating position, it became clear to me I did not know enough about either the oil or grain trade. Despite being enjoined to secrecy, I went to Agriculture to talk with Assistant Secretary Richard Bell. While USDA, as I well knew, for years had opposed long term commodity agreements, it turned out Bell was advocating one with the U.S.S.R. In fact, in addition to helping with my education, he turned his department's opposition into support.

Somehow, Kissinger heard of what I had done. He was furious, chewing out Chuck. Several days later in a cabinet meeting Earl Butz, the secretary of agriculture, allegedly complained to President Ford that State was not keeping Agriculture informed of its plans for grain negotiations with the Soviets. Kissinger denied the charge, citing my talk with Butz's staff!

For oil, Chuck arranged for me to talk with officials in the Federal Energy Administration.

As I developed the details of our negotiating position, my morale got another boost. Nationally syndicated columnist Joseph Kraft reported that Henry Kissinger, starting in Saudi Arabia, planned "a far reaching diplomatic shuffle." What thrilled me was reading that I was to replace Joe Greenwald as ambassador to the European Economic Community. No assignment could please me more. Joe, however, was understandably furious at learning from the press that he was to leave Brussels to replace Enders as assistant secretary for economic affairs. There were other changes, all allegedly related to "what has hitherto been a schizophrenic American approach" to oil-exporting countries and OPEC. Apparently Henry wanted to accomplish much at one swipe. Chuck Robinson seemed as pleased as I with Kraft's column; not, I thought, because I was to leave, but because Enders was to move to Canada.

In September Chuck led our delegation to Moscow. We had to tolerate the fact that the KGB watched our every move, including accompanying one to the john. Chuck shamed them the first morning when he went for a run. His keepers could not keep up. Thereafter, when he ran he had a different team and a follow car watching him.

Negotiating with the Soviets was different, very different from negotiating with other countries. In my experience, only the Israelis, although in a different way, were as difficult. Lengthy plenary sessions concentrated on generalities fortified with toasts, tea, wine, and vodka toasts. Nikolai Patolichev, Soviet minister for foreign trade, proposed toast after toast, to each of which Chuck responded. Chuck thought we should not show weakness by seeking rest breaks. Painful, this rule, which fortunately he eventually relaxed. I, for one, was prepared to accept Soviet dominance in bladder control.

Slowly progress was made on grains (but not on oil) in the plenary sessions. Chuck followed up in one on one sessions with Patolichev. Robert Blackwell of our maritime administration reached a satisfactory agreement on shipping. Blackwell's negotiating leverage was formidable: if the Soviets wanted our grains, our longshoremen had to be convinced to load it into ships.

With this limited success, Chuck was instructed we should return to Washington.

As difficult as some of this visit had been, it also had some pleasant highlights. Soviet hospitality included a wonderful visit to the Moscow circus and a weekend trip outside Moscow to the colorful, old towns of Vladimir and Suzdal, complete with a lavish luncheon and endless toasts! The drive back to Moscow in the twilight was scary. Our cavalcade drove at over seventy miles an hour into traffic coming out of Moscow. Fortunately, oncoming traffic moved to the side or off the road. I guess Soviet citizens were accustomed to getting out of the way of ministers with police escorts.

Upon return to Moscow, life improved. Ambassador Walt Stoessel invited senior delegation members to stay at the residence. He had a fine chef and a racket ball court which got a lot of use, even on the coldest days. We learned no one could beat Walt at the game.

When negotiations resumed it was agreed to establish a working group on grains. I chaired our side. Richard Hill, the Department of Agriculture assistant secretary who had been so helpful in Washington, replaced a junior expert from his department. Again progress was slow. The Soviets seemed more interested in the appearance of balance than in the reality. My memory is shaky, but as I recall it their problems related mostly to our escape clause (Article V). In our view, it was highly unlikely we would ever have such a poor harvest of wheat and corn to need to invoke this clause. Nevertheless, told to reach agreement, I advanced a number of proposals intended to protect our substantive requirement while meeting Soviet problems about appearance. My life was complicated by the delegation's State Department lawyer, a genius at raising objections. After a bit, Chuck agreed to my proposal to use Joe Bell, a lawyer from the Department of Energy, as my legal advisor. Joe and I eventually drafted a Rube Goldberg add-on for a Soviet escape clause that the Soviet negotiator accepted ad referendum. However, common sense prevailed. The next day the Soviet negotiator proposed we return to the status quo ante Rube Goldberg. I presume someone in Washington convinced Ambassador Dobrynin that enough foolishness was enough.

With a draft grain agreement in hand but still no oil agreement, Chuck decided to send me home.

When I got to Washington, the good news was being back with Miren and family; the bad news was Henry Kissinger was furious. We had, he yelled, sabotaged the oil agreement. I should not have left Moscow! He also had his counselor, Hal Sonnenfeldt, rake me over the coals. That was worse.

As I was about to go to an Economic Policy Board meeting to explain the draft agreement, Henry told me that in no circumstance should I agree to a grain sale. He wanted to keep the pressure on the Soviets for an oil agreement. At this cabinet-level meeting my arguments were unanimously rejected out of hand. I think it was Bill Seidman who in exasperation told me, "The president wants a sales agreement now." I ceded, fearful, however, of Henry's reaction. Brent Scowcroft took me aside to assure me Henry would get over it. He did, but after giving me another thorough tongue-lashing.

As we prepared for the agreement to be released publicly, I suggested to Henry we should brief key members of Congress, starting with Senator Dole. He exploded. "Brief Congress! Damn it, no. Not now. You and everyone else want to consult Congress. Get out of here." etc. etc.

Later that day he called me from his aircraft en route to China to tell me, more or less apologetically, to handle the White House announcement and proceed to brief selected congressmen.

Shaken by his three blowups at me in one week, I asked an old friend, George Vest, Henry's spokesman at the time, if I had had it. On the contrary, George said, he would not have behaved that way if he did not think well of you. I recognized the secretary's frustration with the Moscow negotiations and the pressure he was under preparing to fly to Peking, but I didn't like being yelled at. Still it was a small price to pay if I were indeed to be nominated as ambassador to the European Community.

On October 20, White House Spokesman Ron Nessen read a presidential statement announcing the agreement. To take questions, Ron introduced Secretary of Agriculture Earl Butz, Assistant to the President for Economic Affairs Bill Seidman, Administrator of the Federal Energy Administration Frank Zarb, Maritime Administrator Robert Blackwell, and myself, wrongly identified as "deputy under secretary of state." Earlier that day I had sent a draft presidential statement to Seidman and Scowcroft. Totally rewritten, someone had greatly improved it.

I also provided a fact sheet, the grain agreement text, the text of an oil letter of intent, and proposed answers to foreseeable questions. In addition, that morning I briefed representatives of interested governments. This kind of staff work is standard operating procedure (SOP) prior to a presidential announcement.

Secretary Butz followed up the presidential statement with praise for the agreement. Then the fun started with sharp questions about oil. Frank Zarb answered honestly, "We have an agreement to talk...."

The press, clearly skeptical, hammered him with more than twenty follow-up questions.

Bill Seidman told a questioner about the attitude of the Maritime Union, "They have been briefed." You should ask them about their attitude.

A wise guy, aware Kissinger had controlled the negotiations, asked, "Mr. Butz, have you lost the power to make agricultural decision in the administration?" The secretary brought the house down with his reply, "No, sir. I am free to decide our office hours."

Then someone asked me about the effect on détente. I referred the questioner to the president's statement. Then came my turn to fend off skepticism about oil: "Mr. Ambassador, why should the Russians buy grain at market prices and the Americans buy oil through beneficial prices?"

I talked knowingly of differences in pricing grain and oil, throwing in references to credit terms, transportation differentials, sulfur content, and residues, concluding "This is enormously complicated and there is just no such thing as a world price for oil." That gibberish silenced my questioner. A few more questions, Secretary Butz got in the last word, and we were out of there.

Unfortunately, the oil deal Kissinger envisaged came years later. Now, we buy tons of oil from Russian companies "at market prices."

On December 19, 1975, President Ford nominated me "to be the Representative of the United States to the European Communities with the rank of Ambassador." That made for a splendid Christmas.

My confirmation hearings went well. In late January in Chuck's office, I was sworn in. Most guests were family. Miren again held the bible for my oath.

19

USEC (1976–1979)

To return as U.S. ambassador to the European Communities was like going home. From 1958 to 1962 I had been a charter member of the United States Mission to the European Communities (USEC); then, while serving in Washington from 1962 to 1967, I had returned countless times. Moreover, I still had friends in the European Commission, starting with Commission Secretary General Emile Noel, who with a handwritten note sent to Washington welcomed me back to Europe,

The first three years with Miren in Brussels were the happiest years of my life. The last year, 1979, was the worst year of my life, pure hell. Miren was diagnosed with cancer, suffered inordinately, and died in November.

Miren and I were financially strapped, but we had each other, wonderful children, a chateau residence with excellent guest quarters in a former stable, a large garden, and authority for official travel to nine European Community member countries. Miren spoke flawless French, made friends easily, and soon resumed her enameling, eventually exhibiting her Cloisonné pieces at an art show in the Palais Egmont. Still grieving for Salongo, our Zairian dog killed by a car in Washington, she was reluctant to get another dog until she saw an Old English sheepdog puppy. Wellington, as we named him, she could not resist.

Unlike Zaire, I was confident I was as prepared for the job as anyone could be. I understood how the Community functioned, could generally predict how member states would view matters, and had lots of experience with the issues: trade negotiations, monetary stability, energy supply shortages, agriculture, and inflation.

To make things even easier, the USEC staff was first rate, starting with Bob Morris, a friend and colleague of many years, as DCM. He had more European experience than I.

A first order of business was to present my credentials. Nowhere else are an ambassador's credentials presented to two separate "heads of state." De Gaulle's attack on the "supra-national"
role of the Commission had led to this peculiar practice. First, I presented to the president of the Council of Ministers of the European
Communities, at that time Prime Minister Gaston Thorn of Luxembourg. After fifteen minutes with him, I crossed the street to present
to the president of the European Commission, M. François Ortoli,
a French acquaintance from my previous assignment in Brussels.
This time, no honor guards, national anthems, or palm wine!

Another anomaly of my new job was the presence in Brussels
of two other American ambassadors, one to NATO, Robert Strausz-
Hupé, one to Belgium, Harvey Firestone, to say nothing of a nearby American general, Al Haig, the Supreme Commander of NATO
military forces. Fortunately, we were friends and rarely got in each
other's way.

Normally our ambassador to Belgium, not the multilateral
missions, would host the American Fourth of July national day
reception. Miren and I would, of course, attend. Since 1976 was the
Bicentennial of our Declaration of Independence, as an exception I
decided USEC would also host a small reception, limiting our guests
to individuals officially related to the European Communities.

Commission President Ortoli attended and spoke eloquently.
As I offered a toast, my hand began to shake. Had I not steadied it
with my other hand, my champagne would have spilled. It was the
first time I was conscious of a tremor that bit by bit was making my
handwriting illegible. I feared it might be Parkinson's disease. The
next time I was in Washington, a neurologist to whom I had been
referred by the State Department assured me after tests it was "an
essential tremor." What was "essential" about it escaped me, but
since he assured me it was not serious, I did not probe.

My top priority at USEC was pushing forward the Tokyo Round
of multilateral trade negotiations, the same negotiations Bob Morris and I had been instrumental in launching in our White House
years. The Community was critical, being our largest trading partner. As always, the EEC was being particularly difficult about agricultural issues. Still the British were as unhappy as we with parts
of the common agricultural policy. Maybe, we thought, that would
help.

Sir Christopher Soames was perhaps European foreign minister
in his dreams, but in reality far from it. He soon had me around
for a private lunch. Lady Soames, Mary Churchill, talked with us

before lunch, only mentioning her father once. When she disappeared we turned to weightier matters, like specialty steels and nonfat dried milk. Sir Christopher adopted what I assume were meant to be Churchillian airs. Subjected to his lively wit, excellent wines, superb food, Havana cigars, and intelligent conversation, I was impressed. Bob Morris later tipped me off that Soames' favorite "claret" was Haut-Brion '66. Accordingly, I acquired a case in a London wine auction. Serving it to Sir Christopher may not have changed Community positions, but it did no harm to either of us!

Early on when a U.S. negotiating team headed by Ambassador Clayton Yeutter came to Brussels, Soames gave a dinner at his residence. As often occurs in trade talks, voices were raised. To Soames's horror, his dinner guests were soon shouting at each other. The next morning he called his team members in and remonstrated with them. "In my house, such behavior is unacceptable." While I did not like the row, I took it in stride. For Sir Christopher, gentlemen did not shout at the dinner table.

The week of Soames's dinner for Yeutter was exceptionally busy. Miren and I had working lunches or dinners at the residence every single day. Harder on her than on me, but she handled it with aplomb, starting with a lunch for Ambassador Walker, in town to talk about government procurement. A delegation of our Environmental Protection Agency (EPA) discussed toxic substances with Community experts. Then Yeutter came and left. The head of the U.S. Auto Safety Agency held talks with European officials about automotive safety standards. The week was topped off with two days of the semiannual US-EEC consultations with a full agenda of economic and development issues, culminating with political discussions at dinner chez nous. With six Americans of assistant secretary rank or higher in town that week, all of whom deserved and expected ambassadorial attention, scheduling was complicated.

By the time the VIPs left, the USEC staff was exhausted by notetaking and preparation of reporting cables. Miren and I were also stressed, but we took courage from the prospect of a trip to West Germany. I was to speak in Munich and participate in a war game at Garmisch-Partenkirchen. Knowing we would be pampered by the army, we relaxed.

Soon after our return, Ambassador Fred Dent came to town for a speech intended to help get the trade talks moving. Afterwards the USAF flew Dent and me to Strasbourg, where the European Parliament was meeting, for talks with top-level commissioners,

Ortoli, Soames, and Finn Gundelach. We were warmly received but to no avail. Not only was the lame duck Commission dug in on agriculture, but it was also waiting to see the outcome of the impending American elections.

Before there would be a new U.S. president, there would be a new European Commission. The nine governments agreed Roy Jenkins should replace François Ortoli as Commission president. Jenkins, a distinguished British Labour Party member known for his pro-Europe views, had served in the British cabinet as home secretary and as chancellor of the exchequer.

I decided to visit London to call on him before he took office in Brussels. Our embassy in London arranged an appointment. I also called on David Owen, then minister of state in the Foreign Office, and spoke at a Mid-Atlantic Club luncheon.

Jenkins was most cordial, but alluded to his plans for his presidency and for his team of commissioners in terms that struck me as somewhat unrealistic. His optimism was refreshing, but he had not, in my opinion, grasped fully the hold governments had over Commission appointments. With Jenkins at our talk was Crispin Tickell, a Foreign Service officer who was to be his chef de cabinet. I would get to know Crispin much better than Roy Jenkins, the often aloof Commission president.

While in London, I also went south to where Deborah and Rohan lived in Council Housing. Great to see them and comforting to note their commune life days were behind them.

Back in Brussels, I learned USEC had been challenged by the Japanese mission to a softball game. Despite my fifty-four years, I started and played three innings. Memorable innings. I hit a home-run, doubled, scored twice, and had three RBIs. After that game, except for family catch I retired from baseball for life!

As we had done in Chile, Miren and I loved to visit vineyards, taste wines, and buy as much of the good stuff as we could afford. Touring picturesque Alsace was particularly delightful. To this day, Alsatian Gewurztraminer is my favorite white wine. Moreover, I consider L'Auberge d'Ill at Illerhausen to be the best restaurant in the world. The village of Riquewhir, largely unchanged in hundreds of years, enchanted us. I was drawn to Riquewhir partly because I believed, wrongly I later learned, that my grandfather Roesch had been born there. As we wandered about we encountered a bearded artist, M. Grun, whose paintings appealed. After Miren left me in no doubt that his fulsome nudes were not for us, we bought a bright canvas of Alsatian red tile rooftops. I am admiring it as I write.

On a trip to Burgundy, we got to know Louis Latour, a famous and venerable vintner. He took the time to show Miren and me around and sell us cases of superb Beaujolais type wines and bottles of classic Burgundies from his own vineyards. The downside: he told us it would be a "crime" to drink his classic wines before they had aged at least three more years. Well and good, but we were low on finances and could only recoup the cost of the wines by serving them at official representation meals. We just couldn't afford to keep them long in our wine cellar.

Later we were invited to Reims, where I was inducted into L'Ordre des Coteaux du Champagne. The ceremony was held in a cave lit with torches. Speeches, a touch on my shoulder with a sword, and I was a Chevalier of the order. Then we ate sumptuously and drank many different champagnes. The next day we breakfasted, with champagne, of course, al fresco among the vineyards. A memorable, if ridiculous, experience!

In Dublin to meet ministers handling Community affairs and to deliver a luncheon speech, we were house guests of Ambassador and Mrs. Walter Curley. After dinner the ambassador led a focused discussion. His surprising topic was the role of women in Irish public life. So much better, I thought, than the usual aimless table chatter. Then he and I listened to the U.S. election results. To our dismay, Jimmy Carter defeated Jerry Ford. As a career officer, I knew I might or might not stay in Brussels, but Curley was stunned. He knew Ford's defeat meant an unwelcome return to private life for him.

As ambassador, my job was to deal with members of the European Commission and the permanent representatives (ambassadors) of member states. Initially, I called on each. As commissioners changed I had new calls to make. Gradually I made the other calls required by protocol. I spent many, often sterile hours on these calls. I tried, of course, to concentrate on getting to know those involved with my priority concerns, e.g. trade, finance, and energy.

Three commissioners working with Roy Jenkins were already known to me: François Ortoli, now vice president in charge of economics and finance, Vice President Finn Gundelach (agriculture and fisheries), and Vice President Henk Vredeling (employment and social affairs). Knowing them helped, but except for Vredeling, whose portfolio was of little interest to me, they were understandably careful about what they told me.

The Italian vice president, Lorenzo Natali, was in charge of enlargement negotiations with Greece, Spain, and Portugal. It struck me as important that we know how they were going. He tried to be helpful, but his mastery of his portfolio was limited.

I found both German Commission members (Haverkamp and Brunner) to be well disposed; more helpful than most.

Long interested in development issues, I tried to develop good relations with Claude Cheysson, a French Socialist watchdog of Paris's overseas interests. Not easy, he struck me as basically anti-American. Once, I tried to discourage Commission assistance to the bloody pro-Soviet Ethiopian military revolutionary junta led by Mengistu. Cheysson was not dissuaded by my argument. He told me I should not be concerned. A revolution had been needed to rid the country of Emperor Haile Selassie. He added: blood shed went with revolutions.

The Irish commissioner, Richard Burke, and the second British Commission member, Conservative Christopher Tugendhat, were pleasant but overshadowed by others. Tugendhat thoughtfully invited me to dinner to meet Margaret Thatcher, but I was with Miren at the hospital in Washington on the appointed date. Two others, Luxembourg's Raymond Vouel and Italy's Antonio Giolitti, were unimpressive, at least to me.

The Belgian, Viscount Étienne Davignon, was brilliant, generally helpful, and a key trade negotiator.

My staff was made up of agricultural, financial, energy, trade, customs, labor, development, cultural, and information experts. They developed and maintained contacts in the Commission and Council. Economic Counselor John McCarthy and Agricultural Counselor John Montel were outstanding officers, well known to me before my arrival. I was extremely fortunate to have such a strong staff.

President Carter was no sooner inaugurated than I was alerted that Vice President Walter Mondale was to come to Brussels for meetings with both the NATO Council and the European Commission. His arrival three days after assuming office and his pledge of policy continuity was an extremely welcome reassurance for our European friends. They were particularly pleased with his statement that the Community as such should be represented at the coming London Summit. Eventually, it was agreed that President Roy Jenkins would attend as would whoever was president of the Council of Ministers when the economic summits were held.

Mondale gave a new priority to an old agenda item, macroeconomic policy coordination across the Atlantic, urging a reluctant

Europe to follow more expansive economic policies. As the meetings at the Commission ended, Mondale filled his pockets with offered Havana cigars. This permitted me to follow suit. All in all, it was an exceptionally satisfying visit, capped off for me when I learned I would remain as our ambassador to the Communities.

Robert Strauss, chairman of the Democratic National Committee, was announced as Carter's nominee for special trade representative. I wondered if a Texan lawyer and political fundraiser without a background in international trade was the right man for the job. It was not long, however, before I concluded he was exactly the negotiator we needed. He mastered the issues, but it was his personality and people skills, making others like him even as he fleeced them, that made him exceptional.

Before his first visit to Brussels, Strauss telephoned me, soft soaped me, then asked that I arrange a joint press conference for him with Wilhelm Haverkamp to follow their talks. Haverkamp was a well-meaning German trade unionist. He had replaced Sir Christopher Soames as commissioner in charge of external relations. He readily agreed to Strauss' proposal.

Their get-acquainted talks went well and Strauss turned the joint press conference into a love fest, praising Haverkamp and his views. Wilhelm was delighted with his warm relation with his new American friend and what the international press corps reported until several Community governments, led by the French, took him to task for not defending the Community point of view more vigorously.

While Strauss was in Brussels and, I think, on every subsequent occasion, this busy man took the time to visit his former daughter-in-law and grandchild. I was impressed.

When President Carter announced that, for economy reasons, henceforth no one of his administration would fly first class, Strauss, asked for his reaction to Carter's edict, declared, "I fly first class until there is something better." He paid the difference in fares, including for Concorde flights.

Before his next Brussels visit, Strauss again asked me to arrange a joint press conference. This time, Haverkamp declined to participate. Result: Strauss held his own conference and spun his account of their talks so as to suggest more agreement had been reached than actually was the case. The press tore into Haverkamp. The French again were furious. "Willi" learned he was damned if he joined Bob for a press conference and damned if he didn't.

When Haverkamp led a Commission delegation to Washington, Bob and Helen Strauss gave a memorable private dinner for him in their Watergate apartment. All in all, Strauss won us an ally in Haverkamp. However, as the GATT talks slowly progressed toward a conclusion, Finn Gundelach, my Danish friend, for agricultural issues, and, for everything else, Étienne Davignon, a Belgian with a fantastic knowledge of the world steel industry, immersed themselves in the negotiations. Haverkamp still frequently spoke for the Commission, but Finn and Etienne did the heavy lifting.

Roy Jenkins, as far as I could see, stayed above the fray. While friendly and well disposed, he was a big picture man, not one to immerse himself in details. This was also true of his decision to launch a campaign for closer monetary integration, an effort I wholeheartedly welcomed despite some doubts in Washington. His effort largely foundered. Nevertheless, his vision, in the tradition of Jean Monnet and Robert Marjolin, foreshadowed creation of the EURO.

Jenkins' speeches to the European Parliament were masterful, furbishing the reputation for eloquence he had earned in the British Parliament. He wrote lucidly. His tribute to Jean Monnet, a man who had changed the face of Europe, is a gem. He quoted a favorite dictum of Monnet: "There are two kinds of people: those who want to be someone, and those who want to do something." No doubt about Monnet. Jenkins also wanted to accomplish much. He fell short, not knowing as much as Monnet knew about how to do it.

On vacation in 1978, Jenkins wrote me in his hand to point out that he had been right and I wrong about the date on which the Marshall Plan ended (December 1961). He continued: "But this does not detract from my view that you are more often right about Europe (more important than dates) than almost anyone I know, and that both we and the U.S. Govt. are equally lucky to have you where you are."

Signed "Roy," his note made me wonder if I should not err more often.

Strauss' panache was fascinating to watch. At a negotiating session in 1978, Roy Denman, speaking while Haverkamp listened, advanced in writing a new proposal, intimating that it met our position. Strauss studied it, then without a word crumpled the paper and threw it back on the table.

In early 1979 in Washington, I sat in on a negotiating session with the Canadians. After a while, a frustrated Strauss delivered a lecture. He said he was a "closer," not one to hem and haw forever. It was time, he said, to close on a deal. While there was no immediate result, I think he shook some Canadians who badly needed shaking. In the end, they closed.

That the Tokyo Round was a success was due in good measure to Strauss and his able deputies: Al MacDonald in Geneva and Allen Wolff in Washington. Yet it seems to me Bob's decision to move commercial matters from State to Commerce was unnecessarily damaging to the concept of a unified Foreign Service. He argued it was necessary to ensure favorable congressional action. No doubt his political judgment is better than mine, but in this case he so wanted to succeed that he paid too high a price.

While I supported Strauss and his team, occasionally I criticized their actions in classified cables. A sharp blast from me about our approach to "rules of origin" drew an equally sharp reply from Allen Wolff, even as he acknowledged I had "properly increased our sensitivities to such issues as Danish butter cookies." In the end, the rules of origin issue was settled in a manner satisfactory to us and to the EEC, especially the Danes.

On April 18, 1977, President Carter received Roy Jenkins in the Oval Office. It was a cordial meeting with no disagreements. At the briefing for the president in the cabinet room the day before, I was astonished at Carter's detailed knowledge of how the European Community functioned. He came close to knowing more than I. It was both disconcerting and reassuring. Clearly, President Carter was both interested in and well-disposed to European efforts to integrate.

On this visit to Washington, I saw my mother for the last time. I knew she had been ailing, unable to travel, but neither she nor Dad had told me how serious her medical condition was. It was a shock when I got his telephone call saying she had died. Dad told me she went peacefully, sitting in her usual chair in the living room. I flew home for the funeral and to help Dad, who did not need much help, carry on.

On the flight, I thought about the good times Mother and I had had together: camping and hunting quail and doves in Arizona, family games, dominoes, rummy, three handed bridge, beach combing in Hawaii, visiting Grandpa and Grandma Roesch, sharing an apartment in Chicago after World War II, her joy in my contributions to her seashell collection, visiting her Virginia home, "Channelside," and watching fireworks at Manor Country Club with her and her grandchildren. Less happy were my memories of being sent away to school as a twelve year old and again as a high school senior. It had hurt even as I acknowledged there had been good reasons: in 1935, the inadequate school at Fort Huachuca; in 1939, Dad's transfer with his regiment to Panama as war broke out in Europe.

Dad, I found, had long been resigned to her passing. After her funeral and burial in the Arlington National Cemetery, where he too would one day be buried, he was worried about two things. First, selling their home and moving out; second, finding two missing large diamond rings which my mother had insisted she wanted to keep near at hand rather than in a safer place. We searched in vain. One of mother's nurses, we concluded, had taken them. He asked me what of their possessions Miren or I would like. Miren, consulted by phone, asked for some of mother's seashells. I wanted several of her pastels and a few books, including his copy of Grant's memoirs. It turned out, to our regret, that in his haste to clear out the house he forgot each of these requests.

Later I learned he disposed of his entire library. Simpler than sorting, he explained. The seashells, mother's pride and joy, he turned over to the Smithsonian Institution. At first, he said, they had not been interested, but he had persisted, so they sent someone to look. Amazed, they took the entire collection, including her extensive library about shells.

He sold the house to the first buyer, admitting he might have gotten more had he tried. However, he thought the price was fair and he wanted to put the memories behind him. Also, he said, he knew and liked the buyer, another Manor Club member. He moved to an apartment in Leisure World. It was not far from the Club, where for ten more years he played golf and gin rummy with his friends. That winter he resumed his annual trips to Arizona. In Phoenix, where he now spent winters, he had many friends from childhood days, including one Georgia Newcomer, whom he telephoned weekly. I drove him to Phoenix in 1987. He visited with a frail Georgia in a nursing home. Apparently he said farewell to her then, since he never again telephoned her and dismissed my suggestions that he do so.

With the strain of mother's condition behind him, I noted that he neither talked of her nor welcomed my questions. Once, however, when he was ninety-four and living with me in Costa Rica, he apparently dreamed of her, as I heard him calling, "Doris, Doris, are you there?"

Although generally I take a dim view of political appointees as ambassadors, I recognize there are often notable exceptions. One such exception was Kingman Brewster, Jr., the new ambassador in London. Kingman had been an outstanding president of Yale. He was appointed to the Court of St. James by Carter for his intellect and achievements, not his campaign contributions.

In November of 1977, Kingman invited a few of his colleagues in Western Europe to London for informal discussions at Winfield Park, his magnificent residence. The session was unforgettable not for our talks, although they produced results, but for drama on the world stage. Together with another visitor, Andrew Young, our new ambassador to the United Nations, we watched on BBC the groundbreaking speech of Anwar Sadat to the Israeli Knesset.

I had despaired of Middle East peace. Since my Damascus days, I had watched Arab emotionalism persistently overcome rationality. Sadat was a different Arab leader. A brave man, he would prove at Camp David in 1978 that peace between Israel and an Arab country was possible. Three years later, he would be assassinated for his daring.

Kingman proposed that we hold regular meetings of the ambassadors to NATO, France, Germany, Italy, the United Kingdom, and the European Communities. He suggested that each ambassador might be accompanied by one and only one officer. He not only did not want anyone from Washington, but he also later successfully blocked an effort of the National Security Advisor, Zbigniew Brzezinski, to be represented at our quarterly meetings.

The group agreed in advance on the main agenda items and, if needed, on which mission would prepare discussion papers for circulation in advance. As I recall, Tap Bennett circulated papers on intermediate range missiles as well as force size and composition. I did one on "Plans for Monetary Union." The status of the Geneva trade negotiations was almost always reviewed. Discussion of nonproliferation issues, including those involving differences in the IAEA and EURATOM safeguard systems, was frequent.

Kingman's idea produced the most useful coordination mechanism of my years in the Foreign Service.

Normally, meetings of ambassadors, AID directors, economic officers, and the like are dominated by the secretary of state or other Washington officials. They are effective in laying down the party line. However, too often lacking candid discussion, they contribute little to getting the party line right.

Occasionally a meeting of the "Group of Six" generated a collective policy recommendation for Washington consideration. Powerful medicine! Every meeting provided each of us an opportunity to ventilate concerns and to probe for understanding of other mission and country positions. The mix of security, political, and economic expertise was particularly useful to all participants. I must add that we also got to see more of Europe as in turn we met in London, Paris, Rome, Bonn, Berlin, and Brussels. For me, the meeting arranged by Ambassador Walt Stoessel in Berlin, instead of Bonn, was particularly fascinating. We were cleared through checkpoint Charlie to tour East Berlin. In a holdover from the days of four-power occupation of Germany, we returned to Bonn by rail in the American high commissioner's railway car!

When it was the turn of Brussels to host a group meeting, Tap and I agreed after discussion and consultation with Kingman that the American ambassador to Belgium, Ann Cox, would be included in the meetings. She appreciated this and understood why she was not invited to sessions elsewhere. Six ambassadors, six silent staffers, and, in Brussels, another ambassador, were manageable. With fourteen NATO Members and nine European Community countries, to include everyone would have destroyed Kingman's creation. Of course, the downside was resentment and complaints from some at other posts and Washington.

Often the host ambassador invited a distinguished European to give a talk, complete with questions and answers. I invited Commissioner Etienne "Stevie" Davignon, a Belgian who had served under Foreign Minister Paul Henri Spaak, a Community "Founding Father." His tongue in cheek reply: "Without any illusion on the possibility of influencing American diplomats, I could hardly reject an invitation to try from one their most brilliant representatives."

I took public diplomacy seriously, speaking frequently and in every one of the nine European Community countries. While normally I stuck to a fairly non-controversial approach, that was not always the case. In a 1979 interview after saying our relations with the Community were in "first-class shape," I observed that the EEC lacked "dynamism," demonstrated by its "startling" inability to create new jobs while showing a "woeful ignorance" of Japan's strategic importance.

The substance of my talks, speeches, and interviews has largely faded in my mind. Moreover, I find what texts I saved to be deadly dull. However, I vividly remember three incidents.

Trying to be the friendly "Yank," I almost drank too much in

Ireland. I left Dublin convinced the Irish drink more before dinner than anyone else, even the Russians.

In the Netherlands, I spoke to the American Chamber of Commerce, gave a press conference, met with Dutch economists at Erasmus University, and spoke at the University of Amsterdam, described by Ambassador Bob McCloskey as "unfriendly territory." There I was met by a small demonstration against "The Neutron Bomb." To my surprise, once I was introduced the demonstration ceased. After ten minutes or so, I noted the passive behavior, adding that demonstrating American students would be asking tough questions about the bomb. That did it. Thereafter we had a lively discussion.

After luncheon remarks in Luxembourg, a tablemate's blatantly anti-Semitic remark provoked me, for the only time in my life, to walk out of a function. Ambassador Jim Lowenstein followed me out and later fielded apologetic telephone calls from embarrassed government officials.

In 1977, Miren, Joe, Joanna, Veronica, and I drove to Italy in our Pinto. Tight for the kids, but we got to Rome, Florence, and Venice, stopping in Austria on the way back to Brussels. That Christmas, Deborah and her latest boyfriend visited. He was pleasant but seemed somewhat peculiar. On their return to England, the authorities grabbed him. He was an escaped convict!

Official visitors, including Paul Volcker, Bob Bowie, Tip O'Neill, Dick Kennedy, Gerald Smith, Ed Muskie, Sam Gibbons, and many other members of Congress, came in an endless stream.

No visitors attracted more attention than President and Mrs. Carter. Miren and I were perforce among the airport greeters, attended a large luncheon given by King Baudouin, where to my amazement I introduced two Belgians who had never met, a prominent industrialist and a labor leader, then I joined the president for his visit to the European Commission. Carter said all the right things, as did Jenkins, only more eloquently. Their remarks had been exchanged well in advance. Thus there was no discussion, only symbolic harmony. At the end of the day, Miren and I and dozens of others saw the Carters off at the airport.

Another visitor was Secretary of Energy James Schlesinger. He impressed me as a pompous ass. First, for no good reason after driving with him to his hotel, he had me listen as he telephoned various big shots in Washington. He kept his party and flight crew on tenterhooks by suggesting he might stay over "to bird watch."

Maybe I was also influenced negatively by several Secret Service agents. Miren took Mrs. Schlesinger and Mrs. Brunner, the wife of the European commissioner in charge of energy, to a tour of Bruges and lunch. The agents stuck Miren with a large bill. It took months and much effort for me to be reimbursed by the government for their lunch. The secretary's discussions with Commissioner Brunner and others went well. Almost made me overlook the annoying aspects of his visit.

A domestic crisis erupted just before Secretary of Agriculture Robert Bergland was to dine at our residence with key Europeans involved in the trade negotiations. Miren fired Joseph, our outstanding but temperamental chef, after he had chased Juanjo around his kitchen with a carving knife. As important as a good chef is to an ambassador's success, this was too much. We advertised. Miren interviewed candidates. No luck. With time running out, in desperation she hired Dioko, a Zaïreois.

Dioko's dinner for Bergland was sensational, topped off with a fabulous chocolate desert. Thereafter, for important guests I asked for that desert. I asked until I learned Dioko was going broke buying it at a fancy pastry shop. He had wanted the job so had made the first purchase to impress us. Then he was afraid to confess. Once he no longer bought us fancy deserts he was still broke. On his day off he gambled away his salary. He and our kids got along famously. I was saddened to learn my successor fired Dioko.

Ambassador Schaetzel, my longtime friend and boss for years in Washington, was a frequent visitor. While I do not always appreciate my predecessors returning and wanting to meet with my "contacts," or worse, mucking around on their own, I welcomed Schaetzel's visits. He was known as more European than the Europeans, was welcome at all levels, and incisively drew out his interlocutors. I profited from participating in his meetings.

I also benefitted from one of Bob's brighter ideas. He had decided it would be well to introduce prominent Americans to the European integration movement. After obtaining foundation funding, he persuaded the likes of Daniel Boorstin, librarian of the Library of Congress, John Gardner of Common Cause, and Chief Justice Warren Berger to spend up to a week in Europe learning about the Community. When these distinguished Americans were not being entertained by Europeans, Miren and I housed and fed them. In hosting these visitors, Miren, some of mission staff, and I learned much about subjects outside our normal focus. For example, Chief Justice Berger's meetings at the European Court of Justice helped me understand important differences in U.S. and European law and practice.

After my mother's estate was settled, for the first time in our married life Miren and I could contemplate extra expenditures. We had often visited the Brussels antique market, but to look, not buy. Now we bought a few items, including some scrimshaw. One treasured carved sperm whale tooth, marked 1812-1817, shows Commodore Hopkins and the *Franklin*, the first U.S. frigate.

We also bought a used Mercedes and drove to Wurtzberg in Germany to attend a tennis camp run by U.S. Army. What a difference there was between that Mercedes 350SLC and our Pinto!

That fall, Miren began to complain of pain in her arms. Doctors were mystified. In November, the regional State Department doctor arranged for Miren to be examined at the Landstuhl Army Hospital. Their diagnosis was "trigeminal neuralgia." No treatment was prescribed. Miren and I thought the diagnosis was wrong, but we had no idea what the real problem was.

We went ahead with a planned Christmas trip to Chile. Miren was delighted to be back with her family, but when we drove south she was in great pain. The pain did not subside. Upon return to Brussels, the State Department's regional doctor arranged for me to accompany Miren to Georgetown Hospital in Washington. The new diagnosis was cancer. Chemotherapy was started. Eventually, Miren went into remission. We returned to Brussels, carrying written follow-up instructions to a Belgian cancer clinic.

There, she had trouble tolerating more chemo. Soon the Belgian doctor told me her white cell count was dangerously low. He recommended stopping treatment, except for pain relief.

Miren wanted us to spend some time together in a resort in the Ardennes. While there, I told her the Belgian doctor's diagnosis and recommendation. She immediately said she would fight. Also, weak as she was, she insisted on making love.

Since she preferred a return to Georgetown Hospital, chemo and all, to going peacefully in Brussels or Santiago, Miren and I flew home. Don Pedro, Nelli, Kepa, and Sonia again came to Washington. I rented an apartment. Mincho, Michu, and Coca soon joined me.

Miren fought. She fought for months. Even in her last week she demanded to go to physical therapy. Only once did I hear her complain. I overheard her ask, *"Dios, que hice yo por ser tan castigada?"*

Miren worried more about her children than herself. Before

leaving Brussels, she instructed me on what each was to receive of her jewelry. Concerned that their father might complicate things, she took legal steps to name me as guardian of Coca and Juanjo. She asked our friend Ray Sternfeld to help get Guillermo a job at the Inter-American Bank. Ray arranged a probationary job. Mincho did well and still works there. Michu was now of age, no longer the irresponsible girl about whom her mother had once been so worried. Michu dedicated herself to caring for her mother. Until the end, she hardly slept.

Miren asked me to bring Pedro back from Brussels. I called him and explained that his mother wanted a chance to say goodbye to him. He dithered. Kepa then telephoned him. He still did not come. Why? Judging from my telephone bill, he was chasing girls. Nor did he arrive in Santiago in time for his mother's funeral. I never forgave him.

20

Washington (EB) (1979–1981)

As my time at USEC was coming to an end, my concerns were about Miren, not my professional future. To keep me close to Miren in the Georgetown Hospital, I worked out a non-job at the Industrial College of the Armed Forces.

Later, Henry Owen asked me to come work for him at the NSC, an attractive offer that gave me another possibility to think about.

Then, in Brussels for the semi-annual U.S.-EEC consultations, Richard Cooper, under secretary of state for economic affairs, urged me to succeed Jules Katz as assistant secretary for economics and business. Dick argued both that I was needed and that having a real job would help me deal with the inevitable passing of Miren. Without enthusiasm, I agreed.

Upon returning from Miren's funeral in Chile, I sadly tried to resume life, knowing it would never be the same. Michu soon left for Chile, where she married Jorge Grimm, telling me about it after the fact. Mincho and Coca lived with me in the Dellwood house, as did Juanjo when he was not studying at Pennington. A Catholic charity found us a Chilean housekeeper, without whom I doubt I could have managed. Before long, Michu returned with Jorge and moved in for a few months before finding their own place.

Since by law I could not assume charge of my new job until sworn in, and I could not be sworn until confirmed, work was studying and getting to know my likely new staff. Not only was I submerged in piles of briefing memos; I was advised that I should promptly get to know numerous members of Congress as well as key economic correspondents. My brief on "1980 Active Legislation" included over twenty measures about which I might have to testify. My task appeared to be overwhelming. Why, I asked myself, had I agreed to take on these responsibilities?

Worse, both the political and economic outlooks were grim. The Iranian hostage crisis continued and the Soviets had just invaded Afghanistan. Inflation was running at over 12 percent, economic growth was stagnating, and we were in the midst of another oil crisis.

On Miren's and my eighth wedding anniversary, I decided to return to Annapolis, where we had celebrated our brief honeymoon. While there, I replied to the many letters of condolence I had received.

After the usual delays, the president sent my nomination to the Senate. Secretary Cyrus Vance swore me in on January 4, 1980. My invitees were limited to family members.

That very evening I was invited by Stuart Eizenstat to an interagency meeting called to formulate our response to the Soviet Christmas Day invasion of Afghanistan. It was proposed to annul the U.S.-Soviet grain agreement. When I got the floor, I pointed out that the terms of our agreement required us to make minimum deliveries regardless of political considerations such as Afghanistan. A heated discussion ensued. Eventually it was agreed to announce an "embargo" on sales. As we broke up, Vice President Mondale muttered, "How to shoot yourself in the foot."

It struck me as an amazing coincidence that the U.S.-Soviet grain agreement I had helped negotiate in 1975 was the first issue I dealt with in 1981. It also earned me faintly hidden hostility from some.

On January 7, the White House announced that the shipment of "all" agricultural products to the Soviet Union was suspended. However, the fine print indicated that export licenses would be issued to meet our commitments under the U.S.-U.S.S.R. Grain Agreement. We would not license shipment to the Soviets of all the grain they sought, thereby denying them roughly 17 million metric tons. To meet our commitment, in 1980 we would license 3 million metric tons of corn and wheat in addition to the 5 million metric tons already shipped.

I had won respect for the terms of our agreement, but had frustrated White House Counsel Lloyd Cutler, among others. In June, I received a note initialed "W.C.," attaching a satiric cartoon labeled "U.S. Olympic Team." It showed "American Grain Trading Companies" marching at the Moscow Olympics. Apparently I was wrong in thinking that while Deputy Secretary of State Warren Christopher might regret the facts, he would appreciate my insistence on the rule of law?

One of the many problems with imposing sanctions is that unless all significant suppliers cooperate, the intended effect is undercut. Knowing this, we convoked a meeting of the world's major grain exporting nations. On January 12, Under Secretary of Agriculture Dale Hathaway and I made the case for unanimity in reducing grain shipments to the Soviet Union. The best we could achieve was agreement that other exporters would not replace the 17 metric tons the U.S. would deny to the Soviets.

Argentina originally balked at even this, but eventually signed an ambiguous communiqué. As the future unfolded, Argentina was not the only country that cheated. Nevertheless, U.S. economic sanctions somewhat constrained Soviet economic management. They and the Olympic boycott conveyed a clear political message.

My new position was certainly challenging, but it was also frustrating. Much of my career had been dedicated to reducing trade barriers. Now, I concentrated on the energy crisis, sanctions against the U.S.S.R. because of Afghanistan, and sanctions against Iran because students had seized our embassy and sixty-three Americans in Tehran, an action in which the Ayatollah Khomeini acquiesced. Not only did we have sanctions, but there was also constant pressure from the White House to strengthen them.

Regularly I accompanied Deputy Secretary Warren Christopher or Under Secretary for Political Affairs David Newsom to White House meetings chaired by Brzezinski. Pressure for more sanctions was unremitting. Remembering the White House decision-making process I had watched George Shultz preside over, I was often appalled by how Brzezinski ran meetings. Riding to and from these meetings gave me a chance to talk issues over with my seniors, but seldom did I get anywhere. Warren Christopher was not given to bucking city hall, and David Newsom, although more sympathetic to my view, was not much of a fighter, at least about economic issues.

Another persistent problem of concern to me consisted of cases where "human rights" conflicted with export opportunities. Often it was proposed that we block or try to block loans by international lending institutions or simply veto loans by our Export-Import Bank. While I welcomed Carter's emphasis on human rights, I believed that the policy should be balanced against political and economic costs. Too often, I thought, we were doing disproportionate harm. Yet, almost always, the committee, chaired by Christopher, approved the recommendations of the assistant secretary for human rights, Patt Derian.

A committee decision to reject financing to U.S. companies with a contract for a piece of the large Ixaipu hydro-electric project above the Iguazu Falls in South America cost U.S. firms millions, but was clearly inadequate to change the policies of the military dictatorship in Brazil or the Stroessner dictatorship in Paraguay. Faced with my vehement private critique of this decision, Christopher assured me that he would give more weight to U.S. business interests in Carter's second term. Small comfort!

Morale was terrible in the Bureau. My predecessor's resignation expressed his disgust with the reduced economic role of the State Department, but only added to the worries of my staff. Before I was sworn in, Frances Wilson, EB's exceptionally able Executive Director, had spelled out these concerns in a series of briefing memos for me. Worse, it was far from clear how the broad principles of the president's decision would be implemented. Uncertainty fed rumors and magnified fears.

After I was sworn in, I cabled all posts inviting comments as to how we could help each other stay on top of economic issues. I called on all to work positively to make a success of the president's plan for trade reorganization. Noting that the department's role in commercial promotion, investment, and commodity policy had been weakened, I asserted "our responsibilities for the integration of economic considerations into foreign policy are unchanged....I emphasized our need for more convincing political-economic analysis."

In the short run, I had no choice but to work with Director General Harry Barnes, who had been given responsibility for negotiating with Commerce and other concerned agencies. I urged him to develop positions that would reassure my people. Of course, Barnes was under instructions to settle matters, not to prolong discussions. Moreover, he was a political cone officer with little interest in economics. While he would agree in talks with me and my staff to stand firm on key issues, he would then cede much, much too much ground in his negotiations. To say the least, my people and I were frustrated by the process. If we could only grin and bear it in the short run, I resolved to introduce a more positive element to the long run outlook for EB.

It took a while, but eventually the secretary signed off on my proposal that an independent study be conducted of the economic function of the Foreign Service and State Department. I persuaded Ed Martin, a hard-charging predecessor of mine as assistant secretary; John Leddy of the Civil Service, a former boss of mine when he was assistant secretary for European affairs; and Frances Wilson, who knew the issues backwards and forwards, to undertake the study.

Their report, completed in December, was first class. Unfortunately, it was dead upon arrival. In May, Secretary Vance had resigned over Carter's decision to try to forcibly rescue the hostages in Tehran. In November, Ronald Reagan defeated Carter in the election.

The new team had other things on its mind than the economic function of the Department of State. I, of course, commended the Martin Report to my successor, Bob Hormats, a highly competent friend of long standing. Bob, however, was interested in promoting Bob Hormats, not in sexless institutional issues.

While worried about poor morale and caught up immediately in issues involving sanctions against the U.S.S.R. and Iran, I also had to get to know a staff of over two hundred and learn about many issues new to me. Fortunately, Ernie Johnston, an experienced levelheaded officer, agreed to be my principal deputy. Ernie's knowledge and policy advice were invaluable. In Frances Wilson, I had the best executive director in the department. She knew the strengths and weaknesses of not only every person in the Bureau but also of almost every economic officer anywhere in the world. As such, she was close to indispensable.

Five deputy assistant secretaries, with Ernie's and my "guidance," such as it was, oversaw our substantive responsibilities. I came into my job well prepared to deal with finance, trade, and development issues, almost totally unprepared for transportation and telecommunications issues, and inadequately prepared to handle energy policy issues. Early on, however, I recognized the central importance of the energy crisis and concentrated much of my personal effort thereon.

Under Secretary Dick Cooper, who had persuaded me to take the job, came from an academic background. A well-known expert in international monetary matters, he was an easy going boss. In fact, he encouraged me to run EB with minimal reference to him.

Dick used a weekly luncheon with Fred Bergsten, assistant secretary of the treasury for international affairs, Bob Hormats, deputy special trade representative, and now myself to keep track of significant issues. All members of this group were basically opposed to protectionism. Each of us, however, was sensitive enough to political pressures to recognize that at times some ground had to be conceded in order to minimize damage to an open trading system. I found our discussion of cases to be helpful. That they helped us avoid overt interagency warfare was an additional enormous plus.

When I took over EB, Dick was engaged virtually full time in trying to arrange multilateral financial sanctions on Iran. He worked closely with Treasury, basically needing no help from me or my people.

Brashly I suggested to him that a United Nations or international embargo of Iranian oil exports would be simpler and more effective. He agreed it would, but gently explained that the administration did not want to worsen the already severe world oil supply shortage. Not only the United States but also the industrial world depended on Middle East oil. Not one of our allies was prepared to willingly lose access to Iranian oil.

Revolutionary upheaval in Iran had decreased Iranian crude production and increased uncertainty. The combination had pushed up pump prices of gasoline and diesel. Consumers were complaining. In these circumstances, a substantial price increase was not politically viable, either domestically or internationally.

Nevertheless, Dick said, if I wanted he had no objection to my proposing such an embargo. After discussion with my staff, I recognized that a general embargo of Iranian oil exports was not a viable option.

One of my harder-charging colleagues, Assistant Secretary for East Asian and Pacific Affairs Dick Holbrooke, invited me to a meeting of his chiefs of mission in Singapore. Needing to learn more about the economic problems of the Far East, I agreed to attend. Then Holbrooke twisted my arm to also visit Taipei, Seoul, Hong Kong, and Jakarta. My main memory of this trip is of the barrage of criticism of our Foreign Corrupt Practices Act to which I was subjected by American business representatives. Given local practices, I was told, bribery was a requisite for doing business. I, of course, stressed the importance of American firms abiding by the law. I had the feeling that I was judged as not sophisticated enough to appreciate the facts of life in the orient.

Upon returning to Washington, I was told to attend an ANZUS Council Meeting, chaired by Secretary Vance. My role was ornamental. I resented the almost two days ANZUS kept me from my work backlog. Mingling with foreign ministers, listening to dull— to me—speeches, attending receptions, and a couple of fancy meals did not compensate for the time lost.

Back at work, my staff insisted my personal involvement was required to handle a brewing storm over strategic stockpile policy.

State, citing national security reasons, had long blocked reductions in our reserves of critical materials. Now, however, congressional interest in selling some of our stockpile was building. Sales would reduce the budget deficit and ease price pressures. Stonewalling no longer seemed possible, so I agreed to chair an interagency policy review.

After lengthy discussions, I agreed that some small releases of tin made economic sense. My concession on tin led negotiators from the Departments of Interior, Commerce, and the General Services Administration to abandon, at least temporarily, their demands for other releases. They also agreed tin releases would cease at the first sign of disruption of the market. We informed Malaysia, Thailand, Indonesia, and Bolivia of the decision. I was proud of having achieved agreement where previously there had been acrimony.

It was not to be. Before sales were made, Paul Boeker, the outgoing ambassador to Bolivia, protested. Secretary Vance convoked us and had us outline our conflicting views. Paul asserted that the chances for democracy in Bolivia would be destroyed by any stockpile sale of tin. While the agreed safeguards against market disruption might work, he argued, it was a political problem, not an economic issue. Vance ruled against tin releases, thereby scuttling the interagency agreement. Politics had trumped economics.

Market prices shot up. Users, expecting a stock release, protested. My colleagues in other agencies were furious. An indignant Senator Robert Byrd called me. He did not give a damn about Bolivian democracy. He insisted I have the secretary personally explain to him the decision. When I reached Vance, an annoyed secretary made the call. That was that. Except that in July a bloody military coup ended Paul's edition of Bolivian democracy.

Pressure from the White House for more and more restrictions on exports to the U.S.S.R. was unremitting. After a great effort with our NATO allies, we increased Coordinating Committee for Multilateral Export Controls (CoCom) restrictions on many items. We also pushed hard, with some initial success, for restrictions on export credits. I felt the brunt of pressures for more sanctions. I would listen to Zbig Brzezinski in the situation room, then be told by Warren Christopher to find ways to do more. To my astonishment, careful staff work on proposals was noted for its absence. At one meeting, mention was made of the possibility of imposing maritime sanctions. When the meeting minutes were sent to the president, he approved this idea. It had never before been mentioned, much less scrutinized. It took weeks to reverse this presidential decision! Not having much of a merchant marine, unilaterally we could do little. Our NATO allies were horrified by the proposal. Freedom of the seas, indeed!

I admit to having abandoned common sense at least once in face of top-level pressure for more sanctions. Told I should agree with Commerce on new proposals to put before our allies, I found myself arguing with Philip Klutznick, the capable secretary of commerce. Eventually we agreed on a cable of instructions for our NATO delegation. I was ashamed of it and of having ceded far too much. However, it was so outrageous that when I tried to clear it with George Vest, the assistant secretary for European affairs, he exploded. He got the ear of Secretary Vance. I was not unhappy this time to be overruled.

When invited to speak about "Economic Peacekeeping," a euphemism for sanctions, to the Council on Foreign Relations in New York, I had no choice but to follow the company line.

Treasury somehow persuaded my bosses that I should represent the United States at a meeting in Manila of the Asian Development Bank. When I complained that I had other priorities, I was soft soaped about the honor I was to have. No one from State had ever led the U.S. delegation. Of course, the reason Treasury wanted someone else in the lead was its failure to meet its funding commitments.

So in Manila, I had the "honor" of explaining that in the future we would try harder to meet our obligations. Staying in a hotel suite for the first and only time in my life, giving a speech of apologies to the governors, and talking privately with assorted finance ministers did not make it fun.

From Manila I was scheduled to fly to Tel Aviv to conduct negotiations Israel wanted concerning how we would supply them with petroleum products in a crisis. However, in Athens, my last stop before Israel, an embassy officer met me to tell me that President Carter, annoyed with the Israelis, had canceled my trip. I was told that I could either fly home and return to Paris for my regular meeting of the International Energy Agency (IEA), or I could relax in Athens before going to Paris. Some choice!

An old friend, Ambassador Bob McCloskey, let me catch up on badly needed sleep at his residence. Then he beat me at tennis. Only an insatiable taste for famous sights led me to abandon Bob's hospitality. I rented a car and enjoyed sightseeing in Delphi, Marathon, and the countryside.

The energy crisis of 1973, triggered by the Seven Day War and the Arab oil export boycott, had led to the formation of the IEA. When another energy crisis burst on the world in 1979, the IEA was there to coordinate member country responses. I went regularly to its meetings. Les Goldman, assistant secretary for international affairs of the Department of Energy, often joined me.

Les was ambitious, brash, and politically well connected. He had a legitimate claim to attend IEA meetings, but also clearly sought to replace me as head of the American delegation. We got along reasonably well, but the relation was not easy. To be effective with other country representatives, I had first to reach agreement with Les on how to advance U.S. policy, for example, on stock pile requirements, inventory drawdowns, import quotas, and spot market purchases. We did it, but...

The best way to deal with the crisis was to reduce demand to match supply. All IEA members took conservation measures. President Carter had the thermostats turned down in government buildings. The United States also adopted a national speed limit of 55 mph. Normally our German allies joined in collective measures, but not for speed limits. Even after the Iraqi attack on Iran in September 1980 worsened the world energy crisis, the Germans drove as fast as they wished on their autobahns. Les and I were totally agreed about the need for speed limits, but to no avail.

Besides conservation, it was also important to increase supply. Saudi Arabia helped, as did some IEA countries: Norway, the U.K., and the United States. Canada did not.

On the contrary in late 1980 Canada announced a new energy policy, including disincentives to production and measures against foreign countries. The reaction in Washington was one of shocked disbelief. I was sent to Toronto for talks. My private comments were blunt. I noted that some in the United States termed the Canadian action "rolling expropriation and confiscatory." Publicly, later in the month, speaking in Chicago, I observed that Canada "seems to be out of step [on energy policy] with the rest of the world."

In May, I testified before two subcommittees of the House Foreign Affairs Committee. I defended an administration decision to allow the sale of marine engine cores, incorporating U.S. technology, for four frigates under construction in Italy for the Iraqi navy.

I walked into a buzz saw. Never, before or since, have I had a worse day before Congress. That I had not known, since my briefers did not know, of a commitment Secretary Vance had given to

Senator Javits, made a tough day far worse. For several hours, one by one, Representatives Hamilton, Bingham, Bonker, Fountain, Solarz, Rosenthal, Gilman, and Fenwick berated me and the Department of State for arming Iraq, an enemy of Israel and one of four U.S.-designated "supporters of terrorism." Each representative had found a perfect issue to furbish his or her election credentials.

On May 21, pursuant to instructions, I sent the new secretary of state, Edmund Muskie, a one-page briefing memorandum, subject: "My Priorities."

My top priority was energy. I wrote:

> The energy problem, particularly oil, is central to our domestic economic health (inflation and growth), to the stability of the international economic system, to our foreign policy (Camp David, Palestine, and Allied unity) as well as to our national security (undue dependence on oil from the highly volatile Gulf area).

I listed my other priorities as:

1. Resisting Protectionism - Here and Abroad;
2. Economic Peacemaking - otherwise known as economic sanctions to free our hostages and punish the Soviets;
3. Resources and "North-South" Problems.

I wrote:

> You will find you cannot run an effective foreign policy without development assistance. A large defense budget and diplomacy are simply not enough.

After five hectic months in EB, my father and I had a most agreeable break. We attended Mincho's wedding to Isabelle van Stratum in Brasschaat, Belgium. Then we went on to Paris, where Dad and I watched Bjorn Borg, on his way to winning the French Open at Roland Garros. We took in a show on the Champs-Élysées. At a reception given by my old friends Ambassador and Donna Hartman, we met Fred Perry, a British tennis champion I had admired for more than forty years.

That June, I served on a selection panel for promotion to the rank of career minister. Our chairman was Phil Habib, surely one of the great Foreign Service officers of all time. When we were having trouble narrowing the field to a prefixed number of promotions, Phil announced that the situation was intolerable. He marched us to a confrontation with the under secretary for management, Ben Read. Phil browbeat Ben into adding a couple more promotion slots. They were well filled. As chairman of another panel a few years later, I tried to do as Phil had done. I failed.

Later in June, I was the principal speaker at the swearing-in ceremony for the 148th Junior Officer Class. I relished the opportunity to speak about the Service I love. "My generation," I noted, "could be faulted for many things, but not for a failure of American foreign policy. I hope you can say the same thirty years hence."

Pointing to a dangerous, more diffuse world, I observed that our margin for error was much less than previously. I called for "creativity and discipline." Creativity because new problems, in new circumstances, require new solutions. Discipline because of our political process and because, like it or not, ours is a hierarchical service. Our effectiveness depends on disciplined implementation of decisions taken legitimately. We are not elected. The president and the members of Congress are elected. Their mandate comes from the people. We are responsible to them.

The next day I flew to Tel Aviv to negotiate with the Israeli government arrangements to implement the U.S.-Israeli Agreement of June 22, 1979, on Oil Supply. There ensued four rounds of negotiations. My patience and sanity were tested before Deputy Secretary Warren Christopher and the Israeli ambassador in Washington successfully wrapped up matters.

Christopher found the right words to bridge differences that need never have arisen, while the Israelis made a key tactical move. I had undiplomatically warned Ambassador Evron prior to the arrival of Israeli Minister of Energy Yitzhak Modai that the minister was quite capable of frustrating agreement. The ambassador told me not to worry; this time the minister would be kept under control. And he was.

Upon arrival, Modai was instructed by Prime Minister Menachem Begin to attend several events around the country to promote the sale of Israeli bonds. He only returned to Washington in time to attend the White House signing ceremony. There, in his remarks, he referred to Prime Minister Ben-Gurion! His erroneous reference was much repeated on Israeli TV.

Why had I developed a jaundiced view of the minister?

Largely because of what Yitzhak Modai tried to achieve, presumably with his government's approval, at least initially.

The peace treaty between Israel and Egypt required the Israelis to return the oil fields in the Gulf of Suez to Egypt. The Israelis sought and were provided a commitment in a Memorandum of Agreement of June 22, 1979, to make oil available for purchase by Israel if Israel could not find enough on its own, through normal procedures, to meet domestic requirements. It was agreed that experts would meet at least annually "to review Israel's continuing oil requirement and to develop any necessary contingency implementing arrangements."

I thought this would be a simple, straightforward task. Indeed, it should have been. However, Yitzhak Modai purported not see it as we did. He pushed for oil we had not committed to supply. As a result, it took five meetings to reach agreement on what had, in reality, already been agreed!

On October 17, 1980, five complicated pages were signed to supplement the two-page memorandum of 1979. Ridiculous!

Before Peter Borre and I arrived in Israel, Modai had told the press an emergency existed and the agreement should be implemented immediately! Since there was no emergency and Israel was meeting its oil requirement, this made no sense. Later, Modai backed down a bit. Arguing that oil prices were now higher than when the memorandum was signed, he appeared to be asking us to subsidize Israeli oil imports. At another point, he suggested that we should supply Alaskan crude, rather than have Israel make commercial arrangements for its oil imports. When he pressed price considerations, I replied that our commitment depended not on price, but on a shortage in quantitative terms.

As we saw it, what mattered was the U.S. commitment. Why spell out complicated implementing formulae? There was no good reason, only Israeli insistence.

The first round of our talks ended in deadlock, but tourism and Israeli hospitality were outstanding. Not only did we walk everywhere in fabulous Jerusalem; we were taken to Masada, the hilltop fortress that symbolizes Israeli determination never again to be conquered, as the Jews had been in the first century by the Romans.

Memory fails me, but I think it was after a second round of deadlocked talks that Prime Minister Begin wrote to President Carter asking for a more forthcoming American position. The president replied cautiously, but in friendly terms, basically reiterating no more than we had already promised.

Before replying, Carter had chaired a cabinet room discussion during which, to my astonishment, he referred to a footnote in my report on the negotiations. The president's amazing mastery of such details struck me as a waste of presidential energy.

When talks resumed in Tel Aviv, I repeated the well-known American position. Modai ranted and raved. Then Ambassador Sam Lewis was summoned by Prime Minister Begin to be lectured in his turn. How could Hinton ignore President Carter's letter? Of course, what I had said was compatible with the president's letter. The Israelis misinterpreted it. Or, more likely, they tried to distort its meaning to fit their own aims.

Politically, both sides wanted, even needed, agreement, so finally agreement was reached.

At the signing ceremony, President Carter noted, "Both nations hope this agreement will never be activated."

It never has been!

That August, with Poland paralyzed by strikes, found me in London for secret consultations with the British about what to do if the Soviets intervened. My role was minimal, but I appreciated participating in talks considering options running from doing nothing to war. Despite my dislike of sanctions, it was easy to conclude that well-conceived, widely enforced economic sanctions were preferable to war. Fortunately, the Soviets backed away from intervention.

Later in August, with the IEA on vacation, Dad, Coca, Juanjo, and I went to Alaska. Joe met us in Rapid City, went with us to Seattle, then drove Dad's Cadillac back to Washington.

Dad had long wanted to visit Alaska, having been to every other state. At 85, I thought he might not have many more years to fulfill his wish. It was a memorable trip, including a spectacular train ride from Skagway up and over the famed Chinook pass. On a long bus journey through the Canadian Yukon, our bus driver led us in choruses of something he called the beaver song. Juanjo can still sing verses of it. We topped off our trip with a flight around Mount McKinley. Coca, however, did not enjoy one bit the turbulence of that ride.

Our plan had been to pay a surprise visit en route to Seattle on my Aunt Clara and Cousin Patty, whom we had not seen since the 1930s. But car problems so delayed us that we had to go straight to Seattle. Our surprise would have had a sour taste, since Clara had died just before we would have arrived. Nor did I ever see Patty.

We exchanged Christmas greetings for years. Then she insisted that henceforth she be called Annette. I complied, but it was a hard adjustment after seventy years of calling her Patty. Women are strange!

Ronald Reagan won the presidency that November. What, I wondered, would his election mean for me?

At the United Nations, years of pressure from developing nations for a "New Economic Order" were coming to a head. Our delegation, headed by Ambassador Donald McHenry, while defending the U.S. position of great skepticism, nevertheless was privately agitating for an American accommodation. I forget how it came about, but somehow I found myself in New York with instructions to throw lots of cold water on the "New Economic Order." Long sympathetic to LDC ambitions, I nevertheless had no trouble carrying out my mission. The so-called Group of 77, in fact much larger, had cobbled together extremist proposals. Few of their proposals made sense to me. Our ambassador gave a luncheon for me to meet key players. I threw the cold water. McHenry was unhappy with my performance, but it was effective. I think Don got over it.

By law, the State Department provided one board member of the Overseas Private Investment Corporation (OPIC), an agency that insured private investments. Dick Cooper asked me to represent the department. I enjoyed doing so. Quarterly board meetings kept me somewhat involved in development issues, a longtime interest of mine. I had to be on top of the issues before the board, but not much study was needed.

In December, Marvin Cohen, chairman of the Civil Aeronautics Board, suggested I lead the U.S. delegation to negotiations with the Japanese. It was thought we should send a weighty group, since the Japanese attach importance to symbolism. For me, when Dad said he would love to return to Hawaii, the idea of Honolulu in January, rather than Washington, was irresistible.

I immersed myself in the jargon of air traffic rights from First Freedom to Sixth Freedom, gateways, capacity limits, slots, beyonds, pricing, and special rules regarding charters. Since Chairman Cohen, my deputy for transportation Boyd Hight, and numerous American experts would be on our delegation, I knew I need not worry about my lack of expertise. Moreover, United Airlines and Pan American, as well as other U.S. carriers, suffering from blatant Japanese violation of prior agreements, would have their people nearby to advise.

I was encouraged by learning that both countries were dissatisfied with the existing situation. We were preparing a radical proposal for revision of the existing agreement. It was intended in part to respond to the Japanese argument that our basic air agreement, negotiated in 1952, was unfair. They alleged that the U.S. had taken undue advantage of its then status as the occupying power.

In Honolulu, I was surprised to learn that senior corporate officials of Japan Airlines were full members of the large Japanese delegation. I was less surprised, given my many years of often frustrating trade negotiations with Japan, by Japanese stonewalling. While I had known that issues would not be resolved until the Reagan administration took over, I had expected more sign of give as we explored each other's positions. I was disappointed, but note that my successors took quite a while to reach a new agreement. The Japanese are tough.

After the talks ended, Dad and I rented a car and toured Oahu. I was amazed at how he recalled details of his adventures in 1922, but had trouble remembering where at Schofield Barracks we had lived in the 1930s. The experience taught me something about the vagaries of memory.

As Inauguration Day loomed, the transition team released a list of senior State Department officials who would be in charge of the various bureaus. Many Carter appointees were dropped, as were some career officers. I was shown as still being in charge of EB.

As such, it fell to me to lead a negotiating team to Algeria. We were to make a last effort to settle a liquefied natural gas (LNG) contract price dispute between El Paso, a U.S. pipeline company, and Sonatrack, Algeria's national oil company. Les Goldman had held six unsuccessful sessions with the Algerians. He left behind bad feelings and a complicated mess. My team and I also failed. We just did not have enough time to fix matters. However, we left Algiers with an amicable agreement that no agreement was possible.

The original contract was signed in 1969 at a price of 30.5 cents per million British Thermal Units (BTUs). Ten years later, gas deliveries were finally underway but world petroleum prices were soaring. Sonatrack "adjusted" the LNG price to $1.95 per million BTUs, a price said to reflect "parity with Algerian crude oil." El Paso, caught between what Algeria wanted and what U.S. regulators would approve, had asked the government to intervene. Hence, the unusual role of Les, and then me, negotiating about the price a private company would pay a foreign government for LNG.

Had Peter and I handled the negotiating from the outset, I think we would have reached a satisfactory deal. But we did not. El Paso had to write off $365 million largely for tankers it had had to buy for carrying LNG from Algeria to U.S. terminals. Even so, El Paso let me know they were pleased with what I had done. They explained that they had been afraid DOE would "come up with a fake agreement which would put the company in a pinch." Amazing. I succeeded by failing!

Back from Algiers, I concentrated on keeping the EB ship afloat so that Bob Hormats would take over a smoothly functioning organization. As one small step to maintain morale, I planned a series of in-house, informal, off-the-record roundtables. I led off with a talk about links between international politics and economics.

I also started work on my swan song, "Some Consequences of Global Economic Interdependence." It was a summing up of what I had learned about international economic issues in my many years of involvement, not just my one-plus year at EB. I delivered my thoughts to a business audience in Dallas on April 8, 1981. Discussing five challenges, one of which was population growth, long a concern of mine, I attributed "revolutionary conflict" in El Salvador in part to its having the highest population density in Latin America.

With the change of administration, Dick Cooper, my supervisor, promptly returned to academia. He left without writing my efficiency report. David Newsom, under secretary for political affairs, filled in for Dick. His appraisal, I thought, was a ho-hum effort to meet a bureaucratic requirement. Not knowing much about my work, he neither advanced my career nor harmed it.

21

El Salvador (1981–1983)

Serving as ambassador in war-torn El Salvador was the most challenging assignment of my forty-eight years as a Foreign Service officer.

President Ronald Reagan had won election, in part by vigorously attacking Jimmy Carter's Latin American policy. He alleged that Carter had sold out Somoza to the Marxist Sandinistas, surrendered "our canal" to Panama, and responded weakly to the leftist threat in El Salvador. He promised to change course.

Even before the new president took office, word was out that there would be drastic changes at State. As soon as the new administration assumed office, Bill Bowdler, assistant secretary for Latin American affairs (ARA), was fired summarily. Other senior career officers were also given walking orders.

Wondering what this meant for me, I talked with Dick Kennedy, the new under secretary for management, who was a friend from my White House days. Dick said, "Deane, it's policy that all assistant secretaries must be replaced. You, however, are well thought of and will have another job." Asked what job would interest me, I replied, "A challenging ambassadorship."

The following week, I was asked to report to the secretary's office. I had known Al Haig in the Nixon Administration and again in Europe, where he served as supreme allied commander Europe (SACEUR) when I was ambassador to the European Communities. After warm greetings, he came to the point: "Deane, we would like you to go El Salvador, but if you don't want to go, we'll give you a good job."

Startled, I replied I would gladly go, if I could make arrangements for Juanjo, Miren's fourteen-year-old son, to be cared for in my absence. In effect, Al said, "Good. Let me know."

When Miren's sister, Begonia Yaeger, assured me she would watch out for Juanjo, I confirmed that I would be honored to serve in El Salvador. I had recalled my father's admonition, "Good soldiers march to the sound of the guns."

Why did the secretary pick me? Presumably because he knew me and knew I was a widower.

But I knew little about the situation in El Salvador. First with Cyrus Vance, later with Ed Muskie, during their staff meetings I had tuned out discussions of the maneuvers of Salvadoran politicians, ambitious colonels, corrupt businessmen, factious rebel groups, and Nicaraguan Sandinistas.

Hoping to recover as best I could, I called Bill Bowdler, who agreed to meet with me despite his fury with the Reagan administration. Bill, a true professional, greatly helped me in understanding the mess into which I was heading.

At the time, I was dating Hazel Denton, an attractive lady working at the World Bank. She was appalled at the thought of my going to El Salvador. A Catholic, she recalled the horrible murder of four Maryknoll nuns the previous December. Her fears were magnified by daily graphic TV and press coverage of Salvadoran violence. Never mind, I tried to reassure her, it will only be for a couple of years. I will visit you in Washington; you can visit me. She said she would be too scared to visit. Her reply suggested to me that our relationship did not have much of a future.

President Reagan had said he personally wanted to ask potential ambassadors to serve. I was told he would soon call me, but no call came until I was spending a weekend at a lodge in Shenandoah National Park. Being found there surprised me, but a call from the White House surprised the lodge staff even more.

The president indeed asked me to represent him as ambassador to El Salvador. Although he recognized it was a trouble spot, he was optimistic that I could quickly handle the situation. I assured him I was honored by his confidence, but frankly doubted matters could soon be brought under control. Reflecting on our brief chat, I was encouraged by his spirit, but worried that his optimism was not justified.

In early April, my nomination was sent to the Senate. The importance of the job was evidenced by the fact that it was only the second ambassadorial nomination submitted by President Reagan. Bureaucratic inertia or overload was evident from the fact that it was already April.

Only now could I go seriously to work, giving priority to calls on key senators and choosing my DCM.

With El Salvador front page news, I found it easy to get appointments on the Hill. Many senators had friendly admonitions for me. Senator Pell, once a Foreign Service officer himself, asked me if I had talked to Robert White, my controversial predecessor. Knowing the traditions of the service, he was surprised when I replied, "No." He understood, however, when I explained that I had called White to arrange a lunch, only to have Bob cancel at the last moment. Interestingly, the next day, Bob called me. At lunch, I profited from his trenchant observations about Salvadoran personalities, if not about policy.

John Bushnell, after Bowdler's ouster, was acting ARA assistant secretary. I had known John from our days in Central America. He and almost everyone else in ARA recommended that I choose Charles Gillespie as my DCM. I met with "Chuck" and was favorably impressed, but was concerned he might be more the Bureau's man than my man. Consequently, I continued to interview candidates, including Ken Bleakley, a leader of "The Young Turk" reform movement of the American Foreign Service Association (AFSA). Ken spoke Spanish but had not recently served in ARA. I thought he would be a good manager as well as politically astute. That he was from a different mold from me tipped the balance in Ken's favor. I never regretted my choice.

Another key vacancy was that of the Military Group (MilGrp) commander. Colonel John Waghelstein, a Special Forces officer, was proposed by the Pentagon. I met with him. He had cogent comments on errors made in Vietnam, where he had served with distinction. He clearly understood the political importance of land reform. He also assured me he would not try to build an empire. We both recognized that the limit on trainers would pose problems, but he assured me he could live with the ceiling. He was my man. A better officer could not have been found.

James A. Hickey, Washington's Catholic archbishop, was a leading critic of our supply of weapons and training. I called on him. While we disagreed about policy, he offered to introduce me to Bishop Riviera y Damas of San Salvador during the bishop's imminent visit to Washington. Riviera y Damas had taken over after the assassination of Archbishop Oscar Romero. I would have gotten to know the bishop in any case, but a first meeting under Hickey's auspices helped me build a fruitful relation.

No less shocking than the murder of the nuns had been the killing of two Americans, Michael Hammer and David Pearlman, along with Jose Rodolfo Viera, the head of the Salvadoran Institute of Agrarian Reform. They were machine gunned in early January 1981 having coffee in San Salvador's best hotel. These American land reform experts had been sent to El Salvador by Bill Dougherty, head of AIFELD, the Latin American arm of the AFL-CIO.

I knew Bill from my days in Guatemala and Chile. To see him again was high on my list of priorities. While I did not need his lecture on the need to bring the killers to justice, I nevertheless enjoyed listening to the forcefully expressed views of this bulky, blustery man. Moreover, he served the best pastrami sandwiches this side of New York City.

I also paid courtesy calls on many officials, including Secretary of Defense Caspar Weinberger, Deputy Secretary of State William Clark, and Richard Allen, the president's national security advisor.

At the C.I.A., I met with a bevy of officers, ending with Director Bill Casey, a man I had long admired. We had worked together on economic problems in the Nixon and Ford administrations and had met again in the 1970s when he visited Brussels, researching his book on the Office of Strategic Services (OSS). At the Agency, I learned to my dismay that Admiral Turner, Carter's C.I.A. director, had closed the station in El Salvador. It was now back in business, but badly crippled without agents in either the FMLN, the leftist guerrilla movement, or the extremist right wing group, Organización Democrática Nacionalista (ORDEN).

The Senate organized itself slowly. It was May before my confirmation hearing was scheduled. The chairman of the Foreign Relations Committee, Senator Chuck Percy, a BMOC when I was a lowly freshman at the University of Chicago, kindly sponsored me. Since there was so much daily press and TV coverage of El Salvador, the hearing room was jammed. Lots of questions; many senators putting their concerns about Central America into the record. However, I benefitted from the administration's political honeymoon and was spared from most hostile questioning. There were some attempts to place me, an avowed independent, on the political spectrum. Senator Jesse Helms expressed concern over my membership in the Council of Foreign Relations. I explained the Council's nonpartisan function of studying international issues, concluding with an offer to nominate the senator for membership. He ignored this. If my memory serves me, the committee unanimously reported out my nomination.

At the end of May, I flew to El Salvador to be met by Ken Bleakley, my DCM, who had arrived well before me, the Salvadoran protocol chief, and senior embassy staff.

Ken and I drove to my new residence, which featured a large terrace and a swimming pool. It was distinguished by then being the only residence in the Foreign Service guarded by marines. More security was provided by State Department civilian security officers augmented with Delta Force military living a few doors away. The residence was comfortable, but I found its bare walls in need of color. So I visited Galeria 1-2-3, managed by an attractive young lady, Ana Christiana. She helped me start and later build a collection of Salvadoran art. My first acquisition: a striking oil by Roberto Huezo of a church.

Visiting the embassy Chancery, my impression was of a fortress. Marines with M-16 rifles were on the roof behind sandbags. Why? I asked. Answer: to counter drive-by attacks by rebels firing rocket propelled grenades (RPGs). The marines were a great deterrent, but did not entirely end such attacks.

Before I could conduct official business, I needed to present my credentials to President José Napoleón Duarte of the Revolutionary Junta. Ken Bleakley had done well, scheduling me to meet with the Junta on Monday, June 1, only a weekend after my arrival.

That weekend schedule called for a visit to the Salvadoran Air Force base at Ilopango, followed by a helicopter trip to Sonsonate, where we were training a new rapid reaction battalion. At Ilopango, an American colonel inadvertently fired his .45. As a round ricocheted off the cement floor, I wondered about the competence of our trainers.

On our helicopter flight, I nervously watched thunderheads piling up ahead. They reminded me of my near death day in Zaire. As I was about to ask the pilot to turn back, he did just that, with unneeded apologies for taking us to an alternate site.

We landed where the first U.S.-trained rapid reaction battalion, the Atlactle, was garrisoned. We found Colonel Domingo Monterrosa, the reaction force commander, bunking with his men, unusual for Salvadoran officers. He was a soldier's soldier, having risen from a *campesino* background. He impressed me. To this day, I find his role in the tragic December 1981 massacre at El Mozote both puzzling and far out of character, but recognize that the evidence of his battalion's guilt is damning.

Earlier, DCM Bleakley had called from the airport to ask what should be done about an American general, who having neither sought nor received country clearance had simply arrived on a flight from SOUTHCOM. We agreed that he should be told to return directly to Panama.

The grapevine let me know that the commander in chief's (CINC) cabled protest to the Pentagon provoked an outraged reaction to Hinton's decision until Deputy Secretary Frank Carlucci calmed people, by explaining why diplomatic country clearances make sense.

President Duarte, after accepting my credentials, suggested that I forgo reading my prepared remarks. Despite the uncomfortable straight-back chairs on which he, Junta members, the foreign minister, and I were seated, his suggestion made for a more relaxed, if largely non-substantive, discussion.

"Napo" Duarte, a passionate Christian Democrat and an engineering graduate from the University of Notre Dame, had been elected president in 1972. Tragically, for him and for the county, before he could take office, the military, spurred on by long dominant "oligarchical" families, intervened. He was imprisoned and tortured. An international outcry saved his life and Duarte went into exile in Venezuela.

In March 1980, with encouragement from Colonels Gutierrez and Majano, Duarte returned and joined the Junta. On December 22, after the expulsion of Majano from the Junta, Duarte became its president. He and I had our disagreements, but we fought together to make the 1982 elections a success.

That afternoon (June 1, 1981) at the urging of Howie Lane, my fine public affairs officer, I met with a large press contingent. To no one's surprise, the first question, from a CBS reporter, was about the investigation into the murder of the American nuns. The second was about human rights abuses by members of the Salvadoran security forces. These questions quite rightly raised issues that would be central for me as long as I was in El Salvador. And longer.

Chris Dickey of the *Washington Post* asked if we were also investigating a possible cover-up of high-ranking officials in the nuns case. After my reply, Chris asked two follow-up questions, citing both Watergate and cover-up allegations of my predecessor. I replied that there was evidence in the Watergate case and invited Ambassador White or anyone else with evidence "to bring it forward." This was the first of many tough exchanges with Chris, a fine correspondent, whom I came to view as difficult, but a friend. Other journalists had many more questions, mostly antagonistic. It was a baptism of fire; it helped me in identifying issues and attitudes. European journalists seemed highly hostile and, I thought, badly informed. Latin Americans were mostly better disposed than my compatriots.

Radio Venceremos, the propaganda outlet of the Frente Farabundo Martí para la Liberación Nacional (FMLN), the next day broadcast Marxist lies alleging that Reagan "sends us not a diplomat but a C.I.A. agent with twenty-five years experience in plotting against freedom...threatening our people with napalm, bombs, and helicopters..." This scandalous attack helped convince me the tight security surrounding me was sensible.

As always in a new post, I had to devote much time to courtesy calls on ministers, other key Salvadorans, and ambassadorial colleagues. Visitors and visits also took time. Lt. General Gordon Sumner, a hardline Republican inserted into ARA to keep an eye on Tom Enders, the newly appointed assistant secretary for Latin America, was my first visitor, arriving only days after me. Despite my initial misgivings, we got along fine. Those days small arms fire was a frequent danger, so together we learned some rules for survival, e.g. wait twenty minutes after nearby firing stops before moving on. Also, respect the curfew. If caught out after curfew, overnight in place. This rule led to some great improvised parties.

At the end of June, I went to Panama accompanied by Colonel Waghelstein to meet General Wallace Nutting, the SOUTHCOM commander. The CINC said nothing about the country clearance issue, but he arranged a helicopter ride for us, which, I was told later, was meant to scare me. It did. Even Wag was nervous, he told me later, when the rotors got dangerously close to a river surface.

Shortly thereafter I approved a return visit by the CINC to El Salvador. To my surprise, he came with a dozen or so staff officers and lots of ideas about what I should be doing!

I had met Foreign Minister Fidel Chávez Mena in Washington before arriving in El Salvador. He proved to be a good friend. Short in stature and intense in manner, Fidel was, as was Duarte, a founding member of his country's Christian Democrat Party. A businessman and a confidant of the president, Fidel was easier to talk with than his boss. We frequently met at breakfast, Fidel taking notes and outlining his ideas on paper, as I wondered what he did with his scribbles? He had negotiated an agreement with Honduras to submit their disputes to the International Court of Justice in The Hague. It was a politically courageous and far sighted step. Fidel was an excellent sounding board for me. However, when I pressed my concerns over human rights, he admitted that while he shared my concerns he was powerless to stop military excesses.

As I settled into my new job, I was overwhelmed by requests for meetings. Two remain in my memory. One, perhaps a surprise to my interlocutors; another, a surprise to me.

A group of landowners and businessmen, among them Lopez Andreo, Enrique Alvarez, Hugo Barrerra, and Juan Maldonado, calling on me at my residence, found it hard to believe that Ronald Reagan would support the expropriation of large landholdings and the nationalization of banks. They were highly critical of Duarte and Jose Antonio Morales Ehrlich, whom they seemed to view as communists disguised as Christian Democrats. My efforts to explain the political rationale for our support of the Junta's reforms left most shaking their heads in disbelief. Ken Bleakley and I salvaged from this meeting agreement that Ken would explore with Chamber of Commerce members how government policies might be made more acceptable to the business world.

I had been in San Salvador for several weeks when late one day Minister of Defense Guillermo Garcia called asking for a meeting at my residence. I wondered what he wanted. Ministers do not normally return calls. When he arrived, to my surprise, Garcia was accompanied by Junta member Colonel Guttierez and Colonel Vides Casanova, commander of the National Guard, among others. After preliminaries, I was informed that the High Command wanted me to know there would be no more coups and they were grateful for American military assistance. I was astounded, something I tried not to show, but most grateful for their message, a reaction I hope I conveyed.

I'm still not clear in my own mind as to what led to this extraordinary meeting. Although coup rumors, traceable I believed to radical right wing groups, were afloat, we had not thought a coup was likely. Roberto D'Aubuisson, the number one likely coup plotter, was in Guatemala. The High Command's welcome message meant to me that they would support Duarte and stick with the reforms. They were reaffirming that the longtime alliance between the military and the so-called oligarchs was dead. I also interpreted their call as meaning that if D'Aubuisson or someone else still planned trouble, he would fail.

Ken, working with Juan Maldonado of the Chamber of Commerce staff, began a series of meeting with Chamber members. Washington welcomed this effort, correctly thinking that the split between the government and the business world was dangerous. To our disappointment, my parallel discussions with Duarte revealed a mind closed to seeking reconciliation with *los pendejos* with whom we had met.

Naturally, we maintained contact with this and other business groups, but with little success in building bridges to the Junta.

Some ministers were also seeking better relations with the business community. In those cases we made limited progress, as long as the president did not get his dander up. El Salvador needed aid. Occasionally we could tailor our assistance to improve situations of concern to the business community. Atilio Vieytez, both minister for economic development and a personal friend, was such a helpful broad-minded minister.

Every day brought appalling reports of bodies, often mutilated, found here and there. Some killings seemed to be attributable to the left, but far more looked like victims of right wing "death squads." The embassy kept count of such reports; sad statistics indeed. We also tried to note what army or police unit might be involved. In general, it was thought that while financing came from members of the oligarchy, rogue individuals or even rogue units were paid to carry out the terror campaign.

Complaints about Salvadoran human rights abuses from concerned individuals, largely from the United States but frequently from elsewhere in the world, filled my inbox. Not only did I read every letter, but I also required replies to be sent, which I signed. Until the public affairs office (PAO) obtained a computer, our secretaries were close to overwhelmed.

In meetings with the military and police, I constantly expressed concern, inevitably meeting with denials of involvement. Evidence of who was carrying out the killings was rarely available, but my staff and I kept after answers, just as we continued to press for action on the cases of the nuns and the murdered American labor leaders.

A young FSO, Carl Gettinger, had met with one of the suspect national guardsmen and while driving him about, incredibly recorded his confession. This led to five arrests, but bringing these murderers to trial proved to be unimaginably difficult, in part because Salvadoran criminal law, based on the Code Napoleon, made testimony from a confessed criminal unacceptable as evidence against the other defendants. I never did fully understand these legal points, but thought Duarte and his attorney general were trying hard to convict. Still frustration on my part and that of many others was paramount.

In my discussions with Duarte about the case, to my surprise, he accused my predecessor of withholding evidence from him. He also once said that had Ambassador White returned to San Salvador after our elections, he planned to declare him persona non grata.

Thanks to Gettinger, we had made important progress in pursuing the case of the murdered nuns. However, the investigation of the murder of the labor leaders was bogged down. This led Bill Doherty, head of the American Institute for Free Labor Development (AIFELD), to assign a fulltime investigator, Gordon Ellison. Eventually he, too, worked wonders.

As important as these issues were, I wanted to better understand the overall situation, particularly the economic and military outlook. After analysis, I planned to cable my recommendations and then to return to Washington to try to push them through the bureaucracy.

Politically, we had put our eggs in the election basket. Clearly my staff and I had to help make the elections work. That task was clear.

The economy was in a tailspin. Peter Askin, the AID director, was running a $63 million program. Not enough, I was certain. But how much assistance would be needed? Washington had a team at work, but I feared its ideas might be too modest. So Bill Wood, an economic officer, and I made our own analysis of the balance of payments situation. Bill has probably never forgiven me for how hard I pushed him. We did a projection, concluding that several hundred million more in economic assistance was required.

As for the military situation, after talks with my officers and key Salvadorans, it was clear to me that we faced a long struggle. I concluded that we needed a basic look at what it might take to win. This to replace the series of ad hoc responses we had so far made to enhance defense assistance.

I cabled my conclusions and recommendations to Washington. I urged a substantially larger economic support program and a study of requirements for military assistance. I proposed that the study be led by a Spanish-speaking general officer from the Pentagon. Aware of the administration's insistence on holding down expenditures, I suggested part of the increased assistance be in the form of loan guarantees. I copied my message to SOUTHCOM. General Nutting was somewhat supportive, except that he argued the study of requirements should be led by his staff.

The evening before leaving for Washington, going back to my residence, eleven bombs exploded along our route, starting lots of fires. My convoy accelerated. I was far more frightened by driving fast in crowded streets than by the small bombs.

When I got to Washington, my proposals for increases in economic assistance were laughed at by old friends. No way, I was assured, was the administration, committed as it was to restraining expenditures, going to approve large increases in aid for El Salvador.

On the other hand, my new Pentagon acquaintances welcomed my idea for a serious study of military requirements.

I also pushed for the resources I knew were needed at the Inter-American Development Bank (IDB), the International Bank for Reconstruction and Development (IBRD), better known as the World Bank, and the International Monetary Fund (IMF).

At the IMF, analysts were even more pessimistic than I. They feared yearly capital flight from El Salvador was running at over $250 million and estimated the deficit on current account at $240 million, up from $90 million in 1980. There was a possibility, I learned, which eventually materialized, for compensatory finance, since coffee harvests were sharply down. I was also told that a standby loam might be possible, but they ruled out extended finance structural lending.

At the IDB, I learned from President Antonio Ortiz Mena that the bank was looking for additional ways to help.

At the IBRD, Ernie Stern, an old friend, told me disbursements on approved loans had been stopped because required site inspections had been judged to be too dangerous. That problem was soon fixed by the Salvadorans providing inspectors extra security.

In Washington, I arranged for Wellington, the family Old English sheepdog, to join me in San Salvador. He added much to my bachelor life. Introducing Wellington to Napoleón Duarte was a particular pleasure. Wellington seemed to like his tropical life, except that the loud green parrots, flying every morning and evening over our house, drove him into a frenzy. Wellington generally got on well with my guests, but he nipped an aide to Senator Chris Dodd. Once Wellington lifted his leg on a chair occupied by a guest. I had to apologize for Wellington, but told myself that he knew his politicians.

That August 30 Dr. Judy Cisneros was gunned down. A remarkable woman who had become a friend, she had helped form the largest *campesino* union in the country. For this she had been threatened many times by the right. But the left killed her. Why? Probably because as head of Salvador's Demographic Association she was working on projects the United States was supporting. It mattered not that the association's birth control efforts were linked to needed maternal and child welfare programs. I had found Dr. Cisneros to be amazingly balanced in her judgments, insightful, and dedicated. I hate funerals, but I went to Judy's, despite the objections of my security types.

Since I wanted to meet people and see the country for myself, I scheduled as many helicopter flights as possible. The Salvador Air Force was cooperative, but having to rely on them to get around the country was limiting.

My visits had a serious purpose. I wanted to know and judge the brigade commanders. On every trip I would talk with commanders, some other officers, and leading civilians. Always I tried to discourage abuses of human rights, arguing the need to "win the hearts and minds" of the population. Officers listened but I doubt that I made much impression. To my regret, Salvadoran mentality made it exceptionally difficult for me or other Americans to talk with ordinary soldiers.

On an early trip, after flying over Morazán we had landed at San Miguel, capital of the department of the same name. A senior colonel was in command there. He did not impress me. He waddled out to meet us wearing a dirty t-shirt. His troops had a reputation for brutality, but for little else. I soon concluded that few departments were commanded by competent officers. It was discouraging, but there was almost nothing we Americans could do about it. The *tanda* system was virtually sacred to the officer corps. Every officer of a *tanda*, formed by graduation from the military academy, protected every other officer of his group, however incompetent. My efforts to induce Minister of Defense General Garcia to change incompetents were unavailing.

In September, I accompanied Duarte to Washington. He made the congressional rounds and talk shows trying to explain the overall Salvadoran situation. He was well received but often provoked a skeptical reaction. Few understood his explanation of the legal complications that hindered prosecuting the killers of the nuns.

At the time, administration opponents were pushing proposals to make most assistance dependent on certification that El Salvador was making progress in respecting human rights. Duarte wanted improved respect for human rights, but sought to prevent this legislation. He failed. So did the administration. Thereafter, every six months, certification became an acute political issue.

Certification, to a small degree, provided us leverage. Essentially, however, it was far more useful to American politicians, facing voters, than to the embassy. I tried to use it, but recognized that it was much too blunt an instrument to induce real improvements in human rights. How could I convince Defense Minister General Garcia, among others, that President Reagan would cut off assistance to El Salvador? He just did not believe it.

Domestically, the American public was outraged by constant

press and TV portrayal of uncontrolled violence in El Salvador. The reasons for administration policy were not widely understood. The American public was appalled by the situation. Ronald Reagan, the great communicator, with some success explained to the country what was at stake. There was, however, no way to make the policy popular.

In the absence of broad public support for Reagan's policy, certification allowed congressmen on both sides of the aisle to hedge. Democrats sought to embarrass the administration while avoiding charges of opposing aid to a regime fighting a communist takeover. Many Republicans also found in certification electoral protection with their constituents.

As Junta president, Duarte had a brief, cordial meeting with President Reagan, leading to a more substantive meeting with Vice President Bush, as well as meetings with key Cabinet officers. All welcomed his commitment to hold elections on March 28, 1982. He also spoke at the United Nations in New York.

After New York, we returned to Washington for a meeting with the families of the nuns, arranged by Archbishop Hickey. Mary Rose Oakar (D of Ohio) had urged this and Duarte had agreed. He, as I, badly wanted justice done. William Ford, the family spokesman, found Duarte's description of the situation unacceptable. When I tried to amplify Napo's explanations, Ford exploded. He said he was offended to hear his ambassador defending the Salvadoran military. I replied I resented his distorting my remarks. Archbishop Hickey calmed us. Napo and I assured the family that we would continue to do our best to bring the killers to justice.

While in Washington, I had stayed a few days with Hazel. Upon my return I wrote to thank her. I noted, "We have a strange relation—real affection, passion, and a lack of commitment."

Since Hazel would not visit me, I wondered if Kay Stocker, an FSO whom I had known for years, might do so. To find out, I wrote her. I told her about my initial impressions. El Salvador is "fascinating, complicated, dangerous in a way, delightful in another." Here, I'm a "personality." "Let's hope I play my role with humility and judgment." In jest, I added, "If I can restore peace, save the economy, and establish a lasting democratic government, I will have earned my pay."

I also told her of being smothered by security. For example, I wrote of going to play tennis with Atilio Vieytez. With guards I would arrive in a three-car convoy. With his guards Atilio arrives in another convoy. We play where there are still more guards. It did not frighten Kay; she had served in Vietnam. She agreed to come for Christmas.

I was informed by Washington that, were the Salvadorans to agree, we would send a military assessment team to be headed Brigadier General Fred Woerner. Terrific news. Not only had my recommendation been accepted, but I also knew Fred. We had worked together in Guatemala in the late 1960s.

One of our political objectives was to enhance the standing of Duarte vis-à-vis the military. To this end, rather than going first to the minister of defense, I invited the president to lunch and told him of our thinking about a study of requirements. I hoped he would persuade Minister of Defense Garcia to cooperate. He willingly did so. While Garcia may have been puzzled by Duarte's role, he knew a study could produce more U.S. assistance for the armed forces. He promised Duarte cooperation, later reiterated this to me, and provided it to Woerner and his team.

Neither Duarte nor I had any illusions about where power resided in El Salvador. Minister of Defense Garcia was far more powerful than anyone else. Duarte had figured this out long before my arrival. He had concluded that only with military support could he hope to improve things. Not all members of his Christian Democratic Party agreed, but enough did. Nor did all the military agree with Garcia and the High Command supporting Duarte.

Fred and I both wanted his report to examine more than the Marxist threat, but he only got veiled references into the final report about other extremist threats. Specific language warning about the political danger posed by "death squads" was unacceptable to Garcia and his staff.

General Nutting had long been pressing to have his "psychological" experts included in our limited number of trainers. Finally, I agreed to a briefing by his team. When they arrived from Panama, Fred sat in. He commented later that it was the worst briefing he had ever attended. Why the general thought officers who did not even speak Spanish could effectively engage in "psychological warfare" escaped me.

The Woerner report called for eight additional infantry battalions, two additional rapid reaction battalions, the provision of equipment appropriate for the expanded force, some patrol boats for the Navy, and more helicopters and fixed wing aircraft for the Air Force. Fred thought two of his recommendations were critical:

First, a change from a defensive posture, augmented with large unit sweeps, to an offensive strategy based on vigorous patrolling.

Second, out-of-country training of officers for the larger force.

In the American army, officers are often promoted from the ranks, as I had been in 1945, but there was no tradition of Salvadoran enlisted men becoming officers.

Instead General Garcia asked me to arrange to send the cadets at Salvador's military academy to our Infantry School at Fort Benning, Georgia. I cabled his request to Washington and to SOUTHCOM. General Nutting proposed that the cadets be trained in Panama. He argued that training in Panama would be more cost effective. I agreed, but was unable to sell Garcia on Panama.

To resolve matters, I proposed that General Nutting come to San Salvador to discuss the issue face to face with General Garcia and President Duarte. He, a few of his staff, Colonel Waghelstein, and I met with Duarte, Garcia, and other members of the High Command in the Presidential Palace. Nutting made the case for Panama. Garcia said he understood our desire to hold costs down. Then he spoke of the country's young cadets and of how hard it was to send them into battle. Were they not to train in El Salvador, it was vital that they go where the United States trains its infantry officers. Duarte also insisted that national pride required that their cadets be trained at Fort Benning.

In private after the meeting, I told General Nutting I thought political and psychological factors outweighed cost considerations. Therefore, in my judgment, the training should be at Benning. He said he would think more about it. However, back at SOUTHCOM he again recommended Panama. The General's strong point was not political acumen.

The cadets trained at Fort Benning.

Indignation over the murder of the nuns, particularly by Catholics; agitation by leftist groups, such as the Committee in Solidarity with the People of El Salvador (C.I.S.P.E.S.); echoes of our debacle in Vietnam; and a generally critical press all discouraged FSOs, apart from unmarried junior officers, from bidding for positions in El Salvador. I had a bevy of gung ho juniors on the staff, but personnel could not find me a badly needed political counselor. As elections loomed, I scoured personnel's list of qualified, but reluctant, officers, finally talking Robert Driscoll into taking this critical job. His Colombian wife, Margarita, gallantly agreed to his assignment. None of us regretted the outcome.

Dr. Jorge Bustamante, appointed by the Junta to head the Electoral Commission, repeatedly resigned over slights or issues. Each time Robert Driscoll convinced him to carry on. They made a formidable team. Robert's savvy and energy also helped enormously in the post-election crisis.

In a letter of October 24, 1981, I wrote:

> Phone call from Washington. Eventually I organize my security forces and head into the night for an emergency meeting. Then report. Six calls all told to Washington. Then to bed. At 5:40 a.m. the bombs start going off. Four big ones, ugh. fortunately at that time of day not many people are around so there were few casualties. Now the Salvadorans, like Londoners during the blitz are used to it. They also are mighty resistant. They just clean up the mess and rebuild.

Hugo Barrera, a prominent rightist businessman, and his wife, fairly frequently invited me to their home. I knew, of course, that it was my position, not my personality, that earned me such invitations. One night Hugo took me apart for what he called a serious conversation. Robert d'Aubuisson, he told me, was thinking of returning from exile in Guatemala to run in the upcoming elections. Would the United States allow it? Given d'Aubuisson's reputation as both an inveterate coup plotter and possible instigator of the assassination of Archbishop Romero, Hugo's question gave me pause. However, we and the Junta were encouraging the left to lay down their arms and participate in the upcoming election. If members of the FMLN would be welcome as political participants, why not rightists? Assuming the government did not press criminal charges and that d'Aubuisson limited his activities to political campaigning, I thought we would not object to his participation in the elections. We left it at that. I think d'Aubuisson would have returned whatever I thought or said, but who knows?

A few weeks later, d'Aubuisson did return. Before an enthusiastic crowd, he announced formation of ARENA, a new political party. It was backed by Hugo Barrera and many other rightist businessmen. Duarte accepted the situation, but privately told me the same "oligarchs" who were financing "death squads" were behind Arena and d'Aubuisson.

To ease the pressures of my hectic life, I relaxed at meetings of the "Statistical Probability Study Group." Its members included

DCM Ken Bleakley, Jim Blystone of my security team, Colonel John Waghelstein, Gale Rozell and Tom Stukel of AID, and Al Schaufelberger, a navy Seal.

Some family members were far from supportive. Deborah in London contributed in my name to a Trotskyist organization protesting human rights abuses and the American role in El Salvador. Not surprisingly, except to her, the Marxists promptly leaked news of "my contribution." She apologized. Joe wrote: "You stink of the C.I.A....Why not resign and speak the truth?" Otherwise, it was good to have a long letter from him.

We needed good intelligence on the FMLN, but had no sources inside its leadership. This was one sad result of the Carter-Turner impact on the C.I.A. Obviously efforts were needed to correct this, but as far as I know we never succeeded.

I also advocated agent penetration of the death squads and interception of the communications of rightists in Miami thought to be financing death squads. Station Chief Pat Scheid seemed to agree, but if he were pushing, it was not evident to me. He was neither an activist like Miles Copeland in Damascus nor quietly trustworthy like Stu Methven in Kinshasa. Of the many station chiefs with whom I have worked, he was the least impressive.

In an early conversation with Director Bill Casey, I observed that since the Marxist Sandinistas were sending arms to the FMLN in El Salvador, I hoped the C.I.A. would complicate their efforts by engaging in operations in Nicaragua. As usual, Bill listened but said nothing about his thinking. As far as I know, it was only after I left San Salvador that the agency seriously tried to disrupt Marxist operations on the Pacific coast of Nicaragua.

In the meantime, the Contra effort from Honduras—something I had not envisaged—had become a major political issue in Washington. I had nothing to do with the contras, but recognized a clear need for leverage on the Sandinistas.

To his credit, Pat Scheid succeeded in recruiting a death squad member. We now had a source who could not only help us understand their activities but also warn us of planned actions. To my dismay, however, Pat received instructions from Washington to ship the new source home. I protested vehemently, cabling Casey asking for his intervention. The reply, sympathetic to my view of the value of a source that might save American lives, was that agency lawyers insisted we could not keep a known murderer in our pay!

On another occasion, Pat told me about a captured Nicaraguan arms smuggler who had confessed and was providing valuable information. Pat's report triggered instructions for him to send the prisoner to Washington. It was contemplated that he would tell his story to the press. Since I feared the prisoner's confession might have come from torture, I objected. My objection produced a categorical instruction to stop arguing.

That was that. Off the prisoner went. Questioned in private, he stuck to his confession. Before the press he told a different story. His account of Salvadoran torture was a public relations disaster, providing a field day for critics of the administration.

When I took Senator Tom Harkin (D-Iowa), who had won plaudits exposing torture in Vietnam, to call on Duarte, he tried for a repeat performance. He asked if we could visit, without warning, National Police Headquarters. Duarte said, "Let's go." Duarte, Harkin, an aide to Harkin, and I went directly. Once there Duarte showed us where in 1972 he had been tortured by the police. Harkin's aide kept exploring the building while consulting a small hand-drawn map. Eventually he found a locked room. Were there, as he alleged, torture chambers behind the door? Napo ordered it opened. Nothing! I was embarrassed. The senator and his aide should have been.

While I had vowed never to marry again, many Salvadoran ladies assured me I would before I left. Aida Rivera, who worked in the embassy, insisted I come to dinner to meet the ideal lady to share my future. I went. My hostess was wrong. However, a vivacious younger woman, Patricia Lopez, caught my eye. I was captivated by her uninhibited spontaneity. On the spot, I asked her to my Halloween Party. She accepted. Sixteen months later we married.

At Christmas, good as her word, Kay Stocker met me on San Andres, a Caribbean island with comfortable beach hotels. After a few days of fun in the sun, she accompanied me back to El Salvador where, holding my breath, I introduced her to Patricia. Kay must have been troubled by my obvious affection for another much younger woman. Certainly I was bothered by my own behavior. However, Kay, apart from warning me that Patricia would probably break my heart, behaved like the trooper she is. We remain friends to this day.

Ray Bonner's report of the El Mozote massacre was front paged by the *Times* on January 27, 1982. That is just a day before President Reagan was to send Congress "certification" that El Salvador was making "a concerted and significant effort to comply with internationally recognized human rights." Coincidence? I do not think so.

Bonner had gone to El Mozote at the invitation of the guerrillas. They escorted him from Honduras on a walk of several days to El Mozote.

I had been skeptical of early massacre reports, but Bonner's story and a similar *Washington Post* account led me and other embassy officers to dig harder for the truth. Two officers tried to reach El Mozote, got close, but with the town once more in guerrilla hands, could not go all the way.

That known representatives of the FMLN offered to escort embassy officers to El Mozote and my belief that General Garcia's denials amounted to stonewalling led me to conclude that something "had happened that should not have happened." Why then did I not accept the escort offer? Simply because overall policy precluded any action that might appear to bestow recognition on the FMLN.

By early 1982, vigorous electoral campaigning was underway. The slogan "Ballots Not Bullets" was catching on. Six parties, registered with the Electoral Commission, would be on the ballot: Partido Alianza Republica Nacionalista (ARENA), Partido Orientación Popular (POP), Partido Democrata Cristiano (PDC), Partido Acción Democrática (AD), Partido de Conciliación Nacional (PCN), and Partido Popular Salvadoreño. Ballots would also show each party's symbol, needed to help illiterates distinguish the party they supported.

The Marxists, however, not only rejected proposals that they participate in elections, the FMLN threatened to disrupt them. Already they had launched an offensive against the country's infrastructure. Coffee and cotton mills, warehouses, bridges, and the electric system were attacked. High-tension lines, carried across the country on towers, were particularly vulnerable. Long power outages became a fact of life in San Salvador. Eventually, our AID program financed helicopters that carried crews to repair transmission towers about as fast as they were blown up.

To my surprise, on my birthday, in addition to a good time with Patricia, her best friend Lilli Molina, and Lilli's delightful if good-for-nothing husband, Jose Roberto, I was presented by the S.P.C.A. (not the Society for the Prevention of Cruelty to Animals but the Salvadoran Press Corps Association) with a large iced cake. It had a map of El Salvador made with frosting and showed an American aircraft carrier off the coast, lots of tanks, and many parachutists, identified as the 82nd Airborne. If journalists seriously thought we were going to intervene, I intended to disappoint them.

With elections a week off, the FMLN struck. I was awakened

early by a phone call from a highly agitated General Garcia. Guerrillas had attacked the Ilopango Airfield during the night, destroying on the ground over half of the Salvadoran Air Force. Garcia asked us to replace the losses. I promised we would try. In the event, we did more. Within days not only were more helicopters delivered in USAF cargo planes, but we also began to supply ground support fixed wing aircraft.

It was a convincing American response to a disaster that, I thought, should never have occurred.

Colonel Bustillo, the Air Force commander, had been repeatedly warned that Ilopango was vulnerable to such an attack. American officers had proposed measures to correct its security gaps. Bustillo had not acted. It seemed to me that he should be replaced, at least temporarily. I said so to Garcia. Nothing happened. Then, perhaps foolishly, I expressed my view at a larger meeting at the Defense Ministry, citing the relief of the responsible American commanders after Pearl Harbor. I met total resistance. No proconsul I. "Accountability" was not then an operational concept for Salvadoran officers.

For the elections, literally hundreds of TV, radio, and press journalists from all over the world descended on El Salvador. A sizable observer team, led by Senator Nancy Kassebaum (R-Kansas) and Father Theodore Hesburgh, president of the University of Notre Dame, fanned out over much of the country. They were impressed by the incredibly large turnout. So were we all. Journalists who before had focused on rightist "death squads" now reported enthusiastically of peasants defying leftist death threats to walk miles to vote.

The elections briefly looked like a game changer. Unfortunately, the positive effects did not last long.

I wrote my kids about "Absolutely incredible elections...Have you ever seen a friendly riot to move the police out of the way so that people can get to the polls to vote? And the police lost. Now the people who voted for peace and against violence, totally repudiating the extreme left, are puzzled that the politicians seem not to have gotten the message."

The day after the elections, I did eight TV interviews and received a congratulatory call from Secretary Al Haig. However, as tough as things had been before, I knew the real political crisis was upon us.

D'Aubuisson had done well. He began talking of assuming the presidency. Indeed, the right had a majority of elected deputies in the Constituent Assembly. Arena won nineteen of sixty seats. The PCN, the governing party with its military allies until the 1978 coup overthrew General Romero, won fourteen seats. Duarte's Christian Democrats with twenty-four of sixty seats had a plurality, but had no chance of governing. Three seats were won by minor parties. Should d'Aubuisson secure PCN support for his presidential bid, he would win. I knew he had to be stopped.

Publicly I stressed the need for national unity to confront the Marxists. Privately I worked to convince the security forces that d'Aubuisson would be the kiss of death for their hopes of continued American equipment, money, and support. I hoped Garcia and the High Command would see the danger d'Aubuisson presented to their interests. I also began a search for a potential president.

The ideal president, I concluded, should be a highly respected civilian acceptable to the army. This was a big order, but after talking broadly with political leaders, key military officers, and private citizens, I thought I had found such an individual. His name escapes my memory, but he lived on an island somewhere in the Mediterranean. On my recommendation, the State Department sent a senior officer to talk him into the job. To my regret, he declined to return to his war-torn country.

One by one, I invited to lunch many individuals suggested as possibilities. One was Álvaro Magaña, president of Banco Hipotecario, El Salvador's largest mortgage bank. I was intrigued to learn that he was a fellow alumnus of the University of Chicago. An economist, he had written about tax reform, had been an enthusiast for Kennedy's Alliance for Progress, and had worked at the Organization of American States. Somehow, however, I had not met him until he came to lunch.

My showing of *West Side Story* one night provided a welcome break from politics. Our guests, numbering over a hundred, were largely cultural types.

At a joint press conference with Lopez Nuila, director of the National Police, we showed items recovered after the attack on Ilopango. I observed that "Soviet MUV-2 type explosive detonators don't grow on coffee trees in El Salvador". Questions, however, focused on d'Aubuisson's intent to win the presidency. I declined to answer. Joanne Omang of the *Washington Post*, who a few days before at a residence lunch had challenged me to prove outside support for the guerrillas, dismissed the detonators. Rather she wrote: "For the United States it is almost as though the convoluted maneuvering of the Salvadorans trying to form a coherent government were a side-show."

Joanne's report outraged me. Even though I know it is difficult, if not impossible, to win battles with the press, I wrote her my
opinion of her reporting. I also expressed surprise that she did not
understand why I had refrained from public comment on the delicate political situation.

One afternoon, Tom Enders called me in high dudgeon. "How
could I have let it happen?" The news ticker in Tom's office was carrying a story from San Salvador that d'Aubuisson had been elected
president. "Relax, Tom, d'Aubuisson has won the booby prize! He
has been elected president of the Constituent Assembly."

When I paid my courtesy call on Assembly President
d'Aubuisson, I noted with dismay that his bodyguards were the
scruffiest, toughest-looking individuals I had ever seen. They
looked like killers and could, I thought, be death squad members.

I had again assured Tom that Roberto d'Aubuisson would not
be El Salvador's president, but we still needed a good man and
time was running out. Worried, I cabled asking that General Vernon Walters be sent to help me with Salvador's military. Al Haig
recalled him from Buenos Aires where he was meeting with the
Argentine military about what they called the Maldives War.

By the time the general arrived, Garcia had informed me privately that Magaña would be the next president. The decision had
been taken collectively by all the officers in San Salvador. From the
army standpoint, it had helped that Magaña's bank had frequently
lent money to officers in need. While he was not a rightist, he had
never publicly criticized rightist excesses.

Since the Assembly was to elect the president, news of the army's choice was passed privately to the leaders of the major political parties, including d'Aubuisson. Most deputies understood the
matter was settled. Still the Constituent Assembly had to meet and
vote.

As previously scheduled, General Walters and I met with the
High Command and a large group of Salvadoran officers. In flawless Spanish, Walters said all the right things. Only the election itself remained.

That evening I gave a dinner for Walters and twenty other
guests. In keeping with my theme of national unity, I invited not
only Garcia, Guttierez, and Vides Casanova of the High Command,
but also leaders of the six registered parties. D'Aubuisson, as president of the Assembly, was on my right, in the place of honor. I
doubted he would cause trouble, but I worried that John Carbaugh

of Senator Jesse Helms's staff might. Carbaugh certainly and probably the senator as well wanted d'Aubuisson to be president. To minimize the risks, I seated Carbaugh out of d'Aubuisson's view.

When the Assembly met, Álvaro Magaña was duly elected provisional president with PDC and PCN votes. Unity was fractured, however, since most Arena deputies voted for my friend Hugo Barrera. Assembly President d'Aubuisson abstained. Three vice presidents, one from each of the major parties, were elected. I might claim, with some justification, to have suggested this. However, since the scheme, meant to be symbolic of national unity, did not work well, I'll leave the credit for others.

On May 2, d'Aubuisson bestowed the presidential sash on Álvaro Magaña. Junta President Duarte's gracious remarks were more notable, I thought, than Magaña's modest, cautious reflections on the outlook. Napo was a politician. Alvaro, never before active politically, showed it, even as he said the right things. I delivered congratulatory messages from my president to both. Reagan's lengthy message to Napoleón Duarte in part said: "Mission Accomplished."

At the next regular meeting of the diplomatic corps it was proposed and unanimously agreed to invite President and Mrs. Magaña to a formal dinner. The corps split, however, when someone proposed that only the wives of ambassadors should attend. This was clearly meant to exclude my fiancée. The ambassador of Honduras, Roberto Suazo Tomé, spoke up, noting that when First Lady Concha Marina had entertained their wives at tea she had included Patricia. I observed that they had been friends for many years. I hoped the corps would invite her to the dinner. They did.

Later in May, Archbishop Rivera y Damas closed the "Legal Aid Office of the Diocese." The Office had collected data and grim photos of hundreds of atrocities. Its bias, however, was evident. It attributed not a single one to the guerrillas, not even those about which the FMLN boasted.

Another office of the archbishop continued to track atrocities. Its data, also horrifying, reflected Rivera y Damas' effort to publish the truth and avoid political propaganda. The archbishop in his weekly homilies condemned both sides for violent actions. He also spoke against our military assistance programs.

Even though the PCN had helped elect Magaña, it was still basically oriented to the right. Arena and PCN deputies began to whittle away at the Junta's agrarian reforms. The Assembly reaffirmed the Junta's reforms, but it also passed legislation removing a provision prohibiting renting of land on which cotton, sugar cane, rice, corn, and beans were planted, while declaring that rentals do not convey to the renter the right to ownership. This was meant to stimulate agricultural production, not to change the reform program. However, confusion followed. Some rightists illegally took back land that had once been theirs. The Foreign Relations Committee of our Senate voted to reduce assistance programs. Magaña, concerned by such misguided actions, sent me, by personal note, a decree "reaffirming that the reforms continue." He illustrated it by personally delivering land titles to over a hundred *campesinos*. Even d'Aubuisson interpreted the Assembly action as limited.

Wanting to lessen confusion, I asked that a personal message from me be passed to Chairman Long of the House Appropriations Committee. I wrote, "the situation in El Salvador may be misunderstood and some members of Congress may be over reacting". I then flew to Washington to try to explain what was happening.

It was an uphill fight. The agrarian reform program was complicated and hard to explain. Moreover, I had to acknowledge that the Assembly's action created a new element of uncertainty. On the *MacNeil-Lehrer NewsHour*, Senator Dodd and I had a sharp exchange. He insisted the program had been "suspended," which it had not been. Dodd was playing domestic politics. I met with Senator Helms, an outspoken opponent of land reform. I said I understood his opposition to the confiscation of large estates, but was surprised that he was opposed to giving land to small farmers. When I explained what was involved, he said he would support the so-called 207 program. And he did.

I also went to New York, meeting with the Editorial Board of the *New York Times*, I said the reform program was not dead and "it's not going to be killed." I argued that the proposed aid cuts would undercut stability and "play right into the hands of the extreme left."

In its story of the meeting, I was described as "a blunt-spoken professional diplomat" who had said of El Salvador, "It's a hell of a mess, too much indiscriminate killing, a sick society, an agonizing situation, but if the other guys take over it would be a hell of a lot worse."

My expressed view of Raymond Bonner, the *Times* correspondent in El Salvador, as "an advocate journalist" provoked the foreign editor to defend Bonner. I knew he would, but I thought it important to challenge Bonner's objectivity. The first one-on-one interview I gave in San Salvador had been with Bonner. He distorted my remarks. Later he charged falsely that Americans had observed Salvadoran torture training. He tried to undermine the election success with a series of stories about minor fraud. His reporting on agrarian reform had been slanted and, I thought, clearly inaccurate.

I did have brief second thoughts about this spat when the Committee to Protect Journalists expressed concern that my view "possibly endangered Mr. Bonner's security." To my regret, it probably did, but nowhere near as much as Bonner's stories had, which is a tribute to his courage, if not his judgment. We later exchanged handshakes when he came, along with 676 others, to my Fourth of July Reception.

Since our trainers were prohibited from carrying weapons, other than sidearms, an alarmist media report of an American officer carrying an M-16 in the countryside led me to investigate. Colonel Waghelstein confirmed the report, so I ordered the officer out of the country. Since I recognized that trainers in the field might be exposed to hostile action, I cabled Secretary Haig asking that the weapons prohibition be dropped. He agreed and tried to do so, but he was gone before that happened.

DCM Ken Bleakley had long advocated changing the status of San Salvador to permit family members. We finally persuaded the department that security, at least in San Salvador itself, had improved enough to end the unaccompanied rule. My security staff still had to approve trips outside the capital city, for example, to the coast or to a nearby lake.

In August 1982, I returned to the States, having been invited to an Aspen Institute seminar, happily accompanied by Patricia. It was an intellectually stimulating, restful two weeks. We had a wonderful time, even though I was weakened by a bad case of amoebic dysentery.

In Colorado, it was great to introduce Patricia to Joe and Kathy. They approved.

In Washington, so did Dad, when he recovered from the shock of learning we were not married.

I called on Secretary George Shultz. We knew each other since I had worked with him ten years before when he was secretary of the Treasury. When I entered the secretary's office, Under Secretary Larry Eagleburger, an old friend, told the secretary, "Deane is the only man since Hitler to lose Berlin." To this, I replied, "Yes, but I got it back." The secretary warmly greeted me.

The FMLN had captured Berlin, capital of Usulután, a public relations coup. The army, stung at having for the first time lost a departmental capital, soon retook it, but found part of the city in ruins. AID poured resources in. When I took Congressman Long on a visit, we noted a school built by AID named "Colegio Clarence D. Long." I hoped this ploy would improve chances for appropriations. Long beamed, so I knew that at least it had not hurt.

Later I wrote my kids, "George Shultz is so much quieter and placid than Al Haig. Incredible contrast. Lots of good questions, but little guidance."

Al had never publicly criticized the Salvadorans. George, to my delight, soon told the press, "If they don't clean up their act, support is going to dry up. They have been told that and they know that will happen."

Before leaving for Aspen, I told the department of my intention to marry. Since Service regulations required me to interview an employee wanting to marry a foreigner, I prepared a Memorandum of Conversation between Ambassador Hinton and Employee Hinton. I reported ambassadorial approval of the marriage. Endless security checks were also positive.

Back in San Salvador, I learned of welcome political progress.

On August, 3, after intense negotiations, President Magaña and key political leaders had signed the Pact of Apaneca. It purported to be the "basic platform" of the government. On paper, at least, it expressed agreement on goals, including democratization, respect for human rights, economic recovery, and "improving Agrarian, Bank, and Foreign Trade Reforms." To accomplish this, a Peace Commission, a Commission on Human Rights, and a Political Commission were created. The document called for the Assembly to complete a constitution as soon as possible and thereafter for municipal and presidential elections.

Where progress was not evident was in dealing with human rights abuses. It was nice to have a commission, but we needed action. The breaking point for me was the Lopez Sibrian case. The investigation carried out by Gordon Ellison, retained by the American Institute for Free Labor Development (AIFLD) of the AFL-CIO, into the murder in the Hotel Sheraton restaurant of two American land reform experts, Michael Hammer and Mark Pearlman, as well as Jose Rodolfo Viera, a labor leader and president of the Salvadoran Land Reform Institute, led to the arrest and confession of two former members of the National Guard. They in turn implicated two serving officers, Lt. Lopez Sibrian and Captain Eduardo Avila, who they said had at the hotel given them the submachine guns used in the killings. Lopez Sibrian was said to have told them whom to kill.

The Army protected its own. After much stalling, steady pressure from me, and obstructive resistance from Garcia, the minister finally decided that Lopez Sibrian could be tried by a civilian court, not by court-martial. The judge handling the case allowed Sibrian to blacken his red hair and shave off his mustache before appearing in a lineup. Even though separately identified by the killers, the judge ordered him released, alleging insufficient evidence for trial. No doubt the judge feared for his own life. Captain Avila did not even appear in court.

My frustration was shared by many in Washington. Leaders of the AFL-CIO were rightly outraged, as were my colleagues in State. Representative Solarz, Senator Dodd, and other democrats used the case to attack the Reagan administration.

For months I had respected Al Haig's injunction that we privately, not publicly, protest human rights violations. Now I concluded the time had come to speak out.

On October 29, in prepared remarks to a luncheon of the American Chamber of Commerce, I declared:

> Since 1979 perhaps as many as 30,000 Salvadorans have been MURDERED, not killed in battle, MURDERED.... [My] message is simple. El Salvador must make substantial progress in bringing the murderers of our citizens, including those who ordered the murders to justice, in advancing human rights; and in controlling the abuses of some elements of the security forces. If not, the United States, in spite of our other interests, in spite of our commitment to the struggle against communism, could be forced to deny assistance to El Salvador.

As I had expected, the reaction from the Salvadoran media was one of outrage over my remarks. What I had not expected was a *New York Times* report that President Reagan disapproved. The State Department noted that my text had been cleared in advance. Salvadoran praise for my remarks was limited, often expressed only privately, as in a letter I received from Ignacio Ellacuria, the Jesuit rector of the University of San Carlos. Press reports alleged I had been told to shut up, but I received no such instruction. However, the uproar led me to be careful for a while. Roughly a year later, I learned that Vice President George W. Bush speaking in San Salvador made many of the same points. Vindication, I thought.

For Thanksgiving, Patricia and I relaxed in Belize. The break is memorable for two reasons. First, I decided never again to snorkel, having brushed against fire coral only to have our boatman ward off infection by dumping gasoline on the wound. Second, and far happier, Patricia and I, after a long discussion of our age difference and her mother's view of our relationship, set Valentine's Day 1983 as our marriage date.

Back in San Salvador, we celebrated Patricia's son Sebastian's fifth birthday at the residence. Christmas was the best in years, as a number of my children came down from the States.

The FMLN celebrated the new year by blowing up the only bridge across the Lempa River. Their spectacular success temporarily cut north-south communications. Since the strategic importance of this bridge had not been lost on us, our trainers had laid out fields of fire to protect it from attack. Unfortunately, the troops we had trained to defend these positions went to town to celebrate the new year while the FMLN demolition teams floated quietly down the river and carried out their mission unopposed.

El Salvador was such a short flight from Washington that every weekend brought congressional visitors on Air Force special flights. So many came that Elliot Abrams, assistant secretary for human rights, suggested we give a prize to a members who did not visit.

Regrettably, few came to learn; rather they came to reinforce their record, telling their constituents that they knew what was right, since they had been there. Despite the pressure of other work, all in the embassy tried hard to take good care of all our visitors. I met many upon arrival. Mike Senko, a junior officer, won many kudos with good humored visitor pampering. Generally, key country team members and I briefed the Codels shortly after their arrival. Most Sunday evenings I invited them to the residence for a drink and to listen to their reactions.

Three visitors made a particular impression. Joan Didion, whose marvelous books I had not then read, with her husband lunched with us, earning me a place in her report on "Salvador." Ambassador John Negroponte came from Honduras. After we exchanged impressions of our respective problems, he surprised me by announcing that he wanted to succeed me in El Salvador. Highly ambitious, he wanted to stay where the action was. Ambassador Gavin, from Mexico, a onetime movie star who impressed Patricia, came, he said, to understand what was going on. Later I learned his real mission had been to check me out.

My immediate boss, Tom Enders, once called to ask me to take particularly good care of Wyche Fowler, a Georgia Democrat he described as a swing vote and "a real comer." Accordingly, I asked the president to lunch with us. It was a disaster. Magaña was unusually late, no problem, but he arrived dead drunk. After a bad half an hour, I convinced an aide to take him home. When on the phone I told Tom, he calmly remarked that with Álvaro's problems, it was understandable.

One Sunday, a dirty, disheveled Marine officer broke into a debrief session telling me, "Ambassador, you must do something." He loudly explained he had just returned from the fighting at Suchitoto, "where Salvadoran soldiers are dying needlessly because there are no medics. Fix it!"

Oliver North was right. His observation was news to me, since our trainers were forbidden to be in combat zones. This Marine Corps major simply presumed that as a member of the White House NSC staff he could do as he pleased. Thanks to him, we began training medics. Soon senior U.S. medical officers were providing valuable counsel to Salvadoran commanders. I asked for a waiver for fulltime medical trainers from the fifty-five-man ceiling on trainers and got it.

Later Ollie asked me what he could do for me. I told him of my frustrated desire for a secure phone at home. Three days later I learned the department had taken one for me away from an indignant Ambassador Tom Pickering in Lagos, Nigeria. Tom would have felt better about his loss had he known then that he would rejoin his phone when assigned to replace me in San Salvador.

Always wanting to see for myself, bit by bit I visited every department. For a crazy reason, I decided to return to Cuscutlatan. I was determined to check on the fighting near Suchitoto, Cuscutlatan. Persuading the Salvadoran Air Force to take me there was not easy. Eventually a helicopter was assigned. However, as we landed, a nervous commander wanted me gone almost before I was on the ground. He alleged the enemy was less than a thousand meters away. Maybe they were, maybe they weren't, but I thought it was no time to argue. We left with the chopper blowing up an enormous dust cloud. Still I had touched the ground at embattled Suchitoto, whereas in Morazán, where the FMLN was even stronger, on my initial visit I was only able to overfly Perquín and San Francisco Gotera.

Colonel Waghelstein pushed hard for small unit aggressive patrols. Still, most senior officers were content to launch large sweeps. FMLN guerrillas generally avoided much contact with such sweeps. As a result, progress in the war was hard to discern. Yet, I thought General Nutting went too far when he told the *Miami Tribune* in September that he was "pessimistic" about the war's outcome.

As we and Washington reviewed the situation, Enders and I agreed a prioritized "national strategy" was needed. Energized by Tom, the plan emerged under the guidance of Craig Johnson, office director for Central American affairs. One night Craig, key staff, and I were at the residence talking things over when we were rudely shaken by a quake so strong it created high waves in my swimming pool.

It was decided to start our stepped up security and development efforts in the Department of San Vicente, through which arms, landed on the Pacific coast, were being smuggled to more active combat zones, in the Departments of Chalatenango, Sonsonate, Cabañas, and San Salvador itself. Incredibly close to the capitol, the FMLN operated from the Guazapa volcano. We hoped an increased security presence and particularly more visible development efforts would improve intelligence about the FMLN. Regrettably, it fell short.

Critics attacked the concept as resembling failed efforts in Vietnam. When I departed El Salvador it was still not right to consider the "National Strategy" a failure. However, it certainly had not succeeded.

In December, President Magaña travelled to Costa Rica to meet with President Reagan. Of this meeting, I remember two things.

With invaluable help from an officer and his computer in our embassy in San Jose, we cobbled together a last minute benign communiqué, after having previously been assured by the Salvadorans that they did not want one.

As we assembled in the meeting room, I told Secretary Shultz that our observers in San Vicente confirmed a massacre of civilians by a Salvadoran unit. He asked me to inform the president. Reagan listened; National Secrity Advisor William Clark intervened to say the president would, of course, raise our concerns about violations of human rights, but not specific cases. I thought the president missed a chance to make an impact on our Salvadoran allies. Magaña assured Reagan that he shared the president's concern.

Bit by bit, all things considered, I became disillusioned about Garcia. Mainly, but not entirely, it was because of his unwillingness to lean hard against human rights abuses and abusers. Finally, I proposed to Washington that we seek his removal. By return cable I was asked: who would replace him and was I certain he would be better? I believed the new man would be General Vides Casanova of the National Guard. Given the Guard's poor reputation, I had to admit that I could not be sure Vides would be a real improvement. Garcia stayed as minister of defense.

In Sensuntepeque, Cabanas, I met Colonel Sigifredo Ochoa. He impressed me. Trained in part by the Israelis, he had successfully emphasized small unit patrolling. Popular with my Milgroup officers, Ochoa also seemed to have good relations with civilians. Great, except that I knew of his reputation as a coup plotter with ties to the extreme right. Yet surprisingly, Ochoa was instrumental in ousting General Garcia.

Garcia became alarmed at Ochoa's popularity and decided in January to transfer him to Uruguay as military attaché. Such assignments are a traditional way of dealing with problem officers. In this case, however, Ochoa rebelled, saying he was not going anywhere. Defying a legitimate order of the minister of defense was unprecedented. While many officers sided with Ochoa, many more did not. A split in the army during wartime concerned us, but there seemed to be nothing we could do. Then reports reached us that at d'Aubuisson's instigation, Colonel Bustillo, the Air Force commander, was planning a coup.

My officers and I used every contact we had to head it off. Colonel Waghelstein told Bustillo that if he went ahead he would lose vital American support for his Air Force. I warned d'Aubuisson, "No coups."

The crisis appeared to be resolved when negotiations within the Salvadoran armed forces led to a pledge from Garcia to resign soon and the departure of Colonel Ochoa for Washington, rather than Montevideo. Then, in April, Garcia reneged and Colonel Bustillo sent the Air Force flying over the Defense Ministry. Belatedly, the president intervened, replacing Garcia with Vides Casanova, who turned out to be a substantial improvement.

On the eve of our wedding, I had a V.I.P. visitor, Jeane Kirkpatrick. As ambassador to the U.N., she held cabinet rank, and was well known for her scholarly foreign policy studies. Her vehement opposition to communism and belief that "traditional authoritarian governments are less repressive than revolutionary autocracies" appealed to many Salvadorans. Her program included hospitality at my residence, the usual round of meetings, a dinner given by the president, and a Foreign Ministry reception, where she was decorated.

I enjoyed talking with Jeane until she attacked Tom Enders. She accused him of a willingness to sell out to the communist government of Nicaragua. To advance her argument, she produced a recent memorandum of Tom's proposing stepped up pressure on the Sandinistas, but also new negotiations with Managua. I agreed it was somewhat ambiguously drafted, but assured her that Tom was the last person in the world who would sell out to the Sandinistas. Talking with our enemies and selling out to them were, to my mind, entirely different matters. Not so for Ambassador Kirkpatrick.

I now know that on February 17, 1983, President Reagan wrote in his diary:

> Our Ambas. Hinton under the direction of the same kind of St. Dept bureaucracy who made Castro possible are screwing up the situation in El Salvador. I'm now really mad.... heads will roll, beginning with Ambas. Hinton.

What provoked this? I doubt that the president was upset about my marriage three days earlier. My guess is that Jeane Kirkpatrick poisoned his view of the situation.

On the eve of our marriage Radio Venceremos broadcast a series of hilarious conversations allegedly between Patricia and me, portraying her as an oligarch agent seducing and subverting the imperialist ambassador. Nice of the FMLN to celebrate with us.

Patricia's and my marriage was the social event of the season. Almost every significant figure in town, starting with Donna Mariña and my father, attended our reception. Earlier Napoleón Duarte's son, the elected mayor of San Salvador, had married us in a civil ceremony, witnessed by my friend Atilio Vieytez and Patricia's friend Carmen de Balzaretti.

I had had a fright the week before. D'Aubuisson dropped by, reminisced with Patricia about how as a young lieutenant he had served under her father, then mayor of Puerto El Triumph, drank me silly, and threatened to come back the night before our marriage to take me out on a bachelor binge. I worried about what I should do if he carried out his threat, finally deciding I would be a coward and refuse. To my relief, he only came to our reception.

Dealing with Washington was becoming ever more complicated. Increasingly there were signs of splits within the Reagan administration. I saw evidence of discord between the C.I.A., Defense, NSC, and State as I received differing ideas by telephone. I insisted that only written instructions from State were to guide my and other embassy interventions with the government.

In late February, Richard Stone was nominated to be ambassador at large to serve as the president's special representative to Central America. Power was shifting from State to the NSC. In March, Ambassador Stone came to El Salvador. I met his flight and, of course, set up a schedule for him, including dinner at President Magaña's home. Stone, a former senator from Florida, spoke some Spanish, a real asset, since many senior Salvadorans, especially the military, spoke little or no English.

The senator talked convincingly of seizing the political initiative. He told Magaña that the pope would endorse early elections during his forthcoming visit and asked Magana to welcome the proposal. The president promised to do so. When privately I asked the senator how he knew what the pope intended, he told me he had worked it out with the papal nuncio in Washington.

On their flight home, Stone and his aide talked too loudly and foolishly of his triumphal visit. A newsman who overheard them naturally broke the story! Not exactly a diplomatic triumph!

Juan Pablo II's visit thrilled us all. Each member of the diplomatic corps had their picture taken greeting His Holiness. He blessed a rosary Patricia had with her. We attended a Papal Mass, along with seven hundred thousand others. The pope spoke lovingly of Archbishop Romero, against violence, advocating peace and dialogue. No mention of elections. Magaña, nevertheless, announced they would be held on March 25, 1984.

My life became even more complicated when Stone wanted me to participate in his almost daily NSC conference telephone calls. He also visited several times more. Much ado, little accomplished, was my assessment.

Better news, at least by my standards, was the May replacement of General Nutting by General Paul Gorman. The new CINC soon flew up to see me. We accomplished more in two hours of discussion than Nutting and I had in almost two years. It helped that Paul was accompanied not by a bevy of staff officers, but only by Brigadier Fred Woerner.

May also brought a helpful visit by Attorney General and Mrs. William Smith. He had taken an interest in the legal problems of El Salvador and wanted personally to commend to the president the reforms developed by a U.S. judicial assessment team. The team was a response to my pleas for help, pleas that President Magaña had encouraged. Obviously the Salvadoran legal system needed improvement, but I was not competent to deal with the legal issues involved.

The team's suggestions were numerous, including establishing a protection system for judges and witnesses, requiring warrants for arrests, except for offenders caught in the act, and changing the rules of evidence. Whether anything came of them, I do not know.

Sonsonate was the least conflicted of the departments, probably because of lingering fears generated in 1932 by the ruthless suppression of the communist revolt led by Farabundo Martí. The effectiveness of what came to be called La Matanza appealed to many, but, unlike 1932, the U.S. and the world were watching in 1983.

In February 1983, *campesinos* at a cooperative in Sonsonate were seized and summarily executed. There was evidence that a Colonel González had ordered the operation. After my protests to President Magaña and Defense Minister Garcia, the president asked the Human Rights Commission to investigate. The commission eventually recommended indicting González. Garcia also launched an investigation, which concluded that no soldiers had been involved. Moreover, the colonel conducting the investigation dismissed the findings of the Human Rights Commission as "biased."

Once again, I protested, advocating the arrest of those involved, starting with Colonel Gonzáles.

What happened next is something of which I'm not proud, recognizing that I may have made a mistake, but I did what I thought was right.

The President and Sña. Magaña had invited Patricia and me to lunch at their *finca*. After lunch he asked me to walk outside with him. There he told me he would order Colonel González's arrest, but I should know that if he did he would not be president twenty-four hours later. What did I think? A Hobson's choice if ever there was one. After a moment's reflection, I replied that I thought we needed Magaña to remain as president more than we needed González under arrest.

That May, Al Schaufelberger was assassinated by the FMLN. He was the first official American killed in the struggle. Al was deputy MilGrp commander, a great guy, a poker-playing buddy, a Navy lt. commander, and a Seal. As the senior Naval officer at post, he oversaw key efforts at interdicting arms shipments into El Salvador. His loss was tragic for his country, his parents, and for me personally.

In June, I learned from news reports that Tom Enders had resigned as assistant secretary, "having lost the confidence of the president," and that I was to be replaced in El Salvador. While I was surprised by the manner in which I learned of my imminent departure, I was not surprised at being transferred. Indeed, two years of San Salvador was thought to be enough. I had understood for some time that my next job would be as ambassador to Argentina. The thought of Buenos Aires had appealed to both Patricia and me. But now I learned it would not be. The president had granted Tom's wish for the embassy in Madrid. Frank Ortiz, uprooted from Madrid, asked to be sent as ambassador to Buenos Aires. My future was left in limbo. To media inquiries in San Salvador and later in the States, I replied, "It is up to the president."

As planned, Patricia and I left for the States to be with President Magaña during his visit. He and Sña. Magaña were to stay at Blair House, a courtesy not extended to Duarte. They also had a full meeting with the president while Mrs. Reagan entertained Concha Mariña and other ladies at a tea. Patricia thought that Nancy had not been overly friendly. A luncheon was hosted by Secretary Shultz at the department's seventh floor impressive antique furnished facilities.

At a Blair House reception hosted by the Magañas, Shultz told me he wanted me to go to Brazil. When I protested that I spoke no Portuguese and was not adept at languages, he said, "Start studying!" I started to study, but was particularly troubled since Tony Motley, leaving Brazil to replace Tom Ender, was bilingual, having grown up in Brazil.

While in Washington, I asked to call on the president. He and his NSC advisor received me. Clark, beyond a hello, said nothing during my talk with the president. If Reagan was still mad at me, he did not show it.

Indeed, he wrote in his diary on June 9, 1983:

Ambas. Hinton just relieved as Ambas to El Salvador stopped by. He's a good man & did a fine job under extremely difficult circumstances. I hope he can convince some of our left leaning Congressmen how wrong they are.

Back in San Salvador, Patricia and I were feted with seemingly endless *despedidas*, three of which live in my memory. At one, I was given a poker table with the names attached of the regular members of our "Statistical Probability Study Group." The table included a plaque for our missing colleague, Al Schaufelberger. While I drank, my buddies cleaned me out of almost $1,500! The table, however, made and makes my loss worth it. The other three University of Chicago alumni in El Salvador entertained me at another boisterous evening of toasts, jokes, and ridiculous souvenirs. Finally at a Foreign Ministry reception, to my gratification and the surprise of those present, when Minister Fidel Chavez Mena started to drape the ribbon of a decoration over my head, President Magaña took it from him and did me the honor of personally bestowing it.

22

Intermission (1983)

In mid-July, Patricia, Sebas, and I moved into my Dellwood home in Bethesda.

Here I made two mistakes that months later, too late to correct, Patricia told me she had resented. She said she had been upset both by my leaving Jorge and Michu in the main bedroom while we took a guest room and by my leaving her to join my father for bridge on a night when she was recovering from the removal that day of two wisdom teeth.

For me it was entirely natural since the kids were paying rent, even if well below market, that I should not displace them, and my weekly visit to my dad for bridge was something to which we both looked forward.

Had Patricia told me at the time how she felt about these matters, I could and would have done differently. To my regret, this lack of easy communication in our marriage, for which we were both guilty, was never fully overcome.

Secretary Schultz, as he had said he would, sent my name to the White House for Brazil. Soon, however, I learned that the president would nominate Diego Asencio, who spoke Portuguese. I thought it a wise decision.

Without an assignment, I pondered retirement. Tony Motley, who had replaced Tom Enders as assistant secretary for Latin America, invited me to lunch to suggest that I take the embassy in Lima. I thanked him for his consideration but said I would rather retire than struggle to improve our relations with another troubled Latin country.

Testifying before the Bipartisan National Commission on Central America brought back memories of El Salvador. Some were good memories of friends and of ordinary *campesinos* as they voted in large numbers, hoping for peace; others were horrible memories of the toll taken by rightist death squads and by FMLN fighters. I wanted the commission to understand the situation, to tamp down the violence, and to support what I argued had to be a reformed army.

While uncertain about my future, I was kept busy responding to requests from the Bureau of Public Affairs to speak about our Central American policies at colleges around the country.

Almost everywhere I encountered demonstrators opposing administration policy. Fortunately for me, their highly vocal opposition was nonviolent. I noted, however, that while resistance to communism in El Salvador was a relatively easy sale, support for the Contras in Nicaragua was far harder to sell to our young people. In October, our invasion of Grenada stimulated many questions but little objection from students.

My visit to Salt Lake City stands out in my memory for various reasons. My chauffer told me, "We Mormons marry not 'until death do us part' but for eternity." I was impressed, at least until on the way back to the airport he mentioned that he was divorcing! My reception at Brigham Young University (BYU) was entirely different from any other school at which I spoke. The students were polite and neatly dressed; no jeans, T-shirts, or long hair at BYU. Moreover, they were supportive of the president's policies.

My morale got a needed boost when David Newsom invited me to lunch and asked me to accept the Jit Trainor award for "Distinguished Service in the Conduct of Diplomacy." The award came complete with a Georgetown University chair, on which I am now sitting. Subsequently I learned I had received the Presidential Distinguished Service Award. The Presidential Award came with welcome cash, but the Trainor Award citation, presumably written by Newsom, conveyed an almost poetic feel for my service in El Salvador.

One day, Larry Eagleburger, then under secretary for political affairs, called me to say he and the secretary hoped I would go to Pakistan. Would I? Damn right I would! Pakistan sounded like a dream assignment.

Eventually I received the obligatory call from President Reagan. My nomination was immediately submitted to the Senate. So little time was left before the Senate planned to adjourn that I would need unanimous consent. But Senator Helms's staff had put a hold on my nomination, and the department's Office of Congressional

Affairs (H) told me I would probably have to wait for the next congressional session to be confirmed.

When I asked what could be done to move things along, I was told I might call someone on Helms's staff. I called the senator. I was told he was on the Senate floor, but his secretary took my message.

The Senate adjourned. And when the record was searched, I learned to my relief that I was among those confirmed.

23

Pakistan (1983–1987)

Before flying to Islamabad, I was surprised to find that Afghanistan was hardly mentioned in my briefings, other than at the C.I.A. Yet three years after the Soviet invasion, Afghan *mujahideen*, or "freedom fighters," were still resisting. What a contrast, I thought, with the struggle in El Salvador, where public interest was high, partisan politics raged, and interagency battles had so complicated my life.

I sought out Soviet experts, in and out of government, to get their assessment. Without exception, they said the Afghans would eventually be crushed. Hal Sonnenfeldt and Arnold Raphel, then the deputy assistant secretary of state, knew about "covert" support for the *mujahideen* but discounted Afghan chances to carry on the fight for long.

During my daylong briefing at Langley, C.I.A. career officers spoke of a welcome chance to repay the Soviets for arming the North Vietnamese. I found Director Bill Casey enthusiastic about support for the *mujahideen*. He did not believe they could win, but was confident they were weakening the Soviets. Casey volunteered that the Islamabad station chief was first class. This made me wonder if he had thought, as I had, that my station chiefs in San Salvador were weak.

While at Langley, I also heard a good deal, much of it critical, about Congressman Charlie Wilson of Texas. He had used his committee clout to earmark money for the C.I.A. to buy Swiss Oerlikon cannons, arguing that the Afghans needed them to defend against Soviet airpower. But while more funding was welcome, telling the agency how to use it was not. Someone suggested to me that a payoff was involved. These weapons, with the ammunition required for their rapid rate of fire, were too heavy for the *mujahideen* to easily move into and about the mountains of Afghanistan. Agency officers said they were simply unsuited for a guerrilla war.

However, Wilson proved right. The *mujahideen* needed better antiaircraft weapons. He and Chairman Clarence Long had recently visited Pakistan and heard firsthand about this deficiency. They also recognized that weapons easily traceable to the United States had to be ruled out. The C.I.A. insisted on deniability. Thus, it had procured Soviet SA-6s from Egypt. I was told they now intended to provide the British-made Blowpipe. Later in Pakistan, I learned that these obsolete SA-6s often malfunctioned, while the wire-guided Blowpipe put those using it at great risk of countermeasures.

One of the last things I did before flying to Islamabad was to call on Representative Clarence Long at his Baltimore office. He wanted to help and thought the Oerlikons were a good idea, but told me there would not be a dime for Pakistan unless a young woman whose name I have forgotten was released. She had been raped but was the one being charged with sexual misconduct. Knowing the chairman meant it, I promised to do all I could to secure her release.

For starters, I raised the case with Ambassador Ejaz Azim. Ejaz assured me he had informed his government of the problem. He thought it likely that they would find a way to drop the charges. When I reached Pakistan, I learned he had been right. President Zia-ul-Haq had understood the importance of Long's goodwill and had somehow fixed things. I concluded that there was something to be said for dictators.

Indeed, during approximately three years in Pakistan, I learned there was a lot to be said for and against Muhammad Zia-ul-Haq. Shrewd, persevering, with a fine sense of humor and a generally warm personality, he was at times ruthless. Always focused on his objectives, he was an accomplished liar. He lied to me about Pakistan's nuclear program and to my Soviet colleague about Pakistan's support for the *mujahideen*.

Pakistan's credentials ceremony was colorful. The chief of protocol drove me from my residence in a limousine to Rawalpindi, where we switched to a gilded horse-drawn carriage escorted by an honor guard of mounted lancers. After reviewing the Presidential Guard and listening to our respective national anthems, I was introduced to the president. In turn, I introduced senior members of my embassy to him. I had been concerned that I was only scheduled for fifteen minutes with the president, but Zia gave me far longer. He also exited to greet Patricia, whom an aide had noted photographing the outdoor ceremony.

Zia responded at length to my question about how he viewed Pakistan's neighbors. Born in British India, he said:

I want and Pakistan needs good relations with India, but Indira Gandhi does not seem to share my desire. Only with China, our best friend, are there no serious problems. Afghanistan is in crisis, resisting occupation by the Soviets, who threaten Pakistan and perhaps seek a warm water outlet on the Gulf.

He graphically illustrated the threat with a map, on which he placed a bright red arrow aimed from Afghanistan at Pakistan. Iran, which he called "a sister Muslim state," was embroiled in a regrettable war with Iraq, another sister Muslim state. Iran's unpredictable Shia clerics, he added, increased uncertainty in Pakistan's neighborhood.

Nuclear issues, which together with Afghanistan would be central to our relations during my years in Pakistan, were not mentioned by either of us. After India tested a nuclear device in 1974, Prime Minister Zulfikar Ali Bhutto had launched Pakistan's nuclear program, famously declaring Pakistanis would "eat grass," if necessary, to have their own bomb.

After a politically turbulent year that followed General Zia's promotion to the critical position of army chief of staff, he overthrew Prime Minister Bhutto. Eventually, he had him tried and executed. Zia changed many of Bhutto's policies, but not the nuclear weapons program. That he strengthened. He kept Dr. Abdul Qadeer Khan in charge of the Kahuta centrifuge facility. We knew they were enriching uranium there, but we did not know how much was produced, or at what level of enrichment.

With credentials presented, I got on with my job. As always at a new post, I had to spend much time making courtesy calls on ministers and diplomatic colleagues. Over sixty countries had resident ambassadors and only a few of these—Cuba, Libya, and Iran—could I ignore. I also had to call on the martial law administrators, who served as governors of the four provinces: Punjab, Sindh, the Northwest Frontier (NWFP), and Baluchistan, as well as visit our consular officers in Karachi, Lahore, and Peshawar and familiarize myself with their problems, in addition to getting to know my own large staff. It was a fascinating but daunting challenge.

Pakistan had been conceived of by its founding father, Muhammad Ali Jinnah, as an Islamic state, free from domination by the Hindus of India. Not all but a great majority of its population confessed the Islamic faith. And General Zia was a devout Muslim.

That he prayed five times a day is not in doubt. National Day celebrations were adjourned for prayers. I was with him on a train once when he had it stopped so he and other devout Muslims could get off to pray.

He was also a fundamentalist. Soon after seizing power, he had proclaimed *sharia,* or Islamic law, to be in effect, with punishments including amputations for theft, stoning for adultery, and jail and/ or lashes for consumption of "intoxicants" in public places. He also established *sharia* courts. However, he was astute enough to recognize a need to move cautiously. In my time, these harsh punishments were seldom applied and the *sharia* courts were mostly symbolic.

Some thought Zia was only giving lip service to Islam. I disagreed. Yes, it helped him politically, both within Pakistan and in the wider Islamic world. Yet his backing of Jamiat-e-Islami and of extremists, like Gulbuddin Hekmatyar, indicated to me more than a narrow political calculation.

Doctrinal disputes split Pakistan's Muslim majority into many groups. Considering this, his decree prohibiting the propagation of the beliefs of the Ahmadiyyah was also extremist. Once, under instruction, I asked him to review "with compassion" a human rights case involving an Ahmadiyyah woman. He readily agreed to review the case, but stressed that he would apply the law—his law.

On another occasion, I was astonished by the tone of a speech in which he called for Islamic banking and for the abolition of interest. I did not understand the Urdu, but there was no mistaking his fervor. The normally cool, calm, calculating Zia metamorphosed into a passionate advocate. Maybe some bankers were resisting, as well they might. An economy without interest payments can work, but at a high cost in efficiency.

After the 1977 coup, Zia had promised elections in ninety days. When I arrived in late 1983, they had still not been held. There was an ineffective Consultative Assembly, or *Shura,* every member of which he had appointed. We wanted elections, but maintaining Pakistan's support for the *mujahideen* in Afghanistan was a higher priority. I tried, in a low-key manner, to encourage political movement towards democracy and the rule of law, both privately and, more carefully, in public remarks.

In 1984, Zia held a referendum that linked the adoption of *sharia* law with his own election as president for a further five years. Not surprisingly, *sharia* was approved and Zia elected.

In February 1985, he authorized "nonparty" elections, making clear his disdain for political parties. Nevertheless, most of those elected did have party affiliations. Zia appointed a Sindhi, Muhammed Khan Junejo, as prime minister. Parliament gave Junejo a vote of confidence.

To my regret, parliament spent far more time debating widely varying interpretations of *sharia* than it did discussing education, health, foreign, or economic policy. The judicial system, based on British practice, was embedded in the constitution. Now a debate raged over whether Islamic law, on which there was little or no agreement, should supersede the constitution. Could a *sharia* court overrule the Supreme Court? For me, such debates were evidence of a dysfunctional society.

In a letter to my children at home, I wrote:

> It's Eid and all through Pakistan not an official is stirring. Washington still thinks, however, that the world needs saving and keeps sending me urgent instructions. I've explained patiently that the world will just have to wait until the government returns to work.

Pakistan had "a world class foreign minister," Lt. General Sahabzada Yaqub Khan. Born in Rampur, India, into an aristocratic family, Yaqub had served as an officer under British command in North Africa. Captured, he used his time as a prisoner of war to gain fluency in a number of languages. He had served as Pakistan's ambassador to France, Washington, and Moscow and was harder than Zia for me to get an appointment with.

When he did receive me, he demonstrated a Kissinger-like capacity for geopolitical analysis. His views, outlined in embassy reporting, were gratefully received in Washington. While careful not to undercut his president, we noted that his interest in a negotiated settlement in Afghanistan was greater than Zia's. His annual presentations of Pakistan foreign policy to the parliament were magisterial. He hardly participated in any subsequent debate.

The election law of 1985 also provided that future ministers would have to vote and be elected. The aristocratic foreign minister made it perfectly clear that he would not deign to campaign. We wondered if he would tolerate being jostled at a polling booth. He did not have to; somehow it was arranged that he vote in solitary splendor. Unopposed, he won a seat in the Senate. I was glad he would remain foreign minister, despite my doubts about how he did it.

His election, however, was not the only flaw in "Pakistani democracy." Martial law remained in effect. Prime Minister Junejo advocated its end. Eventually, Zia agreed, but only after having the constitution amended so that the president would have the right to dismiss the prime minister and the Parliament.

Junejo, a large landowner in the Sindh, was almost a political unknown. When he entertained the diplomatic corps at his estate, we were transported into a feudal past. Advised to bring our shotguns, we stood in a firing line as beaters drove partridge towards us. In the evening after a feast, male dancers entertained us with traditional dances. Not a female in sight.

Furthermore, while Zia had always dealt effectively with the drug cases I raised with him, after Junejo took office, the first time I took a drug problem to Zia he grinned and reminded me that there was now a prime minister to deal with drug issues. As devout Muslims, both Zia and Junejo furthered antidrug actions and programs. Policy did not change, but Junejo was less effective. I wondered if he was out of his depth.

When the Soviets shelled Chaman, a border town in Baluchistan, I asked Foreign Secretary Niaz Naik to approve my travel there. He refused. The next time I had an appointment with Junejo, I told the prime minister his foreign secretary, who was present, had denied me permission to travel to Chaman. Junejo looked puzzled and asked, "Why do you want to go to Chaman?" I said to show and tell Pakistanis that they had good friends. Nor, I added, would the gesture be lost on the Soviets. He told Niaz to authorize my travel.

Niaz waited, however, until the prime minister visited Chaman. Good for Junejo, I thought. Only then was my visit authorized.

The government was particularly sensitive about visitors to Baluchistan, where low-grade guerilla resistance persisted. I never had a problem getting authority to visit Quetta to call on the governor or to attend ceremonies at the Pakistan Army Staff College where American officers also studied. But every time I asked for permission to take the train through the Bolan Pass, I was turned down.

I wanted to travel that route not only because it is famous for having the world's steepest gradient for a steam train, but also to see the colorful seasonal migration of the nomadic tribes and their livestock. Then, at a reception, I saw the minister of railways and told him about my interest. He, to my delight, said, "I'll arrange it." And arrange it he did, complete with numerous guards and an entire car just for us. My guards even let me take pictures, something otherwise strictly forbidden in the pass.

My first visitors in Pakistan were Senators John Tower and John McCain, both important supporters of the Afghan resistance. A full day had been scheduled for them, with a helicopter ride to Peshawar, military briefings, a visit to an Afghan refugee camp, lunch in the mess of the famed Khyber Rifles, a look into Afghanistan from the pass, a helicopter ride back to Islamabad, and dinner with President Zia. I soon learned that this was a fairly standard program for VIP visitors.

However, bad weather forced us to land at an army base at Mardan. When we finally got to Peshawar by road, the senators opted to return in time for dinner with Zia. They canceled the drive to the Khyber, but wanted to do most of the rest of the program. So we returned to Islamabad in the dark on the Great Trunk Road, jammed with trucks and buses. Traffic reluctantly moved out of our way as we barreled by with a screaming motorcycle escort. It was a frightening ride. Still, we made it in time for dinner and a good talk with Zia, who brought out his map with the big red arrow.

In May 1984, Vice President and Mrs. Bush arrived from New Delhi for a four-day visit. Zia and company went all out to entertain their guests and to show Pakistan off. Zia, along with some flower-throwing girls, met them at the airport. He also hosted a small informal supper that evening. And as the vice president had a digestive upset, Zia thoughtfully cut the evening short.

For me, the visit provided a number of memorable highlights:

Listening to the two presidents, as we drove up to the Murree hill station, discuss the sensitive nuclear issue for one. Bush was firm in his warnings; Zia assured him Pakistan's program was "peaceful."

Lunching in the famed Khyber Rifle Mess and taking my first look into Afghanistan from the pass.

Bush pledging support to tens of thousands of Afghans, assembled to salute him.

Watching American Secret Service agents jostle with Pakistani bodyguards to position Bush's limousine ahead of Zia's.

***

In Lahore, at a special shopping exhibit arranged by the governor of the Punjab, I bought a large tapestry showing camels, donkeys, and peasants. However, when asked if I would defer to the vice president, I, of course, agreed. That night, I learned from the salesman, who had tracked me down, that he had a similar tapestry for sale. Framed, it now hangs in our dining room.

Also in Lahore, at 7 a.m. I watched a young Navy doctor "ordering" the vice president not to run in the over-100-degree heat. After some argument, Bush caved.

For embassy staff, visitors were mainly a burden; but for me, VIP visitors were a ticket to study Zia as his thinking evolved and to talk with other Pakistani leaders and with senior Americans. Many came from the Pentagon, including Secretary Caspar Weinberger and assorted generals and admirals.

For General John Vessey, Jr., chairman of the Joint Chiefs of Staff, Pakistan's generals organized a pheasant hunt in the NWFP, with far more beaters than Junejo had fielded. I also shot better, getting four of eleven. When Vessey stopped in the middle of nowhere to communicate by satellite his thoughts about the latest Soviet nuclear disarmament proposals, the Pakistanis were impressed. I was amazed I had not yet known we had portable satellite capabilities.

In 1987, Zia agreed to lead assorted Pakistan brass to visit an American task force at sea off Karachi. We arrived on the *Kitty Hawk* (CV 63) by helicopter, watched flight deck catapult launches and landings, and toured the carrier. General Akhtar Abdur Rahman Khan, director of Pakistan's Inter-Services Intelligence (ISI), kept glancing at the task force commander. Clearly puzzled, he let his curiosity overcome his reticence and asked me about the admiral's nationality. I said he was Japanese-American. He had trouble believing it.

Some distinguished American guests, such as President Richard Nixon and Secretary of State Alexander Haig, were feted at virtual state dinners and housed in the Presidential Palace. I particularly enjoyed the Haig visit, as it brought back so many memories. Patricia found the Haigs to be great company, as she had Barbara Bush.

At Zia's dinner for him, Nixon asked me to call on him the next day. His questions were as sharp as any visitor ever asked. After some discussion, he asked me to walk with him on the open terrace of the building where he queried me about Pakistan's nuclear program. He did not need to point out—but did—that his suite was probably bugged.

Charlie Wilson visited as well, and his first trip was shortly after Vice President and Mrs. Bush left. Charlie was a fascinating character. He told me and Station Chief Howie Hart, after a lively discussion, that we were not doing enough to help the freedom fighters. He bragged he would get us more resources, and he did. His accompanying friend was a beauty who got along well with Patricia, as did Charlie.

The evening we were to see Zia, he came downstairs asking for whiskey. To my amazement, he threw down three or four straight shots in nothing flat. He knew, he said, we would not have alcohol later. Our meeting went well. Zia clearly recognized Charlie's importance, and Charlie promised more help for the Afghans.

After much shopping, Charlie left, promising to return soon. He did return many times, each time with a different "knock-out" of a friend.

He mentioned he wanted to go to Afghanistan to see the action for himself. I advised that the United States could not risk an American, much less a congressman, being captured by the Soviets. Undeterred, he made his interest known to Zia, who also vetoed the idea. Charlie, nevertheless, explored how he might do it with a *mujahideen* group.

On a 1986 trip, he put his plan into action, only to be stopped by Pakistani authorities and returned to Peshawar. He was furious at being frustrated; Zia was furious at Charlie for risking so much out of personal vanity. They had it out. Zia finally promised to explore how Charlie could visit Afghanistan "safely."

In early 1987, when Charlie was once again our guest, I learned from DCM John McCarthy, who had taken Charlie to see Zia, that Charlie was going. Zia had asked him not to say publicly that the government was aware of his expedition. McCarthy had strongly warned against the trip, but to no avail.

Recognizing the inevitable, I wrote, "Wish I were going with you, but someone has to think of the national interest. Don't do it. But above all have a safe trip." Before leaving, he left me a reply, "Thanks for understanding (Sort of). This is something I simply have to do. Occasionally one has to put one's money where one's mouth is....Warmly, Charlie."

ISI officers and trusted Afghans escorted Charlie into a part of Afghanistan where the Soviets had not operated for months. He had his picture taken dressed as an Afghan and riding a horse. He returned to Washington to trade his vote in the Intelligence Appropriations Subcommittee to anyone who would in return vote more money for the *mujahideen*.

Playboy, romantic, committed to the Afghan cause, I liked Charlie, at least most of the time. Not, however, when he behaved like a spoiled brat. Before a 1986 trip to Pakistan, he asked the Department of Defense to authorize the defense attaché to provide air transportation for him and his lady friend. The Pentagon approved for him, but not for his friend. The attaché, a Colonel Lee, was so informed.

In Karachi, Charlie encountered Mil Group Commander Brigadier General George Baxter, who was also assigned a C-12. George, not knowing of the Pentagon edict, flew both Charlie and his lady friend to Islamabad.

In Islamabad, Charlie berated the defense attaché for declining to fly both of them to Peshawar. Colonel Lee said he would like to do so, but his orders prevented it. Charlie exploded, ordering him to fly his baggage to Peshawar (which he did) and threatening to take the attaché plane away from Islamabad. Charlie called Zia, who arranged for a Pakistan Air Force plane to fly both him and his lady.

When I met Charlie the next evening in Peshawar, I tried to persuade him that the attaché was right to obey his orders, but to no avail. The next annual appropriations bill explicitly withdrew the previously authorized aircraft for the defense attaché.

Charlie had put his personal ego ahead of an officer's orders. His spiteful, childish behavior deprived the embassy of a tool needed to fulfill its mission. By the time Charlie's amendment came into effect, it did not penalize me or Colonel Lee but a new team of Americans in Pakistan. What he did for the Afghan cause offset the bitter taste of such behavior, but not entirely.

Another regular visitor was Bill Casey. He saw Zia often, but always met with General Akhtar. Casey pushed Zia and Akhtar to step up operations against the Soviets in Afghanistan and even mentioned possible actions into the Soviet Union itself. Zia was willing but cautious. He argued it was important to keep the Afghan pot boiling but crucial that it not boil over. He did not want to provoke a Soviet invasion of Pakistan. Frequent Soviet cross-border air raids, occasional artillery barrages, and persistent sabotage were bad enough. When Afghan incursions into the Soviet Union led to particularly strong Soviet protests, we halted such actions for a prolonged period of time.

I enjoyed and profited from Casey's visits, though he was tight-lipped and muttered often. Once, when I complained about the State Department's refusal to upgrade communications for the consulate in Peshawar, he offered to fix the equipment problem and provide the consulate an extra "communicator." Of course, I knew the deal gave him a man in Peshawar, but since Consul Ron Lorton needed better equipment, I agreed. State was upset with me. Too bad.

I normally accompanied Casey to his meetings, though not on his trips to view the training of Afghans or to logistical facilities. The station chief briefed me regularly, but watching Casey's dialogue with Akhtar and eventually with the *mujahideen*'s political leaders was more enlightening.

We knew we needed to know more about our Afghan allies, but learning was slow going. Casey, bit by bit, managed to loosen the rule precluding American contacts with the Afghans.

Whereas Charlie shopped for weapons for his collection and for carpets, clothing, and furs for his lady friends, Casey loved bookstores. He was an omnivorous reader or, more accurately, scanner of almost anything he found in English or French.

When I arrived at post, appropriations for C.I.A. support of Afghan operations totaled $60 million annually. Zia had rejected as "peanuts" Carter's offer of $400 million for military and economic assistance, but covert C.I.A. aid had been another matter. At least it was after Pakistan negotiated rules that kept control firmly in their hands. When I left, the C.I.A. program, after steady expansion, had grown to almost $700 million a year.

After each visit, Casey flew to Saudi Arabia to brief an ally that was pledged to match the U.S. effort dollar for dollar. Bill occasionally muttered about tardy Saudi contributions. Still, as far as I know, the Saudis kept their part of the bargain sooner or later. There were also modest contributions from other Arab countries, China, Israel, and the United Kingdom.

The Saudis also provided much help to Afghan refugees in Pakistan and some to those in Iran. I now know I should have paid more attention to this aid; it supported Wahhabi-run schools that preached an extreme version of Islamic thought.

Two other issues—covert Afghan aid distribution and corruption—did concern me. Was our aid going where it would do the most good? How much was being skimmed off by corrupt officials? Getting the facts was slow, hard work.

As an indicator of corruption, the station watched prices for weapons in the black market. That supply and demand remained more or less in balance was reassuring, but we were still concerned that the government might be storing weapons we had provided for distribution. Certainly the Afghan fighters, not known for truthfulness, complained that they were short of this and that. Verifying the true situation seemed beyond our capability. Not only were we enveloped in "the fog of war," we were constrained by Pakistani rules and sensitivities.

When the program was established, it was reasonable to accept the Pakistan government's conditions, even though they limited our role to supplying needed equipment and weapons. In short, we served as a "quartermaster," supplying what was needed to Pakistan without contact with the Afghans.

I thought, and Casey agreed, that we needed to know more about the use being made of our growing program. We also needed to get to know the Afghan leaders we were supporting. Thanks to Casey, we began to have meetings at ISI with the political leaders of the seven parties to whom weapons were supplied.

It was immediately apparent that the seven disagreed among themselves about almost everything. It was appalling. My reaction was that they should be locked in a room and only allowed out after they agreed to cooperate. Casey, in his mild way, told Zia of his concern. Zia laid down the law and the Seven Party Mujahideen Alliance was formed.

It was progress, but far from enough. I pressed the station chief, Bill Piekney, to learn more. Yet it was mid-1986 before a reluctant General Akhtar gave Piekney a basic breakdown of aid, in weapons and money, for each group. It showed, as we had suspected, that fundamentalist political leaders, starting with Gulbuddin Hekmatyar, received roughly thrice as much assistance as the more moderate ones.

Our efforts to shift the balance were largely unavailing. Akhtar argued that assistance was proportional to efforts demonstrated in the fighting. This was a sensible criterion, and he was largely correct.

However, there was one important exception. Ahmad Shah Massoud's allies from the Panjshir Valley provoked repeated Soviet attempts to eliminate him. Massoud, a Tajik, was an effective fighter who deserved much more support. But General Akhtar maintained that only members of the Alliance were eligible. Burhanuddin Rabbani, also a Tajik and leader of the political party to which Massoud belonged, qualified and received assistance from ISI. Rabbani, however, sent little of it on to Massoud. It is true that the logistical difficulties of getting supplies from Peshawar to the Panjshir were great.

Eventually, I met the Alliance leaders one-on-one. In 1987, when President Reagan decided to invite them to the White House, I was instructed to issue oral invitations. Rabbani jumped at the chance to meet with our president, as did three others.

Gulbuddin Hekmatyar bluntly declined. He was grateful, he said, for our assistance to the Afghan cause, but the Afghan struggle with the "Godless Soviets" was not to be weakened by making it appear as an East-West battle. Two other Alliance leaders also declined.

Months later, again under instruction, I tried to convince each of the need for more Alliance flexibility in the peace negotiations. I failed, but will never forget my meeting with Mohammad Nabi Mohammadi, leader of the Harakat-i-Inqilab-i-Islami (Islamic Revolution Movement). Sitting above me on his raised charpoy, he lectured me on our nuclear disarmament negotiations with the Soviets. To see him, I had had to agree to breakfast. Nabi did not eat, but urged me to finish my fly-covered scrambled eggs.

Nonetheless, our humanitarian aid program provided happier encounters with some other Alliance leaders, including Sibghatullah Mojaddedi and Sayyid Ahmed Gailani.

As a 1933 British field manual explained, "Afghans are hardy, brave, proud,....prepared to die in accordance with their code of honour, yet treacherous."

The Soviets steadily increased pressure. By late 1984, helicopter gunships were inflicting terrible casualties. Some Afghans switched sides; others spent less time fighting, more time resting in Pakistan. It seemed to me that unless we provided the *mujahideen* with better antiaircraft weapons, the Soviets would prevail.

Eventually, Charlie's Oerlikons arrived in country, and, as predicted, they proved difficult for the Afghans to use. As far as I know, they never shot down a Soviet aircraft. Once, deployed in a valley facing a key Soviet supply route, they did take out a convoy of trucks.

I thought the U.S. Stinger, a fire-and-forget shoulder weapon with advanced heat-seeking technology, would make a real difference. But guidance from Washington was clear. The administration opposed a transfer of Stingers. I also thought we had to respect Zia's judgment. He had made it clear that he thought supplying Stingers to the Afghans could make "the pot boil over." Moreover, the Pakistanis had earlier asked for them for their army, and we had declined to supply such technologically advanced weapons.

Then, in November of 1984 Zia told Senator Sam Nunn of Georgia that Stingers should be supplied to the Afghan *mujahideen*. By making the request to the chairman of the Armed Forces Committee, I thought, the decision to reverse his long-standing view demonstrated Zia's feel for American politics.

Yet, while Zia was no longer an obstacle, opposition within the Reagan administration remained widespread. As the issue was fought out in Washington, I was an interested party. Conservative Republicans, most prominently Senators Orrin Hatch and Gordon Humphrey, pushed hard for a policy reversal.

A hawkish protégé of Hatch, Deputy Assistant Secretary of Defense Michael Pillsbury was another visitor at this time. I had met him before when he visited with Fred Iklé, the under secretary of defense. Pillsbury vociferously advocated in favor of supplying Stingers to the Afghans. Such advocacy was fair enough in confidential administration discussions; but I hit the roof when he pushed his view on the Pakistanis. A member of the executive branch criticizing our policy in front of foreigners led me to cable Washington and express strong objection to a "loose cannon."

As decision time approached, Arnold Raphel kept me informed by secure phone. Arnie was opposed to the transfer, but I assume he recorded my favorable vote. Then in March 1986, President Reagan settled matters by approving the transfer of Stingers to both the Pakistan Army and the *mujahideen*.

Six months later, during their initial use on September 25, Afghan fighters shot down three Soviet M-24 helicopters. Further successes followed, and soon Soviet tactics changed. Their aircraft began flying above Stinger range, making the Stingers much less effective. The *mujahideen*'s morale soared, and peace negotiations picked up steam.

The embassy's role in the lengthy and tortured talks, which eventually led to an agreement and the withdrawal of Soviet forces, was limited to reporting whatever we learned from knowledgeable individuals, mainly Zia, Yaqub Khan, and Diego Cordovez, the United Nations negotiator.

Since Pakistan would not meet with the Soviet-backed Afghan regime, Cordovez conducted "proximity talks" in Geneva, meeting separately with the Pakistani and Afghan delegations. After each session, during visits to Moscow, Tehran, and Washington he would directly inform the governments concerned. He often visited Islamabad as well to talk with Yaqub and Zia. From time to time, he would brief me and Political Counselor John Wolf. We appreciated his faithful accounts but recognized that he was an optimist. How else could he have conducted the talks year after year? Still, he had fairly good reason for optimism by mid-1987, which is when I left Pakistan.

In 1986, Benazir Bhutto returned to Pakistan under house arrest. She soon had the political stew simmering. After her release, I invited her to tea. She thanked me for my efforts to secure her release and was surprised when I told her I had not been involved. I knew it had been the regime's decision.

Following a late December dinner with Benazir, Zia semijocularly told me I was seeing too much of her. In February, knowing my weakness for good cigars, she sent me some with a note: "Please don't tell General Zia, otherwise he'll say the Cubans are funding the PPP."

My reply: "Puffing on a Bhutto Havana brings warm thoughts of appreciation and heretical thoughts about interference in the internal affairs of Pakistan...."

In 1984, on my first trip back to Washington, I discussed with Deputy Assistant Secretary Howard Schaffer what we might do to slow down Pakistan's nuclear program. Howie heard me out but discouraged me from publicly discussing nuclear issues. He said the Pakistanis knew our view and would stop well short of a bomb. From my reading of our intelligence, particularly that collected by the station in Islamabad, I feared he was wrong. Howie struck me as someone who did not believe in rocking the boat. While I did not let his view deter me from trying, I recognized that he might have been right. My efforts did little more than annoy Zia and others. I believed, however, that I should try and not just leave it to the president and secretary to express our concerns.

I started, carefully testing the water, in Karachi on May 7, 1984, where I spoke about United States–Pakistan relations in nuanced, almost philosophical, terms. Late in my remarks, I mentioned "two issues which seem to me to hold the potential of truly serious discord between us." One was the peace process between Israel and its Arab neighbors. "The other relates to the future of your nuclear program."

Noting that "President Zia has repeatedly stated that Pakistan's nuclear program is for peaceful uses," I added, "We respect his word, but that does not keep either the American Congress or others from expressing concern about Pakistan's unsafeguarded nuclear facilities." The suggested remedy: India and Pakistan should both adhere to the Nuclear Nonproliferation Treaty (NPT), as had 119 other countries.

Audience reaction was polite; press reaction varied. Karachi's leading paper, *Dawn*, played up Patricia with a knock-out picture of her in a Pakistani Salwar Kameez. Not a bad beginning.

However, in October, a dull speech about economic issues to the Council on Security Studies in Lahore somehow led to a lively question-and-answer session. After assuring the audience that we would honor our pledge to help repel an attack on Pakistan from a communist power or a communist-dominated country, meaning Afghanistan, I was led to discuss the difference in our commitments elsewhere. Pressed about India, I said, "I don't think we would be neutral were either Pakistan or India to commit an outright act of aggression." To me, it was a balanced statement.

The Pakistani press welcomed my view, although often wrongly interpreting it as a promise, under any circumstances, of help against India. The Indian press went bananas. To my amazement, the Indian government called in Ambassador Harry Barnes to protest. The Indian ambassador to Pakistan, a friend, under instruction, demanded an explanation from me, which I gave him over drinks, together with a complete transcript of the proceedings in Lahore.

In the uproar, my replies to questions concerning nuclear policy drew little comment.

Since I knew how sensitive the Indians were on the subject of Pakistan (and vice versa), perhaps I should have ducked the question. My boss, Assistant Secretary Richard Murphy, learned of my remarks while in New Delhi. Visiting me shortly thereafter, Dick asked me if I had had in mind our commitments under the United Nations Charter. I was grateful that he, at least, understood.

War between Pakistan and India began almost simultaneously with independence in 1947. The issue was Kashmir, which had a majority Muslim population. Pakistan tried to occupy it; India declared the Maharaja had acceded to India and so resisted. An eventual ceasefire partitioned the territory, pending a definitive settlement, yet to be achieved.

By the time I arrived in Pakistan, the two countries had fought two more wars. Indians and Pakistanis seemed unable to understand each other. Indeed they hardly tried. Rather, both countries engaged in covert efforts to destabilize the other. It was an understatement to say their relations were tense.

While each government from time to time tried to improve matters, such efforts were doomed by suspicion, distrust, and political demagoguery. Simply reading about these sensitivities was inadequate. Living with them helped, but comprehension of the depth of mutual hostility came slowly.

On my first visit to New Delhi in February 1984, Ambassador Barnes took me to call on the foreign secretary. I had hardly sat down before I was subjected to a diatribe about Pakistan and U.S. policy. It was an undiplomatic but revealing experience.

In late 1984, the Pakistani and Indian armies collided on the Siachen glacier. When the Line of Control in Kashmir was established, it had been assumed that it was not necessary to extend the line into the high mountains of the Karakoram Range. Fighting at over 6,000 feet, frostbite and avalanches led to far more casualties than did standard military action. I found this struggle absurd. It seemed to me that the disputed area might well be demilitarized. Unfortunately, common sense appealed to neither country at the time.

When a Pakistan minister reached an agreement with India to loosen long-standing trade restrictions, he was repudiated. Nationalist demagoguery had won again.

In early 1987, Consul General Arnold Schifferdecker telephoned from Lahore to pass on Indian radio reports of imminent war. I had trouble believing this, but he was right. The danger of war was real. Apparently India had issued an ultimatum. As far as I could make out, India was demanding the withdrawal of Pakistani armored units sent to the Punjab frontier in response to "Brass Tacks," a large maneuver of Indian forces in Rajasthan.

American diplomacy went into overdrive to calm the situation. My instructions and those of my colleague in New Delhi were almost identical.

Public and political opinion in both countries inflamed the situation. Pakistani media was virtually unanimous in calling for the rejection of Indian demands. General Zia skillfully defused the crisis. Quietly, he ordered some withdrawals of his forces. Publicly, he proposed attending a cricket match in India. Rajiv Gandhi announced Zia would be an honored guest. War was averted. Once again, I thought there was much to be said for "dictator" Zia. Prime Minister Junejo could not have done what Zia did.

In March of 1985, I had an interview with the editor of *Nawa-I-Waqt*, a Lahore paper. He first wanted to know my reaction to Pakistan's elections, which was obviously positive, but he was also interested in nuclear issues. After saying we accepted Pakistan's assurances that its program was peaceful, I pointed out that "the previous government never tried to hide its desire to have nuclear weapons." Might not a future government also seek weapons? However, "if the [new] civilian government of Pakistan were to find its way to accept international safeguards, it would reassure the world."

I noted that the five-year congressional waiver from the stringent provisions of American law on nuclear matters would soon need to be renewed. I thought that the issue would be difficult since Senators Alan Cranston and John Glenn, among others, would oppose a renewed waiver. Signing the NPT, or at least agreeing to full-scope safeguards, would greatly facilitate matters.

In July, President Zia, reacting to an alarmist report released by Senator Cranston, charged that the senator was "ill-informed and politically motivated." He added that Pakistan had "neither the capability nor the intention" to develop nuclear weapons.

However, our intelligence about Pakistan's nuclear program was alarming. So were some indications that China might be assisting. In September, President Reagan wrote to Zia drawing a red line on Pakistan's enrichment of uranium above 5 percent. The following November, Foreign Minister Yaqub handed a reassuring reply to Reagan at the White House. Word of this exchange helped with Congress, but I doubted that it slowed down what was going on at Kahuta.

While I continued to give speeches and interviews, in 1985 public interest in nuclear issues largely gave way to political matters, above all to the war in Afghanistan and Soviet aerial incursions into Pakistan.

At some point, I learned from the station chief that a Geiger counter, hidden in a fake rock along the road to Kahuta, was missing. Its data had helped our experts judge how much uranium was being enriched.

Later, at a dinner given by Zia for high-level C.I.A. visitors, the president pulled our chain, telling us about a curious rock a goat herder had found. He pretended to wonder what it might be. After a short pause, I volunteered our experts to assist in analyzing it. We were not surprised when, polite as always, after thanking me for the offer Zia said he would reflect on the matter.

Visiting Washington, I was fairly certain that concern over enrichment was secondary to our desire to push the Afghan war. Even so, I asked Secretary of State George Shultz which was more important. He looked at me, clearly amazed at my having asked, and sharply replied, "Afghanistan is more important."

I understood and fully agreed that the centrality of our relations with the Soviet Union came first. Nevertheless, I worried that our Afghan policy could be wrecked by what I was convinced was Pakistan's pursuit of a nuclear bomb. I suspected that Zia would ignore the 5 percent red line and other warnings in the firm belief that, for us, Afghanistan trumped nuclear fears.

I was far from alone in being concerned. In September, Michael Armacost, under secretary of state for political affairs, and Donald Fortier of the NSC visited India and Pakistan, trying to promote better relations between the two South Asian rivals and seeking to avert a nuclear arms race. I applauded the effort but thought they were too diplomatic in their approach. By cable, I argued for an early confrontation rather than waiting for Congress to trigger a disaster. Not surprisingly, they opted for cautious diplomacy.

Zia met with Prime Minister Rajiv Gandhi at the United Nations in 1985. He told reporters that he hoped the meeting would "pave the way for a better relationship." He also pledged that he would sign the NPT and accept international safeguards and inspection, "if India agreed to do the same." Unfortunately, this condition was highly unlikely to be met, as he must have known.

In December, the National Defense College in Rawalpindi invited me to once again speak off the record. I decided the time had come to focus my text on nuclear nonproliferation policy. After noting that Chairman Gorbachev shared President Reagan's view that "nuclear war cannot be won and must never be fought," I stressed that "the United States is prepared to extend nuclear cooperation to any country, including Pakistan, provided that that country is party to the NPT or is prepared to adopt full-scope safeguards for its nuclear facilities." I paid tribute to Pakistan's many "bold" proposals for agreement with India on a regional solution of the nuclear problem. Then, I came to what seemed to me to be the "gut" issue. Would, as many Pakistanis believed, a nuclear weapon be a force equalizer, a way to offset India's overpowering conventional capability? I thought not, since Pakistan "could not rationally use its weapons." At some length, I spelled out why this was so. Finally, I pointed out the dangers of both a horrific nuclear miscalculation and, given clear congressional concerns and American law, of a cut-off of U.S. aid to Pakistan.

A lively question-and-answer session followed, and India came up repeatedly. I deplored the existing "distrust and even hatred," remarking that neither country had anything to gain by "keeping open the wounds of the past." Pressed, I agreed Democrats appeared to be better disposed toward India than Republicans, but I argued that basic national interests almost always determined policy, not politics. This probably explains why they did not invite me a third time.

In January 1987, A. Q. Khan boasted to an Indian journalist that Pakistan had developed nuclear weapons "capability." He subsequently denied this, but I believed the statement rang true. Internationally, speculation grew that "Pakistan was a screwdriver away from a bomb."

In February, with valuable drafting help from Political Counselor John Wolf, and after clearing the text with State, I went public with remarks "intended to provoke you [Pakistanis] into thinking hard about the pros and cons of nuclear weapons for Pakistan."

Additionally, a more careful redo of my off-the-record remarks to the National Defense College, my "Reflections on Nuclear Issues in South Asia," made the case against atomic weapons and made clear that the decision "is Pakistan's to make, and only Pakistan's." It also spelled out "the new strength and maturity" in the U.S.-Pakistan relationship.

Still, it was no surprise when my remarks provoked a firestorm of press criticism. Publication in some cases of my full text was, however, I thought, a positive result.

In March, President Zia said the public should focus on the beneficial uses of nuclear energy "rather than on fallacies, fantasies, and fabrications" that make "my dear friend Deane Hinton's life more difficult." Later that month, Zia told *Time* magazine, "Pakistan can build a bomb whenever it wishes."

***

Generally, my forays into public diplomacy were not as focused, but almost always I volunteered to answer questions. This helped me learn of and reply to the concerns of ordinary Pakistanis. My interviews with leading newspapers and magazines were particularly useful in getting American views before the public. I spoke to widely varying groups, among them the National Honor Society, the First Pakistan National Coal Conference, the Lahore Business School, the English Speaking Union, and the King Edward Medical College. With a desire to understand Pakistan beyond the main cities, I also gave talks in Multan, Faisalabad, Peshawar, and Hyderabad. Naturally, I also tried to respond to all interested American journalists, whether print, radio, or TV.

Pakistanis, who are polite to a failing, never called me "a fascist pig," as I was labeled when I spoke on "Contemporary South Asia" at Columbia University. Still, I often provoked adverse reactions and controversy. Nevertheless, as I left, I was pleased with an appraisal in Pakistan's leading newspaper. After noting accusations that I had betrayed the basic code of diplomacy by stirring up controversy with comments on nuclear policy, narcotics, the Middle East, elections, and Pakistani politicians advocating direct negotiations with the Kabul communist regime, *The Nation* wrote:

> Now, however, one realizes that Hinton provided a new substance to the art of diplomacy during his stay in Pakistan. Instead of hushing things up and projecting a goody-goody image with hypocritical smiles, he brought into public the differences supposed to be settled and discussed in comfortable conference rooms by vague and elusive diplomats. It is for the people of Pakistan to accept or reject them. This clarity of issues is a tremendous contribution made by Hinton.

Of course, my main persuasive efforts were in private, but they did not work either, even when President Reagan weighed in. The president was markedly different from other senior Americans I had known. At a key NSC meeting on Afghanistan, he spent the first twenty minutes or so telling stories and joking with Charles Wick, head of USIA. Later, after some serious discussion, he instructed me to persuade General Zia to release the Soviet prisoners detained by Pakistan.

In July of 1986, Prime Minister Junejo visited Washington at the president's invitation. The intent was to show that we welcomed the end of martial law and to get the measure of the man. He was given a red carpet welcome, a state dinner at the White House, and meetings with the president and senior cabinet members. His visit ended with a trip to Disney World in the presidential plane.

In Orlando, all went well until the prime minister declined, for religious reasons, to eat the lobster he had been served. After an embarrassing delay while a fish course was prepared for him, he appeared to leave happy and expressed great satisfaction with his reception in the States.

For me, the highlight of the trip was joining the president and Mrs. Reagan before dinner, when they entertained the prime minister upstairs in the White House.

The president raised nuclear issues in a restricted meeting. Junejo said Pakistan's program was entirely peaceful. However, he pled unfamiliarity with details like the red line on Pakistan's enriching uranium beyond 5 percent. We had reason for concern that the red line had been exceeded, and Junejo promised to look into the situation upon his return to Pakistan.

On September 9, I followed up with the prime minister in a private meeting. He assured me that Pakistan was not enriching above 5 percent. I remarked, "This would be welcome news for the president." But I also observed that our differences over nuclear weapons policy were unfortunate. When Junejo wondered if we could help Pakistan with its energy problem, I replied we could and would if Pakistan met conditions specified by Congress. I suggested, "We could talk quietly and confidentially of how Pakistan might adopt full-scope safeguards." Even though Foreign Minister Yaqub Khan had told me such a scenario "was not worth talking about," I thought that "with political will" it could be done. For starters, we would need "to verify that enrichment levels are under 5 percent." Junejo promised to reflect on the matter, and I reported "Eyes Only" to Under Secretary Armacost.

I believed Junejo would come around. His political standing would get a real boost with a breakthrough on Pakistan's critical energy problem. Indeed he soon authorized talks.

I followed up by cable and went next to Washington. It was hard, slow going, but I eventually obtained authority to conduct confidential talks. While I doubted that Zia, for whom security was critical, would let talks go far enough to resolve matters, there was little else to try.

Congressional resistance to the administration's request for a six-year waiver of the Symington-Pressler Amendment helped me get approval to try talks. It dramatized the view, increasingly shared by key individuals in Washington, that we were headed for a disastrous breakup in our relation with Pakistan.

On March 29, 1987, I had a long meeting with Zia and Foreign Secretary Abdul Sattar to discuss how we might conduct talks aimed at reaching an understanding. They had agreed to "a serious dialogue" and the foreign secretary had been named to conduct one-on-one talks with me. Foreign Minister Yaqub Khan still viewed the effort as a waste of time but acquiesced to the "prime minister's directives."

Sattar was the senior career diplomat in the Foreign Ministry. He was well known to me and to Mike Armacost. In the past, we had held extensive talks with him about many issues and had frequently played tennis together. I thought him able and tough but well disposed towards the United States. His choice was good news, even though I expected he would endeavor to spin the talks out.

Nevertheless, I could not hope to reach an understanding in the short time I had left in Islamabad. But I did hope to clear the way for my successor, Arnie Raphel. I told Zia that the most important statement in my "Reflections on Nuclear Issues in South Asia" was: "We must this year win approval of both houses of Congress to extend the present Symington waiver. Congress, not just the president, will decide if we are able to continue aid past 1987."

Noting that the administration could probably hold the line as long as we had a shared interest in evicting the Soviets from Afghanistan, I challenged him and Sattar to think of how the relationship could survive post-Afghanistan.

Zia said it would be difficult and agreed, "as a working assumption," that we should look at the nuclear issue as if the Afghan problem were solved. He preferred, however, a more regional approach and disliked the emphasis on Pakistan.

With the constrained green light from Zia, and after some more back and forth with Washington—which understandably gave me less scope for maneuver than I had sought—Sattar and I met on April 23, May 5, and June 3.

Sattar began our first meeting by asking me to explain our objective. I said we wanted to preserve and strengthen our relations, and for this we needed an understanding on Pakistan's nuclear weapons program. We believed it would be in Pakistan's best interest to sign the NPT. I suggested that we adopt the Jean Monnet approach and put the nuclear question on the other side of the table while the two of us worked together to find a solution.

He replied that there were two practical reasons—political and security concerns—why it would be extraordinarily difficult to sign the NPT. He followed with a long historical exegesis about political support for Bhutto's nuclear policy and about the U.S. arms cutoff during the disastrous 1965 war with India, which had led the public to view the United States as an unreliable ally. He pressed hard for a nondiscriminatory U.S. policy vis-à-vis India and Pakistan. Why, he asked, didn't the Symington amendment also apply to India?

We touched on many other points before adjourning "for reflection." The crux, he said, was Pakistan's "irresistible desire for self-reliance," its need for "self-confidence."

He hinted that a treaty might provide the needed confidence by pointing out that our executive agreement, while valuable vis-à-vis the Soviets, is "of no relevance to the South Asia security problem."

On May 5, we spent much time on India in tough, frank discussion. Sattar pledged that Pakistan would offer India "a complete test ban" and try to resuscitate a 1981 agreement by their foreign ministers that "nuclear development should be exclusively for peaceful purposes." He objected to legislation singling out Pakistan, such as the Symington amendment, and urged the United States to adopt a "regional approach" in legislation concerning South Asia and the Middle East. He noted that his formulation excluded Israel.

He concluded our second meeting by agreeing to my "quixotic" suggestion that we discuss ways Pakistan might go ahead with the NPT, but added that we should also consider "how the United States can contribute to promoting the security of Pakistan and confidence on the part of Pakistan in the U.S. connection."

After this session, I noted in my report, "The key remains what we can do about Pakistan's security concerns." I repeated my suggestion that we use "ambiguous language" that might appeal to the Pakistanis without committing us to much of anything. I noted that the Soviets had done this with "the smoke and mirrors" they had included in their Treaty of Peace, Friendship, and Cooperation with India. I also suggested that we consider offering not to cut off assistance to Pakistan if it were attacked. While I recognized that a NATO-type treaty commitment was impossible, given congressional realities, with the stakes so high I urged that we seek imaginative ways to reassure Pakistan.

In our final and longest session, Sattar informed me that Junejo had written to Gandhi and proposed a test ban treaty, either bilateral or regional. He promised a vigorous diplomatic follow-up. He also said that an investigation, ordered by Junejo, of our claims that Pakistan was evading our prohibitions on the export of sensitive nuclear components had turned up nothing. He continued, however, that since the prime minister recognized "rogue" elements might so act, Pakistan would welcome more specific information about our allegations. If supplied, they would act. After a recapitulation of our discussion, I told Sattar we were involved in a "Greek tragedy" and were on a collision course.

Regrettably, I was right.

Our talks had led to no major breakthrough. But I was satisfied; I had tried, made progress on secondary issues, and, I thought, prepared the ground for my successor or a rumored special presidential envoy. And although I failed in my efforts to stop Pakistan's nuclear program, I had some success with other initiatives.

Knowing how important our local employees are to the embassy's overall efforts, I invited key Pakistanis on our staff to lunch at the residence. It was a great success and was much appreciated. To my amazement, I learned that never before had such a lunch been held.

I also proposed bringing back Peace Corps members. Shortly after I left Islamabad, my successor, Ambassador Arnold Raphel, cabled to tell me the first volunteers had arrived.

But a more important success was establishing an Afghan humanitarian aid program. As Afghanistan became a popular cause, both Congress and eager beavers within the executive branch pressured for various humanitarian projects. A few experienced NGOs, such as the International Committee of the Red Cross and the International Rescue Committee, were doing good work. Unfortunately, many NGO efforts were almost worthless or had backfired, complicating relations with Pakistan. To bring order to a deteriorating situation, I proposed a study of the relevant problems and possibilities to Najmuddin Sheikh, the officer in charge of American affairs at the Foreign Ministry. He liked the idea. After some delay, presumably to consult higher authority, he gave me a green light. AID administrator Peter McPherson assigned Larry Crandall to the study project.

Larry did an excellent job. His report, presented to Najmuddin and me, recommended a clear path forward. Next, we needed to convince Zia. Larry joined me in presenting the plan to him, and Zia told us he would think it over. Eventually, he agreed, on condition that we work closely with the Seven Party Mujahideen Alliance.

I told Larry he was my candidate to carry out the plan. He demurred, pointing out that he was slated to attend the National War College and did not want to lose that prize assignment. I told him Afghanistan was much more important. McPherson agreed and assigned a highly annoyed, but disciplined, Larry Crandall to my embassy. Months later, Larry told me that organizing and running the AID humanitarian program was the most satisfying thing he had ever done.

One of his major problems, however, was not accounted for in the plan. It arose from the congressional mandate to get Defense Department surplus items to the Afghans. The McCollum Amendment was a good idea; but in practice, it left much to be desired. Far from all of the items supplied from Defense Department stocks were usable. Far worse, after much hesitation Prime Minister Junejo only agreed to the McCollum program provided the rules governing the C.I.A.'s covert imports were also applied to humanitarian imports.

The beauty of humanitarian assistance, I had convinced Najmuddin Sheikh and Zia, was that it could and would be delivered openly. The McCollum program was humanitarian as far as our Congress was concerned, but Junejo's decision made it covert for Pakistan. The resulting emphasis on secrecy meant that C-5 flights with McCollum surplus items landed about midnight. They had to be unloaded, their cargo inventoried, and then delivered to approved Afghans before dawn. But since there was a congressional mandate, Larry and his small staff had to struggle manfully; but it detracted from their basic function.

Apart from McCollum items, Larry used contractors, under his close supervision, to establish an efficient program concentrated on providing food and medical supplies to the Afghans. A problem he never solved, however, was to teach donkeys and mules, bought for the humanitarian program, not to carry weapons and ammo once they disappeared into Afghanistan.

For fiscal year 1986, the administration requested $14 million for this new program and $625 million for the final year of the $3.2

billion five-year economic assistance program. Appropriations for the regular program provoked much congressional opposition because of concerns about nuclear weapons, but eventually passed. The humanitarian program, on the contrary, was inordinately popular. Charlie Wilson developed into a rabid supporter. Indeed, McPherson soon found that Congress was appropriating more for the program than he sought or OMB approved—an unusual problem for AID.

As our five-year economic assistance program was ending, the Pakistan government began building pressure for a major increase. Minister of Planning Mahbub ul Haq told the press it had to double. Privately, I told him he should not be building false expectations. However, Mahbub and others kept on, even after Secretary Shultz said that doubling "is simply not in the cards." As the date for talks approached, the two countries' positions were far apart. I was worried that the gap might be unbridgeable.

One day, I was surprised by a telephone call from Zia, asking if he could stop by "for tea." After some amiable conversation, the president came to the point of his visit. He said that if our existing program were somehow increased by a billion dollars, all would be well.

Our under secretary of state for security assistance, science, and technology, William Schneider, Jr., led our delegation. Mian Muhammad Yasin Khan Wattoo, minister of finance and economic affairs, led theirs. After three days of difficult talks, agreement was reached—subject to U.S. congressional approval—on a package of economic assistance and military sales of $4.02 billion for six years. It was spread over a year longer than the earlier package, had a different mix—more PL 480, for example—and a bit of creative accounting; but it was a billion dollar increase. Zia approved the deal.

Pakistan fascinated us. Despite the heat, flies, snakes, and all-too-frequent state visits, we loved it. State visits, counting time to and from the airport for arrivals and then departures, took at least nine hours, including less than sixty seconds with the honored visitor. Coca-Cola in wine glasses at state dinners did not help, nor did the normal absence of all but diplomatic corps females. Quite accurately, an Argentine colleague once remarked, "Only thing wrong with Pakistan is that it lacks wine, women, and song."

In Islamabad, Lahore, and Karachi, we knew many socially active Pakistan ladies. In rural areas, as in Afghan refugee camps, it was markedly different. When Patricia and I would call on key individuals, she would be escorted into the women's quarters. I talked with the men, she with the women.

Once, on the Makran Coast, Larry Grahl and I had to leave a meeting with local officials to rescue our wives from a near-riot. Despite warnings to stay with our vehicles, they had wandered into Turbat, where unveiled women, much less Western women, were never seen. Hundreds of men had gathered around them. Perhaps they were only curious, but the situation was frightening.

Snakes were common behind our year-old residence. Built on a virgin plot on the edge of town, snakes had not yet been frightened away. To accomplish that, we first tried mongooses, but jackals finally eliminated them. Then we got geese, which were too messy. So we tried peacocks. They seemed to work better but were awfully noisy.

Pakistan's geography includes many of the world's highest mountains and some of the hottest places on earth. Its history is long and complicated, its layered cultures too many to list. But, importantly, they include Mohenjo-Daro (roughly B.C. 3300 to B.C. 1300), a Bronze Age city of the Indus Valley Civilization; the Buddhist Kingdom of Gandara (B.C. 1000 to A.D. 1100), which was conquered by the Persians of Cyrus the Great (reign: 559–530 B.C.), then by Alexander the Great (327 B.C.), who died in what is now Pakistan. There was a Hindu dynasty, replaced by Muslim conquerors, followed by the British who ruled until the formation of Pakistan in 1947.

Serving in Pakistan gave us many opportunities to travel, and having two C-12 aircraft made it more enjoyable. Not only did these planes permit me to make official visits to much of the country, but they also allowed Patricia and me to visit other countries, especially in the region. We attended chiefs of mission meetings in Nepal, Bangladesh, Sri Lanka, and India, relaxed on the beaches of the Maldives, and visited Greece and Cyprus with Sebastian on the way back from home leave. Returning from a trip to Washington, I once spent three fabulous days in Istanbul. And in India, we, of course, visited the Taj Mahal.

The embassy had a number of highly competent attaché pilots. Before long, I could tell who was piloting by how we landed. Army pilots were my favorite, since they flew like careful commercial passenger plane pilots. Navy pilots, carrier-trained, hit the runway hard. Air Force pilots, trained on B-52s, glided a long way before touching down, while those trained to fly fighters descended fast and leveled out at the last moment.

One day, I was called and informed that our two-plane Air Force had been knocked out on the ground. Shades of General MacArthur! We, however, had no warning. A 747 belonging to Pakistan International Airlines had carelessly gunned its engines and blown unsecured baggage containers into our C-12s. Uncle Sam was eventually reimbursed, but repairs took a long time. Later, a 747 pilot neglected to lower his gear until it was too late, thereby endangering several hundred passengers. Fortunately, the plane did not catch fire, but several days passed before it could be moved off Islamabad airport's runway, thereby grounding our Air Force once again.

In nearby Fatehpur Sikri, a now largely abandoned city built by Mughal Emperor Akbar, we heard about the Sufi holy man to whose powers the emperor attributed the birth of his son. In gratitude, he had built a shrine for the holy man. It is said that if you tie a string to the shrine's latticework and make a wish, your wish will be granted. I wished for a son. Nine months later Deane Patrick Akbar George Hinton joined our family!

Weighing in at 7 pounds 12 ounces, Akbar was born in Wiesbaden, Germany, since the embassy doctor in Islamabad thought Patricia's caesarean would be safer in an American Air Force hospital. Quite so, but she almost did not make it to Wiesbaden.

On September 5, 1986, four terrorists of the Abu Nidal Organization, with Libyan participation in the planning, seized Pan Am Flight 73 in Karachi. After seventeen confused hours, Pakistan commandos stormed the plane, prompting the terrorists to retaliate with automatic rifle fire and grenades. In all, twenty-two persons, including two Americans, were killed. More than a hundred passengers were injured. The terrorists were arrested, tried, convicted, and sentenced to death by a court in Pakistan.

Patricia had originally been booked on that ill-fated flight. Her last-minute decision, endorsed by her doctor, to spend an extra week in Pakistan before heading north, saved her from a horrible experience.

Watching my son's birth was a new experience. In the 1940s, '50s, and early '60s, letting the father watch, if not ruled out, was discouraged. Yet in Wiesbaden, I not only watched but also filmed our son's birth. It was a wonderful experience that brought me closer to Akbar and to Patricia.

In Fatehpur Sikri, it is also said that if your wish is granted, you should return to the shrine, untie a string, and make a donation of gratitude. Descendants of the original holy man maintain the shrine, living off these donations. I decided that when Akbar was old enough to appreciate India and I was still young enough to travel there, I would return to the city, untie a string, and let him tie one and make a wish.

When years later the Indian consul in Panama asked me why we wanted visas for India, I told him the story of what I viewed as Akbar's miraculous birth, given my age at the time. I wanted to return and untie a string. The consul, looking skeptical, asked me if I really believed in the shrine's powers. "No," I replied, "but I want Akbar to see India."

For years, Akbar declined to tell me about his wish. Finally, he confessed that his wish was never again to travel in India. This disappointed me, but I suspect he'll get over his aversion to the country.

Patricia had insisted our baby would be a girl. Convinced it would be a boy, I even commissioned a well-known miniature artist in Lahore to make a copy of the famous miniature of the Emperor Akbar. Someday, Akbar will inherit that picture.

Perhaps the most memorable trip was the one that took me to Kashgar in China. The summer of 1985, my stepson, Juanjo, was visiting, and we planned to drive to Kashmir. The Indian ambassador to Islamabad made the arrangements for us, complete with an armed escort in the troubled Punjab. Nevertheless, to our annoyance, Embassy New Delhi vetoed the trip.

So instead, Juanjo and I decided to drive some 800 miles to Kashgar, the fabled Silk Road city in Western China. The Chinese ambassador gave us visas, including one for Khala Khan, my driver. He also gave me a letter saying I wanted to travel in my own vehicle and asking the Xinjiang authorities "to satisfy his request as much as possible."

We drove up the spectacularly scenic Karakorum Highway, overnighted at a chilly, if attractive, guesthouse in Hunza, then went over the 16,000-foot Khunjerab pass into China.

At Taxkorgan, we were welcomed by a Mr. Lee, who in broken English insisted that we travel to Kashgar in a Chinese vehicle with a Chinese chauffeur. He was not impressed by the letter from his ambassador in Islamabad.

The call to dinner came at 3 o'clock in the afternoon. We thought it was too early for dinner, but we learned that it was in fact 5 p.m. Peking time! There is, we understood, only one time zone in all of China.

The next day, we headed to Kashgar. The road was terrible, but the scenery along the Pamir mountain range was fantastic. We passed yaks, camels, and a few yurts of nomadic Uighurs.

En route, I told Mr. Lee that we wanted to stay near the bazaar in the historic British consulate, now a hotel. British consuls had been important actors in the Great Game played out by the Russians and British in Central Asia. I thought we should vicariously share in that history.

Mr. Lee ignored my wishes. He had his driver take us to a new hotel on the outskirts of Kashgar. When I repeated where we wanted to stay, Mr. Lee said we would stay in "this fine hotel, the best in Kashgar."

Annoyed, I asked, "Are we prisoners or guests?" After this difficult exchange, Mr. Lee disappeared, probably to consult his superiors.

Upon returning, he said, "OK, you can stay in a central hotel, but not at the old British consulate." After more palaver, we finally arrived at the former British consulate.

There was no one at the reception desk, and no one responded to our shouts. As we turned away, I saw a Westerner and asked where everyone was. He didn't know but advised against staying, saying one had to carry one's water from elsewhere. So we let Mr. Lee take us to another nearby hotel with running water. He and China had won.

The Chinese jeep broke down several times, both while coming and going. While the Chinese driver was unable to fix it, fortunately Khala Khan could.

On our way back to Pakistan, just below the summit the Karakorum Highway was blocked by a large landslide that went into the Khunjerab River. Pakistani army engineers told us it would be several days before the slide could be cleared. This was mighty bad news; we feared we would have to return to China. Then, Khala Khan waded into the freezing river past the slide. He returned to announce that the bottom was firm and thought he could drive us through the river around the slide. As we collectively held our breath, he did just that. During the Second World War, Khala Khan, altogether a remarkable man, had driven a tank for the British in Burma.

Back in Islamabad, there were rumors about an Iranian plot to assassinate me. Coming out of the Embassy compound one night, I spotted a car pull out from a side road. When it began following us, I asked Khala Khan to turn first one way then another. Then another car joined the chase. As we were near the AID Mission, I warned the guards there that we would be coming in at speed. When we did, both trailing cars went on by.

Thankfully, it was a false alarm. One car was from my security staff, the other from Pakistani intelligence! Since neither had told anyone of their plan to follow my car, we were lucky not to have had a shootout.

Informally I had learned that our next post would be Ankara, which pleased Patricia as well as me. Indeed, I had asked for assignment to Turkey right after basic training forty years before. However, it was not to be.

Robert Strausz-Hupé, a friend from my days in Brussels when he had been ambassador to NATO, did not want to leave. Eventually, Secretary Schultz visited Ankara to tell Robert that, at eighty-three, it was time for him to move on. Robert agreed, but once the secretary flew off, Strausz-Hupé called his longtime friend, Ronald Reagan, and asked the president if he was too old to serve. Not surprisingly, the president thought not and told Robert to stay in Ankara. When word of this filtered through, I told Patricia it was time for me to retire.

However, during a courtesy call on Deputy Secretary John Whitehead, he surprised me by suggesting that I take the embassy in Costa Rica. I thought Patricia would love San José. Moreover, given the conflicts in Central America, San José had become a challenging assignment. After confirming that Patricia liked the idea, I told Director General George Vest I was interested. After some delay, the Senate confirmed me as ambassador to Costa Rica.

24

Costa Rica (1987–1989)

In 1974 I had declined the embassy in Costa Rica, asserting, "I am too young to retire." But by 1987, San Jose was no longer an easy post. Its central challenge came from the conflicting views of two presidents about how to deal with the Sandinista regime in Nicaragua.

President Ronald Reagan, whom I represented, thought the Contras were the answer. President Oscar Arias of Costa Rica, to whom I was accredited, thought the Contras were the problem. I was in the middle, where ambassadors frequently are, but seldom is the policy conflict as stark.

For my part, I thought a Contra victory unlikely. They appeared to lack widespread popular support in Nicaragua and suffered from being an American-sponsored mercenary force. A frequently quarreling leadership was another weakness. I was convinced, however, that they provided essential negotiating leverage on the Sandinistas. With only a few mental reservations, I had no problem confronting Arias.

Arias had been awarded the Nobel Peace Prize in 1987 for his idealistic plan for peace in Central America. Clearly, the Norwegians who bestowed the award were criticizing American policy. Not surprisingly, their decision annoyed the administration. As I was being briefed in Washington, I heard kind words for Arias only from Democrats.

During my time in Costa Rica, I thought it had been wrong to have awarded the Peace Prize to Arias, since his plan had not produced results. Then in 1990, while I was serving in Panama, the Nicaraguans, in the elections for which Arias had fought so hard, ousted Daniel Ortega, the Sandinista president. Violeta Chamorro, leader of the opposition, was overwhelmingly elected.

Many, including myself, had been skeptical that a Marxist regime would permit itself to be voted out of office. Ortega had completely misjudged his popularity. Now, I, too, thought Arias deserved his Nobel Peace Prize.

In August 1987 the Democrats arranged for Arias to speak on the floor of the House. He had wanted to address a joint session of Congress, but the Republican administration blocked that. A friend got me a ticket to the gallery. Arias was eloquent but, to me, far from convincing.

What were the guarantees of the promised "democratization" of Nicaragua? Was it right to equate the situation in El Salvador with Marxist Nicaragua? Here, I gave much weight to my experiences in El Salvador. I knew the Sandinistas had intervened long before the Contras came into being. How about Soviet and Cuban support for the Sandinistas?

Arias, I later learned, had an answer to the point about the Soviets and Cubans. He said he had deliberately not dealt with the question, because he did not want to hinder U.S. support for the Salvadoran Government. Sophistry? Anyway, it was only after the collapse of the Soviet Union that Ortega agreed to elections with foreign observers.

Due to maddening bureaucratic delays, it was November 17 when I finally presented my credentials. Privately and publicly, I praised the Esquipulas II Accord, stressing its democratic features. President Arias said little. His brother, minister of the presidency and acting foreign minister in the absence of Foreign Minister Rodrigo Madrigal, talked about their debt problem and the need for more U.S. assistance.

Soon I had reason to call on the president. In his waiting room, I was astonished by the pictures and busts of Oscar Arias. Many politicians collect pictures of themselves with other leaders, but except for one picture with the pope, Oscar's pictures were of himself at various points in his career. Politicians have to have egos to survive, but Oscar's ego struck me as extreme.

While in Washington, I had read of Oscar lecturing President Reagan to the effect that the Contras could not and would not defeat the Sandinista regime. Also, the press reported that he had infuriated Bill Casey by making it clear that he meant what he had said about "neutrality." I knew that the Tower Report convinced the Government of Costa Rica that the United States had lied in pledging not to continue use of an airstrip in northern Costa Rica, approved by Luis Alberto Monge, Arias's predecessor as president, but vetoed by Arias when he took office. Clearly, dealing with Arias against a background of mistrust would not be easy.

Life in beautiful Costa Rica, "sandwiched between bloody Nicaragua and corrupt Panama," was delightful. Having both my infant son and my aged father living with us was a special treat. Dad enjoyed playing with Akbar and Akbar enjoyed teasing him. The ninety-one-year age difference seemingly drew them closer, as did shared love for Akbar's basset hound "Droopy." Dad's vision was too bad to enjoy TV, but he could see a dog. He loved to pet Droopy and was upset if the dog was busy when he called.

Soon Patricia and I received an invitation from prominent businessman Ricardo Falla and his wife. We were told the other guests would be President and Mrs. Arias, so "we could get to know each other in an informal setting." A great idea, I thought, and attributed it, rightly or wrongly, to Oscar. The Fallas became good friends, but we found it hard going with Margarita and Oscar. Patricia thought she was "dull." Early in the evening, he asked me what I thought of the situation in Yugoslavia! His offbeat question and my fumbling for an answer put a damper on the dinner for me.

As I came to know Arias better, I developed an appreciation for his intellect and for his stubborn pursuit of what he thought was right. In March 1989, I told *Time* magazine, "He brings together pacifism, idealism, and neutrality, but also some very hard-edged political skills."

I also admired his ability to turn a phrase. For example, asked about Fidel Castro, he dismissed him, saying, "He still lives in the Sierra Maestra. Doesn't know it is 1989." On the other hand, I remained skeptical of his optimistic belief that he could persuade Ortega to risk free elections. And I deplored what I viewed as his social gaffes.

Gaetana Enders, a friend for over twenty years, called me from New York to ask if I could get her an interview with Arias. Nothing easier, he thrived on publicity and liked to give interviews, especially one-on-one interviews. Gaetana later told me they had talked for well over an hour at his residence but he never offered her coffee or even a glass of water. Incredible! At a luncheon he hosted for Secretary Schultz, Arias did not answer a key question from the secretary until reminded of it by Foreign Minister Madrigal.

Rodrigo Madrigal was an outstanding foreign minister. He led a first class staff, headed by Luis Guillermo Solis. The "peace process" involved many meetings below the head of state level. To try to follow what was going on, members of my team or I met regularly, depending on the level of the Central American discussions, with Arias or with Madrigal or with the minister's staff. We also cross-checked accounts of key meetings with different individuals and against reporting from other embassies and the press.

Arias had two key advisors. His brother, Rodrigo Arias, as minister of the presidency, oversaw virtually all issues, other than foreign policy. For foreign policy, to Foreign Minister Madrigal's discomfort, John Biehl often had more sway than the minister.

Biehl and Arias had become good friends years before at the University of Essex. They had worked together in the electoral campaign, in drafting the "Peace Plan," and in lobbying for the Nobel Prize.

Biehl was a Chilean of Danish extraction who for over ten years had worked for the United Nations on Central American development issues. Of leftist statist political persuasion, Biehl was given to outspoken criticism of United States policies, economic as well as political. His barbed remarks annoyed me. Nor did many Costa Ricans approve of their president having a foreigner as a close advisor. When Biehl's comments about our president infuriated Reaganites, conflict of interest questions were raised. Biehl lost his U.N. job, but remained close to Arias.

An ambassador should, of course, know key individuals. However, after my early approaches were met by Biehl with barely disguised hostility, I gave up. I tried again when George H. W. Bush succeeded Reagan and our Contra policy shifted. Biehl accepted my invitation to a symphony concert, but would not discuss our differences. I should have known better.

With the American community, I hit it off early. Ambassador Lewis Tambs had vetoed holding the Fourth of July reception on the large grounds of the residence. When a committee headed by Jack Fendell asked me to resume a years-old tradition, my immediate "Yes" made me many friends.

Despite our policy differences, Costa Ricans from the president on down were basically well disposed toward the United States and fairly forthcoming about their negotiating situation. Yet, most Ticos were hard to know well. Apart from Arias and Madrigal, whom I knew well because we had so many common interests, I viewed only Carlos Manuel Castillo and Vice President Jorge Dengo as friends.

I had first known Carlos Manuel when I was in Guatemala and he was secretary general of SIECA, an organization promoting Central American integration. In Costa Rica, he had served as central bank president, cabinet minister, vice president, and now was seeking the presidency in the 1990 elections. His views on economic policy were second to none. I, of course, was hoping my old friend would win, but after a 1989 World Cup qualifying soccer game between Costa Rica and the United States, which I observed was attended by every significant Costa Rican politician except my friend, I knew he would lose, as he did. He lacked the common touch.

Vice President Jorge Dengo was high on my mandatory call list, but he turned out to be unique. From the beginning he made two things clear. He wanted to educate me about his beloved country and he knew that his position was largely symbolic. He had a title, a fine office, a reputation as an outstanding manager and electrical engineer, but no line responsibilities. Courtesy calls rarely last long, but Dengo and I chatted for almost an hour. Finally, he lent me a book that he said would help me understand his countrymen. It was an account of Costa Rican opposition to construction of the Pan American Highway. Only during World War II, after years of Costa Rican opposition, had FDR finally persuaded the Ticos to support the project. Dengo was telling me Ticos are isolationists at heart. This was one reason, I decided, why Costa Rica is called the Switzerland of Central America.

Later I learned how right he was. The Peace Plan called for the six signatories to join a Central American parliament. All did except for Costa Rica. Arias found it weakened his case with Nicaragua that he had not complied with a provision of his own plan. I was enlisted to help round up votes in the Assembly. I invited key individuals to lunch, as I did to advance many other issues of interest to the U.S. Soon, however, I was in hot water. Various parliamentarians found it helped them with their electorate to denounce me for "lobbying." In the course of a nationalist uproar, I noted overtones of racism. There were few Native Americans left in Costa Rica. Costa Ricans, it was clear, did not want to risk being outvoted by an Indian-Mayan majority in a Central American parliament.

In Washington in May 1988 for a Chiefs of Mission Conference at Airlie House, I may have overdone criticisms. I urged that views from the field be sought more often. "You never know, you might learn something." I thought the department was overdoing detailed demarches. Rather than telling embassies how to do their job, I recommended telling them what needed to be accomplished.

At the conference Assistant Secretary Elliot Abrams focused a great deal of attention on Panama. He was hopeful that Manuel Noriega, Panama's military dictator, was about to give up. To our regret, before we left we learned that the negotiations to persuade Noriega to leave Panama had failed.

In discussing Panama, I argued it was counterproductive to ignore President Arias. Rather we should consult with him and try to engage his vanity. Elliot, who intensely disliked both Arias and his peace plan, was far from convinced. Still it should have been done, even if it made little or no difference.

Late in 1988, I received an appreciative letter from Secretary George P. Shultz. He presumably wrote many as the Reagan administration came to an end. I treasure mine. While his "no one will forget" line is a gross exaggeration, otherwise his letter showed, I thought, an unusual awareness of my service. In part he wrote:

> No one will forget your courageous efforts to promote democracy and human rights in El Salvador, or the skill with which you managed our important and complex relations with Pakistan. I especially appreciate your determination to speak the truth as you see it, even when your views have been unpopular or controversial.

The election of George H. W. Bush as president and the appointment of James Baker as secretary of state produced major policy changes. On March 24, 1989, a bipartisan agreement with Congress, negotiated by Baker, ended our military support for the Contras. Political support for Nicaraguan freedom and humanitarian assistance to the resistance were to continue. Bush called for the end of Sandinista subversion of others, e.g. El Salvador, and of Soviet-Cuban support for insurgents. This fundamental policy change made relations with Arias much easier. "The Brady Plan," a new approach to Latin American debt, also helped.

Oscar welcomed the policy changes "with great satisfaction." He also took credit for them, some of which he deserved. As was his wont, however, he overdid it. Soon thereafter he wrote President Bush suggesting increased cooperation in the war against drugs. Bush accepted the offer and proposed specific implementation steps. Relations were now more solid than ever. I breathed easier.

Shortly after our elections, I had had a period of serious worry. Rumor had it that I was under consideration to replace Elliot Abrams as assistant secretary for Latin America. I knew I was qualified, but I also knew that at sixty-six it would be a mistake for me to take on such a stressful job. Fortunately, Baker recognized that a younger man was needed. Bernard Aronson was chosen. He was an outstanding choice: bright, energetic, and, interestingly, a Democrat, but one who had been highly critical of Ortega and the Sandinistas.

Soon the president invited Arias to Washington. Aronson correctly viewed this as an opportunity to show that the new administration would work with, not against, Arias. Bernie arranged for an Air Force plane to fly Oscar from Miami to Washington. He then decided we should meet Oscar in Miami. These gestures contributed to a successful visit.

Activities in San José were similar to those in other posts: countless courtesy calls, receptions, lunches, dinners, Marine Balls, press interviews, speeches, and visitors, leavened with tennis and tourism. In addition to the overriding political crisis in Central America, many problems were familiar, e.g. development, economic assistance, debt, and drugs. Instead of Afghan *mujahideen*, here the United States was backing the Nicaraguan National Resistance. There were also new issues—expropriations, official misbehavior, a move into a new Chancery, and an appearance before the Inter-American Court on Human Rights. I was not bored.

Appearing before the court was a new experience but far from a demanding one. I read an opening statement written by State Department lawyers and they handled subsequent oral arguments. Our view that the court lacked jurisdiction prevailed.

Since automobiles imported duty free could often be sold at a handsome profit, Foreign Service regulations basically prohibited profits while leaving some post flexibility in implementation. In Costa Rica profits were to go to a charity chosen by the seller. Unfortunately, some officials could not resist the temptation to cheat. When I learned that a young Foreign Service officer had not only profited from a car sale but had also perjured himself by falsely swearing to its imported value and to its sale price, I asked for a Foreign Service inspector to conduct a formal investigation. Two other cases turned up, but these involved AID officers. The inspector recommended dismissal of the FSO and referred the other two cases to AID. In due course the FSO was fired. To my annoyance, the AID officers were merely reprimanded and transferred.

A young officer, John Naland, filed a complaint against his boss and after some unpleasantness was found to have had good reason for his complaint. John went on to be an outstanding president of the American Foreign Service Association.

A more serious and far from clear case involved congressional probes, the AID inspector general, and high-level interventions from both the Costa Rican and American governments. This case hit the American press in January 1988. I had been briefed in Washington about problems concerning loose practices with the use of counterpart funds and had been urged to press the government to take better control. My efforts encountered resistance but eventually a solution was found.

When I arrived in San Jose, I was surprised to find that the AID mission was to move to new housing that appeared to be more opulent than President Arias's offices. It had been built with counterpart funds generated by our economic assistance. I thought this building reflected bad judgment by the AID director.

Dan Chaij, the AID director who had had these extravagant new offices built, was no longer at post. I had known him and thought well of him when he had served with me as an assistant AID director in El Salvador. Dan was an imaginative and hard charging official. Given the furor, I had to get to the bottom of what looked like a scandal and see to it that nothing like it occurred again.

The problem originated with the Costa Rica government. Ministers had learned from experience that the National Assembly was incapable of expeditiously appropriating Costa Rican counterpart for the kind of development projects we insisted upon. Rather than let hundreds of millions of colones depreciate in frozen accounts, it had allowed, even urged, AID to allocate Costa Rican owned counterpart with minimal reference to it. Dan had taken full advantage of this highly anomalous situation. The government basically approved of what he did.

It took much effort to dig into the record, but I became convinced that generally Dan had done extremely well. By financing a few privately owned banks, he had provided needed competition to a monopoly of government-owned banks. He used counterpart to endow a tropical agriculture research facility (EARTH) and a semiautonomous institution (CINDE) to promote foreign private investment in Costa Rica. He also impacted education, funding hundreds of scholarships for bright Costa Ricans to attend U.S. universities. Here, however, I agreed with our investigators that he had made some serious mistakes.

Dan had authorized about a dozen scholarships for well off students whose parents were influential individuals. Presumably, he did this to gain support for worthwhile projects. However, this use of funds was contrary to approved project agreements.

It was clearly wrong, as was AID funding of CADES, a Seventh-day Adventist educational institution with which Chaij had family connections. Dan's otherwise remarkable record of achievement was tarnished. It little mattered that almost all of the charges leveled against him did not hold up.

Today, Costa Rica no longer requires AID assistance, banking is much more competitive, a government research facility occupies the fancy building that had so bothered me, and both EARTH and CINDE are important, well-functioning institutions.

When I arrived in San José the Chancery was downtown, past cleaning due to pollution from diesel buses, but due to be replaced by a new, much better located building. It was quite an improvement, but security concerns were delaying occupancy. In my opinion, some were valid, some ridiculous, and others out of all proportion. Security officers discovered that a Russian was living in an apartment building across the street with a clear view of the Chancery. Only when it turned out that the Russians had lived there for many years before the land for our building had been acquired was that "threat" dismissed. Another "threat" was "discovered" in an elevator shaft. It was no threat at all, but it took some convincing before the security types admitted error. In the process, the desk officer backstopping us told me the Office of Security (SY) threatened to report me to Congress for failure to take their concerns seriously. I told him that was OK with me.

The building plan provided for a cafeteria in the basement with an exit to an outdoor area with tables and chairs. SY had the exit blocked, alleging that anyone eating outside could be targeted by terrorists. Theoretically, that was right. In the real world I thought it absurd, but my effort to return to the original plan was vetoed. Not accepting this, when in Washington I appealed the case to the under secretary of management. Pros and cons were discussed before the assistant secretary for security. He alleged that a mortar round could be fired that could clear the wall and kill our employees. So it could, but how likely was that? Under Secretary Ron Spiers dismissed us, saying he would take the matter under advisement. Then he decided in favor of SY. Ron is an outstanding officer, but he sure missed that call. Security is critical, but it simply wrong to try to eliminate all risks.

In El Salvador when the Chancery was taking some RP fire, SY proposed hanging steel mesh from the roof so that the rockets would explode harmlessly against the mesh. I said, "No" and made it stick. After my departure the mesh was installed. The Chancery, built to withstand earthquakes, crumbled in the 1986 quake. The extra weight of the steel mesh put extra strain on the building. Fortunately, no lives were lost, but ....

Governments are entitled under international law to expropriate private property, provided fair and prompt compensation is paid. Unfortunately, in Costa Rica there were cases involving American citizens whose property had been seized, but either no compensation had been paid or our citizens considered it to be grossly inadequate. My staff and I tried to assist our citizens in settling these cases. It was slow going. Facts were hard to establish, the law was murky, and the judicial system was overburdened. Some of our citizens in frustration appealed to their congressmen. They asked why the United States was providing millions of dollars in assistance to Costa Rica while they were being screwed. It was a fair question and this congressional pressure helped get high-level attention to their problems. Minister of the Presidency Rodrigo Arias agreed to a systematic review of outstanding cases. A few cases were settled. A few were found to be without merit. Regrettably, more festered, I do not know whether from bad faith, bureaucratic delays, or alleged legal complications. I, too, was frustrated.

Costa Rica is a fabulous country, rightly renowned for its volcanoes, beaches, rain forests, flora and fauna, and all around beauty. Number two son Joe had been uninterested in visiting in El Salvador or Pakistan. When he learned we were headed to Costa Rica, he enthusiastically promised an early visit, citing "world class whitewater rafting!"

When Joe, Kathy, and Waverly visited, Patricia took care of baby Wave while we three ran Pacuare River. It is one of the more beautiful rivers in the world. Thus, I agreed when a friend in the tourist industry asked me if I would give a luncheon at which he could rally resistance to a reported government proposal to dam the Pacuare. Of course, I had no business doing so. Not only was I supporting a private interest, working against possible public policy, but there was no American national interest at stake. I was lucky my luncheon did not win me a public denunciation or worse.

My senior colleague and friend Phil Habib, working on the Central American peace process for the secretary, had encouraged me to take the Costa Rica job. Then, to my regret, Phil resigned in disgust after White House hardliners vetoed the secretary's proposal that he visit Managua to test Ortega's commitment to Arias's peace plan.

Morris Busby was named as his replacement. Unlike Dick Stone, with whom I had had to work in El Salvador, Busby was a Spanish-speaking professional. I liked him, even as I disliked his role and his almost monthly visits, most of which struck me as of limited value.

On a visit after Congress had halted military aid for the Contras, Busby helped persuade Arias to permit us to provide humanitarian aid. This was important. It permitted hospital care for evacuated wounded and small allowances for displaced family members. Other, less fruitful Busby visits followed.

When he cabled asking that we arrange an appointment for him with Arias so he could keep in touch, I objected. A regional ambassador weakens the role and effectiveness of ambassadors responsible for country relations. Visits just to keep in touch would further uncut them. I gather my strongly worded objections created a small furor in Washington. As the Reagan era was ending, I was informed Ambassador Busby's visit had been postponed. Subsequently, the Bush administration named him coordinator for counterterrorism. The regional negotiator's job was eliminated. Common sense had prevailed, finally.

The political leaders of the Nicaraguan Resistance, Alfonzo Robelo and Alfredo Cesar, were different from the Afghan types like Gulbuddin Hekmatyar. Edén Pastora, fabled Commandante Zero, alleged to be involved in drug smuggling, had withdrawn from the struggle before I got to San José. I met him at the home of Defense Attaché Colonel Lent.

In June 1989, Arias proposed to host an October meeting at chief of state level of OAS countries, plus Canada, Spain, and Portugal. The declared reason was to celebrate the centennial of Costa Rican democracy. The undeclared reason was to burnish Oscar's ego. He proposed that themes of his summit meeting should be: democracy, development, disarmament, drugs, and foreign debt. Reactions were muted, but with persistence Oscar pushed ahead, inviting a smaller group of countries. The Bush administration was hesitant. Then occurred an incident of which I am not proud.

Todd Stewart, my DCM, at the end of his absence on leave called from Washington to tell me that Bernie was criticizing me for watering down my instructions. Not only was the charge untrue but as a firm believer that much harm is done when, to maintain good relations, ambassadors dilute their instructions, I resented the allegation.

Shortly thereafter, I was instructed to tell Arias that unless Pinochet were invited, Bush would not attend. While Arias badly wanted the American president to attend, he nevertheless firmly rejected the idea of Pinochet. He told me a celebration of Costa Rican democracy was no place for a dictator. He asked me, perhaps in disbelief, if he could see my instructions. I let him do so. Then he asked if he might keep them. My cabled report included my confession that I had left a copy of my instructions with Arias. However, I was and am ashamed to have let personal pique at Bernie cloud my judgment.

After we agreed President Bush would attend, I was asked to arrange for him to meet separately in Costa Rica with both Violeta Chamorro, the leader of Nicaraguan opposition to the Sandinistas, and Guillermo Endara, whom Noriega had refused to acknowledge as the freely elected president of Panama.

To my surprise, Arias objected. Perhaps I should not have been surprised. I might have guessed he would not want anything to detract from his show. Find a way, I was instructed, Arias notwithstanding. I spoke to Foreign Minister Madrigal, whom I knew would be sympathetic to helping Endara. Madrigal suggested a morning coffee session at the hotel where Bush was to stay. His staff and Political Counselor John Hamilton of mine worked out the details. Lo and behold the secretary generals of the two main Costa Rican political parties issued appropriate invitations to their coffee. It was a success. Lots of photos were taken of the American president's unmistakable endorsement of Guillermo Endara and Violeta Chamorro.

Other highlights—at least for me—of Oscar's festival: Daniel Ortega giving a press conference in Sandinista uniform and Bush's scathing comments later on the uniform's inappropriateness at a meeting supposedly dedicated to peace and democracy; almost playing tennis with my president but settling for lending my racquet to Secretary Baker while watching the U.S. duo trounce Argentina's Miren and Peru's Garcia; failure of the Ticos to win support for adoption of their draft declaration praising Arias among more substantive points; the dinner in the National Theater where Oscar outdid himself offering course after course of delicacies, fine wines, champagne, and liqueurs which made the flowery speeches bearable.

On the side, Arias announced conclusion of a debt-restricting agreement, largely negotiated in Washington, under which the

United States forgave one billion dollars of Costa Rica's debt. I had long urged action on this debt, but since Costa Rica is a small player in international finance nothing would have happened had not the Bush administration decided it had to tackle the overall debt problem in Latin America.

Foreign Minister Rodrigo Madrigal and I talked regularly about the tragedy of Noriega's Panama. The minister may have wanted us to do something about it, but was too diplomatic to say so. Certainly he had trouble understanding why we had not supported the abortive October 1988 coup of Major Moisés Giroldi.

On December 20 I was awakened by the duty officer bringing me a night action (NIACT) cable. It instructed me to inform President Arias that we had intervened to overthrow the Noriega dictatorship.

My first decision, knowing Arias would not welcome the news and certainly not at 3.a.m., was to go back to sleep. When I called him at a more reasonable hour, he was appalled by the news, regretting the use of force.

Juanjo, Miren's youngest boy, was visiting. Immediately after Christmas, he and I flew to Tortuguero for tarpon fishing.

Upon returning I was surprised to see a Marine at the airport. He told me the secretary of state wanted me to telephone. When I did, the secretary said, "This is a heads-up. The president will call you in ten minutes to ask you to take over the embassy in Panama. I hope you will agree."

Startled, I found Patricia and asked her if she wanted to go to Panama. She said yes. Later she said she had misunderstood, thinking I was talking about a trip, not an assignment.

When President Bush called, he said he knew I wanted to retire, but he needed me, "an experienced diplomat," in Panama. I said I wasn't much of a "diplomat." I thought he had the wrong man. He pressed. As a Foreign Service officer, I could not say "No" to the president. He would need a few days, he said, to clear my recess appointment with key members of the Congress, but as soon as my appointment was public, he wanted me in Panama.

25

Panama (1990–1994)

While waiting for a green light from Washington, I relaxed with Patricia and our boys at the beach, read everything I could find about Panama, and pondered some unique aspects of my assignment, starting with the need to work harmoniously both with the commander in chief (CINC) of Southern Command, commanding about 16,000 men located on Panamanian bases, and with the Panama Canal Commission (PCC) administrator.

The president's letter of instruction to ambassadors purports to clarify both my authority and exceptions. I knew the letter was not enough. I would need to develop good personal relations with the CINC and with the PCC administrator.

Finally, my recess appointment was announced. Consul General Johnson administered the oath. Reservations were made for me on a Panamanian airline. When the flight was cancelled, General Max Thurman, with whom I had been in touch by secure phone, offered to send a military aircraft for me. I thanked Max for the offer, but declined it. I knew accepting would send a wrong signal to Panamanians about my role.

On January 8 I arrived in Panama, where I was greeted by the Charge, John Bushnell, General Thurman, a Panamanian protocol officer, and countless members of the media. I read my anodyne arrival statement. The press and local TV ate it up. I was big news in Panama.

John told me he had invited President Endara, First Vice President Ricardo Arias Calderón, and Second Vice President Billy Ford to meet with us at a working dinner the following evening. In the interim, I would check in at my new residence and then meet the rest of the country team.

The residence was well guarded by Marines. A Humvee sporting a .50 caliber machine gun sat in front. When I learned that the Marines, despite the heat, had been told to stay out of the large swimming pool, I countermanded that order.

I found the Chancery surrounded by banks of razor wire. Meeting with the staff, I said we had to return to normal. The razor wire would have to go. There were some objections. Somewhat surprised, I listened carefully; then repeated, "The razor wire goes." Privately, I told the number two C.I.A. officer I did not want him on my staff. Later I had reason to regret that I had not also dismissed the station chief.

Soon I learned the Marines of the Embassy security detachment were bitter about their lack of warning of "Just Cause." With their M-16s locked away, they had been left with only shotguns to reply to considerable RPG and rifle fire from Noriega's irregular "Dignity Battalions." The Marines were otherwise "gung ho," but many of the civilians at post wanted out.

Embassy staff had been drawn down as relations with Noriega's Panama went from bad to worse. As a result, I had to build a staff, starting with a DCM and an AID director. Fortunately, I was about to be reunited with John Dawson, my economic counselor in Costa Rica, who had been recruited by Bushnell for Panama. I would, however, need a new political counselor.

Washington had a candidate for the AID job, whom I was asked to interview. He flew in from Honduras and we had a good talk. He said he would let me know. When he declined, I asked that Tom Stukel, then AID director in the Dominican Republic, be assigned. I also telephoned Tom; he agreed to serve. He asked when he should arrive. I said "Yesterday." He almost made it.

Tom was a terrific colleague, a superb program administrator, a fellow poker player, and a shrewd bureaucrat. Proof of the latter: Tom, evoking my history of fighting for help to the Salvadoran judicial system, ignored my instruction that there were to be no new AID projects in FY'92 and eventually convinced me to agree to seek some funding for Panama's judicial system.

George Reasonover, a friend from days in Pakistan, contacted me saying he wanted to join me in Panama. I asked if he spoke Spanish. He didn't, so I said, "No way." Then I thought again. As my staff assistant he would not need Spanish to help manage the embassy. Personnel exerted itself, and George arrived promptly. I put him to work developing a lean staffing pattern. Specifically, I sought to reduce the C.I.A.'s presence, but to do so without cutting case officers, at least those on embassy staff.

For the critical DCM position, I asked the department for a list of possibilities. When I got to Washington, I found no one on the list satisfactory. However, I thought David Beall, then the assistant secretary's staff assistant, would be ideal. I asked David if he would be interested. He was, but Assistant Secretary Aronson vetoed the idea.

Back in Panama, I outlined the situation in an "Eyes Only" cable to Larry Eagleburger. Result: David was assigned to Panama, where he proved to be a superb DCM. Bernie Aronson was understandably furious that I had gone over his head, but he eventually calmed down, judging from his efficiency report on me.

Personnel lined up possible political counselors for me to interview. I chose a Spanish-speaking officer with a stellar record reporting on the Soviet Union. To my regret, it turned out that I had misjudged. He did not seem to me adequately to sort out malicious gossip from truth nor to recognize that in Panama conspiracy theory was a staple of conversation. He was also thin-skinned. Perhaps I was too hard on him, but when he asked for his assignment to be curtailed, I did not argue.

The director general telephoned me to discuss the case before he approved the curtailment. He also suggested a replacement, who turned out to be a great improvement.

While I had met President Guillermo Endara in Costa Rica, I had not met the two other guests at Bushnell's dinner, First Vice President Ricardo Arias Calderón and Second Vice President Guillermo Ford.

Endara, a lawyer with a LL.M degree from New York University, was for years the right hand man of Dr. Arnulfo Arias. After Dr. Arias's death, Endara became a leading opposition member. In 1989, Endara as a compromise candidate of an alliance of political parties opposed to Noriega was overwhelmingly elected president. Noriega, however, annulled the election results.

At dinner, I noted that Endara was soft-spoken, affable, and almost deferential to his vice presidents. Indeed, he told us the three had agreed all decisions were to be taken unanimously. I thought that while this might reflect political reality, it also seemed like a formula for disaster.

Christian Democrat Arias Calderón, responsible for the police as minister of government and justice, was the last to arrive, but he immediately seemed to take over. Indeed, Endara asked him to explain the overall situation and what was needed from us. A Yale graduate with a doctorate from the University of Paris, he made quite a case for economic help of almost one and a half billion dollars. While I found Arias's intensity to be a bit much, the evening was a splendid introduction to my new job.

Guillermo Ford, "Call me Billy," was known to me from the photo circulated worldwide of his face beaten into a bloody pulp by Noriega's toughs. Politician, glib insurance salesman, "Billy" was minister of planning and economic policy. I liked him and his proclaimed devotion to competitive free markets. Unfortunately, he proved to be something of a lightweight.

The next day, General Thurman and I had a long talk. I liked "Mad Max" as he was referred to by some, including my old buddy Colonel Waghelstein. Max, like me, had been due to retire before being chosen to take out Noriega as CINC South. We both knew what was needed, we both spoke our minds, and when we differed we did not personalize our difference.

I was happily surprised to find that Max had as poor an opinion of his 670th intelligence battalion as I. His opinion was based on poor intelligence performance in tracking Noriega, mine on having read the reporting of the 670th for years. Nor did Max care much for the C.I.A. I thought it depended: some C.I.A. people were great; most so-so. We agreed about NSA and appreciated the performance of intercept operators.

It's hard to believe, but true, that the C.I.A. and a number of military intelligence units, most importantly the 470th, had competed for Noriega's favors. Noriega and company must have laughed all the way to the bank.

Max and I sought to rationalize the USG intelligence effort in Panama. We basically agreed on what was needed, but I do not want to leave a false impression, we did not agree on everything. We differed on the collection effort needed in the provinces. Eventually, we compromised. Max got more provincial coverage than I thought necessary and I got more control over our expanded coverage than Max wanted. Not enough, however, to keep a collector from being apprehended when that eager beaver crossed into Colombia.

One of the extraordinary aspects of the military intelligence establishment was the multiplicity of independent collectors, most of whom had "stovepipe" reporting arrangements to their own part of the swollen Washington intelligence community.

Warned by my station chief, who had once served in the 470th, that there was no chance of success in pulling together these military intelligence outfits, I nevertheless decided to try. Soon I found a potent ally: General Hartzog, Max]'s G-3 (operations), during Just Cause, now commanding USARSOUTH, agreed we needed coordinated reporting. Hartzog's G-2 (intelligence) joined my meetings and we developed a plan. Implementation was delayed by arrival of the new CINC, but General Jouwan eventually approved it. Results were mixed. A number of units brazenly resisted, others invoked agreed exceptions. Still Hartzog and I thought we had made a modest improvement.

Separately, during a yearlong transition, I succeeded in eliminating Panama-based regional C.I.A. components.

Panama's protocol chief tried to delay my presentation of credentials because he did not have a band! My British colleague, who had precedence (he had arrived in Panama half an hour before me), and I both objected, saying we were willing to forgo our national anthems. Foreign Minister Julio Linares agreed we could go ahead.

Arriving at the Presidency to do so, I was horrified to see American troops presenting arms as I entered El Palacio de las Garzas. Fortunately, no newsmen or cameramen were there to report or to further gossip about a non-existent pro-Consul. Our men, I learned later, were there to protect Endara. They meant well in saluting me; they were, of course, not aware of how inappropriate it was to do so at Panama's "White House."

Credentials presented, I was now free to call on the Papal Nuncio, a man with whom I was anxious to talk. Monseignor Jose Sebastian Laboa was still providing asylum to Noriega's aide, Captain Eliécer Gaitán, a badly wanted man. I found the Nunciatura surrounded with much razor wire and American troops guarding it.

The Nuncio, quite full of himself, took credit for convincing Noriega to surrender. He assured me Gaitán would also soon surrender. I asked if he would like us to reduce or eliminate the guards and razor wire. He said, "No, they are useful."

Later, a Latin American ambassador I had gotten to know in Costa Rica told me the Nuncio had complained that I had insisted on keeping the guards and the wire! Truthfulness was not the Nuncio's strong suit! I was not disappointed when Laboa was transferred to Paraguay. His replacement, Msg. Osvaldo Padilla, and I became good friends. It helped that he was both a tennis player and truthful.

Soon after my arrival, the Cuban ambassador phoned and

asked to come see me. This was extraordinary. I said I wouldn't see him unless he told me what he wanted. He hedged, then muttered "arms." So we met. I included my station chief; he brought what I presume was the Cuban equivalent. He told me he had a supply of weapons in his Embassy that he wished to return to Cuba. He asked for assurances that we would not interfere. I assured him we would not, provided we were told when and how the arms would be shipped.

He then asked me, "How is Michu?" I was speechless. "Have you forgotten we met at dinner at the Attoues' in Kinshasa?" He was right. I had forgotten. We had met almost thirty years before.

On January 13 at a press conference, asked my role, I explained, "I am here to support the democratic Government of Panama."

Q: "Does the U.S. plan to keep bases in Panama after 2000?"
A: "No."
Q: "Will bank secrecy be maintained?"
A: "We hope to negotiate a Mutual Legal Assistance Agreement. Honest bankers have nothing to fear."
Q: "How did Mike Hariari leave Panama?"
A: "How the hell would I know?"
Q: "When will troop levels return to normal?"
A: "Ask General Thurman."
Q: "How much aid is coming?"
A: "Under study."
Q: "What are our expectations for Panama's new Public Force?"
A: "Same as Panama's, i.e., an effective police force under civilian control."

I also fielded a barrage of other questions.

Invited to Washington for a meeting with President Bush, upon learning that Max had not been included, I cabled a request for reconsideration. It paid off. We remained good friends until his death.

In his aircraft, Max showed me a C.I.A. assessment different from what I had been given! Max also told me someone was blocking access to me of an intelligence agent he had sent to see me. I was not amused.

In Washington, the meeting with the president struck me as theater. Questioned by the president, I said that while I would prefer more resources than in his plan, I knew about budget stringency. By making careful use of what economic assistance we would have, I thought we could get the Panamanian economy humming again.

In response to another question, I promised carefully to review embassy staffing, opining that some positions, particularly those with regional responsibilities, might be reduced. I knew, but did not mention that the C.I.A. had liberally salted its people into such positions.

While in Washington, I called on Carlos Rodriguez, Panama's ambassador. While there, President Bush telephoned me to urge me to read a cable. Having Carlos overhear the conversation, I thought, would not hurt my standing with him or Endara.

We were to return to Panama from the Andrews Air Force base. Waiting at the Pentagon helo-pad to go to Andrews, Max took me aside and introduced a Colonel Jim Steele. Max identified Colonel Steele as commanding "your military support group." I had no idea what this might be, so I hedged when Max urged me to include the support group (MSG) as an integral part of the embassy.

Upon inquiry, I later learned the MSG was a civil affairs unit, the mission of which was to "conduct nation building operations to ensure democracy...and professional public services are established in Panama." Quite an overlap with the embassy!

It was easy to conclude I did not need Max's offer of 300 or so soldiers. Moreover, recalling my incredible El Salvador psy-ops briefing as well as the foolish psy-ops effort to win Noriega's surrender with full blast noise, I told the colonel that I wanted him on the embassy country team. However, he and his unit could forget about psy-ops. Jim and the MSG proved to be a great help in standing up the police and organizing engineers to repair schools, clinics, and roads

When I learned that Colonel Steele and his deputy were meeting regularly with President Endara, I told Jim such meetings were an ambassadorial prerogative. Nevertheless I hoped he would also attend. Not only do I believe in transparency, but I also thought that having Jim at the meetings would be a good way of letting our military know my views.

Word came that Vice President Dan Quayle would visit Panama. He was to stay with me; more symbolism, but would join Max and the troops to watch the Super Bowl. When the advance team looked at the master bedroom, which I proposed to turn over to my guest, they said no way, since they saw a direct line of fire from an apartment building. So the vice president would have to stay in a small bedroom with peeling wallpaper. He took it in stride. However, when I told him that in Panama the sun rose from the Pacific Ocean, I had to prove it.

When we called on President Endara, I was delighted to note

there was not a U.S. serviceman in sight. However, when we left church, to my horror they were everywhere. My fault; I had forgotten to issue a warning.

After Mass we were scheduled to stop "just by accident" at a restaurant picked out by the advance team where the VP was meant to be able to talk with Panamanians. Yet the first half dozen people approached were Colombians, Peruvians, and a North American! Finally, a genuine Panamanian was found. Despite such missteps, Quayle said he was pleased by his visit.

When Endara was in town, we had breakfast with him every Thursday. The DCM, the AID director, Jim Steele, and I were regulars. The president was usually accompanied by his taciturn relative, Jorge Endara, who ran the Social Security system, and by Panama's outspoken controller, Rubén Darío Carles, known to all by his nickname, Chinchorro.

Either of us could and did raise almost any subject. The DCM and I would list separately what each of us thought should be discussed, then compared notes en route to the Presidency. After Endara and Chinchorro finished with their agenda, we ran through ours. When Washington wanted me to raise an urgent matter with the president, I had no problem in getting an appointment between breakfast meetings. Also, if I said I had an unusually sensitive matter, such as Noriega trial preparations, Endara would invite me to his office after breakfast. Such easy access to a president was unique in my experience.

In his office, I learned he used a top of the line computer not only for letters and speech drafts but also for computer games, to which, he confessed, he was addicted.

Of course, access did not guarantee agreement, far from it, but it did reduce, indeed almost eliminate, misunderstanding. We used our meetings to brief Endara on issues, to encourage him to act, and to explore his thinking. He listened carefully, taking a particular interest in police and judicial matters.

Already a rich man, he was not corrupt, although his political enemies charged that he was. I was bothered by some of these charges, so he and I had a long discussion, charge by charge. I found his explanations to be convincing. He acknowledged that as a private lawyer he might well have helped a firm that later proved to be involved with drugs and money laundering. However, he insisted that neither he nor his law firm knowingly had ever behaved illegally.

Endara as "an act of commiseration and solidarity with his

suffering fellow citizens" fasted in the cathedral. When an AID agreement was ready for signature, Stukel and I went there. Have other economic agreements been signed in a cathedral or do we have a unique claim to fame?

The president listened carefully when I made the case for trade liberalization, but basically he was a protectionist. Nor was it easy to get him to modify his beliefs. To my annoyance he also protected Arnulfista party members whether or not they were doing a good job. He listened to my critical comments about his foreign minister, seemed amused by some of Julio's anti-American antics, carefully frustrated Julio's attempts to intervene on issues assigned to Ricardo Arias or to Billy Ford, but wasn't about to dump an Arnulfista minister who provided him political protection against charges of being an American puppet.

On the other hand, I was convinced he would not tolerate corruption. I may have influenced his dismissal of Juan Chevalier, a fellow Arnulfista and his second minister of government and justice, when I told the president that Chevalier had hinted that hiring his son's firm would resolve a problem of the embassy's.

Endara generally liked to mull matters over before acting. But at times when he felt threatened or angered by suggestions that he was a weak president, he would forcibly react. Worse, his impulsive young wife, Ana Mae, occasionally goaded him into ill-advised action.

A 1991 breakfast meeting with the president illustrates the breadth of our discussions. It included his comments on a Central American summit, a discussion of the latest round of Mutual Legal Assistance Agreement (MLAA) negotiations, Tom Stukel's brief on problems encountered in disbursing AID funds, Jim Steele's report on problems with joint U.S.-Panama police patrols and Army plans for Caminos Fuertes 91, the Drug Enforcement Agency (DEA) role in joint police exercises to seize drugs, our complaints about bureaucratic foot dragging on Coco Solo housing, and my explanation of Paris Club practices for rescheduling debt.

Occasionally, we delved into esoteric matters. For example, someone, reacting to an amorphous threat to assassinate Endara, had placed a .50 caliber machine gun overlooking the Bay of Panama. When he saw it, Colonel Steele pointed out that, if fired, the weapon would endanger lives in Punta Patilla far across the Bay. It took time and patience, two or three breakfast discussions, but eventually the weapon was removed.

Another continuing discussion, in which Chinchorro played a constructive role, involved our shared interest in building a facility in Panama to irradiate screw worm flies, thereby making them sterile and hence unable of carrying the eggs of the screw worm parasite to infect cattle. Our Department of Agriculture wanted to clear Central America north of the Darien Gap of the screw worm. Having once served as minister of agriculture, Chinchorro knew both the economic importance of success and that politically Panama's cattlemen would welcome a program to knock out the parasite.

I liked and respected Endara, but his foreign minister, Julio Linares, drove me up the wall. Having dealt with a world-class foreign minister in Pakistan and an able one in Costa Rica, I found Linares to be a big step down.

During our first substantive discussion over lunch at my residence, he rejected one by one every problem I had hoped he might help resolve, but, he said, he needed my help.

The president and he would shortly visit Colón to inaugurate a school. He asked me to immediately revert to them the potential school building. Despite his negativity, I agreed to try to arrange it.

I persuaded a reluctant general officer to shortcut army reversion schedules and procedures. I phoned Linares to tell him the school had been reverted. He thanked me. However, no school inauguration was held. In fact, for months the reverted building stood empty. The general on whom I had imposed enjoyed ragging me about "my school." I concluded Linares was not trustworthy.

Worse, in March 1990, he forgot he was foreign minister, no longer just a private citizen free to write anti-American polemics. He denounced the DeConcini amendment and the Neutrality Treaty. I complained to him and to the president that the Panamanian foreign minister should not be attacking the treaties, adding that were the treaties renegotiated as Linares suggested, the United States might also seek changes.

Linares had also forgotten Panamanians overwhelmingly supported the treaties. The ensuing public uproar led Julio to a contrite retreat,

Julio often opposed measures we sought to fight the war on drugs. The most important was a Mutual Legal Assistance Agreement (MLAA). For over a year, he and most banks fought to save unimpaired Panama's bank secrecy laws. Mike Kozak, our lead negotiator, thought we had an agreement with Endara in October of 1990. Somehow, however, Julio and the bankers talked the president into changing his mind. This led to a regrettable shouting match between Linares and myself at, of all places, the nuncio's New Year's reception. After more months of negotiations agreement was again reached. Julio, however, unreconciled to the compromise concerning bank secrecy, refused to sign, leaving that to his deputy, Jose Raul Molino.

When I urged Julio to seek ratification of the Vienna Convention, dealing inter alia with money laundering, he declined. Panama's banking sector, he told me, objected! At least he was consistent!

Nor was he always wrong.

On May 24, 1990, out of the blue, Luis Quisado, Linares's nephew, the GOP representative on the Joint Committee (JC), wrote, "Our Government wants back ASAP, all areas temporarily occupied by the U.S. per 'Just Cause'."

Max Thurman wrote me calling this "troublesome." He added, "The request was not in keeping with Panama's interest in maintaining law and order." I agreed, but what to do?

Major General Marc Cisneros made a suggestion: build a backfire. Soon, he had governors and other provincial authorities telephoning Panama City with objections. In response, VP Arias convoked a meeting. After much discussion, he concluded some U.S. forces were still needed in the provinces. Moreover, the joint patrols of U.S. military police and Panamanian police would continue in Panama City.

Linares and Quisado had tried to exploit Panamanian nationalism and up to a point they had succeeded. However they knew virtually nothing about life or security in the countryside. Here they overstepped and were overruled.

We recognized that we had been remiss in not ending some restrictions sooner.

Panamanians loved to stroll on the causeway out to Flamenco. For too long we had blocked access to it and to Fort Amador. Now, we adapted belatedly to the situation. With Panama, we organized a joint ceremonial reversion of the causeway. On May 28, President Endara and I led the way down the causeway.

Soon thereafter, we reached agreement on a continued smaller presence of U.S. forces in the provinces of Panama.

In July 1991, a screaming Linares called to object to a "Sense of Congress Resolution" calling for renegotiation of the Canal Treaties. Ignoring my explanation that the treaties were unchanged and that our Congress was merely letting off steam, he kept shouting.

Later he sent me a note of protest, which still later was published in his annual review of his stewardship of the Ministry of Foreign Affairs. Much ado about nothing, I thought, but he must have thought it would convince others of his steadfast defense of Panama's interests.

Julio liked to complain of U.S. actions. Misreading Treaty provisions, he alleged the Panama Canal Commission was illegally discriminating against its Panamanian employees. The Panamanian administrator of the Canal Commission set him straight.

Julio, again misreading the Treaties, cancelled on base banking arrangements for U.S. forces. Our military understandably were outraged, starting with the CINC, General Joulwan. Julio apparently wanted his bank friends to get the business. With my embassy lawyer to help me explain the Treaty, I took the issue to Endara. He quickly understood, suggested adjustments to the former system, and on-base banking resumed.

Julio at times showed quite a sense of humor. He sent Patricia a cartoon making fun of our differences. He also arranged for his luncheon club of Arnulfistas to include David and me as regulars. We found the club enjoyable, instructive, and inebriating. I was genuinely sorry when Linares passed away from a heart attack while representing Panama at the United Nations.

The CINC, General Max Thurman, was a bachelor, said by his staff to be "married" to the Army. Fortunately we worked well together. Not that we did not disagree from time to time. When Max asserted a free hand to move his forces "to defend the canal," I read the relevant Treaty provisions differently. After a long discussion, we agreed to put the issue to Washington.

The Pentagon instructed us that in Panama, outside of Treaty-designated base areas, prior agreement was needed for U.S. troop movements.

Max and I regularly played tennis. When I began to win more easily, I worried that Max was not well. In July he told me from Washington that he had leukemia. He commended to me Rear Admiral Dave Chandler as his "interim" replacement. He added he was sure I could "beat up" on Dave, "as you have on me" whenever needed.

In November, General George Joulwan took over as new CINC. To get acquainted, Patricia and I had Karen and George to lunch. When he assured me, "I have no agenda," I thought it unlikely he would not want to put his mark on his new command.

On each visit to Washington, I saw Max. We took turns picking up the check at good restaurants. He studied leukemia as he had studied war fighting, having healthy bone marrow cells frozen for later injection. In December 1991, with his leukemia in remission, this dedicated soldier returned for a change of command ceremony at Fort Clayton.

Max fought his disease until December of 1995. Before Patricia and I moved to Costa Rica in 1994, I paid a farewell call on him at Walter Reed hospital.

In early February of 1990, I had flown back to San José to say farewell to my staff, to Oscar Arias, to Jorge Dengo, and to selected colleagues at a dinner Rodrigo Madrigal gave in honor of Patricia and me.

Then with Sebas and Patricia's parrot on board, I drove our Four Runner over the Cerro de la Muerte to Panama. Major General Marc Cisneros met us as we crossed into Panama. He took us up out of the heat to a mountain hotel where we were doubly welcome. Guests had been few and far between after Noriega's overthrow.

The next day, Marc accompanied me on calls on the governors at David and Penonomé. This took much too much time, so Marc arranged for someone to drive my car (and parrot) to my residence while we choppered to Albrook.

The Panama Canal Treaties required the United States to turn over the Canal to Panama at noon on December 31, 1999. One key prior step was for the president of Panama to propose to the United States a candidate to serve as the administrator of the Canal Commission.

Fernando Manfredo, a member of the PRD, Torrijos' political party, had been appointed by President Carter as deputy administrator of the Panama Canal Commission (PCC), when, in 1979, the Treaties came into effect. Fernando now wanted the top job, was well qualified, but was not to get it. The Endara administration was weeding out PRD members, even those who had opposed Noriega. Like a rejected suitor, Fernando was bitter. He subsequently became an annoying critical commentator on Canal issues.

Endara proposed Gilberto Guardia, an engineer with wide experience, to be the PCC administrator. We checked him out. His reputation was untarnished. I invited Guardia to lunch, liked him, and recommended that President Bush nominate him as PCC administrator. I never had reason to regret it.

The Commission was autonomous and ran a smooth ship.

Nevertheless, I had to pay attention to it. I had oversight responsibilities as chairman of the Panama Review committee (PRC). This committee, on which the CINC, the Commission administrator, and I sat, was charged to coordinate American government actions in Panama.

The PRC was almost immediately convoked after my arrival. Its agenda was loaded with "Return to Normal" issues, such as removing economic sanctions.

I welcomed Fernando Manfredo, noting it was the first time a Panamanian national had attended a PRC meeting. He briefed on Canal operations and noted the need for recommendations from the GOP of Panamanians to serve on the Canal Board. We pressed him to speed up the turnover of the PCC's excess housing to the government. The CINC briefed on the security situation and I talked about policy priorities. Our remarks provoked some discussion. It was a start.

I also was an ex-officio member of the Canal Board of Directors, a position which initially worried me, since I wondered what I could contribute to a high-powered body chaired by the secretary of the army, and with prominent businessmen as the U.S. members. With time I came to enjoy board sessions. As an extra benefit, I became well acquainted with its Panamanian members. The directors normally met in Panama but also once a year at an important American port. Given my ex-officio status, the PCC included me and paid my travel expenses to meetings in the United States.

After pushing to restart the tripartite (Panama, Japan, U.S.) "Commission for the Study of Alternatives to the Panama Canal," I had, occasionally, to intervene to try to advance the study.

The Smithsonian Tropical Research Station was another part of the American presence in Panama. Except for a visit to its facilities on an island in Gatun Lake, an annual exchange of Christmas cards, and social engagements when the secretary of the Smithsonian Institution visited, I was not involved with its activities.

The Corozal cemetery, where from 1990 to 1994 I read the President's Memorial Proclamation, was maintained by the American Battle Monuments Commission, the same outfit that cares for our military cemeteries in Europe and the Pacific. However, unless new Treaty arrangements were negotiated, the Corozal cemetery was to revert to Panama when the Canal did.

It seemed to me that getting Panama's agreement to cede to the United States in perpetuity the sixteen acres involved would be easy. Indeed when I first raised the subject with the foreign minister, even Julio readily agreed to the cession. However, despite many reminders he did not act.

Indeed, not only I, but also a number of my successors failed. The Treaty I sought to negotiate in 1990 in order to assure that the American veterans in the Corozal cemetery would rest perpetually in American soil was not, I'm told, agreed until just before the management of the Panama Canal passed to Panama at midnight on December 31, 1999!

Unquestionably I spent more time on police issues than any other. Noriega's Defense Force ideally should have been totally disbanded. That was not practicable, as much as the new government would have liked to have done so. Rather, faced with the urgent need to control widespread looting, it was decided to recruit police, after screening, from the about 12,000 members of the corrupt and brutal former Defense Force. Many bad apples, particularly among the officers, were known and screened out. But many more were initially missed.

Endara from the outset made it clear Panama was to have no army. Moreover, civilian control of the police was essential.

Vice President Arias, now in charge of the police, wanted to clean house, but knew he had to proceed carefully. Also he had no experience with police issues and relied heavily on U.S. Army officers for advice. Indeed, when he and I reviewed his initial proposals for the new police force, I was startled to discover their resemblance to an army table of organization. He accepted my critique and willingly made major changes.

For my part, I received two proposals for reform of how the new National Police Force (PNP) and Judicial Technical Police (JTP) should be constituted. One proposal was from our military, the other from the Department of Justice's International Criminal Investigative Training Assistance Program (ICITAP). As helpful as our MPs had been in training Panamanian police in the difficult early days, it was an easy choice.

The State Department and I not only favored ICITAP, but some members of Congress and Mike Kozak cited the sad history of our support for Noriega to obtain legislation prohibiting future involvement by the military with Panama's police.

VP Arias and I agreed a police academy was a high-priority need. He, however, slowed things down by arguing for the American high school. He was right; it would have been ideal. However,

he badly misjudged resistance to his proposal. Arias, while brilliant, often made the mistake of overreaching. For us, a high school
for American kids was far more important than a police academy.
Eventually we agreed on an adequate site.

In the meantime, ICITAP ran short courses stressing respect for
human rights and the need to avoid even the appearance of corruption. Every policeman now carried a plasticized care reminding
him of his duty toward his fellow citizens. I doubted that many
would change their ingrained habits, but we had to try. Inculcating
a new way of thinking by Panama's police was critical.

The best chance for long-term success lay in gradually training
new recruits at the academy. It would be a slow process. Only three
classes, each of about 400 recruits, would graduate a year. ICITAP
trainers, most of whom were veterans of American police forces,
stressed the rule of law, ethics, police professionalism, and respect
for human rights.

Given widespread unemployment, there was no shortage of
police recruits. Despite poor pay, requirements for selection could
be and were rigorous.

Showing the importance he attached to police reform, President
Endara attended each class's graduation, as I did.

We sought to institutionalize ICITAP's relations with the GOP.
Arias resisted until the abortive police coup. Thereafter things fell
into place, including plans both for a revised police SWAT team
and for training a special presidential protection group.

In February of 1991, we started holding monthly reviews of
police progress in meeting agreed-upon objectives or, too often,
a lack of or inadequate progress. The minister of government, the
PNP director general, the attorney general, and senior police officers attended as did DCM Beall, Patrick Lang, the resident head of
ICITAP staff, myself, and, when in country, David Kriskovich, who
was in overall charge of police training. Soon, given different training requirements, we met separately with the attorney general and
the director of the JTP.

With VP Arias we had carefully prepared detailed agendas,
complete with options. More important, he ran a crisp ship and
made decisions. When, to my regret, he was replaced as minister of
government by Juan Chevalier, meetings became informal, irregular, and at times rather chaotic.

With both ministers our discussions were crowded with budget, procurement, training, maintenance, and other, often boring,
but important issues. For example, police cars!

Initially, Colonel Steele used emergency funds to buy new patrol cars, but gradually they were wrecked or wore out. Noriega's police apparently had had no vehicle maintenance facilities. AID eventually supplied them. Then we arranged for the PCC to train police mechanics. Meanwhile, it was necessary to try to inculcate budgeting and fund controls, entirely new concepts that had not been important in Noriega's time. If it seemed that a nudge would help resolve issues, we would follow up at our next breakfast with the president.

VP Arias reluctantly decided Colonel Herrera, who had been in exile because of his anti-Noriega record, should be in charge of the PNP. It was a mistake. Herrera was a demanding prima donna. When he was finally replaced by a less experienced but loyal civilian, Herrera plotted. We knew of this, but did not think Herrera was dumb enough to think we would permit a police coup. We were wrong!

I had attended Juanjo's graduation from the DEA academy in Virginia, gone on to Miami for a conference, and was asleep when the phone rang after midnight. Kozak was calling from Washington with the news of Colonel Herrera's revolt. He asked me for my approval of a statement. Still half asleep, I suggested a silly change. Mike didn't like it. I woke up enough to approve his draft and went back to sleep.

The next day, back in Panama, I learned that, at police headquarters, Herrera had taken Colonel Steele and a few other Americans hostage. After a tense period, he released them. Later he started to march to the National Assembly. Jim then talked Herrera and the marching mutineers into surrender. Fortunately, no blood was spilled during many hours of tension.

I also learned that many Panamanian officials had panicked. David Beall, like Jim Steele, had been magnificent, deploying embassy officers to the right places, such as the Presidency, while calming Endara and company.

Soon evidence of tension between VP Arias and Endara surfaced. Unfortunately, Ana Mae fanned the flames. To universal amazement she visited the National Assembly, where she denounced Arias and the Christian Democrats for allegedly plotting against the president. Panama's love for conspiracy theories was running wild. Then it was asserted that Arias was spying on the president with American help. We allegedly built him an intercept facility in a building under his control. True, the building was under his control; not true about our role. Charges and counter charges filled the press. I tried to calm things, pointing out to all who would listen the need to hold the government together. Chinchorro sadly let his dislike of the Christian Democrats take him off the deep end. Endara was, many believed, provoked by Ana Mae's taunting into acting. She may well have pillow-talked him into believing he needed to show he was a strong, decisive president.

I do not know exactly what happened but I do know that hesitating Endara called on Carlos Rodriguez to return from Miami to try to fix things. Rodriquez latter told me that Arias had misjudged the situation, overplayed his hand, and left Endara no choice but to dismiss the Christian Democrats from the government. Perhaps so; perhaps not.

Arias remained VP, since he had been elected to that position, but declined to attend cabinet meetings, which was his right, or otherwise to serve in the Endara administration.

At breakfast the next day at General Joulwan's for Colin Powell, chairman of the Joint Chiefs, I noted that Endara had—I thought foolishly—blown away his majority in the Assembly. As a result, I feared he would have grave problems governing.

General George Joulwan and I both tried to work together, but somehow the chemistry was not always right. In part, I suppose because it had been so good with Max Thurman; in part, because there was a substantial age difference; in part, because George played golf, not tennis; and in part, because despite a promising start working intelligence issues, George soon decided to back the 480th in recruiting new agents. That hurt; Max and I had agreed we could do without the 480th!

I recognized that it was hard for him to be living in Panama at Quarry Heights and yet to be limited in his contacts since there was no longer a military to work with and Congress had restricted military ties with the new police. However, he overcame some constraints by aggressively deploying his air assets, including balloons, against drug smugglers. This both advanced the war on drugs and allowed his people to help train the fledgling Panamanian Coast Guard and Air Force. In addition, regular deployments of our engineer and medical units permitted him to develop relations with involved Panamanians.

Then David Beall and I, brainstorming about what could be done to get the GOP moving to prepare to take over U.S. bases, beyond lobbying the president and others, hit on the idea of guided tours. General Joulwan enthusiastically agreed when I put the proposal to him. Indeed he personally led many of the tours.

Endara had appointed J. J. Vallarino to head a committee charged with studying what use could be made of the bases. Soon he and Joulwan were working together. Real progress!

Then a couple of incidents soured my view of the general.

Tragically a GI going the wrong way on a one-way street was shot to death by a policeman. I heard of the incident when Juan Chevalier, minister of government, telephoned to say General Joulwan had summoned Major Arrue, the acting director general of the PNP, to his headquarters. Chevalier wanted to know what I thought he should do. I replied the general was out of order, but what the minister did was up to him. I called DCM Beall and instructed him to tell SOUTHCOM my view and asked that we consult about how to proceed.

Chevalier decided he did not want to cross a four-star American general and told Arrue to go see the CINC. When he did Joulwan reamed him. Joulwan must have thought he was supporting his troops, but I was appalled by what looked like bullying and disregard for a congressional edict. Therefore, I wrote the general an "Eyes Only" letter saying he had been "out of order" in summoning Major Arrue to meet with him. I added I was "disappointed" he had proceeded "over my objections." He did not reply!

He did, however, give a dinner to mark my fifty years of service to the U.S. AID. Planning for the pending drawdown of U.S. forces, he recruited Bruce Stader, an experienced surplus property disposal officer. Joulwan, when he learned of the program, said he would like to speak the next time Stader distributed things to schools, clinics, or elsewhere. Fair enough, since the surplus was generated by his command. With the general's approval, the AID director and I invited Vice President Ford and a number of cabinet members to the ceremony. Joulwan was over thirty minutes late, keeping the Panamanians waiting as well as Tom and myself. I was furious about what I viewed to be insulting behavior toward Ford and our other guests.

He and I had one important substantive difference. We religiously stuck to the public party line that we would honor our Treaty commitments, but we both hoped we could keep a military foothold in Panama. I thought the way we might do this was to speed up the drawdown process, thereby provoking a debate among Panamanians before their upcoming national elections.

General Joulwan disagreed. Nevertheless, when Secretary of Defense Dick Cheney visited, Joulwan arranged for me to make my case to the scretary. I did so during a long, detailed discussion, but was not surprised that the secretary ruled in favor of the CINC. Of course, my proposal might not have worked, but as I had predicted our efforts to negotiate a continued presence at Howard Air Force Base failed.

In early 1992, the inspector general announced that Panama was one of the best-managed posts inspected in 1991. I thought we deserved this kudo; I also thought it would not have happened without David Beall.

Drugs in large amounts flowed through Panama, particularly through the Colón Free Trade Zone. The U.S. market was incredibly lucrative. When we were able to plug one distribution channel, it was soon replaced by another. While we also made progress against money laundering, it was never enough. The "war on drugs" was unending.

My staff included Drug Enforcement Agency (DEA) agents and a Coast Guard liaison officer. I resisted pressure for more agents, knowing there would never be enough. However, it helped that the new station chief enthusiastically joined in the battle. While he and his people had to take care to avoid compromising evidence, their covert collection of intelligence, particularly intercepts, led the DEA to major drug busts.

I talked regularly to my staff about the need to respect Panama's sovereignty. Nevertheless, from time to time, gung ho DEA agents got us in trouble. The lead on raids was supposed to be with the local authorities. Only they were to make arrests. Yet, once the press ran damning pictures of cars with U.S. diplomatic license plates at a raided house. Even worse, detainees swore gringos had arrested them.

The new foreign minister, Jose Raul Mulino, called me in. Unlike Julio Linares, Mulino approved of the drug war. Even so, he rightly read me the riot act. I agreed we had been out of line and pledged to "respect the laws of Panama." To help keep my word, I had the DEA chief turn in the diplomatic license plates on his official vehicles. Until he could get ordinary plates he rented cars. The drug war did not suffer!

I was not as lucky. Coming out of the Foreign Ministry, I suffered an exceptionally nasty grilling by the press.

Word reached us that President Bush planned to visit Panama. Brent Scowcroft, the NSC advisor, called on a secure phone to discuss the idea. He asked about the chance of demonstrations. I said they were likely, but I thought the police would be able to prevent serious trouble.

DCM Beall worked with the White House advance team on the visit. They proposed a speech in Plaza Porras. When David and I discussed it, neither of us liked that idea. I then told the advance that if an outdoor speech was absolutely necessary, it should be in Cathedral Square, near the Presidency. Security there would be more manageable. Thorton Pryce of the NSC also opposed Plaza Porras. The White House advance, however, saying they wanted more room for a larger crowd than would fit in Cathedral Square, insisted on Plaza Porras.

Big mistake! Arrival, cavalcade to the Presidency, Endara's luncheon, and move to Plaza Porras went well. However, after President and Mrs. Bush had been seated we heard noise of trouble, soon followed by whiffs of tear gas. That was it!

The Secret Service hustled President and Mrs. Bush into his armored limousine. Another agent got Patricia and me into my car. Per plan, we drove to our Embassy where Patricia would be safe. Then, I was driven through a bit of chaos to Albrook Field to rejoin the president.

I found him in good spirits making changes in a speech now to be delivered to a radio audience. Before "wheels up" he also made remarks to enthusiastic troops assembled to greet him. His "thank you" letter to me and the entire Embassy staff declared that the "warmth of his reception more than outweighed the efforts of a few dissidents."

Maybe so, but I felt badly about what had happened. I even asked the president's chief of staff, "Do you want my resignation now or later?" Secretary Skinner shrugged it off.

Later I wrote a reflective note to myself reviewing both police performance--not bad, given demonstrator rights to peaceful assembly--and the decision for a Plaza Porras speech. When I had told Brent Scowcroft I thought demonstrations would be manageable, I knew nothing of an outdoor speech. My error was that I had not argued longer and harder against the Plaza Porras speech.

The next day the press said SOUTHCOM had warned the president of trouble. If so, I was unaware of it.

At lunch that day with Shirley Christian, an old friend from our days in El Salvador, she pressed me to comment. Resisting the temptation to damn the White House advance team, I declined to do so.

The day before the president's arrival, Sergeant Zak A. Hernandez was shot and killed and another American soldier wounded while driving toward Panama City in a Humvee. Clear evidence pointed to Pedro Miguel González Pinzón as the assassin.

Inevitably, after three years in Panama, David was slated for transfer. He declined an ambassadorship at a small post, then agreed to serve as DCM Mexico City. David liked challenges!

O.P. Garza was the new DCM. He was a good man, did well, but I found him to be highly reserved, mighty hard to draw out.

In 1993, Secretary of State Christopher, stung by criticism that the department had not done enough to investigate the 1984 El Mozote massacre in El Salvador, formed a panel to look into the performance of the Foreign Service and the State Department.

I was summoned from Panama to testify. While some colleagues were criticized in the panel's report, I came off in good shape. The record showed I had objected to departmental testimony quoting me as denying there had been a massacre.

From my arrival in Panama, I repeatedly stressed the importance of preparing for the day when Panama would assume responsibility for operation of the Canal. There were already studies, but I wanted more. Eventually we had a plethora of studies.

In 1990, Economic Counselor John Dawson examined how the Canal would do were it run as a private business. His study concluded it would do exceedingly well.

President Endara asked J. J. Vallarino's committee, already engaged in planning how best to use areas to be reverted, also to draft legislation for eventual governance of the Canal. After Cabinet consideration of J. J.'s draft, it was sent it to the National Assembly.

AID contracted with Louis Berger for a "Strategic Study." Private business groups and individuals, including Fernando Manfredo, contributed ideas. Our Congress mandated two studies: for one the PCC contracted Arthur Anderson, the second was done by the General Accounting Office.

While future governments would need to make critical decisions about the Canal, the United States and the Endara administration had well defined the options.

New elections were scheduled to be held in 1994. I did not expect to be in Panama then, but even so, I thought I should get to know Rueben Blades, the only candidate I did not already know. He had decided to exploit his great popularity as a salsa singer, songwriter, and actor to run for president of Panama.

Politicians tend to fit a mold, but Blades was different. He declined my invitation to lunch. He surprised again when he agreed to lunch at PAO Peter DeSazo's, even though he was told I would also attend. It seemed it was the symbol of the American ambassador's residence he objected to.

At lunch, he stressed that Panama needed a northsouth railway. If elected, he said, he would have it built. Blades was an interesting candidate. However, with no real need for his railroad nor public interest in it, we discounted his electoral chances. He was a performing artist not a politician.

Ernesto Pérez Balladares, on the other hand, was a political pro, fully able to take advantage of the opposition's loss of unity in opposition to the PRD. In January 1994, after watching him work attendees at a reception given by Gabriel Lewis for President and Mrs. Carter, I concluded Ballardares would probably win. While I hated the thought of a corrupt veteran of Noriega's PRD as the next president of Panama, I resisted even the idea of intervening. It was now time for Panamanians to decide whom they wanted to guide their future.

In July 1993 William Walker was nominated to replace me. He was, however, blackballed by liberals on the Foreign Relations Committee.

As my time in Panama was drawing to an end, Patty Brania, my secretary and right-hand companion in El Salvador, Pakistan, Costa Rica, and Panama, with my approval transferred to Havana. Joe Sullivan, who keeps track of outstanding talent, wanted her in Cuba, where he was heading the American Interests Section. I hated to see her leave, wondered how I could do without her, but recognized that she should take advantage of Joe's offer.

When President Bill Clinton nominated Robert Pastor, I feared correctly that Senator Helms would block Bob. I had planned to serve until a new ambassador was about to arrive. But now, faced with indefinite delays, I decided I had had enough. It helped that O. P. Garza was well qualified to serve as chargé.

At my final breakfast with the president on February 10, 1994, I thanked him for making so memorable and agreeable my four-plus years in Panama. We then discussed a pending call on him by the new CINC of the U.S. Southern Command, General Barry McCaffrey, and what I viewed as Panama's questionable efforts to improve its relations with Cuba and Haiti.

Then, by prior agreement, I summed up where I thought Panama and U.S. relations with Panama stood.

As solid pluses, there were a democratic government under the rule of law, a strong economic recovery, agreements on how to settle Panama's debts, excellent bilateral relations, and fruitful intelligence cooperation. The large judicial backlog and overcrowded prisons detracted from an otherwise good record on human rights. There had been progress on the drug war, but much more needed to be done to make Panama a less attractive transit center. Lots of progress had been made with the PNP, but the administration of the security forces was still weak.

Unfinished business: the Dragseth, Braithwrite, and Zak Hernandez murders, U.S. ratification of the MLAT, a Corozal Cemetery Agreement, GATT membership for Panama, significant privatizations, cuts in the government's swollen payroll, and trade liberalization.

I was impressed by progress made in handling reverted areas and by the outlook for the constitutional amendments needed to assure that at midnight of December 30, 1999, Panama would be ready to assume responsibility for its Canal. All in all, I was optimistic about Panama's future.

It remained for me to give a farewell reception for over 300 guests, to be decorated by Foreign Minister Jose Mulino with the Orden Vasco Nunez de Balboa en el Grado de Gran Cruz, and to take a farewell salute from Embassy Marines.

In Washington at a reception, with my family watching and friends in attendance, I made a few remarks about the Foreign Service's need for diversity, shook lots of hands, and so ended my Foreign Service career of over forty-eight years.

Index

27th Infantry 4

Abbott, A. Tucker 107
Abrams, Elliot 356, 405–6
Acheson, Dean 55–56, 130
Adams Jr., Dr. Samuel 268
Adenauer, Konrad 202
Aggrey, Rudy 270
Akbar. *See* Hinton, Akbar [Deane Patrick Akbar George]
Alessandri, Jorge 240–42
Alfsen, Fritz 65
Ali, Muhammad 278
Allen, Richard V. 332, 252
Allende, Salvador 237, 239,240–45, 260, 281
al-Qawuqji, Fawzi 77, 80,
al-Quwatli, Shukri 67, 80, 82, 87,
al-Sharabati, Ahmad 66, 67
Alvarez, Enrique 336
Amelia 231–32
American Siberia Expeditionary Force 4
Ames, Thomas 17
Amory, Robert 145
Anderson, Arthur 436
Anderson, John 281
Andreo, Lopez 336
Angela. *See* Hinton, Angela Peyraud [first wife]

Arana Osorio, Carlos Manuel 215, 222, 226
de Aretxabala, Don Pedro 239, 278, 289, 311
de Aretxabala, Nellie 278
Aria, Diego 220
Arias, Arnulfo 417
Arias, Oscar 401–8, 413, 427
Arias, Rodrigo 410
Arias Calderón, Ricardo 415, 417, 423
Armacost, Michael 387, 390, 391
Aronson, Bernard 407, 417
Arrivillaga, Guillermo [Miren's 1st husband] 238, 256
Arrivillaga, Guillermo "Mincho" [son of Miren] 238, 256, 289, 311–13, 322
Arrivillaga, Juan Jose "Juanjo" [son of Miren] 238, 256–57, 270, 272, 278, 284, 310, 312–13, 325, 329–30, 398, 413, 431
Arrivillaga, Kepa [brother of Miren] 237, 239, 311–12
Arrivillaga, Maria Luisa "Coca" [daughter of Miren] 238, 256, 257, 272, 311–13, 325
Arrivillaga, Miren "Michu" [daughter of Miren]. 238, 256–57, 272, 284, 311–13, 365, 420

Arrue, Major 433
Asencio, Diego 365
Askin, Peter 338,
Attoue, Mr. 284, 420
Avila, Captain Eduardo 355
Azim, Ejaz 370

Baker, James A. III 406–7, 412
Ball, George 150, 161, 186–87,
    192–94, 202, 206
Balladares, Ernesto Pérez 437,
Balzaretti, Carmen de 360
Baracloough, Bill 208
Barnes, Harry 316, 384–85
Barrerra, Hugo, 186, 344, 351
Barrow, Ralph 66, 72, 84
Bator, Frances 204
Baudouin, King 309
Baum, Warren 132
Baxter, George 378
Beall, David 417, 430–35
Behrnhorst, Carroll 219
Beigel, E.J. 139, 148
Bell, Joe 294
Bell, Mark 216
Bell, Morey 226, 235, 240, 264
Bell, Richard 292
Bennett, W. Tapley "Tap" 307
Berg, Dick 281, 286
Berger, Louis 436
Berger, Warren 310
Bergland, Robert 310
Bergsten, Fred 260, 317
Bernadotte, Count Folke 83–85
Bey, Jamil Mardam 64
Bhutto, Benazir 383
Bhutto, Zulfikar Ali 371
Bider, Lori 249
Biehl, John 404
Bilbao, Mirentxu 289
Bishop, Amasas "Am" 162
Bishop, Meredith 11

Bisingemana, Citoyen 271, 273,
    281
Blackwell, Robert 293, 295
Blades, Rueben 436–37
Bleakley, Ken 331–33, 336, 345, 353
Blumenthal, W. Michael "Mike"
    172, 181, 183, 187, 189–90, 194–
    95, 201, 204, 251
Bobba, Franco 164
Boeker, Paul 319
Boitelle, Benny 135
Bonner, Raymond "Ray" 346–47,
    352–53
Boochever, Lou 162
Boorstin, Daniel 310
Borre, Peter 324
Bosworth, Bill 126
Bosworth, Brian 233
Bourguiba, Habib 85
Bowdler, Bill 329–31
Bowie, Bob 167, 168–72, 309
Bracken, Alice 67
Brand, Bob 91
Brania, Patty 437
Breen, Dick 213
Brewer, Bill 110
Brewster, Dania 60, 129, 144
Brewster, Kingman Jr. 307
Brown, Colonel [pilot] 69–70, 95
Brown, J. Cudd 105
Brown, Lester "Les" 184
Bruce, David 130–31, 138, 224
Brungart, Bob 150
Brzezinski, Zbigniew 307, 315, 319
Buchanan, James 29
Bula, Mandungu 279, 286
Bunche, Ralph 83
Bundy, McGeorge 205
Bunker, Ellsworth 264
Burgess, Ted 70
Burke, Dick 222
Burke, Richard 302

Burrows, Charles R. 213
Busby, Morris 411
Bush administration 411, 413
Bush, George H. W. 341, 356,
    375–77, 404, 406, 412–13, 420–21,
    427, 434–35
Bushnell, John 331, 415–17
Bustamante, Jorge 344
Bustillo, Colonel 348, 359
Butrick, Richard 110
Butterworth, W. Walton 164, 170–
    72, 224, 154, 158–59, 162–63
Butz, Earl 263, 291–92, 295
Byrd, Admiral Richard 11
Byrd, Robert 319

Calvert, Jim 176,
Carbaugh, John 350–51
Carles, Rubén 422
Carlton, Anton 28
Carlucci, Frank 334
Carpenter, Scott 214
Carter, Jimmy 301–3, 305, 307, 309,
    315–17, 320–21, 324–25, 327, 329,
    332, 345, 379, 427, 437
Casanova, Vides 336, 350, 359
Casey, William "Bill" 263, 268,
    332, 345, 369, 378–80, 402
Castillo, Carlos Manual 224
Castillo Morales, Carlos Manuel
    404
Castro, Fidel Cesar, Alfredo 30,
    183, 216, 242, 283–84, 360, 403,
    411
Chaij, Dan 408–9
Chamberlain, Neville 22
Chamorro, Violeta 401, 412
Chandler, Dave 426
Chapin, Selden 56
Cheney, Richard "Dick" 433
Chevalier, Juan 423, 430, 433
Chris. See Hinton, Christopher
    Roesch [son]

Christe, Mina 81
Christian, Shirley 435
Christiana, Ana 333
Christopher. See Hinton,
    Christopher Roesch [son]
Christopher, Warren 314–16, 319,
    323, 436
Churchill, Mary 298
Cisneros, Judy 339
Cisneros, Marc 425, 427
Clark, William 332, 358, 363
Cleveland, Stan 150, 154, 195
Clinton, Bill 224, 437
Coca. See Arrivillaga, Maria Luisa
    [daughter of Miren]
Cochrane, Willard 181, 184–85, 187
Coffin, Frank 190
Cohen, Marvin 326
Colby, William 268
Colley, Mary 53
Colpitts, Andre 233
Colquitt, Adrian 57
Connally, John 248, 250, 260,
Connolly, Chuck 220
Cook, Terrence Cardinal 243
Cooper, Chuck 262
Cooper, Richard "Dick" 313, 317,
    326, 328
Copeland, Miles 70, 86–87, 345
Cordovez, Diego 383
Corse, Carl D. 162, 164
Covey, Oliver 212
Cox, Ann 308,
Cramer, Ben 137
Crandall, Larry 393, 394
Cranston, Alan 386,
Crimmins, John 260
Curley, Walter 301
Cutler, Lloyd 314
Cutler, Walter 286–87

D'Aubuisson, Roberto 336, 344,
    348–52, 359–60

Dad [Joe Arthur Hinton] 3–5, 7–22, 26, 31, 38–39, 45, 53, 57, 93, 136, 143, 157–58, 165–66, 228, 235, 248, 305–6, 322, 325–27, 353, 403
Daladier, Pierre 22
Davies, Roger 79, 88
Davignon, Etienne "Stevie" 302, 304, 308
Davis, Nathaniel "Nat" 220–21, 223, 229, 231, 264, 281, 283, 290
Davit, Alex 63, 72–73
Davit, Peggy 71, 94
Dawson, John 416, 436
Dean, Jim 233
Dengo, Jorge 404–5, 427
Denman, Roy 304
Dent, Frederick 262
Denton, Hazel 330
Derian, Patricia "Patt" 315
DeSazo, Peter 436
Deschnijver, Alain 275
Despino, Madame 12, 284
Devine, Frank 177
Devlin, Larry 273, 282
Dewey, Don 29
Dickey, Chris 334
Didion, Joan 356
Diggs, Charles 268, 281
Dillon, C. Douglas 140, 145, 154, 164
Dodd, Sen. Chris 339, 352, 355
Doherty, Bill 338
Dole, Sen. Robert 294
Dougherty, Bill 332,
Dreyfus, Bertrand 28, 33, 133
Driscoll, Robert 343–4
Drullinsky, Raphael 236
Duarte, José Napoléon 333–37, 339–44, 346, 349, 351, 360, 363
Dufflocq, Adrian 243
Dundas,"Flux" 74
Dunlop, John 291

Dunnigan, Tom 177
Duran, Martinez 220
Durka, Bill 29, 53, 93

Eagleburger, Larry 353, 366, 417
Easum, Donald 268, 277, 281
Eberle, William D. 251–53
Egan, Joe 45
Ehrlich, Jose Antonio Morales 336
Eilts, Hermann 177
Eizenstat, Stuart 314
Ellacuria, Ignacio 354
Ellison, Gordon 338, 354
Ellsworth, Robert 225
el-Nimeiri, Gaafar Mohamed 272
Emmet, Dick 30
Endara, Pres. Guillermo 412, 415, 417–19, 421–33, 235–36
Endara, Jorge 422
Enders, Gaetana 403
Enders, Tom 199, 201, 290, 292, 335, 350, 357–58, 360, 363, 365

Fagetti, Elda 243
Falla, Ricardo 403
Feld, Nick 105
Fendell, Jack 404
Ferguson, Charles "Fergie" 68, 71, 73, 74, 92, 177
Ferguson, Joanna 92
Ferrand, Robert 110
Fina, Tom 148
Firestone, Harvey 298
Fischmann, Imrich 219
Flanigan, Peter M.
Foote, James 51
Ford, Billy 415, 423
Ford, Guillermo 417–18
Ford, Vice President Gerald 433
Ford, William 341
Foreman, George 277
Fort Missoula, Montana 3, 16

Fortier, Donald 387
Fowler, Jim 212, 220, 227, 231–32, 357
Frank, Isaiah 150, 190
Freeman, Orville L. 184, 187, 191–93, 202, 205–7
Frei Montalva, Eduardo 233, 240, 243
Frere, Jean 172
Fried, Ed 194
Frosh, Judy 177
Frosh, Stan 228
Fuentes Mohr, Alberto 220, 225–26,
Fulbright, Sen. William 267, 270
Furnas, Gail 176–77

Gailani, Sayyid Ahmed 381
Gaitán, Eliécer 419
Gandhi, Rajiv 386–87, 393
Garcia, Guillermo 336, 340, 342–43, 347–51, 355, 359, 362, 412
Gardner, John 310
Garnier, Elise 6
Garrett, Johnson 71
Garrett, Margie 71
Garza, O. P. 436–37
Gavin, Amb. John 357
Gazzo, Emmanuele 163
Gettinger, Carl 337
Ghamayan, Fuad 72
Gibbons, Sam 309
Gilbert, Carl 247, 251, 427
Gillespie, Charles 331
Giolitti, Antonio 302
Giroldi, Moisés 413
Giron, Montenegro 225
Givans, Walker 148
Glenday, Vincent 111
Glenn, John 386
Godley, G. McMurtrie "Mac" 142
Goldman, Les 321, 327

González, Colonel [El Salvador] 362
González Pinzón, Pedro Miguel 435
Gonzalo [waiter] 231–32
Gorbachev, Mikhail 387
Gorman, Gen. Paul 361
Gossett, William "Bill" 192, 194, 197
Graf, Barbara 20
Graf, Russ 19, 23
Grahl, Larry 396
Green, Sam 219, 228
Greene, James 260–61
Greene, Marshall 55
Greenwald, Joe 192, 195, 2037, 251, 292
Grey, Bettie 52
Grimm, Jorge 313
Griswold, Gen. Francis 175
Grody, Walt 33
Groth, Edward 100–102, 115
Grow, Colonel [pilot] 274, 286
Guardia, Gilberto 427
Gundelach, Finn 186, 190, 300–301, 304
Gustin, Commander 66
Guttierez, Colonel 336, 350

Habib, Philip 181, 323, 410
Hadzel, Sue 148
Haig, Alexander 257, 262, 298, 329, 348, 350, 353–55, 376
Hallstein, Walter 163, 172, 206
Hamilton, John 322, 412
Hammer, Michael 331, 354
Hannah, John 231–32
Hansen, Alvin 34, 124
Harbert family 9–10
Harbert, Rudolph and Erdine 21
Harkin, Sen. Thomas 346
Harkins, Ray 231, 232

Harriman, Averill 130–31
Harrises, Mr and Mrs Al 107
Hart, Howie 377
Hartman, Arthur 131–32, 245, 322
Hartzog, General 419
Hatch, Orrin 382
Hathaway, Dale 315
Haverkamp, Wilhelm 302–4
Hawes, Maurice 218
Hayworth, Rita 112
Hedges, Irwin 187, 192
Hekmatyar, Gulbuddin 372, 380–81, 411
Helms, Jesse 332, 351–52, 366–67, 437
Henriquez, Silva 234
Hernandez, Zak A. 435, 438
Herrera, Colonel [Panama] 431
Herrera, Felipe 220–21
Herter, Christian A. 160, 167, 170, 192–94, 202, 204–6
Hesburgh, Theodore 348
Hickey, Archbishop 341
Hickey, James A. 331
Hight, Boyd 326
Hill, Dick 30
Hill, Richard 293
Hills, Freddy 106
Hinton, Akbar (Deane Patrick Akbar George) [son] 8, 15, 167, 397–98, 403
Hinton, Angela Peyraud [1st wife] 51–62, 64–65, 67–69, 71–73, 81, 85, 88–89, 91–94, 97–100, 102–7, 111–113, 115, 117–19, 121–28, 132–35, 142–44, 147, 154, 157–58, 168, 172–74, 180, 195, 212, 214–15, 217–19, 227–29, 231, 235, 250
Hinton, Arthur Elmer "Grandpa" 8, 9, 10, 12
Hinton, Christopher "Chris" Roesch [son] 73, 129, 135, 143–44, 173, 211, 214, 216, 227–28, 235–36, 239, 246–50, 255–57
Hinton, Clara [aunt] 12, 325
Hinton, Clarence [uncle] 10
Hinton, Deborah Ann [daughter] 97, 99, 103, 105, 115, 127, 173, 213, 227–28, 235, 300, 309, 345
Hinton, Doris Eileen Roesch. See Mother
Hinton, Emma Harbert, "Grandma" 9 –10
Hinton, Frank [great-uncle] 12
Hinton, Hogan [uncle] 10, 12
Hinton, (Jeffrey) Joe [son] 147, 173, 214, 227–28, 231, 238, 309, 325, 345, 353, 410
Hinton, Jeremiah 10
Hinton, Jim 12
Hinton, Joanna [daughter] 147, 173, 214, 228, 231, 238–39, 309
Hinton, Joe Arthur [father]. See Dad
Hinton, Miren de Aretxabala Arrivillaga [2nd wife] 5, 136, 237–39, 242–43, 245–47, 249–51, 255–57, 259, 264, 267, 269–70, 272, 274–76, 278, 284–86, 289, 294, 296–302, 306, 309–14, 329, 412
Hinton, Patricia Lopez [3rd wife] 346–47, 351, 353, 356–57, 360–65, 370, 376–77, 384, 396–98, 400, 403, 410, 413, 415, 426–27, 435
Hinton, Patty, [cousin] 12–13, 325–26
Hinton, Sebastian [son] 8, 167, 356, 365, 396, 427
Hinton, Veronica Jean [daughter] 157, 168, 173, 214, 228, 231, 238, 309
Hirsch, Jerry 233
Hitler, Adolph 22, 24

Holbrooke, Richard "Dick"   318
Holloway, Jim   176
Hormats, Robert   260, 317, 328
Huezo, Roberto   333
Humphrey, Gordon   382
Hunt, Jim   145
Hutchins, Robert Maynard   28, 34

Iklé, Fred   382
Iler, Mollie   184
Ioannes, Ray   247–48
Irving, AI   149
Ishwani, Ibrahim   75

Jackson, Henry "Scoop"   254
Jaime, Don   232
Janton, M.   186
Javits, Sen. Jacob   322
Jenkins, Roy   300–302, 304–5, 309
Jinnah, Muhammad Ali   371
Johnson, Griffith   186
Jordan, William   264
Juanjo. See Arrivillaga, Juan Jose
   "Juanjo" [son of Miren]
Joulwan, Gen. George   426, 432–33
Junejo, Muhammed Khan   373–74,
   376, 386, 390, 393–94

Kaegi, Richard   226
Kahl, Joe "Jerry"   29–30, 124
Karkashian, John   241
Kassebaum, Nancy   348
Katz, Jules   313
Keeley, James Hugh   65, 82–88, 124
Kennedy, Dick   309, 329
Kennedy, John F.   170–72, 178, 180,
   181, 193, 194, 197, 200, 202, 203,
   349
Kennedy administration   161, 172,
   183–85, 192, 252
Kennedy Round   160–61, 181,
   186–87, 189, 195, 199, 201, 202,
   204, 205–7, 251

Kent, Sherman   152–53
Kessler, Judd   233
Khan, Abdul Qadeer   371, 388
Khan, Akhtar Abdur Rahman   376
Khan, Aly   112–13
Khan, Khala   398–400
Killoran, Tom   283
King, Don   277–78
Kirkpatrick, Jeane   359–60
Kissinger, Henry   178, 242, 248,
   254–55, 257, 263, 281, 286, 289,
   291–92, 294–96
Klein, Herman   177
Klutznick, Philip   320
Knight, Frank   34, 53
Knox, Clinton   147, 149–150, 153
Korry, Edward M.   231, 239–42,
   244–45
Kosciusco-Morizet, Jacques   205
Kozak, Mike   424, 429, 431
Kraft, Joseph   242, 292
Kramish, Arv   177
Krebs, Max   216
Krekler, Hans   171

Laboa, Jose Sebastian   419
Labouisse, Henry   139–40
Lane, Clayton   63, 65
Lane, Howie   334
Larson, Pat   236, 255, 246
Latour, Louis   301
Leddy, John   154, 164, 206, 209,
   212, 317
Levy, Esther   232
Lewis, Samuel W. "Sam"   325
Lewis, Gabriel   437
Linares, Julio   419, 424–26, 434
Lluillier, Jackie   137
Lodge, Henry Cabot Jr.   211
Long, Clarence   352, 354, 370
Lopez, Patricia   346
Lorton, Ron   379
Lowensohn, Fred   137

Lowenstein, Jim 309
Lubell, Harold 137
Lutate, Citoyen Umba Di 271

MacArthur, Douglas II 132
MacArthur, "Wahwee" 132, 240
MacCorquodale, Donald 223
MacDonald, Al 305
MacNeil, Robert 252
Madison, Herb 28, 31, 33, 38, 51
Madrigal, Rodrigo 402–4, 412–13,
   427
Magaña, Álvaro 349–52, 354, 357–
   59, 361–64
Makosso, Mbeka 267
Maldonado, Juan 336
Male, Peter 70
Malula, Cardinal 273
Mamoulaichvili, Helene 135
Manfredo, Fernando 427–28, 436
Mankelberg, Fernando 243
Mann, Thomas 206
Mansfield, Senator 267
Mansholt, Sicco L. 205
Marasciulo, Kay 218
Maria, Jose 289
Marina, Concha 351, 360, 363
Marjolin, Robert 137, 163–64, 304
Mark, Dave 56
Marks, Edward 275, 286
Martí, Farabundo 335, 362
Martin, Edward 193, 316
Martin, Graham 129, 131
Massoud, Ahmad Shah 380–81
Mattison, Gordon 57, 60, 63–65,
   82, 212
Maushammer, Robert 233
McBride, Bob 152
McCaffrey, Gen. Barry 437
McCain, John 375
McCarthy, John 302, 377
McCloskey, Bob 309, 320

McCloy, John 167
McGhee, George 86, 104–5
McGrath, Colonel 77, 80
McGrew, Donald J. 131, 134, 136–
   38, 140–41
McHenry, Donald 326
McNeill, William H. 31
McPherson, Peter 393–95
Meade, Steve 86–87
Mein, John Gordon 213, 215, 218,
   220, 222
Memminger, Bob 72–74, 77, 80–82
Mena, Antonio Ortiz 339
Mena, Fidel Chavez 335, 364
Menzies, Robert 187
Methven, Stu 268, 273–74, 282, 345
Meyer, Charlie 232, 241
Michu. See Arrivillaga, Miren
   [daughter of Miren]
Miller, Bill 132, 137, 164
Miller, Dave 43
Mincho See Arrivillaga, Guillermo
   "Mincho" [son of Miren]
Miner, Bob 132, 137
Miner, Nellie 132
Miren. See Hinton, Miren
   Arrivillaga [3rd wife]
Mobutu Sese Seko 268, 269–75,
   277–87, 289–90
Modai, Yitzhak 323–25
Mohammadi, Mohammad Nabi
   381
Mojaddedi, Sibghatullah 381
Molina, Lilli 347
Molino, Jose Raul 425
Molloy, M.D. 143
Mondale, Walter 302–3, 314
Monge, Luis Alberto 402
Monnet, Jean 130, 137, 139, 150–52,
   159, 161, 168, 171, 203, 224, 304,
   392
Montalva, Eduardo Frei 233, 240

Montel, John 302
Montenegro, Méndez 218–19, 221, 225
Monterrosa, Domingo 333
Moore, Nancy 10
Moose, James S. 65–68, 72
Morgenthau, Hans 54
Morris, Bob 249, 253–55, 297–99, 411
Mother [Eileen Roesch Hinton] 3, 6–8, 11–17, 19–22, 24, 26–27, 32, 35, 39, 41, 43, 47–48, 51–52, 54–55, 61, 70, 93, 115, 136, 143–44, 157, 165–66, 214, 227–28, 235, 305–6, 311
Motley, Tony 363, 365
Mulino, Jose Raul 434, 438
Munger, Ted 107
Munro, Ernest A. 215
Murphy, Richard 187, 384
Muskie, Edmund "Ed" 309, 322, 330
Mussolini, Benito 22

Nacivet, Pierre and Christane 133
Naik, Niaz 374
Naland, John 407
Napoleón, José 333
Nasser, Abdel 207
Natali, Lorenzo 301
Negroponte, John 356
Neruda, Pablo 243
Nessen, Ron 295
Neumann, Bob 270
Newcomer, Georgia 306
Newlin, Mike 268–70
Newsom, David 315, 328, 366
Nickel, Ed 177
Nixon, Richard 170, 180, 220, 242, 245, 249–50, 252, 259–63, 270–71, 376
Noel, Emile 297

Nora, Simon 141
Noriega, Manuel 405–6, 412–13, 416–19, 421–22, 427, 429, 431, 437
North, Oliver 357
Nuila, Lopez 349
Nunn, Sam 382
Nutter, Warren 30, 52
Nutting, Gen. Wallace 335, 338, 342–43, 358, 361
Nyati, Mandungu Bula 279

O'Neill, Tip 309
Oakar, Mary Rose 341
Ochoa, Colonel Sigifredo 359
Oleksiw, Dan 177
Omang, Joanne 349
Ortega, Daniel 401–3, 407, 410, 412
Ortiz, Frank 363
Ortoli, M. François 298, 300–301
Owen, Henry 170, 313

Padilla, Osvaldo 419
Palmer, Amb. Joseph 188
Palmer, Don 212
Pastor, Robert 437
Pastora, Edén 411
Patolichev, Nikolai 293
Paulson, Pep 38
Pearce, Bill 253
Pearlman, David 331
Pearlman, Mark 354
Percy, Chuck 332
Perry, Fred 322
Peterson, Peter G. 245–52, 257, 263
Peyraud, Al 51–52, 92–93, 128, 143, 145, 228
Peyraud, Angela. See Hinton, Angela Peyraud [1st wife]
Peyraud, Bettie Grey 51–52, 92–93, 143, 145, 228
Phelps, Nathaniel 3

Phillips, Ruth 199
Pickering, Thomas 357
Piekney, Bill 380
Pillsbury, Michael 382
Pincus, John 194
Pinkerton, Lowell 73
Pinochet, Augusto 412, 259
Pitkanen, Helena 173
Pollock, Mary 273
Porte, Anton de 148
Porter, Bill 59, 142, 144
Probst, George 30

Quayle, Dan 421–22

Rabbani, Burhanuddin 381
Raetz, Annette 13
Ramallo, PadreLuis 243
Raphel, Arnold 369, 382, 391, 393
Read, Ben 323
Reagan, Ronald 83, 317, 326, 329,
    330, 335–36, 340–41, 346, 351,
    355, 358–59, 360, 363, 366, 381–
    82, 386–87, 389, 400–402, 404
Reagan administration 327, 330,
    355, 361, 382, 406
Reasonover, George 416
Reisman, Simon 191
Renner, John 199
Report, Martin 317
Rey, Jean 203, 251
Rivera, Aida 346
Robelo, Alfonzo 411
Roberto, Holden 282–83
Roberto, Jose 347
Robinson, Charles 290, 292
Rockefeller, Nelson 219
Rodriguez, Carlos 421, 432
Roesch, Christopher 135
Roesch, George "Uncle Rudolph"
    6, 21, 33
Roesch, Grandma 5, 7, 21, 24, 27,
    47, 52, 93, 136, 165, 305

Roesch, Grandpa 5, 6, 7, 13, 15, 16,
    17, 21, 32, 78, 93, 300
Rogers, William P. 250, 254, 258–
    59, 263
Rolf, Milton 7
Rolf, Minnie Louise 7
Romero, General 349
Roosevelt, Archie 87
Roosevelt, Franklin Delano "FDR"
    9, 31, 405
Roquette, François Pierre 6
Rosenthal, Gert 220, 226, 322
Rostow, Eugene 207–8
Rostow, Walt 208
Roth, Bill Matson 194, 201, 203–4,
    206–7
Rozell, Gale 345
Rusk, Dean 189, 206, 208

Sadat, Anwar 79, 307
Salome [cook] 231–32
Sanchez, Nestor 218
Sanderson, Fred 149–50, 195
Sattar, Abdul 391–93
Sause, Oliver 193–224
Sayre, Robert 212
Schaetzel, J. Robert 150, 203–4, 310
Schaffer, Howard 383
Schaufelberger, Al 345, 363–64
Scheid, Pat 345
Scherck, Alfred 91
Schieck, Fred 237
Schifferdecker, Arnold 385
Schlesinger, James 309
Schneider, René 242
Schneider, William Jr. 395
Schoeller, Herr 186
Schultz, Theodore 54, 124–25, 365,
    400, 403
Schuman, Robert 130
Scott, Edith 148
Scowcroft, Brent 262–63, 294–95,
    434–35

Seidman, Bill 294–95
Senko, Mike 356
Serres, Jean 74, 77
Sethi, General 274
Sethian, Bob 79
Sheikh, Najmuddin 393–94
Shlaudeman, Harry 232, 241
Shultz, George P. 124, 253–54, 259, 315, 353–54, 358, 363, 387, 395, 406
Sibrian, Lt. Lopez 354–55
Sievering, Nelson 174
Simon, William 254
Simons, Henry C. 30, 34–35, 124
Simpson, Bob 177
Sissman, Leslie 51
Skinner, Secretary 435
Smith, Gerald 309
Sneider, Dick 177
Snyder, Donald W. 133–34
Soames, Christopher 298–300, 303
Soames, Lady 298
Solarz, Rep. Stephen 322, 355
Solis, Luis Guillermo 403
Solomon, Anthony 206
Sonnenfeldt, Hal 369, 294
Spaak, Paul Henri 149, 308
Spiers, Ronald 409
Spreti, Karlvon 216
Sprott, John 241
Stader, Bruce 433
Standard Stoker Company 6
Stassen, Harold 137
Steele, Colonel Jim 421–23, 431
Sterling, Colonel 74
Stern, Ernest 339
Sternfeld, Ray 193, 312
Stevenson, Bob 177
Stewart, Todd 411
Stocker, Kay 241, 346
Stoessel, Walter 293, 308
Stone, Richard 361, 411

Stookey, Louise 56
Stookey, Bob 53, 113–14
Strait, Ed 177
Strand, Bob 267
Strauss, Robert 303–5
Strausz-Hupé, Robert 298, 400
Stukel, Tom 345, 416, 423
Stutesman, John 177
Sumner, Gordon 335

Taffy. See Hinton, Deborah
Talbot, Phil 212
Tambs, Lewis 404
Taylor, Lawrence 55–56, 113–115
Tempelsman, Maurice 268, 282
Thome, Mami 286
Thorn, Gaston 298
Thurman, General Max 415, 418, 425–26, 432
Tibbetts, Margaret 105
Tickell, Crispin 300
Timmons, Benson Lane 139
Tomé, Roberto Suazo 351
Tomic, Radomiro 240–41
Tomlinson, William "Tommy" 130–31, 133
Toomey, Bill and Odette 132
Torrijos Herrera, Omar Efraín 249, 264, 427
Tower, John 375
Triffin, Robert 164
Tullock, Gordon 124
Turnage, Bill 212
Turner, Adm. Stansfield 332, 345
Tuthill, Jack 164, 194, 202–4, 212
Tuttle, Fred W. 7

ul Haq, Mahbub 395

Vallarino, J. J. 433, 436
van Stratum, Isabelle 322
Vance, Cyrus 314, 317–21, 330

Vance, Sheldon 268, 273, 287
Van der Lee, Jacques 173
Vanik, Charles 254
Velasco, Juan 260–61
Vessey, John Jr. 376
Vest, George 225, 294, 320, 400
Viera, Jose Rodolfo 331, 354
Vieytez, Atilio 337, 341, 360
Vine, Dick 199
Volcker, Paul 163, 309
Vredeling, Henk 301

Wadsworth, George 57, 64–65, 73
Waghelstein, John 331, 335, 343,
    345, 353, 358–59, 418
Walker, Lannon 269, 285
Walker, Amb. William 299, 437
Walters, Vernon 350
Ward, Angus 101–2, 115
Warren, Jake 191–92
Wasson, Tommy 69–70
Watson, Marvin 212
Wattoo, Mian Muhammad Yasin
    Khan 395
Webber, John D. 215
Webster, Glen D. 94
Wehrle, Leroy 211
Weinberger, Caspar 332, 376
Weintraub, Gladys 110
Weintraub, Sidney 231, 233
Wenmohs, John A. 188
West, Gordon 179
White, Robert 331, 334, 337
White, Eric Wyndham 186, 190

Whitehead, John 400
Wick, Charles 389
Williamson, Francis 168–69
Willis, George 144
Willkie, Wendell 31
Wilson, Charlie 369–70, 377, 395
Wilson, Evan 85
Wilson, Frances 193, 316–17
Wilson, Lou 176
Wilson, Peggy 23
Winterburn, G. H. 143
Woerner, Fred 342, 362
Wolf, John 383, 388
Wolff, Allen 305
Wood, Bill 338
Wright, Peter 220
Wriston, Walter 144–45

Yaeger, Begonia 330
Yaqub Khan, Sahabzada 373, 386,
    390–91
Yeutter, Clayton 299
Yost, Bob 150
Young, Andrew 281, 307
Young, Crawford 275

Zaglitz, Oscar 184
Zaim, Husni 87–88
Zaldívar, Andrés 245
Zarb, Frank 295
Zia-ul-Haq, Muhammad 370
Ziegler, Ron 259
Zimmer, Peggy 26
Zumwalt, Bud 176